"The truth is not just a casualty of war but of peace. The official narrative is controlled by an elite few to ensure that the real truth remains hidden within a culture of secrecy. We tend to live more in fear than in love, but California-based travel author turned conspiracy writer Brad Olsen hasn't given up on the belief that the truth will be revealed and that humanity can create a utopia based on love and compassion.

"In Secrets, the first section of his book, Olsen covers the rise of the Fourth Reich in America, shadow governments, media manipulation, back-engineering of alien technology, space weapons, underground bases and more. Next, in Cosmos, he considers UFOs, antigravity, EBEs, Men in Black, crop circles, structures on other planets and yet more. In Utopia, he envisions an age of transparency, superhuman abilities, free-energy technologies, the end of money and the endgame of love.

"Much of Olsen's focus is on hidden UFO agendas, and he wonders if WikiLeaks has a trump card yet to be released—maybe information from British hacker Gary McKinnon who discovered the existence of US Star Fleets capable of interstellar travel!

"In *Future Esoteric,* Olsen reveals many pieces of the puzzle, explaining how we've been duped and what we can do about it. A courageous work that serves to set us free." –Nexus

"This book opens the door to the many mysteries of our world being withheld from us in the 'official narrative.' But at what cost? What is lost when we are not fully informed in our current culture of secrecy?

"The term 'esoteric' implies knowledge available to a select few. This book opens the door to the many mysteries of our world being withheld from us in the 'official narrative.' But at what cost? What is lost when we are not fully informed in our current culture of secrecy? What is our true potential as people? How will future generations view us at this pivotal moment of human ascension?" –Adventures Unlimited

"A provocative look into the world of extraterrestrial phenomena and related history. –Stephen Bassett, executive director Paradigm Research Group

"Brad Olsen has done a vast amount of searching to come up with *Future Esoteric,* and putting it together coherently and beautifully, he has saved us all a ton of time just when we are running out of it.

"Dots are connected and threads knit together, revealing an intentional predicament and leading in the direction of practical, love-based solutions." –Foster Gamble, Thrive

"A new book to shake the world of parapsychology and the paranormal." –Rob McConnell, host of the X-Zone

"In the second half of tonight's program, a newcomer to *Coast to Coast,* but not to the topics that we enjoy here. Brad Olsen sounds like a guy with a job we'd all enjoy to have: he travels the world and then writs books about the places he visits. Cool gig. He's not only a successful writer but also a prominent artist, and a long-time seeker of truths, a passion that has led him that has led him to spend the last four years writing a book with what I would call a sweeping view of our world, and other worlds. It's called *Future Esoteric: The Unseen Realms,* and man, it's jam-packed with the bits and pieces culled from many of the writers and researchers we know so well on this program. Secret societies, cover-ups, suppressed technology, UFO secrecy, reverse engineering, all that. We've got a lot of ground to cover." – George Knapp, guest host of Coast to Coast

"A fascinating compendium of information about the secret government, UFOs, and the road to utopia. Brad's viewpoint on these topics seems to me to represent a growing consensus in the 'extreme alternative information' community; *Future Esoteric* sketches a plausible grand narrative explaining how Earth became a prison planet, and how it can be liberated. Even if you don't buy some of the book's claims, it's worth reading to get a sense of what a growing number of bright, visionary people believe." –Dr. Kevin Barrett, host of Truth Jihad Radio

Future Esoteric
the unseen realms

Second Edition

by BRAD OLSEN

CONSORTIUM OF COLLECTIVE CONSCIOUSNESS PUBLISHING

www.CCCPublishing.com ▲ www.BradOlsen.com ▲ www.EsotericSeries.com

Future Esoteric: The Unseen Realms

2nd edition
Esoteric Series :: Volume II

Copyright © 2016 by Bradford C. Olsen
Updated 2020. 4th printing.
Published by the Consortium of Collective Consciousness Publishing™

As is common in a historic and reference book such as this, much of the information included on these pages has been collected from diverse sources. When possible, the information has been checked and double-checked. Almost every topic has at least three data points, that is, three different sources that report the same information. Even with special effort to be accurate and thorough, the author and publisher cannot vouch for each and every reference. The author and publisher assume no responsibility or liability for any outcome, loss, arrest, or injury that occurs as a result of information or advice contained in this book. As with the purchase of goods or services, *caveat emptor* is the prevailing responsibility of the purchaser, and the same is true for the student of the esoteric.

Library of Congress Cataloging-in-Publication Data:

Olsen, Bradford C.
    FUTURE ESOTERIC: THE UNSEEN REALMS / Bradford C. Olsen
        p. cm.
    Includes index
    print ISBN 13: 9781888729788 (Pbk.)

1. Spirituality—Guidebooks. 2. Metaphysics—Esoteric. I. Title
    Library of Congress Catalog Card Number: 2012914382

Printed in the United States of America.

10 9 8 7 6 5 4

The Dating System used in this text is based upon the modern method of using Before Current Era (BCE) instead of Before Christ (B.C.), and Current Era (CE) rather than "In the year of the Lord" *anno Domini* (A.D.). Those unfamiliar with this dating system should take note that 1 B.C. is the same as 1 BCE and everything then counts backward just the same. Similarly, 1 A.D. is 1 CE with all the years counting forward to the present, or Current Era.

To assist in universal understanding, all measurements of length, distance, area, weight, size, and volume are listed in the metric system.

also by Brad Olsen

2021
Beyond Esoteric:
Escaping Prison Planet

2017
Modern Esoteric:
Beyond Our Senses

2008
Sacred Places North America:
108 Destinations

2007
Sacred Places Europe:
108 Destinations

2004
Sacred Places Around the World:
108 Destinations

2001
World Stompers:
A Global Travel Manifesto

1999
In Search of Adventure:
A Wild Travel Anthology

1997
Extreme Adventures Northern California

1997
Extreme Adventures Hawaii

FUTURE ESOTERIC:

THE UNSEEN REALMS

FRONT MATTER:

BACK MATTER:

SECRETS:

What is being withheld from us, who is doing it, their agenda, and why it matters to you. A peek behind the invisible veil.

DIMENSIONS:

COSMOS:

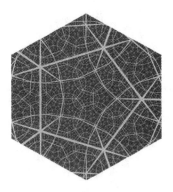

Come oscillate through the spacetime continuum to the next dimensions with us! An essential guide to all things weird and out of this world.

DIMENSIONS:

U T O P I A :

Envisioning free energy for all and an end to money is only the beginning. The Golden Age for humanity is just around the corner.

DIMENSIONS:

AUTHOR'S KARMA STATEMENT

"You can easily judge the character of a person by how they treat those who can do nothing for them."
–Johann Wolfgang von Goethe

"AMERICANS Seeing Things? UFOs in Four States" as reported in the Alton, IL. *Evening Telegraph*, on August 2, 1965:

> *"Authorities in Texas, New Mexico, Oklahoma & Kansas were besieged last night and early today by reports of unidentified flying objects. The Oklahoma Highway Patrol said officers in three cars had seen the objects fly in a diamond-shaped formation for 30 minutes and that Tinker Air Force Base had tracked four unidentified flying objects on radar at 22,000 feet. In Kansas, the Sedgewick County Sheriff Office said the Weather Bureau had tracked objects at 6,000-9,000 feet. One observer said the objects 'were red & exploded in a shower of sparks in nature.' 'Viewers were probably seeing the planet Jupiter and the stars Rigel, Capella, Betelgeuse, or Aldebaran, which were in the part of the sky where sightings were reported,' the Air Force said."*

How many UFO reports just like this have come and gone for the better part of the last century without any serious discussion or agreement about what this phenomenon might be all about? The reason this article caught my eye is because it was a mass sighting in the Midwest on the very morning I was born in Chicago,

Illinois. From the time I was a young boy, I had a fascination with the possibility of extraterrestrial contact with us Earthlings. I drew illustrations of ETs in space suits, and imagined the many possible ways direct contact could manifest. Yet nothing conclusive has transpired in my lifetime other than Hollywood movie depictions of good and bad ETs, usually interacting with armies, both intent on destroying each other. I went through intense periods of inquiry in my young adulthood, really just to satisfy my own curiosity, only to open new doors which led down split paths. As a young man in a search of knowledge and truth, I traveled around the world for three years. As time went on I discovered even more tantalizing clues that led me down different rabbit holes in an attempt to solve this deeply distorted enigma wrapped within a fear-based riddle.

I have considered several theories. Perhaps the entire UFO phenomenon is merely a mass hallucination as NASA and the armed forces would have us believe. Are swamp gas, aural sightings, satellites, planets, twinkling stars or human terrestrial aircraft the best explanations we can elicit? What about the "high strange" incidents viewed by thousands, such as the Phoenix Lights over two states in March 1997, or the millions of people worldwide who swear they witnessed something anomalous? How about an explanation of the other topics in the paranormal handbook such as crop circles, cattle mutilations, and human abductions? Wouldn't any of this warrant the reopening of Project Bluebook or another governmental agency making a new inquiry? Are we all crazy or simply co-envisioning a new modern folklore, one that is collectively believed by millions worldwide? Either the UFO phenomenon is the richest source of mythology since the ancient Greeks, or it is the biggest discovery of humans since fire. My suspicion has always been that certain USA agencies, those who should have the task of informing us, are involved in this cover-up. Like any good detective, first I had to establish a motive. Who might be profiting from keeping UFOs secret?

Second, the task of my detective work was to see through the apparent whitewash of information which denied verification of my own paranormal sightings. To this day, I remember what I saw with vivid clarity, especially a kind of "awe" moment, the kind of life-changing instant when time seems to stand still. It made such an impact that I had to reevaluate my own core beliefs. I wish I could have gone home and read about this "close encounter" or researched the topic just to learn what it was, but all we were given then was the official line of denial and ridicule for any paranormal claim.

My encounter story goes like this: In mid-July of 1997, I was hiking with two fellow campers at the highest point of Crater Lake in Oregon, and the other two hikers both verified this exact description. We recall seeing an intensely bright, exactly straight beam of white light in broad daylight approaching the depths of the lake. About 200 meters above the crater, the slowly moving streaking light transitioned from a solid beam into blips of perfectly square lights, still moving at the same speed in the sky before disappearing. After it passed, the three of us fell to the ground laughing in sheer amazement. We began racing to catch up with the other three in our group, but unfortunately none of them witnessed what we did because they had already entered the woods. Before we got to the trees, only moments later, the three of us saw another beam of light lasting several seconds moving in the direction of Mount Shasta, some 50 kilometers away in California. Two unbelievable sightings within five minutes! It was a moment that solidified my lifelong quest to discover everything that we are not allowed to know. This quest would become the *Esoteric Series* of books.

CHASING DOWN THE TRUTH

It became obvious long before I started creating the notes that would become this book that there was something very large at hand. There were too many unanswered questions, too many blatant denials, too many lives lost or lives irrevocably changed. I made it my duty to examine every side to every issue I present in these chapters, attempting to pin down at least three data points discussing the same information, no matter how disturbing or bizarre the end result might seem. My vetting process for compiling the data in this book was similar to creating reviews in the *Zagat Guides,* looking for at least three similarities and then condensing the information down even further for easy reading. My goal was to combine all the related concepts, recognize clear patterns, and then synthesize the data into a concise format that anyone with a basic education could understand. Despite the format of an "understandable" synthesis, most of the topics in this book also will breed skeptics with their websites devoted to debunking this subject matter. But if there were not debunkers, this information would not be considered esoteric!

I have no agenda other than to pass on the most accurate and truthful information I could find. I have never taken a security oath to the military or any government agency, because neither I nor anyone else has ever questioned my patriotism. I am merely a collector and compiler of anything weird or esoteric. As for UFOs, I noticed there have been far too many sightings for which the authorities had no plausible explanation. It became obvious that we were either being observed by some sort of advanced beings coming in from outer space, or possibly flying with inter-dimensional vehicles based right here on Earth or within our solar system, or some scientific group on Earth had discovered a principle of physics unknown to the rest of us, and that secret research was being employed. More than likely it was a combination of all three of the above possibilities. The more layers of the onion I peeled away, the deeper the mystery became.

Meanwhile, after signing the 2011 petition asking the Obama Administration to acknowledge an extraterrestrial presence here on Earth, the reply was as follows: "The U.S. Government has no evidence that any life exists outside our planet, or that an extraterrestrial presence has contacted or engaged any member of the human race. In addition, there is no credible information to suggest that any evidence is being hidden from the public's eye." The same smokescreen used to deflect public interest in UFOs continues to this day. It seems we live in a society that is devoted to denying the existence of anything it cannot understand.

However, other former U.S. presidents have given us hints that the UFO phenomenon is real. "I know some. I know a fair amount," said George Bush Sr., replying to a question in 1988 about UFOs while campaigning to become President. He also said in a 1988 debate with Dukakis: "I am very careful in public life about dealing with classified information." Jimmy Carter admitted to seeing a UFO.

Some people seem to think that throwing the word "debunked" around means that the debunking has succeeded. Actually, the vast majority of debunking scenarios have more holes than the "conspiracy theories" they're meant to silence. The debunkers construct just enough of a shell to help those who really don't want the truth to be true to carry on believing that it's not. The debunkers provide temporary refuge, once again, for those fearful of new ideas.

By way of a disclaimer, never take what another says to you as "truth," especially the contents you will encounter in this book. Believe nothing and question everything. Your purpose here, if you are to resonate with this material, is to find your own truth. Sometimes others can help you by offering guidance, but for their truth to become your truth, it must pass through the test of your own personal discernment. Sit quietly in meditation and ask the voice inside you to guide your path. Meditate upon that which you will read in these pages and listen to your inner feelings. They are the language of your soul.

A NOTE ON CONSPIRACY THEORIES

In common usage, a *conspiracy* is the combined beliefs held by a group of people not only based on lack of evidence or lies, but with an implied negative intent or message.

The phrase, *"conspiracy theory,"* is usually used as a negative label to discredit a set of beliefs which are regarded as creatively invented, made up due to naiveté or an overactive imagination, or due to a pathological condition such as paranoia.

On the other hand, the use of the term *conspiracy* can be regarded as a "truth-in-labeling" device when it is used to describe a calculated cover-up of truthful events, that is, a cover-up of information to which the public is entitled. In this case, there is a *double conspiracy:*

> *(1) The carrying out of calculated malevolent truthful events parading as accidents or well-intended decisions,*
> *(2) An enormous matrix of devices to cover up number (1).*

In this book, I use the term in this two-fold way. Additionally, I have long believed that the public is entitled to this information.

To further clarify terminology—the secret global cabal (which I describe in detail) behind all elected governments maintains absolute secrecy, which can legitimately be called a *"conspiracy of silence."* This is a conspiracy or a *"truth embargo"* which I and many others wish to disclose, to bring to light events which have occurred and continue to occur, so that all citizens have access to vital information and can draw their own conclusions.

Such efforts as mine and others are then labeled *"conspiracy theories,"* which is an attempt by the labelers to quickly dismiss and discredit the evidence in this book and all of its documentation. My response to these folks is that they are either uninformed, frightened or likely both—a powerful mix for fostering denial and maintaining the status quo. Unfortunately, this is the way we as human beings keep intolerable levels of fear at least manageable, and this knowledge of human nature is the way the perpetrators of the *double conspiracy* hope to keep us subdued.

I hope this book will help us to stare down the fear, walk through it boldly, and discover the truth.

EARTH'S DILEMMA

Here I reveal the book's conclusion at the very beginning. It is my sincere wish that we evolve higher together and overcome the collective obstacles that affect our planet and our collective well-being. This is also the end of my writing in the first person until the final chapter. I created this book to be a research project, not merely a forum for expressing my theories and opinions. It has nothing to do with me. It is about us. So here we go.

"Earth's Dilemma" is a scenario in which our current government, or those who secretly rule those who govern, is complacent in keeping the global population in a deep sleep. Yet, each one of us has free will; each one of us is a free soul; and each one of us possesses a free consciousness. This is your life and all life is precious. Do what you love, do it often, and never forget you have the freedom of choice. If you don't like something, change it. If you don't like your job, quit. If you don't have enough time, stop watching TV. If you are looking for the love of your life, stop looking, he or she will be waiting for you when you start doing the things you love. Stop over-analyzing, since linear thinking can get in the way of deeper intuitive knowing, such as an intuition needed to understand the subjects of "the unseen realms." Life is simple. When you eat, appreciate every last bite. Open your mind, arms, and heart to new things and new people; our differences are superficial. Ask the next person you see what their passion is, and share your inspiring dreams with them. Travel often; getting lost will help you find yourself. Some opportunities only come once, so always seize them. Life is about the people you meet and the things you create with them, so go out and start creating. Life is short. Live your dream and share your passion.

We must strive to be at peace with ourselves and with all people, so we may mutually create a utopian society. If this scenario is possible, maybe it would go something like this: Mutual respect is imperative to an interconnected consciousness. It will be difficult for some of us to come to terms with our own potential while leaving others behind. We must all mutually ascend together. Be as close to nature as possible. Just take it on faith right now that we are the only advanced sentient species that uses a monetary currency. We are the only advanced civilization that allows our own species to be homeless or to die of starvation. We are made to pay to live on a planet we are born into. We have fought wars over power, territory, material goods and money. Humans have shamefully destroyed other species. All this chaos arises over valuing wealth and control. How do we move to the next paradigm? How can we transcend Earth's Dilemma?

The governments currently running the show on Earth have failed us. The real governing bodies are entities we really don't want to meet. We are living through a period of great awakening. The people of our world are beginning to open their eyes and realize the stunning depth of the scams and collusion taking place all around them. These scams steal their wealth, poison them with chemicals, enslave them with financial trickery and control their minds with propaganda. These scams are the very fabric of modern government, the mainstream media, universities, and the so-called "science" institutions. All of our institutions have been infiltrated and exploited, and only now is the astonishing treachery of this infiltration being exposed as it really is. The great awakening taking place will give us the power to see right through the lies in a new Age of Transparency.

ALL YOU NEED IS LOVE

What does it take to change the essence of a man or a woman? We need to examine ourselves from within. Many of us have completely lost our way. We all want to be aware of the changes occurring around us. Sometimes harsh reality is better given in small doses. We're afraid to let go of the old ways. Some will even fight to preserve the old ways, just because it is so familiar. It can be overwhelming to create a new realm of knowing. Everyday there are little things we can do to advance ourselves. Be thankful when you wake up that you are alive. Be friendly to all those around you, even strangers. Tell your children and your immediate family every day that you love them. Offer sincere blessings for the little things in life, from the food you eat to an ambulance screaming by with someone in physical pain. Exercise compassion for others. By doing this we magnetize our surroundings with the vibration we put into the world around us. Little things that we can do, or the thoughts we have, really do make a difference. Change the frequency, and over time, you'll experience attitudes transformed by gratitude. Remember where you are and don't forget who you are. My mantra for the last two decades has been: "I am a master here to co-create heaven on Earth." We can indeed achieve what we ask for!

If there is to be a oneness of humans with cosmic consciousness, or what some conceive of as God, then that divine connection must be love. Humankind can usher in a transcended age by expressing love and kindness toward each other and to the world. For each of us, the mere thought of doing harm to any living creature will someday become repugnant. We need to become incapable of violent acts. Personal ethics and morality should be of the utmost importance. In this way we take a vow of love, morals, respect and altruism which will guide our every action. An initiate may start today by making the goal of seeking wisdom, practicing kindness, and embracing compassion.

The love that you withhold is the pain that you carry. This is a judgment we place upon ourselves. Lifetime after lifetime it goes on and on until we learn the lesson.

We've all made decisions to withhold love. But we can also choose not to withhold love. The greatest thing you'll ever learn is just to love and be loved in return. In the end all that matters is how much you have loved and how you loved. Love is the Absolute Truth. Remember this maxim, and reread this passage if the contents of this book seem frightening, or make you angry. There are great injustices in the world, but they can all be resolved. Love is the Absolute Truth.

Only when humans renounce all violence, stop all wars, share all resources, and fully embrace love can we raise the vibration of our planet. When this happens, a new dawn on Earth will arise, and the exterior manipulations will end forever. Love is the solution to all of our problems. If we can collectively join together and insist on our right to freely evolve, the tyranny of oppressive governments will lose power, and a new power will transform all of us simultaneously. For the first time.

Yours in transformation,

Brad Olsen
San Francisco, CA
August 2, 2012

There are roughly 100+ billion stars in the Milky Way galaxy, plus there are roughly 100+ billion brown dwarfs, or failed stars, in the same galaxy. The Milky Way galaxy is about 90,000 to 100,000 light years wide. For a people in the third dimension it would take them approximately 100,000 years to travel the Milky Way galaxy at the speed of light going 300,000 kilometers per second, or 18 million+ kilometers per minute at 1077+ million kilometers per hour. But what if there were shortcuts?

The Earth travels approximately 958 million kilometers around the Sun every year at a speed of roughly 107,182 kilometers per hour, or 29 kilometers per second. When people look up at the Sun they are viewing events that occurred eight minutes into the past. The Sun itself could be an inter-dimensional gateway.

What if advanced ETs have been coming to Earth for ages? The ancient Mayan story of creation, *Popol Vuh*, states, "Men came from the stars, knowing everything, and they examined the four corners of the sky and the Earth's round surface."

Future Esoteric
INTRODUCTION

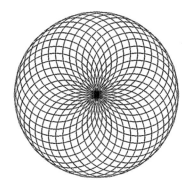

"The day will come when, after harnessing space, the winds, the tides, gravitation, we shall harness for God the energies of love. And, on that day, for the second time in the history of the world, humankind will have discovered fire."
—Teilhard de Chardin

IF you tell someone you study the esoteric these days, they may emblazon you with the charge of being a Satan worshipper or being associated with a death cult. Study of the esoteric has assumed a negative connotation in the modern age, likely trumped by the ascendancy of science and its methodological way of understanding our world. Even to be spiritual has received an unfair assessment by some, because ignorance has a way of making even the beautiful seem ugly.

The word esoteric is derived from the Greek *esoterikos* "belonging to an inner circle," from *esotero*, comparative of *eso* "within." As a philosophical doctrine, it is intended to be revealed only to the initiates of a group, such as the esoteric doctrines of the Greek philosopher and mathematician Pythagoras. Interestingly, the Buddha lived in the same time frame as Pythagoras, but there was no contact between the two men. Pythagoras is considered the first official Grand Master of the Illuminati, members of the secret power elite, who have borrowed this name and have twisted his doctrines for purposes of domination and control. According to the Greek rhetorician Lucian, the division of teachings between exoteric (general knowledge) and esoteric (secret & mystical) originated with Aristotle. Esoteric study was the impetus behind the origin of the mystery schools in ancient Greece.

The literal definition of esoteric is a kind of information understood by, or followed by, a select few who have access to special knowledge. For those involved, esoteric study is viewed as being conducted in private. It can be a secret, discreet, and confidential endeavor. Esoteric research, as contemplated by a select few, can come across as abstruse, arcane or cryptic. It can also mean the study of forbidden subjects, or those derided by science, that is, those weird topics that have no other forum of examination except from within already-biased groups of those who study the esoteric.

DABBLING IN THE ESOTERIC

In any esoteric tradition, the most important factor is that the initiates must truly desire the knowledge they seek. They truly have to want it above anything else. There must be an overwhelming desire for introspection and knowledge. To connect all the pieces of the puzzle, to lift our consciousness and civilization to the next level, we must *all* be students of the esoteric. And in this realm, the truth *is* out there; it is accessible.

To understand esoteric study is to know that it does not progress the way science does. The esoteric is a different school of study, one based on experiences, anecdotes, and even dogmas, whereas science uses testable and objective experimental methodology. Science works very well because other scientists can confirm or refute the findings of the original author, one of the basic principles of the scientific method. If an esoteric science is to be truly universal, it too must be based on fundamental elements of knowledge that can be repeatable, confirmed or refuted and can serve as the foundation for further studies.

Science is unique because it consists of a record of accumulated knowledge, built up over several centuries, with only secondary reliance on intuition. Science is the voluntary acknowledgement by conceptual thinkers that evidence-based decision making is the foundation on which we all stand. In contrast, within the study of religion and esotericism, the essential doctrines are most frequently anchored by the visions and opinions of a single founder and the experiential commentaries of their followers. Scientific discoveries will be referenced extensively in this text, but some of the science to be discussed has yet to be released to the general public. Because of this delay, the validity of esoteric scientific claims in this book will have to await scientific studies performed post-publication. The best examples are the global phenomenon of UFO sightings and free energy technology.

If we accept the premise of withheld information, we have a big problem knowing both what is real and what is true. If we can't trust evidence (replicated reports of seemingly credible individuals) or if we believe those who label strange or unusual claims as a "conspiracy," or if we believe everything the media reports, then we are in a sort of grey zone with no guideposts. We would also have to accept all sorts of other claims without evidence, such as that President Obama was born in Kenya. No evidence? The government must be covering it all up. Defining unusual or esoteric information as a conspiracy is a complete game-changer. Once you give in to this easy dismissal, it is a decision to keep a closed mind. Then, what is the limit? Sooner or later we must decide for ourselves what seems to be correct.

There are those who immediately reject all weird or unusual claims. Others are intrigued and open to further exploration. Of course there are hoaxes out there, but there are also those who seem to have an evil agenda and know how to cover their tracks. On the one hand, we tend to accept only the official explanation, yet on the other hand we see that there is something larger at play, something intent on holding us back from looking beyond—from considering alternatives. The collective esoteric subjects, combined with withheld information by those who seek world control, can be described as the "alternative narrative."

For some people the contents of this book will seem unbelievable. Unfortunately, the beliefs we have always been taught are not a reliable criteria for reality. The very nature of the subjects discussed in this book make them unbelievable, and therefore easily discreditable. It is recommended the reader be intelligently skeptical, but not discard arcane bits of information or perspectives just because the topic is not familiar. At the very least, if the reader is sufficiently intrigued to read through this entire book, he or she can hardly claim the old saw that "there is no evidence." Conversely, the release of this information is potentially catastrophic for certain political, religious and economic vested interests. But if these weren't "dangerous subjects," they wouldn't be considered esoteric.

THE BIG LIE

If the contents of this book are true, it also presents a new dilemma, and that is, what then *is* our reality? For the purpose of this argument we will call everything that we have been told "the big lie." The big lie is an attack upon reality. It undermines and dissolves reality. It eventually undermines all of our social structures based on that false reality, until that reality just collapses. The big lie is very potent and lately it is more and more difficult to counter. The power we need to counter the big lie is to have a true understanding of ourselves. The individual nature of our existence is the spiritual dignity of the human being. To deny the spirit of the individual and instead focus solely on materialism is to become trapped in the big lie. If we want to understand the nature of truth, we need to have incorruptible wisdom. We need to develop a new kind of human wisdom with all its varied aspects. To counter the big lie we need to have a true picture of the threefold human being, that is the universal understanding of mind, body, and spirit. We also need to know who is spreading the big lie.

Two questions emerge: (1) Is it possible that ancient and secret societies exist which have always had control over the real and important information and have been manipulating us throughout history? (2) If so, are they succeeding? Researchers point to the Illuminati and the power elite, the secret society of the huge money interests, who control the information dished out to the masses by planting false knowledge and beliefs into the mass media. This relatively small number of individuals appear to be the ones behind the big lie. Essentially, everything we would like to know, and need to know, has been covered up: information about the electro-genetic magnificence of our DNA being a spiritual antenna, about everything in our universe being a divine interactive creation, about our ascendancy into a new understanding and the fact that we are living the future esoteric right now. It is now harder than ever to understand and differentiate the "shit from Shinola." We've been duped into a system that is designed to consolidate wealth and power rather than provide a real opportunity for all people to thrive. By exposing this agenda, strategically challenging deceptive systems such as central banks and fiat currency and coming up with new ways to organize and cooperate, we can render obsolete this destructive agenda and liberate our planet, plus unleash our true human potential.

Everything of importance has been covered up under the model of the big lie. For example, we are not learning the truth about pharmaceutical products, both the toxicity of vaccinations and the long-term harmful effects of various medications. The pharmaceutical industrialists (better named the Military Medical Petrochemical Pharmaceutical Cartel) have almost total control over the mass media, and thus control over the mass mind. As a result of the power they wield, people are not given factual information to make informed decisions; they are given propaganda. Consequently, the health choices people make are mired in ignorance, make them weaker, and toxify them to the point that they tend to die earlier. This is a fundamental reason for countering the big lie. You can live longer and be much healthier.

There is now what is identified as a global domination agenda, which is a plan by a powerful private banker elite to take over our primary systems. These are the biggest systems in the world, including money, energy, food, medicine, education, media, and influence over government officials who regulate these industries. The elite seek to establish a sole authority over all these global issues, with themselves in charge. They use the media, central banks, multinational corporations, governments, major foundations, and international agencies such as the International Monetary Fund and the World Bank to implement their strategies. So far they have successfully brought down the financial infrastructure of countries across the globe, including Argentina, Chile, Ecuador, Tanzania, Indonesia, Brazil, Poland, Mexico, Bolivia, Thailand, Iceland, the Soviet Union, Japan, Greece and scores of others. They are now attempting to dismantle the U.S. infrastructure by collapsing the dollar to make sure Americans are in more debt than they can ever possibly repay. The "seeing-eye" pyramid is indicative of their basic structure of control. The financial elite are at the top. They use international and national central banks to control corporations, which they loan to at special rates, manipulate national economies and hence their governments, and get everyone in debt to the bankers.

U.S. government politicians, indeed all of the leaders of the so-called "free world" are totally controlled by a secret and wealthy oligarchy. Most of the elite controllers are not even in government, but dictate what the government will do. These are the people who are also behind UFO secrecy. The largest aerospace corporations have now taken over advanced UFO technology for their own purposes and are perpetuating the cover-up. The globalists do not care if you believe in UFOs. But if you do know there are ETs contacting Earth, then you will know there are alternative free energy solutions available and other technology beyond our wildest dreams. But this knowledge, if prematurely accessed, would upset their monopolies based on oil-coal-nuclear energy, transportation, communications, gas fuel, and pharmaceuticals. After all, who would continue to pay all these ev-er-increasing prices for gasoline—the unnecessary burning of fossil fuel that is polluting the air, poisoning our children, choking us all—if we knew beyond a shadow of a doubt that there are non-polluting energy sources out there? This is what the big lie is all about. It all comes back to the old journalistic adage, which is, if you cannot make sense of a story, then simply "follow the money."

It is hard to absorb the enormity of the big lie until you know it personally. It is the greatest story *never* told. The extent to which humanity is being massively manip-ulated can be overwhelming. How can anyone conclude the objective truth about anything in life anymore? We know corporations lie to us. We know governments lie to us. We know the media lies to us. Who can we trust? Yet, we can liberate ourselves once we start breaking through the fog, once we begin to penetrate the maze and start to "get it." But this requires undertaking a real re-education. The other option is to passively allow the programming of our minds to accept a pre-determined version of reality that the elite would like us to have.

Disclosure will remain an individual quest for some time, so forget about official disclosure happening on your TV anytime soon. Until then, study the evidence for yourself. Nobody official is going to tell you the full story, at least not without lying about it or creating a cover story. Choose your sources well and apply a good dose of uncommon sense. Use intuition and pattern recognition. Furthermore, disclo-sure is really just the beginning, and when it does come, do not expect it all in one big revelation. Before that happens, there will be a few primetime TV series to get you used to an alternative idea. "Predictive Programming" is what it is called.

UFOs AND ALIENS: REAL OR HOAXED?

Most people consider UFOs a "socially sensitive" subject. After all, how do we really know if UFOs are real or not? Many consider true objectivity almost impossible. Thus, the information in this book needs to be treated purely as data for your own personal consideration. Consider these views as scenarios. It is imperative readers arrive at their own conclusions, do their own independent research, and become as informed as possible. This then becomes the individual's truth, his or her power, knowledge, and guiding principle in life.

A 2002 Roper poll of American beliefs and personal experiences on intelligent life on other planets (using rigorous scientific polling methods) found that 48% of U.S. adults believe that intelligent life from other planets or dimensions is now visiting Earth, and 67% of U.S. adults believe in the existence of intelligent life elsewhere in the universe. The Roper poll also found that 72% of American adults believe the U.S. Government is not telling all it knows about spacecraft or "un-identified flying objects" visiting the Earth. Fully 14% of Americans say they have had a close encounter with a spacecraft or "unidentified flying object." Two per-cent of Americans told Roper that they have had an encounter with intelligent be-ings from other planets or dimensions. Roper also found that among those adult

Americans who believe in abductions by non-terrestrial beings, 33% claim they either experienced or know someone who experienced a close encounter with intelligent beings from other planets or dimensions.

Yet we are still at a point in history where it is possible (even easy) to believe strongly and completely that we are "alone in the universe," that the human form has only uniquely evolved here on Earth, and that we are already at the highest level of potential human evolution and technological advancement. That's it. End of story. Nothing esoteric found here. "You take the blue pill," said Morpheus in the film *The Matrix* and "the story ends, you wake up in your bed and believe whatever you want to believe."

"You take the red pill," continued Morpheus, "you stay in Wonderland and I show you how deep the rabbit hole goes." If every single UFO or ET video is a hoax, then it is an extraordinarily sophisticated campaign to trick the people of the world. Suffice it to say, this would require big budget Hollywood level SFX expertise and significant equipment to fake something such as the thousands of videos on YouTube alone. Besides, reports of true personal experiences have a kind of intuitive energy which is hard to fake. Hoaxes, on the other hand, have a different, off-putting energy. But when this argument fails, debunkers resort to the label "crazies"—an old and tired strategy. Unfortunately it is all too easy to marginalize those who have a belief in the paranormal.

If UFOs are real, then this discovery will clearly be the most significant event in the history of civilization. So big, it will come to define modern human history, with unimaginable repercussions for society. If they are real, UFOs offer the possibility of technology beyond our wildest dreams. For this reason alone, they have been classified as above top secret for decades. The elite powers view such technological potential as the ultimate threat to their entrenched control of society's infrastructure. Yet, scientists, researchers, military personnel, and astronauts have been talking about UFOs for decades. It appears that "the truth will come out." In recent times, some major governments have begun to make their files on UFOs public. Again, if this is a grand hoax of unpaid computer graphic experts, why would world governments from Belgium to New Zealand, from the UK to Ecuador, France and Brazil, all declassify and present to the public UFO documents? In a new effort to come clean in the United States, the Federal Bureau of Investigations launched a new section on their website in the spring of 2011 called the "Vault." Here can be seen dozens of documents pertaining to UFOs, the Roswell Incident, animal mutilations, ESP and other topics. The FBI and governments of the world who declassify UFO files are not known to be prankster organizations. Also, in April, 2011, the National Security Agency, which was originally formed to handle the UFO phenomenon, declassified select documents under the Freedom of Information Act.

When Professor Peter Sturrock, a prominent Stanford University plasma physicist, conducted a survey of the membership of the American Astronomical Society in the 1970s, he made an interesting discovery. He found that astronomers who spent time reading up on the UFO phenomenon developed more interest in the subject. If there were nothing to it, you would expect the opposite reaction. A lack of credible evidence would cause a scientist's interest to wane. But the fact of the matter is there does exist a vast amount of high quality, albeit enigmatic, data. Hundreds of military and government agency witnesses have come forward with testimony confirming this extraterrestrial presence. According to a recent petition to the White House: "Opinion polls now indicate more than 50 percent of the American people believe there is an extraterrestrial presence and more than 80 percent believe the government is not telling the truth about this phenomenon. The people have a right to know. The people can handle the truth."

The astronomer Father Gabriel Funes, writing in the Vatican newspaper, said he believed that intelligent beings created by God could exist in outer space. "A belief in extraterrestrials does not go against the Catholic faith," stated this Vatican astronomer in 2008. At the same time, many countries of the world were making efforts at disclosure. But the USA, which arguably has the most secrets of all, has remained ever-secretive about an official disclosure.

EXOPOLITICS

The study of the UFO subject, including the idea that extraterrestrials exist and have visited the Earth, is called exopolitics. Exopolitics is defined as the science of relations between our Earth and advanced, intelligent civilizations in the universe. It is concerned with the study of the politics involving ET contact and their possible interactions with humans. Exopolitics is based upon the understanding that Earth is being visited by many advanced extraterrestrial races with diverse ethics, motives, appearances and agendas. The dynamics of the interactions between ET races and their interactions with Earth humanity is the ultimate *Future Esoteric* field of study. Exopolitic researchers are quick to point out that it is not enough to simply study the UFO phenomenon. There are human motives for keeping their presence secret, just as there are motives we can learn from the ETs. Apparently, there are quite a few groups of space entities operating in the vicinity of this planet, and while they have knowledge of each other they do not engage in extensive interchange of ideas. Some of them are working for the benefit of the human race, others to fulfill a "plan," while still others are merely "tourists." According to exopolitics research, something drastic is set to happen around the world shortly, and it can be assumed that entities will flock here to observe how the Earth drama plays out and how humanity will respond.

Advocates for exopolitics have proposed establishing relations with extraterrestrials to take advantage of their presumed knowledge of sustainable energy sources and other matters of global importance. Exopolitics offers a bridge out of the permanent USA warfare state, out of the permanent warfare industry, and into transforming the warfare economy into a cooperative, peaceful, space age society. The exopolitics model retains the view that we live in a highly populated universe filled with intelligent, evolving civilizations operating under universal law, with governance systems mediated by universal politics.

We on Earth are just becoming aware that we live in a populated universe. The structural blinders and belief patterns that have been placed upon us now face a complete restructuring. If the exopolitics model can become the dominant paradigm, we can create a massive change which will turn around the destructive fate of the world. The environmental problems we are now facing are part of the "truth embargo" forced upon us by allowing the military, intelligence agencies and the industrialists to keep everything UFO-related under top secret status. Removing it from "national security" status to the scientific laboratories and the classrooms is the goal of exopolitics. UFOs and extraterrestrials are not top secret threats to be hidden away, but provide social, educational, and very likely, spiritual solutions for our society. Our intelligence agencies and the military are the real culprits of information starvation, and they in turn are owned and controlled by corporate military industrial complex globalists.

Exopolitics and most esoteric topics are very broad and complex subjects. Neither is something that one can expect to learn quickly on a whim. These subjects are best left alone by those who demand definitive proof rather than the pursuit of a general inquiry. The best way to get a handle on the truth is to work with a number of separate data streams and then compare the different outputs for similarities and patterns. There is also disinformation out there with the sole purpose of throwing off truth seekers. Propaganda is easily allocated to the masses on a silver platter, but the truth is like a gold mine. You have to dig through a lot of ore to find the good stuff.

THE LAWS OF CONSISTENCY

In the abstract, *Future Esoteric* constructs a new unified theory of all the "maybe subjects" by combining the three sections in this book: Secrets, Cosmos, and Utopia. We will extrapolate on the esoteric study of UFOs by constructing a unifying theory of all phenomena which we can apply to real advancements within our civilization. One utopian cosmic vision suggests that if we can possibly learn from other highly-evolved ET societies, then we can also create a new society of our own. Perhaps such a society would support a high-technology holographic science, where time travel and interstellar travel is possible. Contact with other interstellar beings would motivate the human race to come together in a lasting world peace. This would be the moment when real and meaningful contact with benevolent ETs could occur.

This utopian unified theory model would practice the Laws of Consistency, which allows for children to receive all new information when it becomes known. Nothing is ever withheld and every tool that is available to one is available to all. There is no such thing as secrets, greed, or hoarding. Knowledge is freely distributed and encouraged to be expanded upon by the next generation. Thus, every new generation becomes smarter than its parents. They inherit the society. They are the ones that continue to go out and expand knowledge, science, and contribute new advancements for society. Every truth is spoken. Everyone is forgiven. There is no monetary system. It is a utopian system where no one is left behind. Work is defined as mentoring, creating, and cooperating with others, and then all human needs are taken care of in an open and fair society. There is free health care but it has nothing to do with pharmaceuticals; it has to do with advanced healing information about color, light, and sound, and our multi-dimensional physicality. This entails the advancement of the soul and repairing of our DNA structure, which can all be healed. We cannot begin to implement these practices with the current power structure in control.

The first thing to realize is we are not just a physicality. Each of us has a soul and it is quantifiable. It is so quantifiable it has a weight. Scientists around the world have weighed humans at the moment of death and discovered the human spirit weighs exactly 22 grams. Before death we create our own adventure in life. People can identify with truth, so lies will eventually come to the surface and fall away. We know what is real, but we have to detach ourselves from the addiction to physicality. When detached from the body we can become completely objective. We can come to know the essence of ourselves. Once we have achieved self-empowerment we will know exactly what to do. We are eternal spiritual beings. There is no age to us. We need to move all our collective power into the essence of awareness of our spiritual being through voluntary introspection. "Out beyond ideas of right-doing and wrong-doing there is a field. I'll meet you there," spoke the mystic Rumi. For in the end, only our actions in life arising from love will matter. If you want to know where to start, develop an inner serenity from which peace activism, the highest calling, can arise. We hope someday you will join us.

WILL THIS BE OUR FUTURE …

> When the Nazis came for the communists,
>   I remained silent;
>   I was not a communist.
> When they locked up the social democrats,
> I remained silent;
>   I was not a social democrat.
> When they came for the trade unionists,
> I did not speak out;
>   I was not a trade unionist.
> Then they came for me,
> and there was no one left to speak for me.

−Martin Niemoeller, German anti-Nazi theologian and Lutheran pastor

… OR THIS?

> Love is the new religion of the 21st century.
> You don't have to be a highly educated person, or have any exceptional
>   knowledge to understand it.
> It comes from the intelligence of the heart,
>   embedded in the timeless evolutionary pulse of all human beings.
> Be the change you want to see in the world.
> Nobody else can do it for you.
> We are now recruiting.
> Perhaps you will join us,
>   or already have.
> All are welcome,
>   the door is open.

−Brian Piergrossi, from his book *The Big Glow*

The ordinary narrative is what we all perceive to be real. It is the alternative narrative that stretches the bounds of reality, such as the Sphinx and Great Pyramids have done for eons. To codify and document esoteric subjects it was necessary to plot three data points containing similar information, especially when those data points extended over years and decades. Given the fact that all disinformation involves some degree of truth, the next step was to rigorously check the links to see if any of the info could actually be independently validated. Subjective intuition also factored into the process of writing about these esoteric subjects.

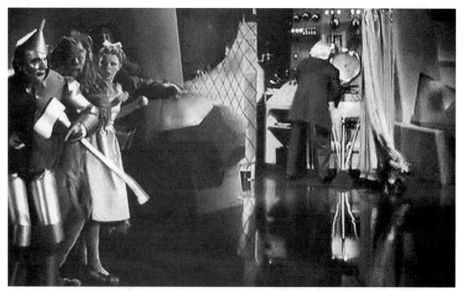

"Don't look at the man behind the curtain!" cried the Wizard of Oz out of desperation, when he knew his cover was blown. There is a similar deception called the "big lie" in the world today. The lie is so vast, so all-encompassing, that everything we thought we knew about the world is an illusion—and there really is a "man behind the curtain." However, the illusion is effective only on the unwary, the unaware, and the uninformed. Just like the magician trying to trick us, once we know that the man behind the curtain is a fraud, the jig is up. The lie is exposed, the spell is broken, and the illusion loses its power over people.

Which way is up in this "optical eye-gasm" by M.C. Escher, the famous graphic artist of "impossible structures?" Similarly, what is the correct path when each side seems plausible when we focus on it? Such is the dilemma of the "alternative narrative."

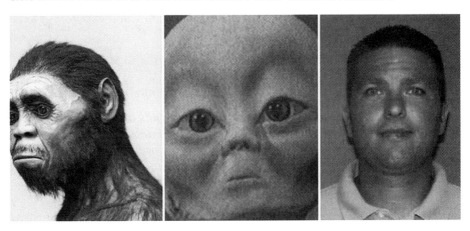

What do proto-humans, the "Grey" extraterrestrial biological entities, and humans have in common? Perhaps more than you'd think. Once the ET truth embargo is lifted, the human race will come into contact with information that will blow the lid off of who we think we are, where we came from, and our true hidden identity. Indeed, sometimes the truth *is* stranger than fiction!

SECRETS

What is being withheld from us, who is doing it, their agenda, and why it matters to you. A peek behind the invisible veil.

"Whosoever controls the volume of money in any country is absolute master of all industry and commerce. ... And when you realize that the entire system is very easily controlled, one way or another, by a few powerful men at the top, you will not have to be told how periods of inflation and depression originate." –President James Garfield, assassinated a few weeks after making this statement in 1881

"These international bankers and Rockefeller-Standard Oil interests control the majority of newspapers and the columns of these papers to club into submission or drive out of public office officials who refuse to do the bidding of the powerful corrupt cliques which compose the invisible government." –President Theodore Roosevelt, 1922

"The drive of the Rockefellers and their allies is to create a one-world government combining super-capitalism and communism under the same tent, all under their control. ... Do I mean conspiracy? Yes I do. I am convinced there is such a plot, international in scope, generations old in planning, and incredibly evil in intent." –Congressman Larry P. McDonald, 1976, killed in the Korean Airlines 747 shot down by the Soviets

"We are on the verge of a global transformation. All we need is the right major crisis, and the nations will accept the New World Order." –David Rockefeller, 1994

"The cruelest lies are told in silence." –Robert Louis Stevenson

"It's not hard to find the truth. What is hard is not to run away from it once you have found it." –Prometheus

"We are a nation of sheep, and sheep are always led to slaughter. There is tremendous power in knowledge, and in secrecy. Take away that secrecy, you make sure you are informed and you can change things." –William Cooper

"If you shut up truth and bury it under the ground, it will but grow, and gather to itself such explosive power that the day it bursts through it will blow up everything in its way." –Émile Zola, 19th century French novelist

"Those who can make you believe absurdities can make you commit atrocities." –Voltaire

"All governments suffer a recurring problem: Power attracts pathological personalities. It is not that power corrupts but that it is magnetic to the corruptible." –Frank Herbert, *Dune*

"The general population doesn't know what's happening, and it doesn't even know that it doesn't know." –Noam Chomsky

SECRETS NO MORE

"The money powers prey upon the nation in times of peace and conspires against it in times of adversity. The banking powers are more despotic than monarchy, more insolent than autocracy, more selfish than any bureaucracy. They denounce as public enemies all who question their methods or throw light upon their crimes." –President Abraham Lincoln

IF indeed we do live in a fair and open democracy, the public most certainly does deserve to have "freedom of information." It can be argued that keeping a secret is a form of lying. Maybe this is even the worst form of lying, especially when withholding certain information can cause harm to others. What is *not* said can speak volumes. There are people who risk their lives to end the age of secrecy endemic in the United States and around the world.

Secrecy is both expensive and can have negative consequences. As former Senator Daniel Patrick Moynihan wrote in his 1998 book appropriately titled *Secrecy*, "The actors involved seem hardly to know the set of rules they play. Most important, they seem never to know the damage that they can do." Regarding the UFO subject and its dismissal by skeptics, he continued, "Conspiracy theories have been a part of American culture for two centuries. But they seem to have grown in dimension and public acceptance in recent decades." If the intelligence community and the highest-ranking officials in this country don't fully understand the game and its consequences they play, how can the general public comprehend the scale and scope of the big secrets in America? The UFO cover-up is simply symptomatic of far larger secrecy problems. This book holds credible evidence that the UFO phenomenon is not a "conspiracy"—not a false set of beliefs. However, perhaps because it is a real phenomenon and such a bombshell, there is a conspiracy of secrecy to prevent disclosure—hence, the dedication to secrets no more.

At a strategic level, the practice of over-classification (that is, over-classified in the sense of keeping unnecessary secrets or spreading outright lies) erodes the public's trust and confidence in their government. We all know by judging from the events in the recent past that there are many instances in which officials of the government have been less than truthful. Recent polls have shown that over half of the American people feel they cannot trust the government. Secrecy, which is rarely justified (contrary to official claims), greatly contributes to this declining trust. Also unfortunately, the manner in which the UFO topic has been handled has increased the level of distrust for the general public, and to a much greater degree for those true believers.

SECRECY IS REPUGNANT

In late April of 1961, President John F. Kennedy made a revealing speech before the American Newspaper Publishers Association about the danger of the powerful elite keeping secrets. He made clear that secret societies were operating among us and wielded enormous control. He called these groups a "monolithic and ruthless conspiracy that relies on covert means for expanding its sphere of influence." Kennedy went on to say in his address:

> "The very word 'secrecy' is repugnant in a free and open society; and we are as a people inherently and historically opposed to secret societies, to secret oaths and to secret proceedings. We decided long ago that the dangers of excessive and unwarranted concealment of pertinent facts far outweighed the dangers which are cited to justify it. Even today, there is little value in opposing the threat of a closed society by imitating its arbitrary restrictions. Even today, there is little value in insuring the survival of our nation if our traditions do not survive with it. And there is a very grave danger that an announced need for increased security will be seized upon by those anxious to expand its meaning to the very limits of official censorship and concealment. That I do not intend to permit to the extent that it is in my control. And no official of my Administration, whether his rank is high or low, civilian or military, should interpret my words here tonight as an excuse to censor the news, to stifle dissent, to cover up our mistakes or to withhold from the press and the public the facts they deserve to know."

A conspiracy, by definition, implies that a group of people performs a treacherous or evil act and attempt to do so in secret. Napoleon said that history is the lie agreed upon. Indeed, the winner of a conflict gets to rewrite the history. It makes victims of everyone not in on the conspiracy. The more insidious the conspiracy, the less likely the victims know that they are being victimized. Nazi propaganda chief Joseph Goebbels famously stated, "If you tell a lie big enough and keep repeating it, people will eventually come to believe it. The lie can be maintained only for such time as the State can shield the people from the political, economic or military consequences of the lie. It thus becomes vitally important for the State to use all of its powers to repress dissent, for the truth is the mortal enemy of the lie, and thus by extension, the truth is the greatest enemy of the State." A grand conspiracy must be identified in the esoteric narrative as two-fold: both as the effort to suppress the truth, and keeping that suppression shrouded in secrecy maintained by the "State."

The key to maintaining a massive secret agenda is a classic pyramid structure, a "need to know" system, where people only understand as much as they need to in order to accomplish their tasks, but no more. That way only the individuals at the top of each pyramid can ever access the full plan. Secret societies and the aerospace-military complex work this way, including the CIA, the banks, the major corporations, the military, mainstream media, and religious hierarchies.

AN OPEN-SOURCE, DEMOCRATIC INTELLIGENCE AGENCY

Today we have the whistleblower website WikiLeaks offering a look behind the government's curtain. Not since Daniel Ellsberg released the Pentagon Papers in 1971 has there been a more effective challenge to state secrecy. In a modern version of the Pentagon Papers story, Army soldier Bradley Manning was arrested in Iraq, in May, 2010, on suspicion of having passed restricted material to the website WikiLeaks.

Bradley Manning started leaking classified information to WikiLeaks in 2010 as a way to protest the conduct of the war in Iraq. He downloaded data onto a CD marked "Lady Gaga," lip-syncing as he supposedly did his job. He posted his reasons for releasing classified information on a blog site: "Hypothetical question: if you had free reign over classified networks for long periods of time ... say, 8-9 months ... and you saw incredible things, awful things ... things that belonged in the public domain, and not on some server stored in a dark room in Washington D.C. ... what would you do?" Bradley Manning, who now identifies as Chelsea, was convicted in 2013 of "aiding the enemy," a violation of the Espionage Act. She is currently serving a 35-year sentence.

WikiLeaks was set up in late 2006 as a disclosure portal, initially using the Wikipedia model, where volunteers would write-up and analyze classified or restricted material submitted by whistleblowers, or material that was in some other way legally threatened. The de facto editor-in-chief of WikiLeaks is Julian Assange, an Australian with a background in computer hacking. It was he who had the idea of creating what he saw as an "open-source, democratic intelligence agency."

A CHALLENGE TO THE ULTIMATE SECRET

People wishing to encourage an open-source, democratic intelligence agency have identified many "black" programs. The black programs are so named because it is very difficult to shine a "light" on their activities and expose the corruption within. There can be governments within governments within governments, and the "black ones," or secret governments, can be invisible to the elected government itself.

Since 2012, Julian Assange remains in London's Ecuador Embassy under political asylum. He faces rape charges in Sweden, but most think it is really because WikiLeaks released a selection of more than 250,000 classified U.S. diplomatic cables passed to the whistleblowing website by Chelsea Manning and others. U.S. officials and other world politicians have denounced Assange as a traitor, and some have even publicly called for his assassination. But Mr. Assange says he has a smoking gun, a secret that keeps his would-be executors at bay. This secret will be released in time, or in the event he is killed or extradited to the United States. According to Julian Assange, "It is worth noting that in yet-to-be-published parts of the cablegate archive, there are indeed references to UFOs." These references to extraterrestrial life in yet-to-be-published confidential files were obtained from the U.S. Government.

Perhaps in response to Julian Assange's claim to have possession of official U.S. diplomatic cables regarding UFOs, both the FBI and the NSA online sites have started posting UFO-related materials on their websites. Also, likely in response to the WikiLeaks announcement, the British government has released the largest number of UFO files of any government to date. Over 8,500 new pages were released in June, 2011, by the National Archives. And in yet another strange twist, the respected *Guardian* newspaper ran the headline: "'Earth must prepare for close encounter with aliens,' say scientists."

DEBUNKERS NO MORE

Those who have debunked UFOs for the last 70-plus years are becoming a dying breed since the National Security Agency (NSA) released many declassified documents pertaining to UFOs starting in April, 2011. Those who have made a career proclaiming the entire UFO phenomenon is just plain nonsense, mass hallucinations, swamp gas or Earthly aircraft were either terribly uninformed, or outright liars. Most damning to debunkers is a document pertaining to U.S. and Soviet scientists decoding messages from a higher intelligence at the time Sputnik was launched in the early 1960s. This single document on the NSA website proves the debunkers are, and always have been, dead wrong.

In April, 2011, the Allen Telescope Array (ATA) at the Search for Extraterrestrial Intelligence Institute (SETI) was temporarily mothballed. At a time when NASA's Hubble, Kepler and other exoplanet-hunting telescopes are detecting hundreds of confirmed and candidate alien worlds orbiting other stars, wouldn't this be an opportunity to point the ATA at some of these worlds—particularly the ones known to have Earth-like characteristics? There seems to be a reluctance to study similarly habitable exoplanets. Even more curious is the timing of SETI's radio telescope arrays shutting down abruptly with little notice "due to budget cutbacks." SETI announced they would turn off their signals on April 15, 2011, only a week before the NSA released documents confirming human contact with extraterrestrials. For UFO researchers, this is a small vindication that their studies were valid all along. Unfortunately for these long-ridiculed researchers, an official disclosure may not be forthcoming.

Contrary to a the widespread debunker opinion regarding the U.S. Government's supposed inability to keep anything secret, quite the opposite is true. In August, 1942, the "Manhattan Project" was tasked to develop the atomic bomb. It was started under the control of the U.S. Army Corps of Engineers during the Roosevelt Administration and not a single leak occurred among the 125,000 people assigned to work on the project. The Manhattan Project utilized four main facilities, including: Hanford, WA; The Clinton Engineer Works at Oak Ridge, TN; the basement of the unused football stadium at the University of Chicago, IL; and the Los Alamos National Laboratory which was built in 1943 on a secluded New Mexico mesa and headed by Robert Oppenheimer. It was, and still is, possible to keep most classified developments top-secret.

CORE SECRETS

A "core secret" is considered so sensitive by the U.S. intelligence community that not only its contents but its very existence is a secret. Within NATO, the UFO phenomenon is classified as "Cosmic Top Secret," which is an even higher secret ranking than plans for the hydrogen bomb. As such, the extraterrestrial presence is the core story in this uppermost level of U.S. intelligence secrecy. Some researchers speculate the U.S. military brass will not, indeed cannot, ever make an official ET disclosure because of these above top-secret classifications.

Within the U.S. Government there are various levels of Special Access Programs (SAP), the first being a division into acknowledged and unacknowledged SAPs. A "Black Program" is slang for an unacknowledged SAP. An unacknowledged SAP is so sensitive that its very existence is a core secret. Indeed, some unacknowledged SAPs are sensitive to the extent that they are "waived" from the normal management and oversight protocols. Even members of Congress in the appropriations committee are not allowed to know anything about these programs, along with the Senate and House committees that allocate budgets and the intelligence committees. In the case of a waived SAP, only eight members of Congress, the chairs and ranking minority members of the four defense committees, are even notified that a given program has been waived. Even when these programs are waived, committee members are not told anything about the nature of the program. In this case, such a program is certainly "Deep Black."

Dr. Edgar Mitchell, the Apollo 14 astronaut who was the sixth man to walk on the Moon, remains an outspoken believer that the government harbors "core story" secrets. Mitchell has revealed why the UFO subject is a core secret, even out of reach of the president, or anyone in government (including Congress) who are all regarded as only on a "need to know basis." Mitchell, who landed on the Moon with Alan B. Shepard in February, 1971, stated flatly: "A few insiders know the truth ... and are studying the bodies that have been discovered." Then he added, a "cabal" of insiders stopped fully briefing presidents about extraterrestrial matters after President Kennedy.

NASA astronaut Gordon Cooper also has expressed his frustration with core secrets:

> *"For many years I have lived with a secret, in a secrecy imposed on all specialists in astronautics. I can now reveal that every day, in the USA, our radar instruments capture objects of form and composition unknown to us. And there are thousands of witness reports and a quality of documents to prove this, but nobody wants to make them public. Why? Because authority is afraid that people may think of God knows what kind of horrible invaders. So the password still is: 'We have to avoid panic by all means.' "*

Astronaut Mitchell had a conversation with a high-ranking admiral within the Joint Chiefs who agreed to investigate the "core story" of alien contact and report back. The admiral, who has been identified as Rear Admiral Thomas R. Wilson, did provide Mitchell with the confirmation that his assessment was "essentially correct."

Quoting an article taken from the prestigious *Janes Defense Weekly*, Mitchell implied that the admiral had discovered that the core story was protected by a "Special Access Program." As reported by *Janes*, such a "black program" must remain unacknowledged when it is "considered so sensitive that the fact of its existence is a 'core-secret,' which can be defined as any item, progress, strategy or element of information, the compromise of which would result in unrecoverable failure." Astronaut Mitchell then added, "The UFO program that the admiral sought would be in this category. Thus by law he would be required to deny the existence of such a program. For a core secret Special Access Program, even a 'no comment' would be a breach of security." So if our top elected officials cannot make UFO inquiries, nor can the highest ranking military officials or the highly-esteemed Apollo astronauts, then who is really in charge?

SECRET JUSTIFICATIONS

The "Powers That Be" strongly believe in the value and legitimacy of using secrecy over the people. They justify their actions because those uninformed, or those not sure what to believe, are scared and any disclosure will cause panic. What if people took their own lives because of the fear of something coming and then nothing happened? They cite the 1938 Orson Welles *War of the Worlds* radio broadcast when a panic broke out because the show sounded like a real hostile alien invasion.

Such a news quarantine on anything UFO-related can be traced back to the World War II era. While returning to Britain from a mission in Germany, air crew personnel were reportedly approached by a metallic UFO on the English coast. The crew took photographs, reported that the UFO appeared to "hover noiselessly," and then the craft suddenly disappeared. Upon hearing the story, Winston Churchill ordered the report to be kept secret for 50 years or more. "This event should be immediately classified since it would create mass panic amongst the general population and destroy one's faith in the Church," said Churchill.

Looked at another way, what if something really bad was going to happen, such as the catastrophic impact of a meteor, would you really want to know? Would it be better for the disaster to be over quickly with little or no warning, or for people to be in terror for months or years before impact? Maybe those pulling the strings behind the scenes justify their actions of secrecy to world politicians by saying chaos and fear would be much worse. They ask leaders how could they possibly manage to control a mass panic before a coming disaster? Would they want their constituents to live in fear? No, they would keep the secret.

The extremely wealthy elite, let's call them the cabal, hold the lion's share of vital secrets. Many of these secrets, such as free energy or anti-gravity technology, would greatly benefit humanity. Unfortunately, the cabal has incredible disdain for the vast majority of people. They regard the mass public as "worthless eaters." There are also reports of their dastardly future eugenics plan to reduce the world's population by upwards of 90%. They believe that there are far too many people alive, especially too many inferior brown-type people, and they have publicly stated their opinions on the Georgia Guidestones. Such plans to create chaos, destruction and mass murder need to be kept out of the public view at all costs. If you are a researcher and you get too close to exposing the cabal, your life is in great danger. They use assassinations like most people go through tissue papers. We are dealing with some very dangerous, ruthless and controlling sociopathic individuals. No wonder they see a need for absolute secrecy, and no wonder many Americans see a need for disclosure.

ULTRA HIGH NET WORTH

When one class of people loses its wealth, another group deposits the wealth in its portfolio. When whole communities are affected by foreclosures, the wealth shifts upward where shrewd investors stand to gain. The rich continue to get richer as the numbers indicate. The number of individuals with at least $1 million in investable assets rose 8.3 percent to 10.9 million investors after markets rebounded following the 2008 financial crisis. The wealth of global millionaires increased to $42.7 trillion in 2010, up from $40.7 trillion in 2007. Most telling are the global ranks of "ultra high-net-worth individuals" (defined as those with $30 million of investable assets instead of only $1 million for regular millionaires), which increased at a faster pace than the millionaires, rising 10%. The richest 1% of Americans possesses more wealth than the accumulated wealth of the lower 90% combined. It doesn't get much better globally, where the richest 2% of adults currently own more than half the world's wealth. In these intentionally orchestrated times of recession and depression, the 1% are thriving with record profits. The extreme concentration of wealth within a tiny percent of individuals is usually the tipping point before an economic collapse, unless you're the one gaming the system. Before the crash in 1929 that led to the Great Depression, elite bankers pulled their money out of the stock market. After the crash, they used that money to buy up cheap stocks and smaller failing banks for pennies on the dollar.

The next stage after accumulating money is to seize power. The people who have established the Federal Reserve are beginning to create exclusive societies for themselves simply to retain and create yet more control. In 2006, while still in office, President George W. Bush had purchased a 98,842-acre farm in northern Paraguay, protected by a semi-secret U.S. military base. The Mariscal Estigarribia sprawling air base complex and the Bush ranch in Paraguay are both located atop one of the world's largest freshwater aquifers. Does Bush foresee a collapse of the U.S. economy or world economy, or a time when he might need to flee an arrest warrant, and feels his family could use an escape plan? Or are they better off staying here, scamming the system for as long as possible, and if they get in trouble, persuade the right people for a bail out? The system is no longer beholden to the people. If it were, there would be no such thing as "too big to fail." The majority of Americans were against bailing out the banks in 2008. According to Vermont Senator Bernie Sanders, "The top six financial institutions in this country own assets equal to more than 60 percent of our gross domestic product and possess enormous economic and political power." Sanders bravely asks a question few of his colleagues will support: "One of the great questions of our time is whether the American people, through Congress, will control the greed, recklessness and illegal behavior on Wall Street, or whether Wall Street will continue to wreak havoc on our economy and the lives of working families."

The highly concentrated influence of the Rockefeller cabal remains a huge threat to American interests, as JFK warned in his "Secrecy is Repugnant" speech. Secret power brokers such as the Council on Foreign Relations, the Trilateral Commission, and the Bilderbergers are examples. Some if not all of the highest-ranking politicians must go through these organizations first before they become government candidates. In this arrangement, politicians who must rely on large sums of money to further fuel their campaigns are then heavily influenced. At the international level, central bankers use the World Bank and the International Monetary Fund to make more money while exploiting the resources of the countries they lend to, sometimes bankrupting them in the process. The bankers covertly encourage war because the government would need to borrow money from them and then pay it back with interest. It is a vicious cycle and with the ultra-rich ultimately calling the shots, they are always on top.

OCCUPY ... THE WORLD

The explosive growth of the Occupy Wall Street demonstrations that began in mid-September, 2011, and spread to cities across America, and then globally within weeks, illustrates the growing awareness and deep discontent of people worldwide. The banking cartel, under any different name, will do nothing to change the status quo. And nothing ever will change under their power. They are happy to create credit out of thin air, charge interest which is never credited, and control people and politicians alike. There is not enough money on credit and principle to ever pay it all back. The whole money system from the time it was created was designed for human suppression and control. When "99%" of the Occupy Movement expressed outrage about the bondage of corporate banking, it struck a chord with a wide audience. Their demand should be no less than an end to private banks, their ability to control credit, and governments having to borrow from private banks at interest. As a leaderless consensus movement in solidarity with Occupy Wall Street and the worldwide Occupation Movement, the 99% organized and articulated a simple message: We will no longer tolerate the 1% wielding the power they gained with a promise to serve in our best interests, but instead are serving only themselves.

How can we break the bonds of mental emancipation we now find ourselves under and the illegal "truth embargo" they impose? People have been trained to believe that which they are told—whether it is truth or a lie, to the point where we are simply victims of the lies. But are we? They are the few and we are the many. If we stay divided, they win. If we all become aware together, even just ten percent of the world's population, then they can no longer keep their vice grip on power. If we fall back into fear or into perpetual conflict among ourselves, then they will win.

THEY USE ALL THE DIRTY TRICKS

The controllers know the initial stage of any war is fought in the public arena. If they can successfully influence mass opinion to get behind a cause, then they might not need to manipulate any further. Great invasions do not happen with thundering smoke and high-tech weaponry. That is the mark of an immature society. Great invasions happen in secrecy. In *The Art of War*, a classic fifth century treatise of Chinese philosophy and battle strategy, General Sun Tzu said, "All warfare is based on deception." The master strategist added, "For to win one hundred victories in one hundred battles is not the acme of skill. To subdue the enemy without fighting is the acme of skill."

The latest platform for molding public opinion has now moved to cyberspace. The recently surfaced "Internet Water Army" is a group of individuals who act as paid mercenaries to inundate the Internet with comments, gossip, or other content to build up or demolish credibility of articles, information, websites or public figures. These paid staffers pose as ordinary people writing comments on blogs and discussion forums that can demolish the consumer ranking of products and services, create false images, or provide the rationale for opposing perceptions to destroy the truth.

Some blame China as the pioneer of the Internet Water Army. China may have started the ominous trend, but the list of abusers is vast. *India Daily* posted an article that clearly asserts that China is not the only group "flooding" the Internet this way, watering down content, or launching cyber-attacks. Scams and slander are commonplace on the freewheeling World Wide Web, no matter your access point. Two scientists at the Canadian University of Victoria investigated the problem of the "paid armies" of fake commentators in China. They created software that was 85% successful at discovering their identities. Although most of the Water Army soldiers reside in the emerging economies of China and India, almost all of their clients come from the Western Hemisphere. The corporations are employing them, the unions are employing them, and even the political parties employ them for smear campaigns. It is harder than ever, now, to discern the truth, especially going up against the very well-financed movers and shakers.

John D. Rockefeller famously said, "I don't want a nation of thinkers; I want a nation of workers." As founder of the National Education Association, couldn't this be considered a conflict of interest?

The mighty "Pyramid of Capitalism" still rules over the people of the world today. The cost of "vulture capitalism" in terms of human death and human misery has become so unbearable that we must now abandon it and establish a new life-affirming social system. The planet can no longer afford such forms of predatory capitalism.

THE FOURTH REICH
IN AMERICA

"We find ourselves faced by powers which are far stronger than hitherto assumed, and whose base is at present unknown to us. More I cannot say at present. We are now engaged in entering into closer contact with those powers, and within six or nine months time it may be possible to speak with more precision on the matter." —Wernher von Braun, suggesting in 1959 an extraterrestrial reality

IN the world of global banking, the United States and Germany have been closely tied together for a century or longer, despite the two world wars fought against each other. There have been many German sympathizers in the USA. After all, in the 19th and 20th centuries, German immigrants were the largest segment of foreigners settling in America. German immigrants new to the USA were hard working, inventive, and saved their money. Their can-do spirit is part of what makes America great. There is a saying that "Germans make the best Americans, but Germans make the worst Germans."

The financial assistance of Wall Street in Germany's post-World War I rebuilding in the 1920s is legendary. Many well-known American corporations invested in Germany and inadvertently aided in the subsequent financing and technological footing for World War II. These companies included General Electric, Standard Oil, ITT, Ford, General Motors, Chase and Manhattan banks, and the Rockefeller and J. P. Morgan interests, among others. Investors and governments in the West were interested in German industry before, during, and after the Nazi era. This made for a sometimes easy transfer of post-war assets, secret technology, and trained personnel when the skills of a former Nazi were desired.

Germany was reportedly the scene of many UFO visits in the decade before World War II, including some landings and close personal encounters. The Nazis credited receiving their advanced technology before W.W. II to a small group of German psychics who made contact with ETs from the star system Aldebaran. The benevolent Vril Society originally had the intention of doing only good in world. Thus, Aldebaran ETs allowed Vril psychics to channel plans for interstellar craft, anti-gravity, and free energy devices. When the Nazis saw a war application, they collaborated with the Vril Society and formed the Bavarian Illuminati Thule Society to actively pursue development of these projects. It is claimed that the first "intergalactic treaty" with ETs was established by the Bavarian Thule and Illuminati societies as early as 1933. In 1936, it is alleged that the Nazis recovered a downed craft in Bavaria. From these various ET contacts, Nazi Germany acquired technology far in advance of what modern science acknowledges, even by today's standards.

THE REICH'S OBSESSION

Senior members of the Third Reich, especially Adolph Hitler, Albert Speer and Heinrich Himmler, were obsessed with the occult and esoteric subjects. Their interpretation of these topics fostered the unique Nazi concept of the mystical powers of the Aryan race and its resulting "decline" and degeneration as a result of miscegenation with lower races. The Nazi's *Teutonophilism* carried a fascination with the Norse runes, Nordic myths, and the concept of a "super man." The Swastika came out of the general climate attendant with the new pan-Germanic nationalism. Albert Speer was clearly very interested in geomancy and charting the ley lines and sacred spots of Germany, and some of his architecture exhibits principles of mystical geometry and numerology. The Vril Society in Germany promoted the idea that there might be a mystical energy within the Earth that could be tapped by the German scientists. It is well-known that Hitler consulted astrologers for propitious dates for his military campaigns and employed dowsers on the battlefield to search for water and minefields.

Adolph Hitler knew the Third Reich needed optimal technological advantages to win the war. He approved the production of the so-called "Retaliation Weapons" in 1942, using all the technology acquired from the Vril and Thule societies. The V-2 rocket, the *Vergeltungswaffe 2* or "Vengeance Weapon 2" was launched toward England on September 7, 1944. The Germans were also frantically working on other secret weapons, including nuclear weapon development, which never came to fruition. Reichsfuhrer Heinrich Himmler, head of the SS, was obsessed with the occult; yet his involvement with the backward-engineered UFO called *Die Glocke* seems tangential, that is, until Himmler's closest associate is considered. In 1942, Himmler chose Dr. Hans Kammler, formerly a high-level Air Ministry officer in charge of engineering, to take over the rocketry program. Soon the world famous rocket and space-travel scientist, Professor Hermann Oberth, was ordered to head their probe.

Dr. Hermann Oberth concluded that the "behavior of the UFO discounts any means of propulsion, including the reaction rocket, known to us," and that the "principle of an 'anti-gravity device' might be expected." This is a watershed statement, especially since Oberth was directly involved with *Die Glocke* and the creation of Nazi UFOs. The outspoken Oberth said in 1954: "There is no doubt in my mind that (UFOs) are interplanetary crafts of some sort. It is also our conclusion that they are propelled by distorting or converting the gravitational field."

Analyzing Oberth's pronouncement from the perspective of contemporary physics, mathematician Ward Locke combined Einstein's gravitational theorems with a later tensor model developed by Hermann Weyl. The math revealed the potential for the generation of an anti-gravity field when the equation begets a negative number. Professor Locke confides that sustaining such a system requires a continued energy input of at least 900 kilo amperes, or the transfer of 1020 electrons per second. Without an effective heat shield the temperature will instantly rise to 28,000 Kelvin, which is nearly equivalent to the surface temperature of the Sun. Although dubious that the Nazis harnessed such a force, Professor Locke concedes that, if true, this might have been the reason behind the short intervals sustained during *Die Glocke's* early tests. The scientists simply couldn't generate enough power to keep it going. Had the Nazis been able to utilize their backward-engineered craft into a military craft, the outcome of W.W. II might have been very different.

After the war, this same group of ex-Nazi rocket scientists were secretly whisked off to the USA through Project Paperclip. Was similar technology channeled into experiments conducted by the U.S. Government? It would seem so, and these experiments are also classified as the most top-secret operations since the Manhattan Project. It would take decades before the use of Project Paperclip Nazi scientists was acknowledged. After the war in 1946, apparently in an effort to rewrite history, the Rockefeller Foundation paid $139,000 to commission the publishing of an official history of World War II that deleted any and all mystical and occult interests of the Third Reich. One of the Rockefeller Foundation's main contributors was Standard Oil.

NAZI ESCAPE ROUTES

The ODESSA, a German acronym for *Organisation der ehemaligen SS-Angehörigen*, meaning the "Organization for Former SS Members," was an international Nazi network established in 1946 by a group of Nazi SS officers shortly after the Germans surrendered in World War II. Plans were drafted for a Fourth Reich before the fall of the Third, and it was to be implemented by reorganizing in remote Nazi colonies overseas. The Nazis decided that the time had come to set up a worldwide clandestine escape network. The purpose of the ODESSA was to establish and facilitate these secret escape routes, later known as ratlines, to allow former SS members to avoid capture and subsequent prosecution for their war crimes.

Most of those fleeing out of Germany and Austria were assisted in relocating to South America and the Middle East. As the former head of the SS, Heinrich Himmler was believed to have been the founder of the ODESSA, but he committed suicide while in custody awaiting trial in Nuremberg. Adolf Eichmann escaped to Argentina with the help of ODESSA. Notorious Auschwitz doctor Josef Mengele also escaped to South America, but he died there instead of being captured, brought to trial, and executed, like Eichmann. It is estimated that over 10,000 former German military personnel made it to South America along escape routes set up by ODESSA, with help from the Vatican and the Red Cross. Some researchers contend that Hitler never died in his Berlin bunker at the end of World War II, but instead escaped to a secret Nazi base at San Carlos de Bariloche, in Patagonia. According to this view, he escaped Germany weeks before the end of the war and was transported by submarine to southern Argentina. There he lived out his natural life in hiding and died of old age in 1960.

Allied reports indicated knowledge of a massive Nazi network called the "New Berlin" facility beneath the ice and mountains of Neuschwabenland, now called Queen Maud Land in Antarctica, prompting a U.S. military response called Operation Highjump. Navy Admiral Richard E. Byrd led the expedition with a powerful military squadron including an aircraft carrier, 12 surface ships, one submarine, more than 20 airplanes and helicopters, and 4,000 elite Navy troops under the guise of a "scientific expedition." Byrd and his massive military armada made an all-out assault on the Nazi Antarctica battalions on February 26, 1947, but were soundly defeated before making a hasty retreat. Upon return to the USA, Admiral Byrd testified to Congress of enemies that have the ability to "fly pole to pole with incredible speed," and discussed an attack on the expedition by "strange flying saucers" that emerged from the sea. Even today, much of Operation Highjump remains highly classified information.

PAPERCLIP NAZIS

Vanquished post-war Axis forces also escaped to Antarctica, while others were brought intentionally to North America to be absorbed into a U.S. scientific talent pool. This secret operation brought brilliant German scientists and officers (some who could have been tried as Nazi war criminals) into the United States by the hundreds, some say thousands, and gave them immunity and new identities where they assumed influential research and corporate positions in such institutions as U.S. Intelligence, the military industrial complex, the space agencies, psychiatric, petrochemical, and other influential corporate positions. Some went to work for the various Rockefeller-connected oil cartels such as ARCO, Standard Oil, Exxon, Zapata, and other companies that were supported by the Bavarian-based secret society lodges. These were the same corporations that had actually sold oil to the Third Reich during World War II and helped keep the Nazi war machine operating. Once the transplanted Nazi scientists were able to infiltrate the military, industrial, aerospace, intelligence, and petrochemical industries, their ideology began to spread amongst the ranks. Within a decade they were well on their way to creating a fascist corporate-government, which began siphoning trillions of dollars "down the tubes" into their military industrial empire.

There were certain Nazis (not considered war criminals) who didn't need to escape, because they were whisked off to new jobs and a new life in the United States with no change in identity. These were ranking Nazi intelligence officers and scientists, along with their young, fanatical protégés, who were welcomed into the USA under Operation Paperclip. Intelligence officers were employed to help monitor the Soviets in the east, and most of the scientists were used to advance aerospace programs. After gaining a foothold, these former Nazis used their clandestine network to loot the coffers of Europe and create corporate front companies in many countries, as well as establish their way into corporate America. They brought with them seemingly miraculous weapon technology that helped the USA win the space race. But they also brought their Nazi philosophy based on the authoritarian premise that the end justifies the means—including unprovoked wars of aggression and curtailment of individual liberties—which has since gained an iron hold in the "Land of the Free." The deep connections between the Bavarian Illuminati, which sponsored the CIA, and the Bavarian Thule Society, which sponsored the Nazi party, allowed for the upper covert-op levels of the CIA to be manned by nothing less than the core of the Nazi SS itself, with the help of fascist sympathizers and fifth column double-agents working within American intelligence. Although some leading Nazi's were "sacrificed" to the Nuremberg Trials, this was done to appease the Allies and establish the illusion that Europe had been de-Nazified.

With a little help from friends in high places, these relocated former Nazis created a cabal which began to infiltrate the highest levels of government. Unfortunately, the Nazis were never stopped in their world control agenda, which can only be understood when one considers how they were assisted in coming to power by those controllers whose vision spans generations rather than limited terms of government office. That generational approach is apparent with George W. Bush's grandfather, the late U.S. Senator Prescott Bush, who was a director and shareholder of companies that profited from their involvement with the financial backers of Nazi Germany. Prescott Bush, father of future American president George Herbert Walker and grandfather of George W., had his company seized in 1942 under the "Trading with the Enemy" Act. He was funding Hitler from America whilst German soldiers were killing American soldiers.

Within months of the end of W.W. II, Nazi scientists and high-ranking intelligence officers were brought into the U.S. under the watchful eye of oligarch Allen Dulles, the first director of the Central Intelligence Agency. The intention was to bring brilliant former Nazi scientists into weapons development, high technology and the intelligence sectors. Nazi General Reinhard Gehlen and his staff were brought over shortly after the war to aid the CIA in gathering intelligence on the developing Soviet menace in Europe. Rocket engineer Wernher von Braun, his mentor Hermann Oberth, V-2 rocket engineer Arthur Rudolph and over 100 other high-ranking Nazi scientists were employed by the U.S. Army and NASA in various aerospace programs.

How did the Nazi element help create the newly formed secret government in the USA? Allen Dulles was a covert sympathizer of the Nazi philosophy of white Aryan supremacy and a member of the Bavarian Illuminati. He stands accused of creating the financing between Nazi Germany, American oil companies, and Saudi Arabia. Together with his brother John Foster and a second partner who also held anti-Semitic views, Dulles established an international financial network to benefit the Third Reich. Near the end of W.W.II, Dulles successfully directed the smuggling of Nazi money back to his Western clients, carefully evading Allied surveillance. Allen Dulles was the first civilian and the longest serving Director of the CIA from 1953 until 1961. Few were surprised when he was appointed a member of the Warren Commission. But the appointment was later criticized by some historians, who have noted that Kennedy had bitterly fired him as CIA chief after the Bay of Pigs fiasco, and, logically, he was unlikely to be impartial in passing the important judgments charged to the Warren Commission. Nevertheless, history remembers him as a top architect of the modern U.S. intelligence system, and his name is memorialized as the new Washington D.C. Dulles International Airport. With friends like Dulles and his ideological views, it is easy to see how the relocated Nazis assumed power in "the government behind the government." Without being subject to any kind of public scrutiny, it is logical to assume their fascist tactics are still operating today.

SPYING ON THE SOVIETS

After W.W. II, General Reinhard Gehlen's organization commanded a vast network of "émigré fronts" of Eastern European nationals whose homelands had been occupied by the Soviet Union. Émigré fronts arise when emigrants leave for a new country by choice, and then seek exile as a temporary expedient forced upon them by political circumstances. Émigré circles often arouse suspicion as breeding-grounds for plots and counter-revolution. It was through these organizations that the Nazi International, via Gehlen's spy organization, managed to exercise a great deal of hidden influence over American politics. Decades later these exile organizations were not only found to be peripheral influences in the assassination of President Kennedy, but they played an influential role in Republican politics during the administrations of Ronald Reagan and George H.W. Bush. In Europe, Operation Gladio conducted attacks against innocent civilians. General Gehlen's organization of émigré fronts of fascist Nazis was alive, well-organized, and politically powerful long after the general's death, meaning that the Nazi International continues to function as a cohesive and influential organization maintaining its original unreconstructed agenda. Careful research shows that the Third Reich never did surrender. Only the country of Germany itself surrendered at the conclusion of W.W. II.

The West German intelligence agency, *Bundesnachrichtendienst* (BND), was established in 1956, along with the Federal Intelligence Service, which was West Germany's foreign intelligence service. Unlike the CIA, it was responsible for both foreign and domestic intelligence. The BND was the descendant of the Gehlen Organization (described above) which was developed and overseen by the CIA beginning in 1949. It was essentially the intelligence network that had been run for Nazi Germany against the Soviet Union by General Reinhard Gehlen. During the 1950s, the CIA controlled West German intelligence through Gehlen and the subsequent BND. In the early years after the war, much of their focus was the Soviet threat. The present day German BND functions in much the same manner as it did under the West German government. The BND's counterpart organization is the CIA and its counterintelligence arm in Germany is the BfV, or the Federal Office for The Protection of The Constitution (first established in 1950) which greatly mirrors the American FBI.

It needs to be established that in the United States there have always been two CIAs, one influential above ground, and the other in the black operations. The CIA was created when the Office of Security Services (OSS) merged with the Gestapo after W.W. II. The Nazi faction is the one that oversees all drug dealing, headed by the senior George Bush. The other faction (called "white hats") is made up of the patriots who work on government salaries and have never made their money from drugs. The first and largest drug smuggling operations were established on behalf of the CIA by George Herbert Walker Bush while he was the President and CEO of the offshore division of Zapata Oil. Fishing boats would deliver the drugs to the offshore rigs where they were transferred to helicopters and crew boats which were never inspected by customs or any other law enforcement agency. Most of the drugs flowing into the United States are owned and controlled by the CIA and military intelligence organizations, plus the Israeli Mossad, the chief security and intelligence organization of Israel.

FALSE FLAG OPERATIONS

False flag operations are covert operations conducted by governments against their own people, which are designed to deceive the public in such a way that the operations appear to be carried out by an enemy. Basically, it is a way for governments to "play victim" in order to mask their own aggression. In planning for a false flag operation, the first step is to create the problem, then offer a solution. This method is also called "problem-reaction-solution." After a problem arises, or a "situation" that will cause a reaction in the public, the next step is to create a measure (a flawed solution) that the public will be willing to accept, each subsequent phony solution further eroding Constitutional freedoms and adding to fear and confusion. An example would be to create an economic crisis for the public to accept as inevitable before the step-by-step dismantling of public services.

The Reichstag fire in February, 1933, was an arson attack on the German Parliament building in Berlin. The event was pivotal in the establishment of Nazi Germany and the Reichstag Fire Decree, which suspended most civil liberties in Germany and was used by the Nazis to ban publications not considered "friendly" to the Nazi cause. Documents uncovered after the war, as well as testimony at the Nuremberg Trial, revealed that the soon-to-be appointed Luftwaffe Commander-in-Chief Hermann Göring was responsible for plotting the fire. This was an inside job, also known as a false flag operation. These covert attacks are used as a justification to pass new laws restricting freedom, or to grant the government sweeping new powers, such as what originally propelled the Nazis to power. In 1939, the Germans based their invasion of Poland around a staged attack against one of their own radio stations and then blamed the sabotage on the Poles.

False flag operations were named after the old technique of attacking a group using an enemy's banner instead of one's own to misdirect the ensuing counterattack. These manufactured and often tragic events allow the elite to acquire resources, reap profit from wars, and erode our rights. They are disguised to generate a predictable reaction—public fear—to help serve the controlling interests. False flag operations are executed because if they can keep the population scared, they can then justify war, or continue to take away people's rights in the guise of public safety and national security. Former Minnesota Governor Jessie Ventura points to the FBI or CIA involvement on various levels of such schemes. In most cases they provide the explosives, intelligence, or weapons.

The best documented case of a false flag in the USA is Operation Northwoods, cooked up in 1962 as a covert CIA operation to paint a plane with Red Cross colors and shoot it down, then blame it on Castro. The plan was to stage a series of events as a pretext to invade Cuba. However, President Kennedy refused to support the plan. According to James Bamford, a bestselling journalist who writes about U.S. intelligence agencies, "Operation Northwoods, which had the written approval of the Chairman and every member of the Joint Chiefs of Staff, called for innocent people to be shot on American streets; for boats carrying refugees fleeing Cuba to be sunk on the high seas; and for a wave of violent terrorism to be launched in Washington, D.C., Miami, and elsewhere. People would be framed for bombings they did not commit and planes would be hijacked. Using phony evidence, all of it would be blamed on Castro, thus giving (Admiral) Lemnitzer and his cabal the excuse, as well as the public and international backing they needed to launch their war." After Operation Northwoods was declared unclassified, *ABC News* documented the incident: "In the early 1960s, America's top military leaders drafted plans to kill innocent people and commit acts of terrorism in U.S. cities to create public support for a war against Cuba. Code named Operation Northwoods, the plan included assassinations, sinking boats on the high seas, hijacking planes, blowing up a U.S. ship, and even orchestrating violent terrorism in U.S. cities."

Another well-known (and in this case successful) false flag operation took place a few years later. It was the Gulf of Tonkin Incident which created a justification for the U.S. to enter the Vietnam War. Former Secretary of Defense Robert Mc-Namara has acknowledged that the second attack on a ship in the Gulf of Tonkin didn't actually take place. In August of 1964, a news bulletin reported two attacks against U.S. naval ships by the North Vietnamese. The first occurred on August 2, the second occurred, allegedly, on August 4. It has since been determined that the second attack did not occur as described. Rather, some reports suggest that the attacks did not happen at all. This is tragically significant because it was the second attack that initiated the Gulf of Tonkin Resolution, giving President Johnson *carte blanche* to invade Southeast Asia. Given that there was no second attack, it is now clear that there was in fact no justification for invading Vietnam, and the U.S. entered the Vietnam War under completely false pretenses.

More recently, careful research strongly indicates that the terrorist attacks on 9-11 were really a false flag operation perpetrated by factions within the U.S. Government, the military and the global elite. A growing number of professional engineers and demolition experts in the U.S., Italy and Great Britain, current and retired Air Force personnel, and a small number of courageous investigative journalists have demonstrated (with diagrams and technical information available on YouTube) the nearly impossible enactment of the official accounts. It appears that the 9-11 attacks were orchestrated in order to set the stage for dismantling U.S. constitutional protections, as a catalyst for the fake "War on Terror," to advance

Israel's domestic security by prompting new wars in Afghanistan and Iraq, and as a way to take over Middle East oil. The evidence is vast, specific and growing that a select few individuals within the U.S. Government, Israel's Mossad spy agency and the financial sector conspired to plant explosives in the three World Trade Center towers, and fired a missile into the Pentagon. The Mohammed Atta hijack plan was well-known ahead of time by intelligence agencies, and the insiders used the advance notice to wire the three World Trade Center buildings with explosives to finish the job. Architects, engineers, physicists, firefighters, scholars, pilots, scientists, whistleblowers, investigative reporters, and filmmakers are all behind the growing "9-11 Truth" movement.

In the wake of the 9-11 attacks, President George W. Bush and his administration deliberately led the American public to believe that the U.S. invasion of Iraq was justified because its government, due to the alleged possession of "Weapons of Mass Destruction" (WMD), represented an "imminent threat" to the United States. As we now know, former President Bush used non-existent WMDs as a pretext for preemptively invading Iraq. The Bush Administration later recanted, claiming it never told the public that Iraq was an imminent threat. Moreover, there is evidence that the Bush Administration had drawn up plans to use military force to overthrow the regime of Saddam Hussein before the 9-11 attacks on the World Trade Center and the Pentagon.

Basically, false flag operations in the U.S. recycle the same old dirty tactics used in the Reichstag fire. After all, Hitler's propaganda mantra was "Keep it simple and repeat the message over and over until it becomes the truth." This was called the "Big Lie" (*Große Lüge*) which was a highly effective propaganda technique. Adolf Hitler coined the expression when he dictated his 1925 book *Mein Kampf*, describing a lie so "colossal" that no one would believe that someone "could have the impudence to distort the truth so infamously."

Hermann Göring confessed the following propaganda observation at his trial at Nuremberg: "Naturally, the common people don't want war, but after all, it is the leaders of a country who determine the policy. And it is always a simple matter to drag people along whether it is a democracy, or a fascist dictatorship, or a parliament, or a communist dictatorship. Voice or no voice, the people can always be brought to the bidding of the leaders. This is easy. All you have to do is to tell them they are being attacked, and denounce the pacifists for lack of patriotism and exposing the country to danger. It works the same in every country."

It should be noted that leaders of smaller and less industrialized nations, who happen to oppose U.S. foreign strategy, are not crazed madmen looking to pick a fight. They are better informed than their citizens and know the consequences of military action. In any war, an attacker does not need equal forces compared to the enemy. The attacker needs at least a five-fold local superiority to establish dominance. No nation begins a war without very definite objectives and a quick victory in sight. Apart from the American War of Independence (1776-1779) and the English challenge to that independence (1812-1814), no single nation has provoked a continental war against the USA. The First World War was joined by America when the Lusitania was sailed into hostile waters in 1915 with armaments from the Morgan banking interests hidden in the hold of the passenger ship. The subsequent sinking by German U boats and the loss of thousands of lives was enough to awaken the anger of the American people and get their support for entering the war. When looking carefully into the history of all the wars the USA has been involved with in the last two centuries, it appears that almost every one started with a false flag operation.

PROPAGANDA MACHINES

The novel titled *1984*, written by George Orwell in 1948, is an English dystopian novel about life under a brutal dictatorship, reminiscent of Nazi Germany. It is a futuristic story of the protagonist Winston Smith, an ordinary citizen and typical target of a fascist totalitarian government and his degradation when he runs afoul of that government of Oceania, the state in which he lives in the year 1984. The novel introduces a language called "Newspeak" and the infamous phrase: "Big Brother is Watching You." The adjective "Orwellian" denotes governmental totalitarian action, ruthless organization, and connotes pervasive, even invasive frightening surveillance of the populace. Winston Smith, an intellectual worker at the "Ministry of Truth," labors at the task of a continual rewrite and alteration of history so that the government is always right. He works tirelessly at destroying evidence, amending newspaper articles, and deleting the existence of people identified as "unpersons." Eventually Winston has doubts, runs afoul and is captured by the Thought Police and interrogated at the Ministry of Love.

Orwell paints a dark portrait of the future where the government assumes total control. In the numerous examples of media manipulation, doctored photography in *1984* is a propaganda technique to sell the public any story the government wants to create, just as the two-way television, called the telescreen, dominates the private and public spaces of the populace. "And if all others accepted the lie which the party imposed," according to the Orwellian doctrine, "if all records told the same tale—then the lie passed into history, and became the truth."

Hitler and the Nazi Party had only a one percent approval rating among the German people in 1921, but following carefully orchestrated party strategies, soon made deals with the media and industrial corporations. They forged alliances with large chemical companies and arms corporations (Messerschmidt and a number of others), and seemingly all of a sudden, the Nazis exploded in popularity and became a majority party. The Nazi's rise to power was due in part to a lackadaisical media, which agreed to licensing agreements and in the process became accomplices with the numerous mergers and acquisitions. Nazi Germany became the ultimate state-controlled media propaganda machine. Now we see the same process taking place in the United States.

NEO-NAZIS IN AMERICA

A neo-Nazi group, the outspoken Nationalist Socialist Movement (NSM) in America, has only 5,000 members, but it was profiled on the fall, 2011, season premiere of *60 Minutes*. Hate speech is permitted under the First Amendment of the U.S. Constitution and is not a crime, as long as it does not incite violence. Neo-Nazis focus their current tirades against immigration laws and the "browning of America." Their goal is an "all white" homeland in the USA. Their strategy is to ask all non-Aryan races to voluntarily leave the country, or force will be used if necessary. The NSM has joined forces with other national neo-Nazi groups, the KKK, various Confederate flag organizations, and other U.S. hate groups that identify with Nazi ideology. Racial hatred has not disappeared, despite the election of America's first black president.

According to author Jim Marrs, the insidious Nazi ideology thought to have been vanquished more than a half century ago is actually flourishing in the USA. He provides compelling evidence of an effort under way for the past 60 years to bring a form of National Socialism to modern America, creating in essence a secretive new empire—or the "Fourth Reich." Surviving members of Germany's Third Reich, along with sympathizers in the United States and elsewhere, were given safe haven by organizations like ODESSA and Die Spinne to live anonymously, while still pledging allegiance to the Reich. They have been working behind the scenes since the end of W.W. II to inject the principles of Nazism into culture, government, and business worldwide, operating primarily in the United States. These principles include militarism, fascism, white supremacy, conquest, and widespread spying on citizens, plus the use of corporations and propaganda to control national interests and ideas.

A NEW WORLD ORDER IS THE MASTER PLAN

The net result is a loss of liberties in America. Right now in the United States, any of us can be imprisoned without warning or due cause, and can be kidnapped, tortured, and assassinated, legally, if the government decides what we are doing is a threat to their plan. All they have to do is name an individual as a suspect in their so-called "War on Terror." Since 9-11, Congress has passed, or attempted to pass, several key pieces of legislation that aim to limit our freedoms under the guise of protecting our safety. Passed shortly after the attacks of 9-11, the Patriot Act substantially expanded the government's powers in anti-terrorism investigations. While supporters of the law believe it acts to provide safety for American citizens by way of increased intelligence, such "safety" comes at the high price of loss of privacy. For example, under the Patriot Act, U.S. citizens who are not the subject of criminal investigations are still included in the government's massive databases; also, citizens who come into "casual contact" with a suspect could be subject to wiretapping. These minor offenses could allow for law enforcement to gain access to highly private personal records. Under the Violent Radicalization and Homegrown Terrorism Act, dissent against a government agency might be enough to classify a person's words as terrorism. This is due to vague language and lack of a substantive definition for "violent radicalization." If an individual is deemed a "suspect" under these loose guidelines, he or she would be subject to the provisions of the Patriot Act or Military Commissions. This includes extraordinary measures to extract a confession. Sound similar to Big Brother yet?

The Department of Homeland Security was behind the police brutality involved in the breaking up of the Occupy protests. After 9-11, the federal government created a federal police force using the doublespeak term "Homeland Security." They now supply tactical assistance to city governments. Former Mayor Jean Quan of Oakland acknowledged that the Department of Homeland Security had participated in an 18-city mayor conference call, advising mayors on "how to suppress" Occupy protests. Finally, the proposed Enemy Belligerent Act would authorize imprisonment and even assassination of American "terror suspects" as has been apparent with drone strikes against Americans overseas without a trial. Welcome to the New World Order.

In fact, it's only going to get worse. *Popular Mechanics* magazine reported that there are an estimated 30 million surveillance cameras operating daily in the United States. Police, schools, banks, and businesses are shooting roughly 4 billion hours of footage per week. Every phone call, social media posting and e-mail we send is collected and archived, and can be inspected at any time.

The all-inclusive implantable RFID tracking chip is gaining momentum for widespread implementation in the prison population and for sex offenders. RFID chips are designed to be inserted under the skin and can send information via radio waves. One chip, developed by a Saudi inventor, even has the ability to kill the host with a cyanide dose. Other chips can burn the host if the person disobeys. For the general population, they will be launched as helpful solutions to eliminating identify theft, lost wallets, keys and purses, and a host of other information breaches. Our driver's licenses and passports already have RFID computer chips implanted in them to track our every move, and new hospital patients are getting these same chips implanted under their skin.

The would-be controllers, through the U.S. Space Command, have outlined a plan called "Full Spectrum Dominance." Sophisticated satellite surveillance, as well as "directed energy" and laser weapons "which are already developed" would have the ability to target dissenters anywhere on Earth. And finally, FEMA, the Federal Emergency Management Agency, has been taken over by these same forces. Originally set up decades ago to assist with emergencies that overwhelmed local agencies, it was placed under the Department of Homeland Security after 9-11 and renamed the Emergency Preparedness and Response Directorate. It's first director warned of its diminished effectiveness as an arm of the Department of Homeland Security and in 2007, it was restored to FEMA. Critics say the lingering emphasis on terrorism threats has undermined its preparedness for natural disasters. In fact, FEMA "containment camps" and railroad cars with shackles have been constructed or refurbished all over the United States for use in what officials call "times of pandemic or civil unrest." Could a well-orchestrated false flag operation set off this civil unrest, allowing the full implementation of the New Word Order? Let's hope not, but seeing the technology they have, and what they have done and are capable of doing, our future could be about as bleak as the world of Winston Smith in Oceania. We have, however, what Winston Smith did not have, which is the Internet and a growing public awareness of the threat.

In this rare photograph, the future "Father of the American Space Program" Wernher von Braun can be seen, half-hidden, directly behind *Reichsführer* Heinrich Himmler as he tours the Nazi's rocket test facility Peenemünde. Von Braun is adorned wearing the elite Nazi regalia of the Black Order of the SS. Anyone who has studied the Nazi hierarchy is well-aware that Himmler's elite order had a "no weekend Nazis need apply" policy.

This is a NASA photo of the region of Lake Vostok in western Antarctica. The lake is a vast, 18° Celsius warm and dark body of water hidden 4,000 meters below the ice sheet's surface. Lake Vostok has not been exposed to surface air for about 20 million years. Another Antarctica mystery is what happened to over 100 of the Fuhrer's Sea Wolves, the U boats that were never accounted for after World War II? Some say they took high ranking Nazis to a secret base in Antarctica, an "impregnable citadel for our Fuhrer," according to Admiral Karl Doenitz in 1943, commander of the U boats.

The first V-1 buzz bomb was developed by the Nazis. After the war, many of the same scientists who worked on cutting-edge aerospace technology for the Third Reich came to the USA under Project Paperclip and helped start up NASA.

A "Flying Fortress" is seen flying over the burning Peenemünde secret rocket base, located in northern Germany near the Baltic Sea. This was one of the primary targets during the Allied bombing raids in W.W. II.

Hitler modeled his SS troops on the Knights Templar and other crusader orders, including the Jesuits and the Masons. This is a famous poster from 1937 showing Hitler in holy armor as a Templar knight, preparing to do battle with Satan.

It should always be remembered the Third Reich never did surrender after W.W. II.

The legacy of the Nazis continued—in that the most brilliant minds among them were whisked away to the victorious nations, namely the Soviet Union and the United States under the ultra-secret program code-named "Paperclip."

SECRET GOVERNMENTS

"Truth: the most deadly weapon ever discovered by humanity.
Capable of destroying entire perceptual sets, cultures, and
realities. Outlawed by all governments everywhere. Possession
is normally punishable by death."
–John Gilmore, American author

PART of the disinformation used by the Anglo-American moneyed elite in order to influence and manipulate government officials is the argument that what they do is for the sake of democracy and nation building. They actively remind politicians, particularly when making a campaign contribution, that they are the financiers and corporate heads who help keep the world going 'round, along the lines of "what is good for GM is good for the USA, and what is good for the USA is good for GM."

This argument is simply a modern disguise of the age-old feudal system, and more recently, the colonial system. Colonized "subjects" were told their well-being depended on their participation and cooperation with the colonial system, a system they were told benefitted workers and owners alike. Small uprisings (dissenters) could easily be squashed by the superior military machine of rulers. Today, the Powers That Be use superior economic clout (the control of wealth) instead of military threat. This sort of process has been ongoing not only for decades, but for centuries. In the 13th century, the challenge to kings and queens of what they thought of as their "divine right" to rule had already been undermined with the popular idea of democracy born with the Magna Carta around 1250. The invention of the Gutenberg Press in 1497 dealt another blow to the hold of the monarchies and the Church (the equivalent of today's 1% wealthiest), when the citizenry learned to read and decide for themselves.

The similarities today are chilling. To the elite, it is much easier to let the common people vote and think they are in control. By allowing democracy to spread worldwide, the cabal can prevent close inspection of their operations which would lead to revolution. Now the elite power brokers merely give the winners of elections their orders, rather than make their pronouncements to the whole country openly. They know where the power lies. Just consider this quote from British Prime Minister Benjamin Disraeli, in 1876: "The governments of the present day have to deal not merely with other governments, with emperors, kings and ministers, but also with the secret societies which have everywhere their unscrupulous agents, and can at the last moment upset all the governments' plans."

Yet, this is in fact a new age. The power elite's control is slipping as is faith in government officials. In 2011, a full 87% of people surveyed in the United States say they mistrust the government, but do not exactly know where to place the blame. The Powers That Be know that their bid for complete control is nearly up, but not before they play one final hand. This is a clever group, and they have changed their game plan many times throughout history. What has not changed is that those in "power" who discover them and threaten to stop them, will be bribed, silenced, or assassinated.

THE MILITARY INDUSTRIAL COMPLEX

At his farewell speech in 1961, President Dwight D. Eisenhower may have been alluding to the growing power of national security agencies that dealt with war, to the ruling elite, or to the possibility of the extraterrestrial presence, or more likely all three. Eisenhower saw these "military industrial" interests as gaining far too much power. His remarkable speech is a tribute to an aging but savvy public servant who was once the highest ranking general in World War II:

> *"In the councils of government, we must guard against the acquisition of unwarranted influence, whether sought or unsought, by the military industrial complex. The potential for the disastrous rise of misplaced power exists and will persist. We must never let the weight of this combination endanger our liberties or democratic processes. We should take nothing for granted. Only an alert and knowledgeable citizenry can compel the proper meshing of the huge industrial and military machinery of defense with our peaceful methods and goals, so that security and liberty may prosper together."*

Unfortunately, Ike unwittingly cast a dye for a secret government that would set a precedent for decades to come.

A few years later Ike's presidential successor, John F. Kennedy, alluded to the secret societies, and it quite likely cost him his life: "The great enemy of the truth," he said, "is very often not the lie—deliberate, contrived and dishonest, but the myth, persistent, persuasive, and unrealistic. Belief in myths allows the comfort of opinion without the discomfort of thought." President Kennedy had a strong suspicion that some CIA operatives were not the loyal civil servants of the president and the people, but had nefarious dealings with a shadow government. He was angered with the CIA's failure at the Bay of Pigs and declared he wanted "to splinter the CIA in a thousand pieces and scatter it to the winds." Kennedy also remarked, "If the United States ever experiences an attempt at a coup to overthrow the government, it will come from the CIA. The agency represents a tremendous power and total unaccountability to anyone." This statement is accurate. Indeed, the CIA functions as a 4th branch of government, operates without oversight, and is actually more powerful than the other three branches.

Just one month to the day after the JFK assassination, on December 22nd 1963, former president Harry Truman wrote an op-ed article in *The Washington Post*. Truman titled his piece "Limit CIA role to Intelligence." In that article, just 16 years after he and the Congress established the CIA, he said (in part),

> *"For some time I have been disturbed by the way the CIA has been divested from its original assignment. It has become an operational and at times a policy-making arm of the Government ... This removal from its intended role ... has led to trouble and may have compounded our difficulties in several explosive areas ... I never thought (the CIA) would be injected into peacetime cloak and dagger operations ... I, therefore, would like to see the CIA restored to its original assignment as the intelligence arm of the president ... and that its operational duties be terminated or properly used elsewhere."*

It would seem from this column that Truman thought the CIA might very well have had something to with the JFK assassination. Interestingly, Harry Truman's column on the CIA was run in the afternoon edition of *The Washington Post*, but immediately removed from the later edition that day. Could it be that Truman struck a nerve? Could it be that all subsequent presidents since JFK are afraid of the CIA?

FOR REASONS OF NATIONAL SECURITY

Accusations of abuse and inhuman acts by the CIA and FBI were investigated by Congress in 1977. These agencies used the excuse of "national security" for every crime they were accused of committing. Under the guise of national security, there has not been an investigation of their highly illegal activities since 1977. The U.S. President, the Congress, and the Supreme Court are aware of them, but are afraid to provoke them. A mountain of evidence points to the fact that CIA assassins have killed thousands, including corporate executives, "rouge" politicians, whistleblowers, and quite possibly John F. Kennedy when he probed too deeply into the lawless abuses of the CIA.

The three-tier standard government security clearance levels are well-known: confidential, secret and top secret. However, just having a clearance at one of these levels does not automatically give access to all information at that level. There has to be a demonstrable "need to know" reason in order to be briefed or to have access to documents on a given project, program, facility or intelligence product. But this system is merely the "white" side of the security system. The rabbit hole goes much deeper on the "black" side. The problem is now the intelligence community itself is beholden to the controlling elite.

The Bilderberg Group, now with offices in Geneva, Switzerland, was secretly established in 1952. They control the media, the banking, and the intelligence empires. MITRE Corporation is a nonprofit group supporting the Department of Defense (DoD), the Federal Aviation Administration (FAA), IRS, Veteran Affairs and the newly formed Homeland Security Administration. The JASON Group are the planetary physicists in a government advisory group. Based on an admission from the Pentagon, The JASON Scholars hold the highest security clearances in the nation and have been assigned the protocol rank of Rear Admiral, and are treated as such on any military installation or in any government office. The Council on Foreign Relations (CFR) is also run by the secret government. All are beholden to the Bilderberg Group, including the CIA and the intelligence services who also work for the secret governments. The National Security Agency (NSA) is especially malignant, because it is not subject to any law, unless that law specifically mentions the NSA. The NSA/CSS (Central Security Services) focuses on cryptology, the science of tracking and decoding signs and signals around the world for national security purposes. They regularly release false documents, news stories, movies and disinformation to throw off truth seekers.

SECRET GOVERNMENTS AND THE CABAL

The Black Operations have encountered great difficulty in maintaining international secrecy for the their activities. Consequently, it was decided that an outside group was necessary to coordinate and control international efforts to provide better protection from normal scrutiny of governments and the press. The result was the formation of a secret ruling body which became known as the Bilderberg Group. The Policy Committee of the Bilderbergers is the closest an investigator can come to getting information about the secret world government. The Bilderberg Group has 39 permanent members. This is an important number to them (13 x 3) because it is significant in Freemasonry, and most Bilderbergers are supreme Freemasons.

In 1913, the United States saw the creation of the Federal Reserve and income tax. The CFR was formed in 1921. The U.S. Federal Reserve, and almost all central banks worldwide, are privately owned by Illuminati bankers, ruled over by the House of Rothschild. "Once *anything* goes, *anything* can come back and haunt us," said Bill Moyers on PBS in 1987, referring to the secret government. Moyers also used another name, the "cabal," which is the government behind the government. This cabal, working with the Black Ops of the U.S. Government, maintains a host of projects together, including a network of Deep Underground Military Bases & Structures (DUMBS). There are currently more than 130 known underground cities worldwide. The DUMBS are built with nuclear powered drills, then the bases are connected with magneto leviton trains able to travel at Mach 2 speeds.

In 1945, President Truman enacted the UN Participation Act, the UN Treaty, and the first known secret government in the U.S. termed OVERT. For his part,

President Eisenhower sealed the deal when he brokered an agreement with his election supporter Nelson Rockefeller to help tackle the ET problem. He knew that he could not do it by revealing the secret to Congress. Early in 1953, the new president turned to his friend and fellow member of the Council on Foreign Relations, and together Ike and Rockefeller began planning the structure of secretly supervising all alien-related events and responses. Within a year their vision was to become a reality. The idea for MJ-12 was thus born. The Majestic-12 was the control group running the secret space program related to all alien activity. Asking Rockefeller for help with the alien issue was to be the biggest mistake Eisenhower ever made for the future of the United States, possibly for all of humanity.

MAJESTIC-12: SUBVERSION OF THE U.S. CONSTITUTION

The U.S. Constitution has been subverted since at least 1947, or possibly earlier. Just after World War II an executive order under Truman created the National Security Council (NSC). It was established to oversee the intelligence community and especially the alien problem. A series of NSC memos and executive orders removed the newly formed CIA from the sole task of gathering foreign intelligence and slowly but thoroughly "legalized" direct action in the form of covert activities at home or abroad. These NSC memos and secret executive orders set the stage for the creation of MJ-12 only four years later. Only a handful of members of Congress from the late 1940s, if any at all, would have known anything more than that Cold War issues were involved in this far-reaching national security legislation enacted at a time of near panic over a Soviet nuclear threat.

The control group that is running the secret space program is called Majority, and any ET connection with the president is called Majestic. By secret Executive Memorandum NSC 5510, President Eisenhower proceeded to establish Majestic-12 as a permanent committee to oversee and conduct all covert activities concerning the alien question. The name was shortened to "MJ-12" with numerical value because each of the 12 members on the panel had a vote. In their rush to compartmentalize and contain their secret, MJ-12 was formed as a highly secretive group within the U.S. Government. Among the 12 members on the MJ-12 board, some were famous scientists and others were top military officials, but their identity on this committee was to remain ultra-top secret. Thus began the "Under Oath" rules which still exist today. If anyone within the military ranks ever has a close encounter with an ET or an observed spacecraft, they are required to take an immediate new oath of secrecy. They are required to sign documents attesting they did not see what the government told them they did not see. The language of the document is full of legalese, but the point is very clear. The person who was witness to a sighting was to never, ever discuss anything whatsoever with anyone regarding what they had seen, heard or experienced during their service in the military—under pain of death as an Act of Treason against the United States of America.

Truman and Eisenhower somewhat unwittingly led us into what was to become an entrenched secret government, and a young idealist who was the next president in line would attempt to get us out. Because he ordered a plan to disclose UFO truth among other provocative actions, highly placed spooks ordered the hit on President Kennedy. It appears that MI5, the CIA, and the FBI were used for the assassination and subsequent cover-up. Because JFK received a full briefing on UFOs and other secrets, and passed this information to his brother Bobby, neither could be trusted and both had to be taken out. Contrary to mainstream media accounts, Bobby was killed from a head shot at point blank range from behind by one of three CIA agents present at The Ambassador Hotel in Los Angeles, and only wounded by the brainwashed assassin Sirhan Sirhan, who was shooting from the front. Bobby's murder was quickly covered up with another "lone nut."

New presidents receive UFO briefings, but are never told everything. Sitting presidents now have at least 24 security levels of clearance above their access level. This is justified by giving the president a "plausible deniability" on the UFO issue. Today, every new president is given an "Above Top Secret" and "Need to Know" clearances, but they do not have the "UMBRA Above Top Secret" clearance to have access to upper-level MJ-12 secrets, or the "Keystone" documents pertaining to ET research.

An independent special studies group, the JASON Scientific Group (separate from the JASON Group but supposedly with the same handlers), was tasked to study the ET issue. JASON members all have top security clearances, and they include physicists, biologists, chemists, oceanographers, mathematicians, and computer scientists. They are selected for their scientific brilliance, and, over the years, have included 11 Nobel Prize laureates and several dozen members of the United States National Academy of Sciences. Four members of the JASON Group sit on MJ-12. They discuss the most highly classified top secrets, regarded as the most sensitive information in the USA.

No MJ-12 documents have been leaked since 1977. It is speculated that MJ-12 remains to this day, but there are now more members on the board and they've changed their name. Their task is the same as it was since their founding: to research any acquired ET craft, study any recovered aliens living or dead, and continue to work diligently to keep it all secret.

THE FIRST CASUALTY

MJ-12 would solicit the views of top leaders in the field. Ambitious, elite scientists such as Vannevar Bush, Albert Einstein, Charles Lindbergh and Robert Oppenheimer, plus career military people such as Hoyt Vandenberg, Roscoe Hillenkoetter, Leslie Groves, Jimmy Doolittle and George Marshall, along with a select cast of other experts, who feverishly and secretively labored to understand the alien agenda, technology, and its implications. The operations to handle the alien issue was established earlier by a special classified presidential order on September 24, 1947, at the recommendation of Secretary of Defense James Forrestal and Dr. Vannevar Bush, Chairman of the Joint Research and Development Board. The goal of the group was to exploit everything they could from recovered alien technology.

James Forrestal, while still the U.S. Secretary of Defense in 1949, started to object to the secrecy. He was a very idealistic and religious man. He believed the public should be told. When he began to talk to leaders of the opposition party and leaders of Congress about the alien problem he was asked to resign by Truman. He expressed his fears to many people. Rightfully, he believed he was being watched.

Forrestal was said to have gone crazy in the halls of the Pentagon. He babbled about the "space people" who were about to attack us, and that we were defenseless. Officialdom explained that his breakdown was due to the "pressures of the Cold War," and maybe so, but his paranoia was not centered upon the Soviets, but on perceived space people. Friends reported that he told them that the weirdos could appear as normal humans and had already infiltrated the most sensitive parts of government. He also thought that they had tapped his phone and read his mail. Forrestal was said to have suffered a nervous breakdown. Although it had no authority to do so, the Truman Administration committed him to the Bethesda Naval Hospital. It was feared that Forrestal would begin to talk again, so he had to be isolated and discredited. His friends and family were denied permission to visit. One can speculate that his paranoia was real, in that he was being watched and followed due to his breaking secrecy laws about ETs. What we don't know is whether or not he actually had pathological symptoms, whether or not he "knew" of possible malevolent aliens, and/or whether real threats from colleagues pushed him into a so-called nervous breakdown.

On the morning of May 22, 1949, the brother of James Forrestal came to take him home, but when he got there James was found dead after falling from his 16th floor room at the Bethesda Naval Hospital. A bathrobe sash was knotted tightly around his neck, raising suspicion that he was murdered, but the death was ruled a suicide. James Forrestal died under very suspicious circumstances. Researches dedicated to disclosure say he was murdered by the CIA because he objected to the secret methods being established that undermined the due process of law, including the safeguards of the Constitution. Many others would also die when they threatened the secrecy of this control group.

NASA = NEVER A STRAIGHT ANSWER

A report was prepared in the late 1950s under contract to the National Aeronautics and Space Administration (NASA) by the Brookings Institute, a Washington D.C. think tank, to identify long-range goals of the United States space program and their impact on American society. The report outlines a need to investigate the possible social consequences of an extraterrestrial discovery and to consider whether such a discovery should be kept from the public in order to avoid political upheaval and a possible "devastating" effect on scientists themselves due to the discovery that many of their own most cherished theories could be at risk. It also says that the information should be covered up because of the "disintegration of our culture" due to the shock it would have, especially to the scientific community.

Executive Order #10501, enacted by President Eisenhower in November, 1953, outlines "safeguarding official information in the interests of the defense of the United States." In this document, national security is outlined as a national defense perspective that includes the military, but also geo-economic and geo-political concerns as well. When this executive order is combined with the Brookings Institute findings, the result is the legal justification for NASA to cover up anything ET-related, and to lie to the American people.

NASA has always been a division to the Department of Defense, and thus, beholden to military regulations. Astronauts are subject to military security oaths and regulations. Apart from the fact that the NSA screens all films, broadcasts and probably radio communications, NASA also stands accused of editing out any information pertaining to an ET presence. Again, they can fall back on the Brookings Study on *The Implications of the Discovery of Extraterrestrial Life and Intelligence* to justify their actions. The study best describes better than any other document the perceived fear that an encounter by our civilization with an advanced race might spell disaster. The report states: "Anthropological files contain many examples of societies, sure of their place in the universe, which have disintegrated when they had to associate with previously unfamiliar societies espousing different ideas and different life ways; others that survived such an experience usually did so by paying the price of changes in values and attitudes and behavior."

There are other political motives for keeping anything ET-related top secret. The announcement of an ET presence on Earth would be front-page news for months. It would stymie and dominate the government's every action and severely disrupt its ability to carry out routine business. It would be the Watergate scandal times a thousand. Agencies like NASA would become irrelevant overnight. The government would face the question of why they continued to fund NASA when they knew that such technologically primitive space efforts were a total waste of taxpayer money.

We all know, however, that NASA's space shuttle program has been permanently retired by the DoD, according to a March 28, 2012, report on CBS's' *60 Minutes*. Under the Obama Administration, the next manned spacecraft contract is being offered to the private sector. Critics consider the private commercialization of space technology a mistake. While it is too early to tell, elimination of the defense department's regulations of military secrecy could be a step in the right direction.

RELEASING BACK ENGINEERED PRODUCTS

The military industrial complex is now multinational. There is a massive secret "black" system which issues oaths of secrecy and even threats, the existence of which is known, while the details remain deeply hidden. Secrecy oaths and threats especially surround the Special Access Programs. They are protected by a security system of great complexity. This structure has been described as a "shadow military" existing in parallel with open or overtly classified programs. It is a permanent government which continues to run the show behind the transparently elected government officials who remain largely unaware of its existence. It is beholden to no elected official, not even to the President of the United States.

The secret government was originally set up by Harry Truman for programs considered too sensitive for normal classification measures. It is likely that the UFO topic is actually classified by one or more laws duly enacted by Congress in the late 1940s (described above) concerning national security—but without any overt reference to UFOs of course—and signed into law by President Truman. Three weeks after Eisenhower learned about ET technology, it went into the black operations, which was overseen by the Special Operations Coordinating Group, a part of the intelligence community, including the National Security Council. Information could be as high as 46 levels of clearance above the president now, who has access on a "need to know" basis only.

Such clearance covering is set-up to allow technology to be relatively openly developed until the time it is ready for application in a black program. The overt cover program is then usually cancelled, having accomplished its purpose. This also occurs today with biological products being supplied to the Monsanto Corporation. Originally, Bell Laboratories were given many items to study and back-engineer under the disguise of research and development. This happened to the X-30 National Aerospace plane project in 1994. It appeared to be an unrealistic, ambitious program that was eventually cancelled. It was in reality a cover for what is almost certainly a black-world hypersonic aircraft according to defense analysts who studied the program. Speculation hints this may be the source of the phantom sonic boom phenomenon reported since the early 1990s. All of this results in very effective isolation, and allows virtually no one in a position of open civilian governmental authority to be aware of the truth. Still, at least in principle, the Special Access Program Oversight Committee (SAPOC) should be cognizant of such a program. But the situation has gotten so out of control that those involved in these deep black programs have essentially become a breakaway civilization.

THE BLACK OPERATIONS

From the secret space program, to the enormous network of underground bases, and to the financing of the largely unaccountable actions of the CIA and the NSA, the U.S. "government behind the government" wields an amazing amount of control and assets. In short, the way the black operations are financed, is first, money is siphoned out of other programs by the CIA, or is simply announced as missing, such as the 2.3 trillion dollars Donald Rumsfeld announced the day before the attacks on 9-11. Money also comes from the CIA drug-smuggling division. The CIA then takes the money and distributes it to the agencies of choice, mostly to the Department of Defense.

The CIA has in its mission statement not to operate domestically, yet their tentacles are all over the place inside and out of this country, seemingly out of control, and certainly not accountable to U.S. citizens. Regional privateer cells comprise an international ring, or "rent-a-terrorist" for the Continuation Of Government (COG). This is where the missing trillions went.

The new American "battle front" is being fought using "information warfare," utilizing sophisticated mind control techniques including psychological warfare, propaganda, misinformation, intimidation, fear, and manipulation. It is, in fact, a usually quiet war being fought mostly with silent weapons, but when unleashed it can become deafening and destructive. *Ordo Ab Chao,* or "Order Out of Chaos," dictates that the old order must be completely and thoroughly dismantled before the New World Order, the Third Wave, or Third Way, can be established.

A one world socialist government is the stated and avowed policy of the United States Government. The United States created the United Nations. In 1961, the U.S. State Department wrote the policy known as *State Department Publication 7277,* a document designed to disarm the American public, while building up the United Nations' armed forces and establishing new global governance. The Black Ops have waged a silent war against its own citizens, and it won when no one was paying attention on New Year's Eve, 2011, when President Obama signed the NDAA "Martial Law Bill" into law. The American broadcast media has been eerily silent on NDAA's passage into law, despite the fact that foreign newspapers and broadcast networks have been covering this as one of their top international stories. The cartoon character Pogo once observed, "We have met the enemy, and he is us." In a twist of irony the fictional character Pogo resided in a swamp, and the District of Columbia was built on a reclaimed swamp.

According to financial journalist Benjamin Fulford, upwards of 90% of the U.S. budget is going to the military and the black operations. Fulford says there is an easy way to check his numbers. Just look at the U.S. external trade deficit and compare it to the U.S. military budget. There are amazing similarities over the years. He says that's the simple reason the military does not produce tradable goods. They are a parasitic entity on the United States, and by extension, the world economy.

WAR IS BIG BUSINESS

Simply stated, war is big business. Perhaps the military industrial complex is the biggest industry ever developed in history. The elite who continue to meet behind closed doors will always push for wider wars, which today leads to incalculable suffering in the Middle East and elsewhere. After all, the money masters have long profited from war and mass murder. War is always by deception. Nathan Rothschild made a financial bet on Napoleon at the Battle of Waterloo, all the while funding the Duke of Wellington's peninsular campaign against Napoleon. He had information delivered to him a day early, sold some shares to dupe London stockbrokers into thinking Napoleon won, then acquired a massive portfolio at rock bottom prices before the market adjusted to the real news that Napoleon lost at Waterloo. The House of Rothschild also financed the Prussian War, the Crimean War and the British attempt to seize the Suez Canal from the French, and also financed the Mexican War and the Civil War in the United States. They also cornered the gunpowder market, selling the key war-making ingredient to both sides of every conflict.

Control of national currencies is the core of their power methodology. The elite financed Mussolini and Hitler, planned World War I and II, and financed all sides in order to dupe the population and consolidate their power. For more than a century, their goal has been to create a single global government. The attempt to create a League of Nations after W.W. I was funded by the Rockefeller and the Rothschild families. The plan failed, but was revived as the United Nations after W.W. II on property in New York City gifted by the Rockefellers. As wonderful as it's made out to be, with its diversity and "peacekeepers," the UN seems to be the front organization for the One World Authority—with NATO as its militant arm and the World Bank as its financial enforcer. All the "think tank" organizations that promote war, as well as the World Health Organization, and the World Trade Organization, were the creations of the Rockefellers, Rothschilds or Morgans. As such, wars have been created in modern history to consolidate power domestically throughout the West. The kings or leaders going to war needed to borrow huge sums of money, which the bankers held. In the last century wars have been created in order to build support for international agencies that would provide the backbone of a formal world government, which is the elite banking families' great dream. These "Round Table" agencies are the United Nations, Council on Foreign Relations, The Trilateral Commission, Royal Institute of International Affairs, Club of Rome, the Bilderberg Group and other less influential agencies. But make no mistake, near total global control lies within the hands of the elite.

Senator Barry Goldwater wrote in his l964 book, *With No Apologies*: "The Trilateral Commission is intended to be the vehicle for multinational consolidation of the commercial and banking interests by seizing control of the political government of the United States. The Trilateral Commission represents a skillful, coordinated effort to seize control and consolidate the four centers of power: political, monetary, intellectual and ecclesiastical. What the Trilateral Commission intends is to create a worldwide economic power superior to the political governments of the nation states involved. As managers and creators of the system, they will rule the future."

HOW DID IT COME TO THIS?

This grim scenario started in 1776 when economist Adam Smith published the *Wealth of Nations*. He believed that for fiat money to work globally, there could be no national currency based on the gold standard. Top bankers developed a plan to get all the world's gold off the market, then divide the wealth among nations according to the wealth they created. But first, it was essential to eliminate the gold standard. Any nation with physical gold would disrupt the plan and be a risk to the rest of the nations. So the new rules stipulated that no one was allowed to own gold.

In 1921, the Bank of International Settlements was created in accordance to a secret plan to confiscate all the world's gold. This occurred through Japan's Emperor Hirohito who was given the green light to invade East Asia and begin to rob about 85% of the world's gold. China had amassed huge gold supplies from centuries of trading its spices, silk, and other commodities. They stored their gold in various locations which remained concealed; however, some was confiscated by the Imperial Japanese Army, while other stocks were shipped abroad, especially in 1938 when seven U.S. battleships full of gold from Asia were sent to the U.S. via the Federal Reserve.

For this, gold bonds were issued. The Nazis were also instrumental in collecting Europe's gold, and by the end of W.W. II, the confiscation of all gold was complete.

There has been a very clandestine battle over the dollar printing machine to control the global financial system. In July, 1944, leaders of the allied countries who were set to win the Second World War gathered in a rural New Hampshire hotel to determine how certain interests would be preserved. This meeting is commonly known as the Bretton Woods conference. Two new Rothschild world banks were created at Bretton Woods. The International Monetary Fund (IMF) and the World Bank were introduced. The participants also decided to grant Britain, France and the U.S. the right to control the world's currency. With a few honorable dissenters (notably like the great British economist John Maynard Keynes) the negotiators were determined to do one thing. They wanted to build a global financial system that ensured the money and resources of the planet were forever under their influence. They set up a series of institutions designed singularly for that purpose, and that is how the IMF and the World Bank were delivered into the world.

The IMF's official job sounds simple and attractive. Its function is to ensure that poor countries don't fall into debt, and if they do, to lift them out with loans and economic expertise. It is presented as the third world's best friend and guardian. But beyond the rhetoric, the IMF was designed to be dominated by a handful of rich countries—and more specifically, by their bankers and financial speculators. Make no mistake, the IMF works in the bankers' interests, every step of the way.

According to Wikipedia, there are only 120,000 tons of gold in the world. But according to David Wilcock's groundbreaking series, *Financial Tyranny: Defeating the Greatest Cover-Up of All Time*, there is actually two million tons of gold held. The total worth of all the world's gold is 11 million trillion dollars. The biggest secret is that gold is not scarce, and when this becomes known, gold prices will plummet. It was all confiscated wealth and kept hidden so no power could rise up against all the nation's fiat currency plan. The reality is that all fiat money is based on nothing but the faith citizens put into it, that is, until the new BRICS bank comes on-line with a new gold-backed currency.

By 1954, the Kuomintang Chinese began to suspect that the United Nations was not spending the interest on their gold money on projects that were agreed upon. For example, the UN was not developing Asia or Africa. Along with the Indonesian President Suharto, they started demanding results. John F. Kennedy issued Executive Order #11110, to return the U.S. dollar to a silver-backed currency. He was assassinated three months later.

When the 1944 Bretton Woods charter was set to expire in 1994, another lawsuit was issued to reclaim the lost Asian gold. The Federal Reserve said no. So in 1998 China sued once again to reclaim its gold. The Feds lost the lawsuit. They were ordered to return the gold to China on the date of September 12, 2001. The gold reserves were held in a massive vault under World Trade Center Building 7, the third building to collapse on 9-11 after two planes crashed into the Twin Towers. The Feds could buy some more time by claiming the gold was destroyed, when in fact it was removed in the days and weeks prior. A few years later China attempted another lawsuit, but this time they were paid in fake gold. So in 2008 the Kuomintang wealthy families in China (not the communist government) realized they were being scammed and caused the dollar to collapse. After the financial crisis of 2008, they were shocked at TAARP fiat money being printed and flooding the market. The Feds once again had found a slippery way out.

SECRETS BENEFIT THE ELITE

The elite involved in the black programs are among the smartest people on the planet, but remain deeply puzzled by much of what they have learned. They tend to regard the public with disdain, like undisciplined and unruly children who are incapable of handling information of extraordinary complexity. Over the past 50 years, the highest courts have accepted and upheld the precedence of national security over the First and Fourth Amendments. So even if the public wanted to know, this wish would not constitute a legal need or right to know. The secret government believes it is doing its patriotic duty by trying to control the situation within the established rules of national security.

The real issue for the controlling elite is not so much about money, but control. Control has always been the dominant goal. The elite Western power brokers who actually run the secret governments remain tremendously powerful, and apparently have tens or hundreds of trillions of dollars at their command. Some of this money has been siphoned off from other U.S. government programs, defense contracts, or simply gone missing, including a new missing $8.5 trillion reported in 2015.

Throughout much of the 20th century, and into the 21st century, the Council on Foreign Relations (CFR) and the Trilateral Commission have been calling the shots behind closed doors. The CFR is one of the most powerful semi-official groups concerned with America's role in international affairs. The CFR does not conform to government policy. The government conforms to CFR policy. For the last 50 years at least, the same international globalists continue to pull the global strings. They primarily seek profit and control over the population. Similar to the three regions of the world in George Orwell's classic *1984*, each regional block is played off against the other. Today we have the European Union, the American block, and the soon to be Asian Union. These will become the three power brokers on the planet. There can never be unity and full cooperation, as one is always going to play off the others.

Clearly one of the top motives is to keep free energy out of public view, mainly because the Persian Gulf region is still flooded in oil. Secret technology could easily be moving the world off fossil fuels completely, but that would mean there would be too much oil left in the ground, resulting in huge revenue losses. That's why secret technologies must be kept secret no matter how they might benefit humanity. Power, control, and riches are very powerful motivators. Let's not forget the first acknowledged billionaire on the planet was oil tycoon John D. Rockefeller. His descendants, as with the ever-secretive Rothschild dynasty, still wield vast influence around the world today. If we can break this petrochemical stranglehold, we'll soon see a clean and free energy future.

When you follow the money and arrive at the top of the pyramid, above even the Bank of International Settlements (which is a global version of the Federal Reserve), you'll find the controllers of the world. They fit the description of a secret society because there is little or no information revealed about what is said at their meetings, what is done or what is decided behind closed doors. No publicity of any kind is allowed. Their members cannot take notes, film or record the discussions or talk about the meetings outside the group. They are sworn to absolute secrecy, often under penalty of death. If the Bilderbergers, the Trilateral Commission, the Masons, the Priory of Sion, the Council on Foreign Relations, Skull & Bones, the Illuminati, the Committee of 300, the White Brotherhood, the Black Nobility and so many others are really working for the good of all humankind, wouldn't it be appropriate to see a live feed on TV or the Internet of their discussions and highest level decision making?

CORPORATIONS VS. DEMOCRACY

What should citizens do when the cabal subverts the will of the people and takes over the space that democracy ought to occupy? Until we lose all of our civil rights we can still let our voices be heard, stay informed, and peacefully protest. In theory, we can re-elect a new government that truly represents the will of the people. But first there is a cancer on elected office that needs to be remedied. That cancer is corporation influence and lobbyist money. Corporations are extremely influential in the decisions the government makes on all levels. If we make election campaign contributions completely illegal, the corporate power over politicians can be seriously weakened.

Robert Kennedy, Jr., second oldest son of Bobby Kennedy, never did run for public office, but has been a tireless environmental activist. He fought against the coal industry, historically one of the most aggressive lobbyist groups. When Kennedy was asked during a June, 2011, PBS interview with Tavis Smiley, "What is the battle between corporations and democracy in this country beyond just coal?" he gave a chilling example of an energy company subverting local government, illegally polluting and disobeying the will of the people. Kennedy replied to Tavis:

> "Appalachia, in particularly West Virginia, is the template for what happens when corporations take over a democracy. It's a company town. What they're doing is illegal. In fact, if you've filled 25 feet of a Hudson River tributary, you would be in jail. If you blew up a mountain in the Berkshires or the Catskills or California or Utah, you would go to jail or a place for the criminally insane. But they have flattened an area larger than the State of Delaware. They've blown up the 500 biggest mountains in West Virginia in the last 10 years and it's all illegal. They've buried 2,500 miles of rivers and streams. That's illegal. You can't do it."

Kennedy went on: "I debated on West Virginia TV a year ago with Don Blankenship, who is the head of Massey, which is the biggest mountaintop removal company. I said to him, 'By your own records, you had 67,000 violations of the Clean Water Act. Over the past five years, you've had tens of thousands of violations of labor laws, of mining safety laws and all these other laws. Is it possible for you to make a profit without violating a law?' He said no. He said these are silly laws. So he acknowledged that his company is a criminal enterprise. Their business plan is to break the law, then get away with it. In order to do that, you have to subvert democracy. So if you go to West Virginia, their democracy essentially doesn't exist."

"When we have a government that tortures people," continued Kennedy, "that suspends our Bill of Rights, suspends habeas corpus, that says the Bill of Rights is a luxury we can't afford anymore, that does extraordinary renditions and whisks American citizens out of the country to places that torture them and eavesdrops illegally on hundreds of thousands of people, as our government is now doing, that is a threat to democracy. But the bigger threat comes from unleashed corporate power. We have to understand in this country that the domination of business by government is called communism. The domination of government by business is called fascism, and that's what you're seeing, that form of government." Kennedy then goes on to offer a solution:

> "Well, our job is to walk that narrow trail in between and hold big business at bay with our right hand and big government at bay with our left and walk that narrow trail in between, which is free market capitalism and democracy. To do that, we need an independent press that is willing to stand up and speak truth to power and is going to inform the public and we need an informed public that can recognize all the milestones of tyranny and we don't have either of those things left in this country."

Unfortunately, Robert Kennedy, Jr. will not seek election for any public office. He has all too clearly seen the danger of running for office as an honest U.S. politician.

CORRUPT TO THE CORE

Woodrow Wilson, the 28th President of the United States, perhaps expressing regret because he was president when the Federal Reserve came to power, warned the American people of a powerful, almost invisible influence to the highest office. "Since I entered politics, I have chiefly had men's views confided to me privately. Some of the biggest men in the U.S., in the field of commerce and manufacturing, are afraid of somebody, are afraid of something. They know that there is a power somewhere so organized, so subtle, so watchful, so interlocked, so complete, so pervasive, that they had better not speak above their breath when they speak in condemnation of it." To understand this warning by Wilson over a century ago is to identify the complex web of deceit between the ultra-elite and a complicit government. On his deathbed in 1924, Woodrow Wilson made the following telling confession: "We have come to be one of the worst ruled, one of the most completely controlled governments in the civilized world—no longer a government of free opinion, no longer a government by a vote of the majority, but a government by the opinion and duress of a small group of dominant men." Wilson lamented: "I have unwittingly ruined my government."

A government controlled by hidden powerful moneyed interests, as Wilson indicated, was nothing new then and it has only increased in spades now. Lobbyists transparently shower gifts on lawmakers on behalf of clients to influence legislation with campaign contributions. Stated simply, amoral moneyed interests target select members of Congress for favors in return. Infamous lobbyist Jack Abramoff claimed to have spent $1 million per year. "We owned them," he said on *60 Minutes* in an interview that aired in November, 2011. One of his strategies was to offer chief of staffers a lobby job later. By doing this, he held considerable power over staffers and elected officials. Lobbyists are routinely offered three times the salary of congressional officers to join them on K Street.

The interview went on to reveal that over 100 Congressional offices were directly influenced by Jack Abramoff alone. Trips, free food and drinks in his Signature Restaurant were commonplace. Lobbyists would request the insertion of language into reform bills to change U.S. laws, deliberately re-written to insert bought favors. In short, Abramoff said corruption and bribery was what he engaged in by giving gifts to people who make the laws for U.S. citizens. He would orchestrate corporate campaign contributions to the reelection campaign of members. Now reformed and out of prison, Abramoff said lobbying is subverting the essence of our political system by plying members of Congress who (as intended) only make tiny attempts at reform. Congress reformed the law by declining free meals, only to be replaced with fundraiser lunches. Abramoff suggests prohibiting members of Congressional staff from ever becoming lobbyists. He says the situation now is "as bad as it's ever been." The people who make the laws are the same people who would have to change the laws. "It's like putting a fox in to protect the hen house," said Abramoff.

The powers of financial capitalism have far-reaching aims to create a world system of financial control in private hands, able to dominate the political system of each country and the economy of the world as a whole. This system is to be controlled in a feudalistic fashion by the central banks of the world acting in concert, by secret agreements arrived at in frequent private meetings and conferences. The apex of this system is the Bank for International Settlements (BIS) in Basel, Switzerland, a private bank owned and controlled by the world's central banks, which are themselves private corporations. The BIS is now composed of 55 member nations, but the club that meets regularly in Basel is a much smaller group, and even within it, there is a hierarchy. In a 1983 article in *Harper's Magazine* called "Ruling the World of Money," Edward Jay Epstein wrote that where the real business gets done is in "a sort of inner club made up of the half dozen or so powerful central bankers who find themselves more or less in the same monetary boat." Those core bankers come from Germany, Switzerland, Italy, England and the Federal Reserve governors in the United States. They are able to dominate the political system of each country, the media and the economy of the world as a whole. Some of the bankers who own the Federal Reserve are not even U.S. citizens. Yet the Internet has somewhat leveled the playing field, or as Ron Paul described, the Internet has become an alternative to the "government media complex."

THE INTERNET KEEPS US FREE

The Internet has now entered the equation and this is unprecedented. Yet at the same time, we are losing traditional print investigative journalism. Now people are informing each other via the Internet, as this is currently the most trusted source of news. Look at the impact social media websites have had on the development of the 2011 Arab Spring. Besides a way of dynamic interpersonal communication, the Internet has become the greatest threat to all the secret societies, especially the secret government behind the government, because we the people still have a chance to take back the USA. In the view of those in the secret government, there is no direct or immediate solution to the Internet's impact. Recall when Egyptian President Mubarak hit the Internet "kill switch" before his ouster. After all, if they can keep us an ignorant populace, we will be a complacent populace. But the Arab Spring proved the people do have the power to enforce change upon the ruling elite.

And what might we see if we were to get a glimpse beyond the technological iron curtain of the U.S. National Security State today? There is evidence of anti-gravity devices which propel advanced American Star Fleets capable of interstellar travel, according to British computer wiz Gary McKinnon. What he found between 2001 and 2002 when he hacked into 97 U.S. Government military and NASA computers is suppressed evidence of reverse-engineered UFO technology and free energy devices that could help reverse climate change.

The most shocking find to McKinnon, the one he thought would be his ace in the hole when negotiating with the U.S. Government, is what he "stumbled" upon in the systems of U.S. Space Command. McKinnon says he found a log of 20-30 names listed as non-terrestrial officers. He did not believe that these were aliens, but he interpreted the statements as evidence that the U.S. military has a secret battalion in space. He read the names and ranks of personnel and ship-to-ship and fleet-to-fleet transfers of material on Excel spreadsheets. McKinnon tried to find a corresponding listing of the space command personnel which he had seen, but was unable to find a match. Interestingly, the names of two of the ships he saw on the transfer logs were the USSS LeMay and the USSS Hillenkoetter. Typically, Navy sea ship names just have two Ss, an acronym for United States Ship; however, there are three Ss here, presumably standing for United States Space Ship.

McKinnon (who suffers from Asperger's Syndrome) claims his actions were benign, as he simply wanted to "prevent old age pensioners from dying of the cold," and free energy technology could help do that. He made his findings without stealing passwords, breaking through firewalls, or using anything more than commercial software and a 56K modem. Although driven by altruistic motives, eventually McKinnon got caught and fought extradition to the USA for over a decade. It is likely McKinnon passed this information on to the whistleblower website WikiLeaks, whose founder Julian Assange also faces extradition to the USA. Assange says he has official USA cables with countries abroad regarding UFOs and other sensitive documents. Many in the hacker chat-room community consider both of these men true heroes of free speech and justice.

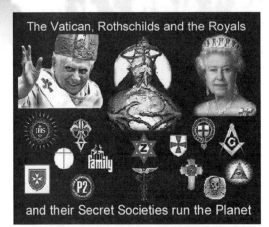

The Vatican, Rothschilds and the Royals

and their Secret Societies run the Planet

A monarchy is a dictatorship government ruled by one King or by one Queen. A monarch is free to do whatever he or she wants without any regard for their subjects. The Kings and Queens of England would be one of the best examples, but the Queen of England actually has advisors, such as Evelyn De Rothschild, who can also create laws and policy through covert manipulation of the British Parliament. "The world is governed by different personages, from what is imagined, by those who are behind the scenes," said Benjamin Disraeli, the first British Prime Minister.

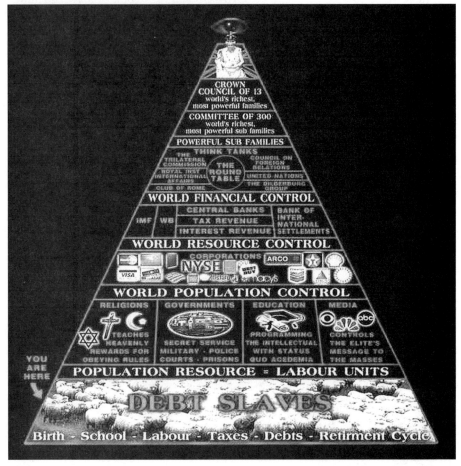

"Heavy physical work, the care of home and children, petty quarrels with neighbors, films, football, beer and above all, gambling filled up the horizons of their minds. To keep them in control was not difficult. ... And when they become discontented as they sometimes did, their discontentment led nowhere, because being without general ideas, they could only focus it on petty specific grievances." –George Orwell, *1984*

MEDIA
MANIPULATION

"Just look at us—everything is backwards. Everything is upside-down. Doctors destroy health, lawyers destroy justice, universities destroy knowledge, governments destroy freedom, the major media destroy information, and religions destroy spirituality." -Michael Ellner

IF the mass public can be easily controlled and shaped to think a certain way, isn't it an asset? If adult public attention can be diverted from sensitive matters, isn't that helpful for an agenda of mass control? If it is possible to distract public attention away from the real social issues and on to matters of no real importance, could that not be a useful tool for a subversive New World Order? Those in power know that if a story is not reported by the mainstream media, even a big story—a dramatic one—most people will not believe it. Media professionals know how to engage the public's emotions. They know how to indulge the human desire for cheap thrills with a constant barrage of sex, violence and all manner of human conflict and depravity. Cynical controllers give people what they want, even in excess—"junk food for thought"—while depriving them of the essential information they need to make informed decisions. These are the silent weapons of the stealth war.

Noam Chomsky demonstrates in his book, *Manufacturing Consent: The Political Economy of the Mass Media,* that the free market economics model of media leads inevitably to generic and narrow reporting. He describes how the U.S. government and its corporate partners exercise control over what we read, see, perceive and hear. The national media networks profit through advertising revenue; in fact, they can only survive by depending on their close links with other huge corporations whose bottom line is profit. Inevitably, this leads to corporations essentially dictating their choice of broadcast or print information. The result? Mainstream news comes from biased sources—both in the choice of what is aired and the spin placed on the information. Mainstream media either knowingly or by rationalization distorts its reporting when the event is perceived as a threat to the moneyed interests. The guardians of our Constitutional freedom of speech and freedom of the press have been bought and paid for. Bedrock principles of our democracy are compromised everyday on TV, newspapers and radio. Instead, what we have is a news system that panders to the interests of America's privileged and neglects its duties to objectively inform the public.

Public radio and television have been the brave exceptions to this trend because their support has come from small contributions of average citizens, philanthropic foundations and government grants. However, with that support diminishing in recent years, they too have accepted advertising revenues from major corporations. Nevertheless, their discerning, objective reporting of both sides of an issue, often in depth, continues to offer a choice to viewers—a stark contrast to the superficial sound bites and omission of important stories of the major networks.

Noam Chomsky has tracked the amount of time the corporate TV news media typically devotes to a particular story. A good example was the beginning of the Occupy Wall Street movement which started in September, 2011. During the first week there was a near-complete TV news blackout. In the second week the protests blossomed at the Federal Reserve building in San Francisco and a dozen other U.S. cities, but still there was scant national reporting. In the third week of protests, the "Chomsky stopwatch" clocked in a short 30 seconds on the *CBS Evening News,* which devoted its main stories to a man who had built his home completely from "Made in the USA" products, and Lady Gaga's message to her fans. Both were allocated three minutes. In the fourth week of the Occupy movement, the protests went global with more than 900 meet-ups in 900 cities worldwide and across America before the story finally got the attention it deserved.

Chomsky points out that the key element of social control is the strategy of distraction—diverting public attention away from important issues by flooding the airwaves with trivia (insignificant information) and cheap thrills. This prevents people from focusing on important issues, ongoing real problems and considering needed changes to bring about solutions. Consider the type of stories given the most prominence. Local network affiliate news outlets often use stories of violence as their lead. In 2010, two-thirds of viewers surveyed (who indicated they receive their news from TV) reported they thought crime was a serious problem. Yet statistics show a general decline in violent crimes across America over the past decade. But this is not the impression portrayed on the local nightly news. Fear-based stories are a dominant theme on TV news and dramas virtually every night. Fear is a tried and true psychological tool to shut down the mind. Fear causes confusion, impairs critical thinking and can immobilize entire groups of people.

SUPERSTITION PEDDLERS ON TV

A standard definition of a vested interest is "any person, group or entity which prevents or controls communication to serve their own purposes, plans or agenda." The status quo position of our government and the media, now largely run by corporate vested interests, has been to "protect the people" from knowledge it regards as frightening, not credible, irrelevant, and most of all, threatening to their bottom line of money, power and control. This largely explains what is *not* told. In fact, the only "protection" afforded by ignorance and secrecy is to hide the private agenda (vested interests) of those in power seeking to maintain control by regulating the flow of information. By doing so, this technique can disarm every perceived enemy through superstition, disinformation, or ignorance. The best way to enslave someone is to allow that person to believe they are already free. Today most Americans still believe we have a free press. This fundamental right guaranteed by the U. S. Constitution has been so gradually and cleverly eroded that many Americans have not noticed it. The controllers exert a strong but subtle influence over our lives.

One such influence is the constant use of terminology tinged with suspicious overtones and suggestive interpretations, that is, subtle editorializing. Play a little game the next time you watch the network news. See how many times a feel-good story is described as "miraculous." Weather forecasters will say: "You might need an umbrella for Sunday services." Another perennial favorite is the "Guardian Angel" news story that runs in the aftermath of any national tragedy. The network news never fails to report on any Jewish or Christian religious holiday, but no other religious group enjoys such attention. There also appears to be great interest in the Pope's activities with a lead in such as "We turn now to the Vatican where the Pope says …"

On Friday, April 29, 2011, at least one network news outlet led with the Royal Wedding story. Only the day before a major national disaster hit several southern states, killing hundreds of Americans. This was the worst natural disaster since Hurricane Katrina. Instead of informing the public on the towns and homes destroyed by the largest recorded tornado in history, the feel-good story of Prince William and Catherine Middleton's marriage took priority. When the mega-tornado story did run, there was not one mention of global warming, potential Earth changes, geoengineering, or speculation (scientific or otherwise) about what might be contributing to such natural disasters; in this case the biggest tornado on Earth at the EP5 level, which destroyed everything in its 200 kilometer-wide path. This within weeks of another huge tornado that had wiped out large sections of Joplin, Missouri. Instead, all three networks used religious jargon to describe "miraculous" survival stories. "It was God's will I survived the tornado," confided one, or "I prayed with confidence in the Lord." When describing the damage to a church, one reporter led his story with "God did not spare his own house," and later, "No services this Sunday in this deeply religious town." But they did show weather photos of cumulous clouds, observing "It looks like heaven out there." In the days following, survivor stories were very popular, such as the "Agent of God" story, featuring a babysitter that saved an infant by covering him, "interpreting" this behavior as something other than simply a natural response.

UN-FREE PRESS

Many people think America has the most liberated mass media in the world. The truth is we do not. It is more likely the most expensive press in the world, costly to its citizens who waste time stumbling around in the dark, to say nothing of having to look at alternative sources to be informed. A little research with documents now available since the expansion of the Freedom of Information Act in the mid-1990s, plus clues from other Internet sources, reveals that not only is the mass media owned by a select few, but the select few have strategically-placed agents from the intelligence community throughout the biggest news media outlets. Their instructions are to kill, alter, or change selected stories. These moles are plugged into the large corporate media outlets worldwide, which (as you've probably guessed) are tied mostly to international corporate and financial interests.

If the U.S. had a media worthy of the First Amendment, instead of mere shills for private oligarchs and propagandists for government, Americans would be much more advanced as a people and a nation. Those who seek to manipulate the conscious and intelligent opinions of society constitute an invisible government which is the actual ruling power of America, and by extension, the world. It is they who pull the strings that brainwash the public mind, who harness ancient corrupt strategies while using modern technology to bind and sway public opinion. News reports are dictated from the top down. Anchors are advised to avoid issues such as Israeli aggression, ISIS as a Mossad / CIA creation, the American Israel Public Affairs Committee (AIPAC), the Council on Foreign Relations (CFR), the Bank for International Settlements (BIS), the Endowment for Middle East Truth (EMET), the Project for the New American Century (PNAC), the MacQuarie Infrastructure Company (MIC), the American Enterprise Institute (AEI), the Trilateral Commission, the Bilderbergs, and of course 9-11 or anything about the lies behind the wars in Iraq and Afghanistan. The mass media creates a story by repeating selected talking points and sound bites over and over, such as the "War on Terror." Corporate interests, both their financial bottom line and what they want people to think, drive the selection of stories. The oil companies are among the biggest advertisers, along with the pharmaceutical companies. These two giant enterprises now account for 70% of the revenue for news shows on TV.

It has become very difficult to criticize big oil, pharmaceutical companies, and the war machine in the news, let alone encourage unbiased investigative journalism. A rare exception (and a hopeful sign) is the airing of two recent stories on *60 Minutes,* one detailing the bogus claims of anti-depressants and few weeks later, an interview of two top Air Force pilots who reported instructions from top brass to continue flying planes that were exuding a mysterious gas which made pilots disoriented and seriously ill. Military top brass stated that they were conscientiously studying the problem, had no solution, but were continuing to order flights with these planes. The pilots reported harassment and threats if they refused to fly these flawed aircraft.

THE BIG GUNS

In 1985, author Eustace Mullins published the book, *Who Owns the TV Networks*, in which he reveals that the House of Rothschild has the controlling interest in all three major networks, NBC, CBS, and ABC, and the news services Reuters and the Associated Press. Rupert Murdoch and his News Corporation media empire are in close lockstep with the Fox conservative message broadcast worldwide. In total, six companies control all the major English-speaking media outlets, including the TV networks, the major newspapers, book and magazine publishing, talk radio stations, and the Hollywood studios. From their beginnings, these media giants have attempted to get everyone to think the same way. They have sought to use mainstream media to make up your mind for you, or at least severely reduce the scope of your concerns.

Ben Bagdikian's book, *The New Media Monopoly*, confirms that the mainstream media conglomerates in the U.S. have consolidated down from 50 companies in 1983, to just five as of 2004. Those five titans of the news media are Time/Warner, The Walt Disney Company, Murdoch's News Corporation, Bertelsmann of Germany, and Viacom, formerly CBS. General Electric's NBC follows as a close sixth. These companies often vertically integrate the entire creative process of a film or television show from conception to end distribution, creating an ideal environment for dispensing propaganda. According to Bagdikian, the big five *manufacture* politics and social values. "The media conglomerates have been a major force in creating conservative and far right politics in the country ... They have almost single-handedly as a group, in their radio and television dominance, produced a coarse and vulgar culture that celebrates the most demeaning characteristics in the human psyche: greed, deceit, and cheating as a legitimate way to win (as in the various 'reality' shows)."

At the 1991 Bilderberg Conference held June 6-9 in Baden-Baden, Germany, David Rockefeller made the following statement: "We are grateful to *The Washington Post*, *The New York Times*, *Time* magazine, and other great publications whose directors have attended our meetings and respected their promises of discretion for almost 40 years. It would have been impossible for us to develop our plan for the world if we had been subjected to the lights of publicity during those years. But the world is now more sophisticated and prepared to march towards a world government. The super-national sovereignty of an intellectual elite and world bankers is surely preferable to the national auto-determination practiced in past centuries." This captain of industry is actually stating flatly that the medieval feudal system (mere slaves serving at the whims of "the Divine Right of Kings") is "surely preferable" to the democracy crafted by the founders of the United States. That David Rockefeller apparently holds this view unapologetically and regards it as rational and even superior is indicative of massive self-deception and sad dissociation from the natural kindness and altruism deep within human nature. The chilling reactions we have to these revelations can be used to bring us to a heightened awareness that we do have choices. We can not be victimized by these forces without personal consent.

YOU WILL KNOW WHAT THEY WANT
YOU TO KNOW

In the service of heightened awareness, readers here are invited to notice other tactics of mind manipulation. In order to create a divided mindset among us, we have been conditioned to think with an "us and them" attitude. We think of "them" in terms of religion, race, language, education, patriotism, class, wealth and every other form of separatism that highlights differences among people. We tend to focus on these differences rather than our similarities. Fortunately, certain authentic older beliefs and the New Age teachings recognize our spiritual oneness, and this has made some corrective inroads.

Another manipulative strategy is the catchall umbrella phrase, "for national security purposes." Many important news stories have a "kill switch" enabling the Powers That Be to eliminate any news item deemed a threat to national security, which is actually any story that might expose their cloak of secrecy. And in this way the Orwellian Newspeak of word collisions can seep into public consciousness through the mass media by deliberately introducing contradictory and impoverished language: War is Peace. Freedom is Slavery. Ignorance is Strength.

The elite rulers know that to control the media is to control the public. This is one of their stated agendas. Control of the mass media and financial institutions also open the door to complete domination of law, government and education. Centralized banking allows a few to dictate their vision to government, military, mass media, education and industry. The Federal Reserve Bank of the USA, the Federal Reserve Bank of England, the Bank of Roth, the Bank of Germany, the International Monetary Fund (IMF), the World Bank, and the Bank of International Settlements are all privately owned and controlled businesses. Mass media outlets criticize these institutions at their peril.

And finally, Hollywood, the entertainment arm of the media, is a natural target. To manipulate this sophisticated group, controllers are less transparent than in the pharmaceuticals foisted on the public (with their "comical" lists of side effects). They do not approach a film producer and say, "Here is our script, and oh, by the way, we are the Illuminati, and we want you to make this movie that promotes our agenda." Instead, they will form small investment corporations that fund movies with ideas they choose. The business entity select the scripts they wish to see developed, then hires the producers, directors and actors. They will never mention their affiliation publicly or reveal their motives, yet they do have a propensity to relish hiding the truth in plain sight. What moviegoers are offered as "science fiction," more often than not, is actually science fact.

It is constructive to observe how the North Korean government runs its state-owned media. Consider how the people of North Korea have been under the spell, so to speak, of their former "Dear Leader" Kim Jung Il and his son the new successor. At Kim Jung Il's funeral in December, 2011, the TV cameras used the transparent device of rotating imagery of crying citizens to convey the false impression of widespread grieving. Since there is no interaction with any neighboring nations, no news from the outside, the North Korean people are manipulated by one source of information, similar to the handful of mass media outlets we have in America. Forces in both countries inform the outlets to stay "on message" and can doctor stories as was done with Kim Jung's funeral, or at least, focus attention where they want it. TV reporters passively or deliberately doctor their material by crafting "everyone thinks" stories, implying a general consensus. The message gets repeated by all official news outlets to *create* a general consensus via "group think." Seeking to understand the situation, the viewer then repeats the talking points to friends, co-workers and family, thus perpetrating the propaganda and gradually solidifying the story as true.

Never forget that the false reason for a preemptive second invasion of Iraq was its possession of "Weapons of Mass Destruction" which first entered groupthink as a pure media fabrication via the Pentagon public relations machine. When this was roundly challenged by numerous groups of Americans, including a lengthy UN-sponsored search turning up no such weapons, the Bush Administration fell back on the treatment of Iraqi citizens by Saddam Hussein (which could not be defended as a security risk to the U.S.) combined with a vague terrorist threat. In fact, enormous defense contracts (won by major corporations) needed for destroying a country and then rebuilding it was a major force driving the invasion of Iraq.

CORPORATE OVERLORDS

Much of the manipulation described here is psychological conditioning. A psychological matrix similar to George Orwell's *1984* has been created to keep the public in a box. An infiltration of institutions and the media makes mass manipulation fairly easy. Those in power have the ability to float nonsensical stories to confuse people. A carnival of ridiculousness keeps many reasonable, intelligent people off important subjects. So much virulent disinformation has been placed in the public arena that most people cannot distinguish between the truth and lies; an enigma wrapped in a mystery. The emphasis on ideological differences, the removal of nuances, and continuous repetition of simplistic sound bites create "low information voters," a Newspeak term to describe citizens who remain uninformed on complex issues.

The greatest flaw of capitalism, and its ultimate downfall, will be the insatiable greed that it perpetuates. This is capitalism run amuck as we see in the 1% where wealth is concentrated. People are scared when faced with the idea of lacking what they think they need, or what they are told they need. But the idea of "never enough" or "just a little more" is the insidious psychological lie which can be our downfall.

But there are many small groups, and their numbers are growing, whose members are calling for a halt in the headlong race of rampant individual spending and a return to a simpler life with fewer material possessions. While corporations and the media foster greed and compulsive consumerism, individuals and organizations throughout the U.S. are combating this trend by beginning to wake up to the false "never enough" attitude, and are fostering a "downsizing" mood instead, along with the idea of sharing resources.

How does a corporation lose its moral compass? A corporation run by many people becomes the sum of its parts. As it grows in employees, it accumulates wealth and grows into its own entity. With that power a company seeks to survive by any means possible. It commissions its own studies to justify its actions. It hires lobbyists to influence politicians. It buys off politicians by making campaign contributions. Wealthy individuals, usually captains of industry, use their money power to influence policy. Every politician relies on money to get elected. Thus, a corporation will continue to push its agenda, no matter how flawed, to ensure survivability. Most individuals within these entities who question policy don't last. Think of how askew the health insurance industry, oil companies and big tobacco have become.

From today's perspective, it is reasonable to suggest that no multinational company should have been allowed to develop in the first place, and now they are behemoths—near mythical monsters! An exaggeration? Just try to kill one! You'd be killing an entire industry, such as offshore drilling, employing thousands. You'd also be killing the sum of its parts. Of the hundred largest economies on the planet (companies and countries), more than half are corporations. Exxon-Mobil passed up Uruguay in the late 20th century as a larger economic entity. Oil companies employ their own mercenary armies. Governments now serve the corporations rather than the people who elected them, and this is described as fascism (a system of government run by corrupt dictatorial authority rather than by the individuals freely elected by its citizens). Need further proof that America has become a fascist nation?

In 2010, The Supreme Court ruled in a 5-4 decision called "Citizens United" that corporations have the same rights as individuals. "I'll believe a corporation is an individual when Texas executes one," read a sign at the original Occupy Wall Street protest. Speaking for the Court majority, Justice Kennedy performed an amazing feat of turning First Amendment rights upside down. "A ban on corporate spending," he said, "*suppressed* free speech for non-profit and for-profit corporations, big and small." This was the twisted logic which made a corporation into a person—a classic example of doublespeak, raising suspicions of the same insidious manipulation taking place in the highest echelons of justice. On the other hand, Justice Stevens, one of the dissenters, said he believed "that corporations were *not* human beings, and that this was a distinction that was significant in the context of elections." He noted with wry understatement "the interests of corporations may have fundamental conflicts with the interests of the electorate." This unfortunate 5-4 decision underlines the importance of appointing independent thinkers to the Supreme Court.

The insidious influence of the hidden government has spread like a cancer into every area of industrialized society. These tentacles, fueled by money and threats, have moved into everything of importance and influence. They have infiltrated groups ranging from the mafia, to Harvard University, to international banking. Ominously, they strive to influence every person's mind. They have been largely successful, that is, up to a certain point.

Once again, notice the awakening that is occurring. Individuals and groups are spreading the word, person to person and through the Internet, nudging each other to remember that our minds are our own. We have a choice. Our minds are not constrained by our brains, and cannot be controlled without our consent. In fact, we have a better idea. We can let go of fear and choose love, that is, love in the highest sense, where it is identical to truth. Those who *choose* to focus on pure love energy are nearly impossible to penetrate with hate-mongering or fear-based propaganda. This kind of love is the most powerful force in the universe. It grows exponentially when shared.

CONTROLLING CORPORATE POWER

President Teddy Roosevelt, who was willing to stand up to what he called the "malefactors of great wealth" over a century ago stated, "These international bankers and Rockefeller-Standard Oil interests control the majority of newspapers and the columns of these newspapers to club into submission or drive out of public office officials who refuse to do the bidding of the powerful corrupt cliques which compose the invisible government." He and Congress successfully passed the Sherman Antitrust Act, which had the clout to break up burgeoning corporations and limit the influence of moneyed interests. His administration also passed the graduated income tax that forced corporations and the wealthy to pay their fair share of taxes to operate the country. His administration passed laws that allowed unions to organize, which created a middle class in this country and enabled the prosperity and the stability that made American democracy the envy of the world. Congress created, among other things, direct election of senators, and in 1907 a law passed that forbade corporate contributions to federal political officeholders or federal political candidates.

The achievements of the Teddy Roosevelt Administration have been reversed in the 100 years since the antitrust acts were passed. Now, even the Supreme Court appears to have lost its Constitutional moorings. The opinions of Alito, Scalia, Roberts and Clarence Thomas regularly favor the rights of corporations over the rights of individuals. In fact, even if it's a corporation versus the government, the corporation wins. We have a Supreme Court which overruled a duly elected president in favor of a puppet controlled by elite moneyed interests. Finally, as described above, we have a Supreme Court which has in effect repealed a 100-year-old law prohibiting corporations from contributing to federal political candidates. It is now legal for the first time in a century for corporations to flood our federal political campaigns with a tsunami of money through Political Action Committees, or Super PACs, and many Americans see this as the beginning of the end of representative government.

To continue a brief American history survey, the Fairness Doctrine law, passed in 1928, stipulated that the airwaves belonged to the public. Broadcasters had to be licensed to use them, but only if they did so to inform the public, promote the public interest and advance democracy. This spawned the beginning of the 6:00 nightly news. The networks didn't want it then, and even now devote only a half hour to national and international news, with the exceptional of public broadcasting. Networks didn't want to spend time on news because news departments were chronic money losers. But they were forced to broadcast the news at 6:00, and even today the news on music radio stations is an artifact of the Fairness Doctrine. Congress asserted that if media outlets were using the airwaves to broadcast, they had an obligation to fairly inform the public. The other rule was to avoid corporate consolidation and control. Both rules are now lost.

REVOKING THE FAIRNESS DOCTRINE

The devolution of the American press began in 1987 when President Ronald Reagan abolished the Fairness Doctrine. Once again, in a kind of upside-down thinking, Mark S. Fowler, the new FCC chair under the Reagan Administration stated that the Fairness Doctrine violated First Amendment rights by giving government undue control over free speech. In a flurry of debate, a District Court of Appeals also undermined the statute by arguing that it was not actually a binding law, citing a "faulty amendment." Nevertheless, Congress overwhelmingly passed a law to reinstate the Fairness Doctrine. But Reagan vetoed the law and a later effort was threatened with a veto by President George H.W. Bush. To the list of Orwellian Newspeak can be added: Freedom is Unfairness.

Perhaps unwittingly, Reagan did away with the diversity and the multiplicity of control. He vetoed the Fairness Doctrine as a favor to the Christian Right, which helped him get elected, and they wanted to take over all of AM radio which is now complete. Talk radio is 95% controlled by the right and the big studio heads who helped Reagan get elected. Their goal was consolidation of the media giants. Rupert Murdoch was also complicit in helping Ronald Reagan repeal the Fairness Doctrine, which has since essentially allowed "Faux News" to tell whopper lies on the air. Media ethics have deteriorated so much that the Florida State Supreme Court ruled it is now legal for Fox to lie during the TV news.

A recent example is Fox News being sued in Florida by its own journalists because they were being asked to lie on "the news." The issue was a story they researched about the manufacture by Monsanto of a possible carcinogen, a recombinant bovine growth hormone (rBGH) shown in some studies to be toxic and was routinely injected into cattle. According to the two reporters who brought the suit and later were fired, their complaint was *not* that they couldn't air the story. "Fox 13 didn't want to *kill* the story revealing synthetic hormones in Florida's milk supply," they said. "Instead, as we explain in great detail in our legal complaint, we were repeatedly ordered to go forward and broadcast demonstrably inaccurate and dishonest versions of the story. We were given those instructions after some very high-level corporate lobbying by Monsanto (the powerful drug company that makes the hormone) and also, we believe, by members of Florida's dairy and grocery industries." The journalists were outraged because Fox protected its corporate sponsor, Monsanto and its "Round-Up" ad, condoning misinformation which could affect the safety of children who drink milk. Fox (and Monsanto) won the case when the Supreme Court of

Florida declared it was not unlawful to lie on TV broadcasts, because in the end Monsanto's commercial advertising paid for the "news."

Fox News is not allowed to broadcast in Canada because the Canadians still have a Fairness Doctrine. It's illegal to lie on the air in Canada. England also has similar rules, as do most countries in Europe. But in the United States, we have lost the Fairness Doctrine and, as a result, we know a lot about Lindsey Lohan's gradual emotional collapse and are aware of Justin Bieber's sex life, but we do not know much about controlling the weather or the causes of the mega-storms that are only increasing in severity. The controllers operate from the disdainful premise that average Americans will behave like sheep. They believe voters are simple-minded and want only pat answers: "government is bad; taxes too high; free markets know best." This is termed "confirmation bias," and more and more people are noticing that it keeps us in ideological trenches. It is red meat spoon-fed. A growing number of Americans are suspicious of condensed data in the form of sound bites, recognizing that key information is lost in its reduction.

While the controllers are not yet home free, the challenges Americans face to regain lost freedoms are formidable. To recap, today we have six giant corporations that control virtually all 14,000 radio stations in our country, all 2,200 television stations, 80 percent of our newspapers, the majority of our billboards, and most of the largest Internet content providers. When it comes right down to it, there are a few individuals deciding what most Americans receive as news. In their corporate culture, the over-riding obligation is to their shareholders. They seem to have lost sight of an obligation to serve the public interest by broadcasting useful information in a democracy in which people vote for programs in the best interest of the Republic. What a quaint notion! Rather, they provide what they perceive we are asking for: entertainment. It is said Americans are the best entertained and are the least informed people in the Western World. We spend more time talking about Taylor Swift than discussing what's really about to destroy our democracy, which is a huge flood of corporate money into the political spectrum as we see in the 2016 presidential race. The Super PACs empower corporations even more, to the point where unseen donors can now make or break a political opponent. And now the Supreme Court recognizes a corporation as an individual, with the same inherent Constitutional rights and powers of an American citizen.

APPEALING TO THE REPTILIAN BRAIN

Robert Kennedy, Jr. articulated our dilemma in his interview with Tavis Smiley on public television: "Our mass media today is designed to appeal to the prurient interests that all of us have in the reptilian core of our brains for sex and celebrity gossip. There has been a sharp decrease in investigative reporting on important matters. 85 percent of investigative reporters lost their jobs in the last two decades. The networks discarded their foreign news bureaus. As a result, the Bush and Cheney Administration were able to say to the American people, 'Oh, we're gonna go into this 800-year-old fist fight in Mesopotamia and they're gonna meet us with rose petals in the streets,' and the American public believed them, while the rest of the world saw the second U.S. invasion of Iraq as unjust and illegal."

TO RECAP

Do you remember when real reporters existed? Those were the days before the Clinton regime concentrated the media into a few hands and turned the media into a Ministry of Propaganda, a tool of Big Brother. Consider a review of ways we have colluded (often unaware) in these alarming developments—and a reminder of our way out. As members of the human collective consciousness, most of us are choosing a negative polarization by default, by the quality of our unmindful thoughts and actions. The stealthy conversion of information into fear is a primary tactic of the mass media. Ever since *Washington Post* investigative reporter Carl Bernstein revealed in 1977 that the CIA was making a comprehensive effort to control the media, we have known the stories that actually do make it out to a mass audience have been vetted, edited, and sanitized by the Powers That Be. And since virtually everything the CIA does is hidden behind the cloak of national security, who then is accountable for deciding what vital information we are allowed to receive? Or perhaps more importantly, what we are *not* allowed to receive?

Thought is creative energy, focused. We get exactly what we put out. Control of the mass media is vitally important to the ruling elite because of its hypnotic powers. We as a society, in our comatose state (despite our free will), in many ways have consented to the state of our planet today. We saturate our minds with the unhealthy dishes served up for us on television that are really a form of addiction. Violence, pornography, greed, hatred, selfishness, incessant "bad news," fear mongering, and "terror" are popular media compulsive addictions. The use of television flashes are employed as mental impulses which on a subliminal level make us agitated. Guns, blood, and actors playing terrified character roles are a common lure for upcoming TV shows.

When was the last time you stopped—just to think of something beautiful and pure? The planet is the way it is because of our collective thoughts about it. We are complicit in not noticing our projections, and in our own inaction every time we "look the other way" when we see an injustice. Thus, we are feeding into the general negativity. It is very important to the controllers of the media that the polarization of this planet remains negative. That means passively condoning our old habits of selfish preoccupation as opposed to positive service to others.

We can begin to break these negative habits by taking time to be quiet and access our inner guide, the wise decision maker. This decision to first turn inward wrests control from seeming outsiders (the mistaken idea that we are victims) and returns control to where it has always been—within—with our choices. From accessing our own higher wisdom and coming from a healing intention, we are able to diminish negativity and fear, and the love and compassion that remains will guide our actions in service to others and the planet.

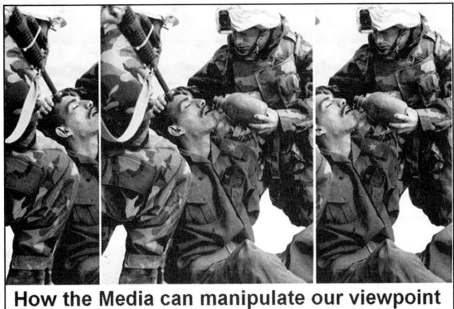

How the Media can manipulate our viewpoint

Don't trust the mainstream media because they are known to be masters at distractions, fabricating stories, and dishing out half truths. Always research things for yourself, consider multiple opinions (including the opposition), and only then will the story be mostly correct.

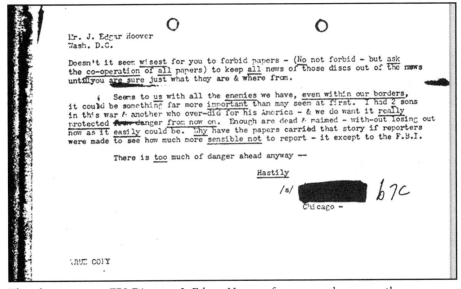

Mr. J. Edgar Hoover
Wash. D.C.

Doesn't it seem wisest for you to forbid papers - (No not forbid - but ask the co-operation of all papers) to keep all news of those discs out of the news until you are sure just what they are & where from.

Seems to us with all the enemies we have, even within our borders, it could be something far more important than may seem at first. I had 2 sons in this war & another who over-did for his America - & we do want it really protected from danger from now on. Enough are dead & maimed - with-out losing out now as it easily could be. Why have the papers carried that story if reporters were made to see how much more sensible not to report - it except to the F.B.I.

There is too much of danger ahead anyway --

Hastily

/s/

Chicago -

b7c

TRUE COPY

This document to FBI Director J. Edgar Hoover from an unknown author, presumably writing from Chicago, was acquired through the Freedom of Information Act. Here we can clearly see a motive for blacking out the UFO story from any mass media outlet, especially when those instructions come from the highest law enforcement office in the land. The letter is also telling because it is known that Hoover was angry because the Army / Air Force would not give him access to the recovered or crashed craft, as can be seen in another de-classified memo.

You will write what we tell you to write! But who is at the top of this information pyramid who decides what can run and what cannot? Someone is telling us how to think, buy, hate, and vote on a daily basis. Tell a lie enough times and the "sheeple" believe it to be their truth. The sanitized and highly edited mainstream media looks a lot different when viewed through the lens of government propaganda, or as the not-so subtle mouthpiece of corporate America.

SHADOW GOVERNMENT

"Men occasionally stumble over the truth, but most pick themselves up and hurry off as if nothing had happened."
–Winston Churchill

A basic dilemma about how the average American views the role of the government regarding state secrets, such as UFOs for example, is the fact that many Americans do not know how the system of hidden influences and manipulation works. The average person has been conditioned to think a certain way their entire life. In many instances, foreign immigrants being granted citizenship have a better knowledge of the legitimate functions of our government than most Americans born here. Civic lessons are no longer a priority in our high school educational system and are seldom found in college curriculums, unless one majors in political science. It also needs to be noted that "The Government" as the media and most people refer to it, is not a single monolithic entity. In reality it is made up of millions of people, all functioning at different levels. There is an unstated assumption that if knowledge of UFOs exist somewhere in the vast bureaucracy, then the entire government is responsible for concealing that information. But like all large pyramid-hierarchical institutions, inadequate communication within the ranks of government (especially between agencies) is a generic weakness. Because one person or officer acquires information, it cannot be assumed the same data is shared with others. In the highly compartmentalized structure of the agencies within the U.S. Government, there is strict "need to know" access only, plus numerous additional top-secret classifications. So it is little wonder most people in government jobs have no access to any kind of "official" knowledge to black projects, UFOs, or anything outside of their jurisdiction.

Beyond the government of the United States and the influential corporations with which they have contracts, there is a "cabal" of extremely powerful people who are calling the global shots. There are only 287 families who own close to 50% of all the world's assets. Many of these family leaders control whole levels of different secret governments, depending on where the governments are based. This corporate cabal remains secret, and its influence over sovereign governments is illegal. In this country, the power of cabals is subverting the U.S. Constitution, Congressional oversight, and presidential powers. Their goals go far beyond the accumulation of greater wealth since the core families have plenty of financial resources. What they seek to keep is geopolitical control. These are transnational entities who are power brokers beyond the Western countries. They control long-standing, continuing interests around the world and strive to keep certain subjects (vital to their interests) secret at all costs.

NO SUCH AGENCY

The National Security Agency (NSA) was created by a secret executive order under Harry Truman on November 4, 1952. The NSA was a completely unknown agency to the nation until the 1980s, hence the nickname "No Such Agency." The secret government was originally created as a buffer for the president, a protective device, so he or she could honestly say, "I didn't know." While such secrecy originally seemed to protect the president from sabotage and other nefarious manipulations, it also prevented the Executive Office and Congress from fully knowing the truth. In the next decades, it served to isolate future presidents from any substantive knowledge of UFOs. According to numerous whistleblowers, the NSA is tasked to maintain communication with all Extraterrestrial Biological Entities (EBEs) and develop the various USA secret space programs.

The NSA is exempt from all laws which are not named in the text of that law, allowing them to be essentially a lawless institution. There was no formal procedure established for either coordinating or approving NSA operations, meaning they answer to no one. Their only guidelines are to stay consistent with "American policies," however that may be defined.

The National Security Agency was created in a large part by the Paperclip Nazis serving on its panels and advisory boards. The NSA in conjunction with the Council on Foreign Relations (CFR) spawned its muscle to establish the Central Intelligence Agency (CIA). It is not generally known that the CIA was originally formed by a presidential executive order to deal with the presence of extraterrestrials, reported by the military. That task would transfer over to the newly-formed NSA. Officially, the CIA was created to deal with national security issues around the shifting geopolitical alliances following World War II.

Soon after the formation of these organizations, the United Nations (UN) was created in 1947. The UN was envisioned as a way to ensure nothing as heinous as World War II would ever happen again. Yet, since the UN was formed there have been more wars and conflicts than ever before. Somehow these conflicts always invite Western nations into combat. The mass media tells us the Western armies enter various conflicts to ensure peace. The statement that we make war to create peace is really doublespeak. If influential policy makers in our government sincerely want to make peace with other countries, why would we enter uninvited, create conflict and kill innocent people? The CIA is responsible for most conflicts in the world, being the agency charged by the U.S. Government with protecting our national interests by interfering in and often destroying the governments of other countries. The CIA has become a criminal cabal based on Nazi principles and answerable to no one. It also hoards secrets that would benefit the human race.

The NSA and CIA claim over 75% of the intelligence budget. Currently, one primary task is still alien investigation and communication. This department originally was kept under top-secret classification in case any aliens were hostile to civilization on Earth. The Russians also have their own version of the NSA with which Americans perceive we are in competition. The NSA reasons that they cannot reveal the ET interaction with Earth society because it would result in economic collapse, religious structure collapse, and national panic leading to anarchy. If the public cannot be told, Congress cannot be told.

This completely covert group (top secret NSA & CIA) denied requests for information from President Jimmy Carter, Senator Barry Goldwater, Congressmen Steven Schiff of New Mexico, and even FBI Director J. Edgar Hoover. While sometimes provocative information has been obtained via the Freedom of Information Act, the government behind the government still is able to keep a tight lid on the UFO issue by dismissing with contempt and mockery those who would press them on disclosure or conduct any kind of serious scientific inquiry. Documents clearly indicate that the secret UFO control group of human beings here on planet Earth is in collusion with one or more ET groups.

It is very likely that there are countless levels and varieties of ETs, given the vast numbers of galaxies and even dimensions astrophysicists now theorize likely exist. It is also likely, as many contactees report, that most aliens don't see the destruction of our civilization (or planet Earth) as either necessary or wise. Wars, conflicts, and enemies everywhere are probably a myopic Earthling's view. The alleged national security issue regarding UFOs is bogus. Even if it were not, wouldn't more information be better than less?

THE ULTIMATE SECRET

A primary top secret subject is the technology collected from crashed UFOs. In the early days, the U.S. Government and others like the Soviets were retrieving crafts and working to develop "backward engineered" technology. This is the term for taking remains from a UFO crash site, or instructions from an alien, and attempting to build a similar craft. At first, recovery engineers did not know what they were working with nor could they understand the technology, so it was a logical decision to classify these projects as top secret under the cloak of "national security." But this logic is now outdated and yet the rigidity of secrecy has increased.

In the U.S., the intelligence community has lied to Congress, eliminated whistle-blowers, or used money, corruption, intimidation, and ridicule to silence people. This is what is called "the inertia of secrecy." By doing this they have painted themselves into a corner. Now with more and more at stake, the secret government practices relentless psychological conditioning. Once they use enough false information, or disinformation, fear is created around an issue. It is then easy to control the worldview on the topic so people either remain afraid or regard the topic as so outrageous as to dismiss it outright. Orthodox religious leaders also viewed potential ET contact in a disturbing way. They simply did not know what to make of contact, nor what effect it would have on their religious teachings. The secret power brokers might also feel threatened by ETs. If you wear a lens of fear, everything looks frightening. If you wear rose-colored glasses, you see everything as rose-colored. So visitors from outer space can be perceived as a threat. You can begin to believe your own propaganda.

Many people would say it is next to impossible to completely suppress this subject. Given the vast amount of information on the Internet, this is correct. This fact amps up disinformation campaigns. Agencies and hired guns do their best to create a cognitive dissonance that ridicules any sightings or evidence, even the mere concept of a UFO reality. A fictional interpretation is encouraged in the movies with hundreds of films and more to come. It is understandable that, after 70 years or so, we are still in the dark and are intentionally kept in the dark. For example, one must wonder what could possibly be hidden in those 27 security clearance levels above the office of the U.S. President. That is a lot of room in which to hide classified information.

A very effective program has been developed over the years to "safeguard" the fact that the United States Government has ample evidence of our planet being visited by extraterrestrials. Pervasive fear reactions have spawned our own secret space program. The first comprehensive disinformation campaign was called Project DOVE. It was, and still is, a complex series of covert media operations by U.S. military intelligence agencies to misinform the public. At times, the public and press are given suggestions that maybe UFOs are real in order to trick the public into thinking that what they are seeing are actually UFOs when, in fact, they are our own secret advanced aircraft. This tactic reinforces confusion and denial about both facts: that there are UFOs visiting our planet—and—we have built (through backward engineering) our own anti-gravity spacecraft and other "futuristic" machines. In this form of counterintelligence, the public is given some actual facts. Starting in the early 1950s, film productions of UFO-related movies influenced public opinion to remain open-minded, while also allowing the Black Operations to keep secret their advanced aircraft. There has always been some form of cooperation between the government and the motion picture industry. The first cooperative venture was the movie called *The Day the Earth Stood Still*. It was a collaborative undertaking between the United States Air Force and the movie industry.

Once again, why all the hoarding of this information? Once the U.S. and the Soviets retrieved several of these exotic ET crafts, combined with technical knowledge we already had, they realized it would mark an end to the oil cartels, coal burning, and the internal combustion engine. It would be the end of transmission lines for electricity, because energy can be extracted from the vibration of the Earth itself, or from fabric of space (not outer space, but the space all around us) and transmitted wirelessly, as demonstrated by Nikola Tesla over a century ago.

In the 1950s, the Lockheed/Northrop experimental craft were called flux liners, named that way because they could pull energy from the quantum flux field. The shadow power brokers knew this information meant the end of their oil monopoly and it had to be covered up. It would be the end of geopolitical hegemony and would threaten the real power structure that has been running the world for a long time. Over $100 billion dollars per year is known to be siphoned off from various U.S. Government agencies and used to support these secret projects. The shadow government's global long-term agenda is to grow the military industrial complex from currently one trillion to several trillion dollars; thus they must maintain a manufactured enemy (which requires a massive defense budget) to keep the wheels of industry moving under their control.

THE UNTOUCHABLE SUBJECT

Our duly elected government may no longer be concerned about covering up the truth about UFOs. Perhaps it is now beyond the oversight of Congress all together, even if they tried to investigate the matter. President Bill Clinton told veteran White House reporter Sarah McClendon that there was a government inside the government which he did not control. Perhaps some people in the government have tried, but they have no power to disclose. Many believe that control over the UFO subject has been compartmentalized away from legal and constitutional chain-of-command oversight and control. Those who run the secret government, according to researcher Dr. Steven Greer, are "risk-averse, do not like significant change, and will not give up control and power easily." They can afford to be patient. After all, elected public officials such as the president are just transient faces who will be gone in four, six, or eight years. The government's alleged position on UFOs appears to have been controlled for the last seven decades by an unelected group, and is now firmly in the hands of industrialists.

In reality, our elected government officials may have no more power to disclose the UFO secrets than the average American citizen. They may be totally out of the loop, as is illustrated by a story told about Clinton's Secretary of Defense, William Cohen. As recounted by Steven Greer, Cohen was approached by an astronaut who gave him a piece of UFO evidence along with the provenance for the piece. Then the evidence disappeared. Cohen spent much time and effort trying to track down where this piece of evidence had gone, but was unsuccessful.

Another possibility is that the president has had death threats by the control group and does not have the courage to demand disclosure. Steven Greer reports that a close friend of Bill Clinton's said to him (Greer): "If the president does what you say, he fears that he will end up like Jack Kennedy." The theory of the president being threatened with death in order to keep him quiet is actually quite a regular theme in the UFO community, given the synchronicity of events surrounding assassinations. There are declassified CIA documents that claim President Kennedy was assassinated because he gave the order to declassify the ET presence only 10 days before he was killed. A related tie-in with the secret cabal is that only seven days before his assassination, Kennedy cryptically said, "There's a plot in this country to enslave every man, woman and child. Before I leave this high and noble office, I intend to expose this plot."

Jimmy Carter entered the White House determined to release the UFO files, inspired by the fact that he himself had seen a UFO and had said so publicly. However, after a UFO briefing, Carter changed his tune and joined the cover-up side. He told actress Shirley MacLaine, "It was true ... there were occupants (in alien space crafts)," and that he wanted to "shine the sunshine laws on it to see how the people would react," but he "couldn't and wouldn't." Carter stated, "I don't see any reason to keep information like that secret but there may be some aspect of the UFO information with which I am not familiar that might be related to some secret experiments that we are doing that might involve our national security—our new weapons systems. I certainly wouldn't release that. But if it were something removed from our national security, in my opinion as president, I would go ahead and release that. I see nothing wrong with that." Carter clarified that if the subject involved national security matters, he wouldn't release that material. Anything the briefers would tie into a threat to the security of the United States would be reason enough for Carter to keep quiet, and that is what he did as president.

History might record the disclosing president as a hero, but there is an equal chance he or she might be seen as a leader with remarkably poor judgment whose decision precipitated chaos. It might be these very human considerations that stop a president from releasing UFO information. The president who makes the ET reality announcement will face numerous unpredictable fallouts, possible harm to himself and his family and quite possibly his entire presidential agenda being overrun by the ET issue.

AL QAEDA BOOGEYMAN

After the end of the Cold War, the cabal realized another perceived national threat was necessary. They decided to create a radical group of extremists who would become the target to further advance a "War on Terror." Once again, the CIA was tapped as the skilled operative agency with their own bag of lawless, terrorist strategies. A neo-conservative think tank called the "Project for the New American Century" released a document that would create a full spectrum threat for the entire globe. It spoke of creating a change in public perception (a "transformation") from *no* perceived threat to a *global* threat. The authors realized how long it could take to bring about such a change. The document said:

"The process of transformation, even if it brings about a Revolutionary Change, is likely to be a long one, absent some catastrophic and catalyzing event, like a new Pearl Harbor."

America acquired its new Pearl Harbor on September 11, 2001. Homeland Security and the Patriot Act were already awaiting implementation before 9-11, and soon after were signed into law without much resistance from the American people. Few objected when these restrictive and often ridiculous regulations (airport searches) went into effect shortly after what is generally regarded as the largest "false flag" operation in history. It was designed once again to invent a new enemy to enrich the international bankers who fund both sides of all wars, as well as specifically to restrict the incentive and the ability to protest unfair government practices.

The "War on Terror" is fake. It is a manufactured boogeyman. Aggressive acts against the United States take place in countries we are occupying, in which we are imposing an uninvited presence. America has created its enemies with its aggression. Terrorism acts are merely blowback from U.S. violent aggression. Terrorism is a tactic. It is a desperation tactic used by victimized peoples trying to protect themselves from the invasion of their sovereign nations, the destruction of their cultures and economies, and the killing of innocent people. A war on a tactic is a nonsensical and dangerous notion, and one that has led us into open-ended conflicts with no achievable goal. The people who have set up these vicious scenarios are the elite global power brokers.

With no actual threatening enemy to justify their vast military appropriations and imperialist wars, the would-be controllers have created the boogey man called Al Qaeda. Terrorism is intangible and needs the label of a person, group, or nation. Iraqi dictator Saddam Hussein functioned as the big bad boogeyman in the 1990s. "Simply stated, there is no doubt that Saddam Hussein now has weapons of mass destruction," said Dick Cheney in a speech to VFW National Convention on August, 26, 2002. We know now that this was a blatant lie. The latest blatant lie is the creation and funding of ISIS.

While the American people naturally dismissed all of Osama bin Laden's statements, there is actually a ring of truth to some of his pronouncements after 9-11. He made a statement to *Al Jazeera* within days following the 9-11 attacks, denying any involvement. "The U.S. Government has consistently blamed me for being behind every attack," said bin Laden. "I would like to assure the world that I did not plan the recent attacks, which seem to have been planned by people for personal reasons. I have been living in the Islamic emirate of Afghanistan and following its leaders' rule. The current leader does not allow me to exercise such operations." The bin Laden "Confession Tape," translated and released by the U.S. Government, was used as justification to bomb and invade Afghanistan. It has many inconsistencies and is largely regarded as a hoax. The vast majority of people in the Arab World, however, also believe 9-11 was an American-Israeli inside job. Such is also the force behind the Islamic State, but the mainstream media and Western pundits make it seem ISIS arose organically in the Middle East.

Osama bin Laden gave another telling interview in October, 2001, again denying involvement in 9-11: "I have already said that we are not hostile to the United States. We are against the (U.S. Government) system, which makes other nations slaves of the United States, or forces them to mortgage their political and economic freedom. This system is totally in control of the American Jews, whose first priority is Israel, not the United States. It is clear that the American people are themselves the slaves of the Jews and are forced to live according to the principles and laws laid by them. So, the punishment should reach Israel." In the same interview, Osama bin Laden suggested that "the United States should try to trace the perpetrators of these attacks within itself; the people who are a part of the U.S. system, but are dissenting against it. Or those who are working for some other system; persons who want to make the present century as a century of conflict between Islam and Christianity so that their own civilization, nation, country, or ideology could survive." But of course, Osama bin Laden was the face of the enemy, so these remarks were hardly reported.

"It's easy to imagine an infinite number of situations where the government might legitimately give out false information," said Solicitor General Theodore Olson, whose wife Barbara was killed on 9-11. "It's an unfortunate reality that the issuance of incomplete information by government may sometimes be perceived as necessary to protect vital interests." Mr. Olson stopped just short of explicitly placing the 9-11 tragedy in the category of "incomplete information." Now we have the Patriot Act, the long occupations of Iraq and Afghanistan, and 850,000 new top secret positions developed since 9-11, mainly in the Department of Homeland Security, which is charged with protecting U.S. citizens while our government is waging the War on Terror. As for pulling one over on the public, the best place to hide the truth is right in front of those you are trying to deceive.

CONTROLLING THE FLOW OF INFORMATION

In the mid-20th century, the Western mass media was controlled by 86 small corporations who competed to deliver the best possible news. Through consolidation, only six companies run it today. It is a well-oiled, very streamlined, very controlled machine run by very few people. This has set a dangerous precedent, as manipulated news no longer allows viewers to make informed decisions. All of these six media organizations have very close ties to arms manufacturers and major financial institutions. Each of these six media organizations primarily gets its information from two sources, the Associated Press and Reuters, both owned by the Rothschild dynasty. That is why there is no bad press about the World Bank or the international banking cartel reported to the population through these outlets. (Public television, as its anchors often note, gets many of its stories from the Independent Television News Network.) The money cartels who own the mainstream media also own Monsanto and wish to outlaw organic food through the legislation called Codex Alimentarius. They also advocate using aerial spraying, and they hoard the world seed banks. General Agreement on Tariffs and Trade (GATT) and the World Trade Organization (WTO) continue to push Monsanto's Codex Alimentarius "Food Code."

The Trilateral Commission was established in 1973 as a way to influence the emerging Middle East and Far Eastern nations. Its founder and primary financial sponsor was international tycoon David Rockefeller, longtime chairman of the Rockefeller family-controlled Chase Manhattan Bank and undisputed overlord of his family's global corporate empire. The Trilateral Commission was unique in that it brought the Japanese ruling elite into the inner councils of the global power brokers, a recognition of Japan's growing influence in the world economic and political arena. Trilateralists have been known to say, "The people, governments and economies of all nations must serve the needs of multinational banks and corporations." To accomplish the purpose of supporting hand-picked political candidates to win upcoming elections, Trilateralists mobilized the money-power of the Wall Street bankers, the intellectual influence of the academic community (who are subservient to the wealth of the great tax-free foundations), the media controllers who are represented in their membership, and the Council on Foreign Relations (CFR), another Rockefeller-financed foreign policy pressure group. The CFR is similar to the Trilateralists and the Bilderberg Group, although the CFR is composed solely of American citizens.

The Trilateral Commission can be said to be the Bilderberg Group dressed in another frock because membership includes Japan's elite. Both groups have the same goals. Both the Bilderbergers and Trilateralists are post-World War II Axis-influenced secret policy groups. They have combined with British, European, and American Nazi counterparts, and are working toward a "one world government," a concept first thought to represent an altruistic coming together to solve humanity's problems and live in peace. Unfortunately, absolute control and unregulated power drive these one world government advocates, which morphs a potentially lofty vision into a deranged dream. By spoon-feeding selected information to the public, they can make up any reality they choose. We have been influenced collectively to ignore certain events in the world, such as six million people dying of starvation every year. Rather, we are encouraged to keep the blinders on and we are distracted by the pressure to work long hours, produce, and consume. We are bombarded with heavy-handed incentives to make a pile of money and buy as many trinkets as we can to gain more status in society. And this is sold to us as happiness, security, and the good life.

LIFTING THE VEIL ON SHADOW GROUPS

What good would it do to uncover these elite overlords and expose what they are doing? For starters, we could have a media that truly serves the people. It would allow sustainable energy sources, the end of poverty, availability of nutritious food, and the emergence of a completely informed and empowered human race. Most importantly, it would put the rule of law back into civilization. If we allow them to succeed, we may have a world in which our children will not want to live. But it does not have to be this way. We can end self-generating debt, starvation, wars, and unnecessary suffering if we can look beyond the great distraction of the mass media. A clear and present danger exists right now and it deserves our urgent attention.

The veil of secrecy that has ruled the world for centuries is beginning to be lifted. It is time to forget the imaginary constraints put before us. We are all people and we are all one, and the current crisis affects each of us equally. Where do we begin? First, we are spiritual beings and as such, we have a better idea. Fear and violence do not ultimately succeed. Only love in its highest meaning succeeds. An idea cannot actually be attacked. Furthermore, the attacker is always coming from fear. To respond in kind is to give power to the perceived attack and keep the cycle of attack/counter attack going. Instead, we have another choice. The power of our minds, used in the service of healing and love, can neutralize the dynamic of hate and treachery. The energy of love (the attitude of seeing beyond a person's desperate acts to his or her spiritual essence as a kindred spirit) is very powerful. Choosing this attitude is the means to the end goal of peace. The *idea* of non-violent dissent (including the absence of hateful thoughts) has to be embraced first, and, then, appropriate behavior follows. The process is that we simply notice, but are not dismayed or immobilized by the chaos the collective ego has wrought (as described in this book) and now we know what *not* to choose. Thus we can change our minds and see beyond our fellow human and our own mistakes. Since minds are joined, this is simultaneously offering a choice to all minds. More to the point, a truthful idea is powerful, invulnerable, and is increased by sharing. From this choice to look beyond grievous acts, and choose love and healing over fear, comes clear guidance as to what actions to take or refrain from taking.

In short, we need to treat each other coming from a state of love, not fear, and address the root cause of the problem—our unwitting, fear-driven compliance. We are not merely pawns in the game of life, but pieces who can move independently. It is up to each of us to change the world for the better *by changing our thinking first.* Do not accept tracking devices from the New World Order, do not accept poisoned food or water, *do* question any justification for war, and keep yourself informed through trusted sources on the Internet and inspired publications. It is time to wake up from the collective ego's hypnotic trance of fear, and then free ourselves from the shackles of those who wish to keep us enslaved.

This souvenir sheet features an image of the late Grenada Prime Minister Sir Gary Gairy, who spoke before the UN General Assembly, urging them to study the flying saucer phenomenon in more detail. In October, 1977, Gairy made the following request before the UN General Assembly, recommending the "establishment of an agency or a department of the United Nations for undertaking, coordinating and disseminating the results of research into Unidentified Flying Objects (UFOs) and related phenomena."

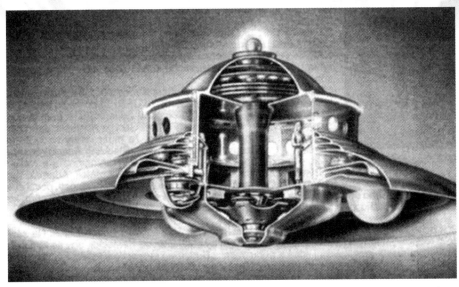

On May 29, 1950, George Adamski took a photograph of what he alleged to be six unidentified objects in the sky, which appeared to be flying in formation. Adamski's 1950 UFO photograph was depicted in an August 1978 commemorative stamp issued by the island nation of Grenada in order to mark the "Year of UFOs." This is a diagram of the inside of a UFO supposedly visited by George Adamski.

The Day the Earth Stood Still is a 1951 science fiction film about an alien and a robot on a diplomatic mission to Earth. Devoid of the computer-generated imagery and special effects that seem necessary for today's movie-goers, *The Day the Earth Stood Still* is quite a landmark in sci-fi films, especially for the early 1950s. It bases its audience appeal on suspense and the personality of the "invading alien" named Klaatu, seen here being shot by a paranoid army force.

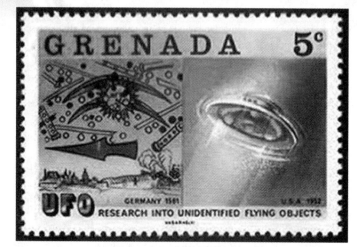

The first in a series of four stamps issued by the island nation of Grenada, in August 1978, commemorating the "Year of UFOs." This stamp includes two images side by side: On the left is a 16th century landscape with mechanical-looking sky activity; on the right is a UFO. It seems to suggest a theme of "then and now."

A radar device and an image of Mars are featured on this stamp. The line of light circles on the right is based on a formation of craft in flight photographed by George Adamski on May 29, 1950.

A flying saucer illustration and a photograph highlight this $3 stamp.

SECRET SCIENCES

"We already have the means to travel to the stars, but these technologies are locked up in black projects and it would take an act of God to ever get them out to benefit humanity. Anything you can imagine we already know how to do."
–Ben Rich, Founder of Stealth Technology Lockheed Skunk Works

IT is now largely recognized that the United States has had a two-tiered technology development program, with some major scientific developments withheld from the public. This technology has been held in the hands of a controlling elite for at least a century, perhaps longer. The "secret" technological base can be traced back to the 19th century or earlier. The reason certain technologies aren't being released in this modern era, especially when they will greatly benefit humanity, is simply because of control and power run amuck. Once again we are seeing the accuracy of the old adage, "Power corrupts. Absolute power corrupts absolutely." If we had the means to perform truly advanced technological feats, say for example, time travel, free energy systems, holographic communication technology, and even to travel to the planets and beyond, then those who control that information would be in a very powerful position. If it were possible to contain these developments within a very small group, a controlling group, they would have the ability, quite literally, to control the planet and humanity.

Over the last century, human consciousness has been saturated with a huge intertwining web of conspiracy theories which are often too overwhelming for the average human to understand, and may in fact produce more questions than answers. It has been very cleverly orchestrated so that no one ever discovers the whole truth about anything, but if someone does blow the whistle, then that person is ridiculed or silenced. What if a global conspiracy of silence does indeed exist? What if we already do have the means to travel to the stars as Ben Rich, the 20-year brilliant boss of Lockheed's legendary Skunk Works claimed in an apparent deathbed confession? What if people are kept blind to it because they commonly associate the word "theory" with "conspiracy?" And what if information buried in a secret conspiracy deeply affects our future, our media, our government, our academic system, our monetary system, our technological advancement, our food supply, and the planet we live on? Just consider that if such a conspiracy of secrecy does exist, it would affect virtually every person alive.

But due to the overwhelming nature of such a possibility, most people do not want to take a look. The implications are very steep. The very idea of a conspiracy theory (as noted in the Introduction to this book) can be manipulated by the conspirators themselves. Efforts to investigate claims made by astronauts, Air Force pilots, scientists, engineers and thousands of average citizens have generally been discussed in the mainstream media as entertainment, imaginative quackery and science fiction. Failing that, individuals who come forth are tainted by labels of gullibility on the one hand and mental illness on the other. This cover-up appears to be such a concerted effort about a phenomenon that doesn't go away that a "conspiracy of silence and cover-up" for a real phenomenon seems a logical explanation.

The TV show *The X-Files* popularized the term "the truth is out there," and it is, sometimes right before our eyes if we'd only choose to notice. There is far more to the workings of the world than what is readily apparent. If one does not take the time to examine the evidence and find out the reasons for layers of secrecy, then the problem will certainly never go away. When the *complete* story line is woven together, what we have is an "alternative narrative" which is comprehensive in scope.

MODERN SECRET SCIENCES

The earliest secret science projects actually started prior to World War I and were concerned with weapons development. The better-known programs were started during and after World War II. The U.S. Army's Manhattan Project was in charge of developing the atomic bomb, while the U.S. Navy dealt with Stealth equipment and invisibility, as witnessed in the Philadelphia Experiment. The secret agenda keepers had to find a way around Congressional oversight and public scrutiny. They did it with the introduction of Special Access Programs (SAPs). By the year 2000, there were already 150 SAPs within the Department of Defense alone. The existence of many SAPs are unacknowledged and have no oversight. All are managed on a strict "need to know" basis. The SAPs, now dominated by private contractors, are completely independent classification systems. It is not known how much money goes in and how is acquired. This runaway secrecy has become so monolithic, so vast, it has spawned not only a secret space program, but also a breakaway civilization living off-planet.

After World War II, the top Nazi intelligence agents were joined with German scientists and brought to the USA under Project Paperclip (discussed earlier). The intelligence officers joined with American anti-communist agents, and the scientists teamed up with NASA. From this merging, the National Security Agency (NSA) was officially inaugurated. Many of the Paperclip Nazis joined the newly formed CIA. Wernher von Braun and other German rocket engineers were employed by NASA and other military organizations. Previous experiments such as "Babylon-Working" and the "Montauk Project" were carried out using Nazi occultists and scientists to communicate with and materialize inter-dimensional beings and ETs. They were the "unofficial" pioneers of projects working on inter-dimensional time travel, as well as the emerging dark sciences such as eugenics and cloning. This is how these projects called the "secret sciences" were officially, yet covertly born, with any leaks of their reality dealt with as "science fiction."

An off-ledger "black budget" was established to fund the secret sciences, which also became known as the "Black Arts" or "black sciences." The black sciences are the "most secret of all secrets" and are guarded by specially screened soldiers. The CIA planned and trained the MK-ULTRA agents, who were specifically programmed, mind-manipulated assassins (if necessary), courtesy of a little known "black world" agency that "takes care of things" outside of normal channels. Starting with Eisenhower and finalized by Nixon, this parallel world that deals with anything ET or backward engineered has been privatized. It is now managed by military industrial complex companies, which are privately owned by the Rockefeller and Rothschild dynasties, among others. There are so many layers and compartments, so many "unseen realms," that even the highest level people involved may not know or comprehend the big picture.

Project MK-ULTRA was the code name for a covert, illegal CIA human experimentation program run by the CIA's Office of Scientific Intelligence. This official U.S. Government program began in the early 1950s and continued at least through the late 1960s, using U.S. and Canadian citizens as test subjects. The published evidence indicates that Project MK-ULTRA involved the use of many methodologies to manipulate individual mental states and alter brain function, including the surreptitious administration of drugs, hypnosis, sensory deprivation, isolation, verbal and sexual abuse, as well as other forms of torture. This evidence is now in the public domain and has been reported in some segments of the mainstream media, with muted public reaction.

Shadow government leaders have long known the advantage of compartmentalizing the secret sciences on a need-to-know basis only. New knowledge was not and still is not available to the regular military ranks, to Congress, or to just any university. The most valuable secrets remain in the hands of a power-corrupt few who have tied themselves to the World Bank for the future funding of their projects. They have developed their "think-tanks" such as Stanford Research Institute and Britain's Tavistock Institute as both fronts and laboratories to keep the public fooled about virtually everything.

ATMOSPHERE WEAPONS

Since its founding, the National Security Agency (NSA) has been a very dangerous group as they control some of the technology that has the potential to harm the natural order of Earth, with the possibility of destroying the planet. These elite scientists, spies, and powerful industrialists have developed top secret projects such as the nuclear bomb, chemical and biological warfare, and HAARP, the misnamed "High-Frequency Active Auroral Research Program," which has nothing to do with studying the northern lights. The HAARP Alaska operation is about weather control, or more correctly named HARP, the High Altitude Research Program. In essence, HAARP is a massive beam cannon, a type of global microwave oven that can move weather systems. The NSA, along with defense contractors such as Raytheon, are behind other cutting-edge technology such as the Stealth aircraft, invisible hovercraft, Extremely Low Frequency (ELF) mind control devices, and the cloning or reproduction of biological human-like species, plus engineering super seeds for agricultural patents used by multinational companies such as Monsanto.

On April 28, 1997, just as the Alaska HAARP operation was becoming fully operational, the *Department of Defense News* made the following curious warning to the public. The report stated: "Others are engaging even in an eco-type of terrorism whereby they can alter the climate, set off earthquakes and volcanoes remotely through the use of electromagnetic waves. So there are plenty of ingenious minds out there that are at work finding ways in which they can wreak terror upon other nations. It's real, and that's the reason why we have to intensify our efforts, and that's why this is so important." Is there any doubt the big players within the U.S. military industrial complex are not completely involved?

Research into the use of microwave weapons and their use for mind control began in 1950s at the Tavistock Institute, one of Britain's leading psychiatric research establishments. The United Kingdom institute was researching strategies of mind control which could be inflicted on the British populace without their awareness. The brain state of most interest to British scientists was the monkey submission response, whereby the dominant monkey caused submissive behavior in its underlings. Having discovered the specific brain-wave pattern for docile, submissive, or zombie-like behavior, it was then recorded and used as the template for the invention of the Extremely Low Frequency (ELF) signal beamed by UK microwave transmitters. Britain was the first discoverer of microwave technology used for radar in the 1940s, and therefore had a commanding lead in the field.

The 1970s brought an even darker side to the story, with the news that the Soviets were microwaving the U.S. Embassy in Moscow. One third of the staff eventually died of cancer believed to be due to microwave irradiation. These weapons transmit ELF signals which mimic natural brain waves. At the flick of a switch, anyone around these microwave transmitters can potentially be turned into submissive zombies who cannot think clearly and become depressed or apathetic. Australian scientists found in 1997 tests that tiny amounts of microwave produced by even the very safest mobile phones can cause cancer in mice when exposed to this radiation.

Although this information is also in the public domain, other opinions and studies offer contradictory evidence. Once again, it is up to the individual to decide.

THE PHILADELPHIA EXPERIMENT

The Philadelphia Experiment was carried out several times at the Philadelphia Naval Shipyard in Philadelphia, Pennsylvania, and out at sea. The experiment, labeled "Project Rainbow," was designed to make the U.S. Navy destroyer escort USS Eldridge invisible, or "cloaked," to enemy devices. The Navy began the project in the 1930s and 1940s featuring Nikola Tesla, the brilliant Serbian-American electrical wizard as a lead engineer. The mission was to make ships invisible from the enemy. The experiment was based on theoretical implications of the Unified Field Theory, a term coined by Albert Einstein. The Unified Field Theory sought to describe mathematically and physically the interrelated nature of the forces that comprise electromagnetic radiation and gravity. According to eyewitness accounts, scientists thought that a variation of the Unified Field Theory would enable the Navy to use several large electrical generators to bend light around an object so that it became completely invisible. Quantum physics experiments in the past decade have succeeded in making small objects invisible, using similarly-described light manipulation techniques; however, the technology might have been known decades earlier and is only now exposed to public scrutiny.

Testing began in the summer of 1943 and it was successful to a limited degree. The first test on July 22, 1943, resulted in the USS Eldridge being rendered almost completely invisible. Some witnesses reported a "greenish fog" appearing in its place. Crew members supposedly complained of severe nausea afterwards. A few weeks later, on August 12, the test was attempted again, and this time there was "a blue flash" and the ship disappeared totally. When the ship reappeared four hours later, some sailors were embedded in the metal structures of the ship, including one sailor who ended up on a deck level below the position where he began with his hand embedded in the steel hull of the ship; the hand had to be amputated. Other sailors above deck continued appearing and disappearing. At that point, the experiment was altered at the request of the Navy, with the new objective being solely to render the Eldridge invisible to radar.

The equipment was not properly re-calibrated, but in spite of this, the experiment was repeated for the last time on October 28, 1943. The experimenters threw the switch on this eventful evening and the ship again went into hyperspace. This time, the Eldridge not only became invisible, but the ship and crew physically vanished from the Philadelphia Naval Shipyard in a flash of blue light and teleported to Norfolk, Virginia, over 320 kilometers away. It is claimed that the Eldridge sat for about 10 or 15 minutes in full view of men aboard the ship USS Andrew Furuseth in Norfolk, whereupon the Eldridge vanished from their sight and then reappeared in Philadelphia at the site it had originally occupied. It was also said that the ship traveled back in time for about 10 seconds.

The three experiments resulted in a variety of problems for the different crews on the Eldridge. There are descriptions of serious side effects for the crew. Some sailors were said to have been physically fused to bulkheads, while others suffered from mental disorders, and still others simply vanished. It is also claimed that the ship's crew was subjected to intense brainwashing afterwards in order to maintain the secrecy of the experiments. The Navy regarded it as top secret security information. In addition, having experimented with a new technology that went awry, there was all the more reason for secrecy. Subsequently, all public references to the Philadelphia Experiment were labeled a hoax. In the end, it was a huge success as well as a huge failure. Of course the Navy denied ever doing it, and then officially shelved any future experiments, at least those involving enlisted men.

CALLING IN DR. BROWN

It seems the Norfolk, Virginia Naval Shipyard could be a key "vortex point" on the Earth's surface, and connected with the abnormal behaviors of aircraft flying in the area, including the nearby Bermuda Triangle. Prior to the Philadelphia Experiment, observers had described strange "warp" effects in the atmosphere of the Norfolk Naval Shipyard. Navy engineers first attributed this to the blast of high-intensity electromagnetic fields from the arc welding going on in shipbuilding. As word of these strange effects reached the highest levels, top brass called in Dr. Thomas Brown to investigate, and it was from these observations that the Philadelphia Experiment was eventually born.

Dr. Thomas Townsend Brown was one of the secret fathers of anti-gravity technology. He worked in the UFO field with electrostatics, attempting to prove that it was possible to make an object move by means of very high voltage electrostatic fields. The reason his name is not famous is because his work was classified for "national security" reasons. He discovered that strong electromagnetic fields produce an anti-gravity effect. Brown created a strong enough flow of current between a negative and positive pole that an anti-gravity "thrust" started propelling his device in whatever direction the positive pole was pointing. In Brown's designs, the negative pole is much larger than the positive pole. When considering a craft designed like this, the entire bottom of the ship is a negative plate, and the small sphere at the very top of the ship as the positive plate. Pilots can navigate the ship by breaking up the negative plate into a series of sections and varying the current flow between them, where the ship "falls" into the gravity field it produces.

Dr. Brown was asked to examine the Philadelphia Experiment "phenomenon" and comment on what the observers saw—that is, the dematerializations and what could have caused them. His knowledge of "dielectric stress" phenomena and the activities associated with arc discharges made him a qualified expert. When Dr. Brown reviewed the material, his conclusions were strikingly different from the majority opinion. While some scientists adamantly insisted that the observed dematerializations were the result of "irradiation" and subsequent vaporization, no such evidence for the vaporizations could be found. Careful analysis of weld-chamber atmospheres proved negative in this regard. No gasified metals were detected in the room air throughout the discharge event. This fact was truly mystifying.

Dr. Brown was confident he knew what was happening between the two shipyards. Despite the fact that he had never observed these effects, his intuition taught him well. Not surprisingly, Brown's principle directly ties in with quantum mechanics. He proposed that there are negatively charged electron clouds and a positively charged nucleus in the atom. The Biefield-Brown effect is what causes the electrons to rush into the nucleus. Having no conventional electrical explanation, the only resolution was found in the Einsteinian proposals concerning electrical and gravitational force unity.

A MIND CONTROL CHAIR

An earlier invention was also used in the Philadelphia Experiment. A mind-altering prototype chair had been back-engineered from a recovered Grey alien craft and was used in the Philadelphia Experiment. This chair was essentially a mind amplifier. The shadow government planned to have specially-trained individuals sit in the chair and generate thought-forms which would be amplified and transmitted. Engineers could transmit a signal which would put people in a pre-orgasmic state in which they would be receptive to programming. The thought transmission worked very well and the experimenters found other capabilities. They discovered that it could also work in conjunction with time travel. A psychically trained individual would sit in the chair and generate a thought-form of a vortex that connected 1947 and 1981. That's exactly what they got—a time tunnel they could walk through. These were some of the earlier capabilities in which individuals started going forward and backward in time. That was the last phase of what was labeled the Phoenix Project.

Around 1979 or 1980 the Phoenix Project time machine was fully operational. The transmitter had enough power to warp space and time. The individual in the chair would have to synthesize the vortex function because they did not have the technical capability. (It can now be mechanically synthesized.) The protocol called for the subject in the chair to think of some creature, and then the creature would materialize. They instructed the individual in the chair to think of all the animals at Montauk Point charging into town, and that's exactly what happened. They nearly succeeded in creating a synthetic being. The problem was that what they created only stayed as long as the mind amplifier was on. It had tremendous power, somewhere between gigawatts and terawatts. The vortex diameter could be projected outward to about seven kilometers.

MONTAUK PROJECT

Montauk is a small seaside resort town on the tip of Long Island, New York, that draws vacationers to its shores every year. Camp Hero, located a short distance outside of Montauk, has roots going back to the Revolutionary War when it was used to test military cannons. Camp Hero served as a coastal defense installation against potential invasions during World War II. Before closing in the early 1980s, this military base at Montauk Point, especially the underground base that was reportedly there, was the center of an otherworldly conspiracy operation which lasted for decades. This "conspiracy theory" alleged that people were being kidnapped and taken to a U.S. Air Force base where they were subjected to mind control and time travel experiments. There was also a tie-in to the ship disappearing from the Philadelphia Naval Shipyard, plus alleged tall reptoid extraterrestrials who also somehow had a hand in it all. All of these experiments have been dubbed "The Montauk Project."

Several witnesses have come forward to say they ended up at the Camp Hero underground base near Montauk for scientific experiments. These witnesses reported seeing ETs working alongside human scientists. The main whistleblower is Alfred Bielek, a retired electrical engineer, who maintains he was a survivor of the mysterious 1943 Philadelphia Experiment and was part of the crew who traveled through time. Mr. Bielek and his brother Duncan jumped off the Eldridge while it was in hyperspace and ended up, in an instant, at the secret base in Montauk on August 12, 1983! The black operations military personnel working with certain ET groups tried the same experiment 40 years after 1943, on the same date and time, and opened up a hole in time between the two eras. If this hole were not closed, according to Mr. Bielek, then our world could have been destroyed.

Mr. Bielek stated that his brother decided to stay in the future with the identity Duncan Cameron, while he himself agreed to go back to 1943 in order to close the hole by destroying the equipment onboard the Eldridge. He did accomplish this task and the holes were closed. However, in Montauk, through contact with the aliens, there was a time tunnel that existed there in 1983. Also during the 1943 experiment, three UFOs were hovering overhead witnessing the Philadelphia Experiment. When the ship vanished, one of the UFOs was caught up in the energy vortex hole and was transported into the future. Bielek's brother, who stayed in the future, became quite fascinated with the time tunnel at Montauk. He stated that the government saw him as a liability and would have killed him except that his molecular structure was connected with the two holes in time in 1943 and 1983. Furthermore, they believed if they killed him, it also could cause a ripple effect that would reopen these holes. Thus, they used the technology they had received from the aliens to regress him to a baby, and sent him back in time to 1927 where he was exchanged for the son of the Bielek family. Somehow his brother got caught in the time tunnel experiment, and again, they had the same situation where if he died, his death could cause the holes in time to re-open. So again, using some strange technology of the aliens, they were able to take the soul (the life force) of his brother and place it in the body of his father's third son.

The military goals and technical connections between the Philadelphia Experiment and the Montauk Project became known as the Phoenix Project, which resulted in the ripping open of a huge hole in spacetime. According to Al Bielek, this was deliberately done by the aliens on the 1983 end to create a rift in the fabric of spacetime, enabling a large number of aliens and ships to come through. All of the alien spacecraft had time travel capabilities, but the rift was needed to get the largest ships through in order to expedite a mass invasion of the Earth by malevolent reptoid aliens. Interestingly, abduction researcher Dr. Karla Turner has reported a spike in human abductions and missing people starting around the mid-1980s. The Phoenix Project may very well be the most esoteric of all the secret sciences, but there are other subjects we will cover now that may not seem so much like a science fiction novel.

TIBETAN ACOUSTIC LEVITATION

Tibetan priests of the Far East were said to have the ability to lift heavy boulders up high mountains simply by creating various sounds. Knowledge of the various vibrations in the audio range suggests to some scientists of sound physics that a vibrating and condensed sound field can nullify the power of gravitation, hence, levitation.

While studying at Oxford, a Swedish physician named Dr. Jarl became friends with a young Tibetan student. A couple of years later in 1939, Dr. Jarl was urgently requested by his student friend to medically treat a high lama in Tibet. Dr. Jarl requested a leave and followed a designated messenger on a long journey by plane and yak caravans to the monastery where his young friend and the old lama were now living and holding high positions. Dr. Jarl stayed there for some time and, because of his friendship with the Tibetans, learned many things that other foreigners had no chance to observe firsthand.

One day his friend took him to a place in the neighborhood of the monastery and showed him a sloping meadow surrounded on the northwest by high cliffs. Perched on one of the rock walls, at a height of about 250 meters, was a big hole that looked like the entrance to a cave. In front of this hole was a platform where the monks were building a rock wall. The only access to this platform was from the top of the cliff and the monks lowered themselves down with the help of ropes. In the middle of the meadow, about 250 meters from the cliff, was a polished slab of rock with a bowl-like cavity in the center.

A block of stone was maneuvered into this cavity by yak oxen. The block was one meter wide and one and one-half meters long. Then 19 musical instruments were set in an arc of 90° at a distance of 63 meters from the stone slab. The radius of 63 meters was measured precisely. The musical instruments consisted of 13 drums and six trumpets. When the stone was in position, the monk behind the small drum gave a signal to start the music and chanting. The small drum had a very sharp sound and could be heard even with the other instruments making a terrible din. All the monks were singing and chanting a prayer, slowly increasing the tempo of this unbelievable noise. The monks, with their instruments, formed exactly one quarter of a circle, with all their sound pressure directed at the "bowl" depression in the ground where the stone was positioned.

During the first four minutes, nothing happened. Then, as the speed of the drumming and the noise increased, the big stone block started to rock and sway and suddenly took off into the air with an increasing speed in the direction of the platform in front of the cave hole, 250 meters high. When the trumpets rose us so did the monks attention, focused on the rock in the air. After three minutes of ascent it landed on the platform. The Tibetans continuously brought new blocks to the meadow, and the monks using this method transported five to six blocks per hour on a parabolic flight track approximately 500 meters long and 250 meters high. From time to time a stone would split, and the monks moved the split stones away. Dr. Jarl had heard about the Tibetans hurling massive stones, but he was the first Westerner who had the opportunity to see this remarkable spectacle.

Dr. Jarl was careful to point out that the stones took three whole minutes to rise, so this was not simply a sudden catapulting effect. Rather, it was more like a slow, deliberate movement. This suggests that the ether vibrates in a harmonic resonance, and the vibrations can be measured very precisely and put into numbers. This act of levitation was not a product of fantasy, but the entire setup was carefully observed, measured and even filmed. Unfortunately, the English Scientific Society for which Dr. Jarl was working confiscated his films of the procedure and declared them classified. They have still not been released.

FORBIDDEN PATENTS

Anything that has to do with free energy, or anti-gravity breakthroughs such as developed by the Tibetans, are under strict control and are not made public. According to the American Academy of Sciences, there are more than six thousand patents that have been suppressed for so-called "national security" or "public safety" reasons. The Federation of American Scientists puts that number at 5,135 withheld inventions that have been classified up to the end of fiscal year 2010. There is no doubt that some of these patents probably need to be suppressed. For example, we don't want everyone to have a backyard nuke. But there are other classified patents which utilize benevolent technology and could be used for the benefit of the human race.

Among the forbidden energy patents, any power system that is more than 70-80% efficient at converting energy will automatically be declared "classified information." Such uber-energy efficient blueprints, or free energy patents, have been around for decades, but have never been released. These patents are kept classified because the cabal wants to have exclusive control of this knowledge. After all, energy manufacture and distribution is the world's largest industry.

Other forbidden "patents" are the biological agents used in germ warfare, originally developed for military purposes. Bioweapons can be made to target certain people or even certain ethnic groups. The A-H1N1 Swine Flu pandemic of 2009 has been tied to being introduced by the UN and WHO as a bioweapon attack. Dr. Robert Gallo is a leading U.S. biomedical researcher who is credited with discovering the Human Immunodeficiency Virus (HIV) in the mid-1980s. Fifteen years prior, Gallo forged a close relationship with the U.S. military when he worked to develop several diseases which could be used as synthetic biological weapons. Gallo, the discoverer of HIV/AIDS, was also the *inventor* of the deadly virus while overseeing military bionetics contractor, Litton Industries.

Dr. Robert Strecker verified these claims in an extensive report, identifying HIV/AIDS as being developed as an intentional human-made virus bioengineered in American labs, and unleashed as part of a covert eugenics program. The head of vaccines at pharmaceutical giant Merck, Dr. Maurice Hillerman, admitted on camera that Merck's Hepatitis B vaccines, contaminated with a virus, introduced the AIDS epidemic in Central African countries and to gay populations in the USA. Furthermore, Hillerman claimed that all of Merck's vaccines are contaminated with cancer and other viruses. Over the decades, elite researchers have learned that all viruses are crystalline in structure, and that the correct frequency can destroy them, as demonstrated by inventor Royal Raymond Rife and others. The Powers That Be have not released this information, likely because their eugenics program for culling the human population continues. They are ruthless in their pursuit to maintain certain sciences secret, including "suiciding" prominent doctors on the verge of a breakthrough. The loss of Dr. Bradstreet in June, 2015, raised eyebrows, just as his findings of GcMAF treating autism, and nagalase as a vaccine-induced inhibitor, started to influence others, who also mysteriously died.

A detailed study by Dr. Marcia Angell, the former editor of the prestigious *New England Journal of Medicine*, says that only 14% of pharmaceutical companies' budgets goes to research and development (R&D) of drugs, "usually at the uncreative final part of the drug pipeline. The rest goes to marketing and profits." And even with that paltry 14%, drug companies squander a fortune developing the so-called "me-too" drugs. These are medicines that do exactly the same job as a drug that already exists, but is changed by as little as one molecule, and re-released as a new product. Then the company can take out a new patent and reap another avalanche of profits. Forget about R&D on the diseases that kill the majority of people, like malaria. Because victims of malaria are poor, there's hardly any profit in developing new medicines.

ROCKEFELLER MANIPULATIONS

The Rockefeller family oil empire got started in 1870 when John D. Rockefeller founded Standard Oil and became America's first billionaire. Standard Oil has since morphed into the world's most profitable corporation, ExxonMobil, and several other massive multinational corporations. In 1911, the Sherman Antitrust Act was passed to oppose these monolithic entities, such as monopolies or cartels that would harm competition. In theory, the act broke up John D. Rockefeller's monopoly, Standard Oil. However, the reality is that the Rockefellers never lost control over the spin-offs, thus retaining a dominating presence in the oil industry despite the intent of the law.

With such immense wealth at their disposal, the Rockefellers diversified into other industries, namely the Military Medical Petrochemical Pharmaceutical Cartel. It should come as little surprise that they were primarily responsible for the global shift to large-scale petroleum-based agriculture, thus controlling the nation's food supply. This shift characterizes modern agriculture practices, which the industrialized West spread throughout the globe under the term "Green Revolution." The Green Revolution was the brainchild of the Rockefeller Foundation's Natural Science Division in partnership with large agricultural corporations.

Using their vast influence, these foundations pushed their agricultural agenda, lobbying Congress and the World Bank for financial support and persuading other foundations such as Kellogg and Milbank Memorial to join the cause. By the

1960s, $3 billion a year was directed toward developing agricultural practices in the Developing World. Today, such development is still supported by powerful foundations with private interests. For example, the Gates Foundation granted the International Rice Research Institute $19.9 million dollars in 2008. The so-called Green Revolution has also been associated with the development and distribution of hybridized seeds and synthetic fertilizers and pesticides. The true costs of the Green Revolution can now be seen with taxpayers paying billions in subsidies to giant agribusiness corporations. Small family farms have all but disappeared. Biodiversity is destroyed. Toxic chemicals poison farm workers and pollute the land, water, and our food supply, endangering the health of everyone.

What if it were possible to discourage critical thinking in the public in such a way that people would never put all the pieces together? One useful way to do this would be to control the educational system. It was the Rockefellers who created the National Education Association (NEA), with help from the Carnegie Foundation and later from the Ford Foundation. What the captains of industry wanted from our schools was an obedient and docile workforce who would be manageable employees and eager consumers. In the early 20th century both the Rockefeller and Carnegie Foundations were donating large sums of money to education and the social sciences. They supported, in particular, the National Education Association. By way of grants, they spent millions of dollars—monies which were used to radically bend the traditional education system toward a new system that favored standardized testing over critical thinking and that facilitated "scientific management" of schools. This was part of a calculated plan to make the school system benefit corporate America, which of course came at the expense of authentic education of American school children. Powerful foundations with private interests, such as the Ford Foundation, continue to support and thereby influence the policy of the NEA to this day.

The Federal Reserve was also involved in creating the National Education Association via the Rockefeller family. An unprecedented U.S. Congressional investigation into tax-exempt foundations has identified the Rockefeller and Carnegie Foundations' engagement in an agenda for vast population control. Norman Dodd, Research Director for the Congressional Committee, found this statement in the archives of the Carnegie Endowment: "The only way to maintain control of the population was to obtain control of education in the U.S. They realized this was a prodigious task so they approached the Rockefeller Foundation with the suggestion that they go in tandem and that the portion of education which could be considered as domestically oriented be taken over by the Rockefeller Foundation and that portion which was oriented to international matters be taken over by the Carnegie Endowment."

Lastly, the American Medical Association (AMA) is largely funded by the Rockefellers, who in turn use their funding to influence AMA research, development, and medical decision making. After all, if you own and control the pharmaceutical industry, it would certainly make sense to secretly run the agency in charge of regulating your products. In an effort to control the medical education establishment and to gain power over this "large and vital sphere of American life," from as early as 1910 the Rockefeller and Carnegie Foundations have been giving money to the AMA. And this vital sphere would also include what is not released to the public, but actively suppressed. The fate of Royal Raymond Rife is an example of the controller's ability to suppress and destroy.

KILLING THE CANCER CURE

The inventor Royal Raymond Rife developed a technique called "coordinative resonance" in the 1930s that was apparently able to destroy cancerous tumors as well as viruses. Rife's treatment was tested on 16 terminally ill cancer patients. Within three months, they were all successfully cured. Through the efforts of Morris Fishbein, head of the *Journal of the American Medical Association*, Rife was essentially shut down and his brilliant and promising work was ruined and all but forgotten. But the idea could not be destroyed and there are still Rife practitioners attempting to use his technology. They are regularly harassed and continue to operate outside of the U.S. and at their peril. Rife's shutdown is only one example among dozens more, according to the *Thrive* website. Rene Caisse had an old Ojibway Indian formula that was also effective for treating cancer. Harry Hoxsey and Max Gerson had natural remedies that worked. But if you look at medical documents discussing these remedies, the AMA cleverly makes them sound like complete quacks. These are but a few examples of the many sad stories of suppression, simply so the elite can maintain control of the lucrative medical industry.

If the medical and the pharmaceutical industry is putting profits over people, shutting down potential cancer cures, suppressing innovations, and gouging money out of an already strapped economy, then why would anyone want to keep this deeply flawed system going? In short, there are many dissenters and organizations working for change. But so far they are no match for the entrenched moneyed interests which have literally bought the government. The drug companies have spent more than $3 billion on lobbyists and political "contributions" over the past decade in the U.S. alone. They have paid politicians to make the system work in their interests. Republican Congressman Walter Burton illustrated how deep this influence goes when he admitted that "The pharmaceutical lobbyists wrote the bill," referring to the health care legislation passed in 2003.

DR. RICH SPILLS THE BEANS

Dr. Ben R. Rich, a former head of the Lockheed Skunk Works (the secret and highly advanced arm of Lockheed Martin), admitted in a 1994 deathbed confession that extraterrestrial UFO visitors were real. He confirmed there were two types of UFOs—the ones we build, and ones "they" build. "We learned how to build ours from crash retrievals and actual 'hand-me-downs,'" Rich said. Nearly all "biomorphic" aerospace designs were inspired by the original Roswell space crafts, that is, from Kelly's SR-71 Blackbird onward to today's drones, UCAVs, and other highly advanced aerospace craft such as the U-2, the SR-71 Blackbird, the F-22 Raptor and the F-117 Nighthawk. All used aspects of UFO technology that have been backward engineered. "Of course the government knew," exclaimed Rich, but it was becoming more difficult for them to manage the Black Operations. Until 1969, the U.S. Government took an active role in the administration of all UFO and ET information. After a 1969 Nixon "purge," oversight responsibility was handed off to an international board of directors in the private sector such as Raytheon, and there it has remained. Ben Rich would not be the only aerospace executive to leak this type of information. Leonard Stringfield, Dr. Robert Sarbacher and Dr. Eric Walker also made detailed confessions of backward engineered UFO technology towards the end of their lives.

By 1988, the Lockheed Skunk Works was operating exotic propulsion spacecraft called ARVs, or "Alien Reproduction Vehicles." Another system called the "flux liner" culminated in the development of three different-sized vehicles. One was about 7.5 meters in diameter, code-named "Baby Bear." Next in size was an 18-meter version, code-named "Momma Bear." The largest craft between 38 and 40 meters in diameter was code-named "Poppa Bear." Each craft had the same general shape and proportions with the exception of its hatch and "synthetic vision system," which remained uniform through all sizes of the craft. The propulsion system was based upon "Zero Point Energy," and it was said to be capable of "light speed or better" according to a three-star general making a presentation on the craft. These "second space program" inventions were being developed in secret, while the above-ground relatively primitive space shuttle program was touted as progress to a fascinated and gullible American public.

It was originally Ben Rich's opinion that the public should not be told about UFOs and extraterrestrials. He believed people would panic and could not handle the truth, not ever. Only in the last months of his physical decline did he change his tune and begin to feel that the "international corporate board of directors" dealing with the "Subject" could represent a bigger problem to citizens' personal freedoms under the Constitution than the presence of the off-world visitors themselves. As someone who knew much about the secret sciences and their motives, and who was a respected business leader, Ben Rich spoke volumes during his final confessions.

In the 1930s, Royal Raymond Rife invented a super microscope that used light in a revolutionary design. It enabled him to see virus-sized microbes, invisible to the naked eye, that could not even be seen with an electron microscope. More importantly, unlike electron microscopes, the microbes, some linked to cancer like the pleomorphic microbe, remained alive. He found that every micro-organism has a "mortal oscillatory rate"—a point at which it will shatter or break apart when bombarded by sound waves, like an intense musical note that shatters a glass. Shortly after he successfully treated several terminal cancer patients, medical officials mounted a furious counterattack against Rife's monumental discovery and effectively shut him down.

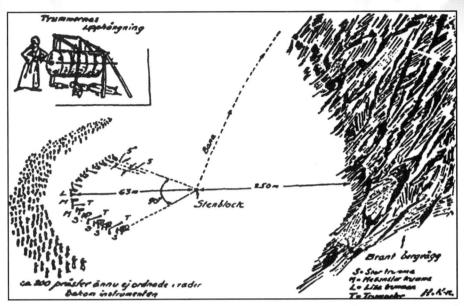

Tibetan Monks levitate stones by using an acoustic levitation technique consisting of drums, trumpets, chanting, and mental projection. These sketches were made in 1939 by Swedish aircraft designer Henry Kjellson who was friends with Dr. Jarl. The steep mountain side is on the right.

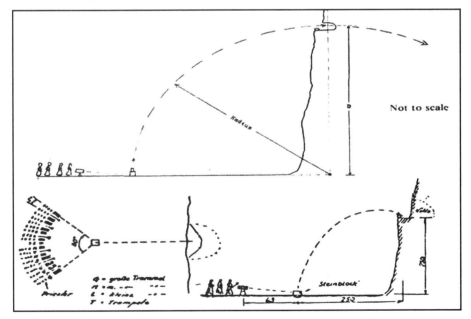

In the center is the stone block and on the left are the priests and musicians. S=big drum, M=medium drum, T=trumpeter. Inset shows the method of suspending a drum and gives an idea of its size. As shown here, Kjellson says the 200 priests are waiting to take up their positions in straight lines of 8 or 10 behind the instruments, "like spokes in a wheel." Unlikely as it may seem, this operation has an intriguing precision, made even more so by Kjellson's meticulously detailed description.

Project Rainbow, better known as The Philadelphia Experiment, took place on October 28, 1943. These Navy personnel are observing the experiment of molecular energy cycles as the U.S. Navy ship Eldridge enters a brief time warp. During the actual experiment, the ship and crew disappeared and were located in another body of water re-materialized, though some crew members had bodies fused into the hull of the ship and were still alive. All the crew, if not insane upon initial re-materialization, were institutionalized for mental disorders or committed suicide directly associated with this event. Consider these images above and below as artistic renditions of the event.

The Project Rainbow experiments utilizing invisibility were also performed on land, most notably at Montauk Point on Long Island, until all Montauk projects were abandoned in 1983. If these experiments were performed in the 1930s and 1940s, just imagine what they have now? Such scientific advancements kept in underground vaults may be dangerous information and technology in the hands of a new generation lacking morality or intellect.

BACKWARD ENGINEERING

"I suspect that in the last 60 years or so, that there has been some back-engineering and the creation of this type of equipment, that is not nearly as sophisticated yet as what the apparent visitors have." –Dr. Edgar Mitchell, the sixth astronaut to walk on the Moon

THERE has been an emergence in the last few decades of a renegade group within the military, the petroleum industry and intelligence agencies whose focus is to cover up everything related to UFOs. This conspiratorial group of plotters is commonly referred to as the "cabal." Made up of extremists, fundamentalists, xenophobics, racists, and paranoid officers, the cabal fears and hates extraterrestrials. Without presidential authorization or Congressional oversight, the cabal has commandeered Star Wars weaponry to shoot down UFOs, has taken surviving extraterrestrials prisoners and has attempted to extract information by force. Another faction of humans called the "controllers" work with what they believe are malevolent ETs. The two groups are collectively called the Military Industrial Extraterrestrial Complex (MIEC). This is a convoluted jar of exopolitical and geopolitical agendas. As we'll see in this chapter, they have become something of a breakaway civilization today because of the mind-boggling technology the controllers have back-engineered for decades.

The process of taking a finished product and discovering new technological principles for dismantling, then reassembling it, is called reverse or "backward engineering." The goal is to reproduce and duplicate the results. Reverse engineering is usually undertaken in order to redesign any system for better maintainability, or, as with alien spacecraft, to produce a copy of a system without access to the design from which it was originally produced. Most frequently backward engineering is involved in the study of a mechanical device, electronic component or software program. It involves taking apart and analyzing its workings in detail in order to make a new device or program that does the same thing without using or duplicating the original. The study of the object, whether a human-made or ET device, is conducted through analysis of its structure, function and operation.

In the USA, "the government behind the government" plays a big role in keeping UFO information secret worldwide. Of course, they are not the only nefarious group doing this, as the Russians, British and other developed countries also have black operations. Their primary motive for top secrecy is to backward engineer the most advanced technology acquired from ETs to be used for their mutual defense systems. Backward engineered technology is promoted within the USA Military Industrial Complex (MIC), which is composed of our nation's armed forces, its suppliers of weapons systems, supply producers, service operators, and its civil government. Apart from weapons development, another motivation for secrecy of an ET presence on Earth is the perceived damage it would cause to the established order of society, especially the collapse of religious institutions. The third reason is because very extreme measures have been taken to keep this secrecy, including undermining the Constitution, murdering the whistleblowers, and outright fraud to name a few. Open disclosure would reveal many crimes.

The study of craft debris has been assigned an above top-secret classification ever since the extraterrestrial disc crashed in New Mexico in 1947. An even earlier discovery of a UFO craft in 1941, in Cape Girardeau, Missouri, was the first known retrieval of a UFO craft in the USA. The government knew it had something big on its hands, but it would take decades to figure out just what it was. The recovered items initiated the first reverse engineering work, but it did not create a unified intelligence effort to exploit possible technological gains, except for some uses within the Manhattan Project. That real work, and the method for keeping it secret, would be launched in a matter of months.

THE DAY AFTER ROSWELL

The extraordinary recovery of fallen airborne objects in the desert of central New Mexico between July 4 and July 16, 1947, caused the Chief of Staff of the Army Air Force's "Interplanetary Phenomena Unit," Scientific and Technical Branch, Counterintelligence Directorate to initiate a thorough investigation. The special Interplanetary Phenomena Unit had been formed in response to two crashes in the Los Angeles area in late February, 1942, after the infamous "Battle of Los Angeles." The draft summary for the Roswell report begins: "At 23:32 MST, 3 July 1947, radar stations in east Texas and White Sands Proving Ground, N.M., tracked two unidentified aircraft until they both dropped off radar. Two crash sites have been located close to the WSPG. Site LZ-1 was located at a ranch near Corona, approx. 75 miles northwest of the town of Roswell. Site LZ-2 is located approx. 20 miles southeast of the town of Socorro, at latitude 33-40-31 and longitude 106-28-29."

In fact, there were two UFOs that collided in midair during an intense electrical storm, although the dates and exact crash locations vary slightly. One craft contained "Orange ETs" and the other was flown by the "Greys." One crash-landed near Corona, northwest of Roswell, while the other crashed onto the Plains of San Agustin near Shaw Mountain, about 200 kilometers to the west. Army Intelligence units secured both sites and removed the craft and the ET crews who were all dead, except one.

In 1957, the USAF published a highly classified report that detailed in depth this crash site in New Mexico. The report lists one crash site for the Roswell craft, but two different debris fields: one site being where part of the craft crashed north of Roswell, and the second being southeast of Corona. Both of these debris fields resulted from the same craft. The second disc crash site was listed as Shaw Mountain, but not recovered until 1949. Alien bodies were recovered at both crash sites. The USAF theorized that the two crafts collided in midair north of Roswell. Other speculation suggests that the crafts were brought down accidentally by high-powered military radars, or as the result of an electrical storm, or possibly a combination of both.

The Roswell crash was headline news on July 8, 1947, when the *Roswell Daily Record* newspaper published a front-page article: "RAAF Captures Flying Saucer On Ranch in Roswell Region." The Roswell Army Air Field (RAAF) also issued a press release stating that personnel from the field's 509th Bomb Group had recovered a crashed "flying disc" from a ranch near Roswell, New Mexico. However, the news was short lived. The next day the *Roswell Daily Record* cover story dramatically changed: "General Ramey Says Disk is Weather Balloon." The article stated: "An examination by the army revealed last night that a mysterious object found on a lonely New Mexico ranch was a harmless high-altitude weather balloon." The infamous Roswell downed flying disc account, accurately reported immediately by the local newspaper, was debunked the following day by the same paper's publication of a press release issued by General Ramey at the Roswell Army Air Field, saying it was a weather balloon. This was certainly a whitewash, being nothing but a cover up story to discredit the initial press story.

The official military story would change once again exactly 50 years later when the Air Force stated that the alleged weather balloon was actually "Project Mogul Balloon," and then added the bogus detail about "crash test dummies" being the explanation for "the bodies." All the military cover stories about Roswell are ridiculous. After all, if the debris originated from a top secret weather balloon test, why was there no recovery or search operation under way until the rancher, Mack Brazel, reported the debris to Sheriff Wilcox four days after the find?

There are dozens of civilians and top officials who since have come forward with what they knew about Roswell, many on their deathbeds for fear of reprisals. The intelligence chief at Roswell, Major Jessie Marcel and the first people to investigate sheep rancher Mack Brazel's find, confirmed in a number of interviews 30 years later that the crash debris had highly anomalous properties and was "not of this Earth." Former Roswell base public information officer Lt. Walter Haut's "deathbed" sealed affidavit was later published. In it he confesses to seeing the spacecraft and bodies in base Hangar 84/P-3. He states that the mysterious "weather balloon" press release was General Ramey's idea to divert media and public attention away from the closer and more important alien bodies and the crash site. Even General Ramey's wife told reporters decades later that her husband was "embarrassed about having to lie about the weather balloon."

The rancher's son Bill Brazel had collected and showed several people a piece of metallic looking debris with memory properties. All who saw it described it as very strong. It resembled a smooth fabric (like silk or satin) and strangely unfolded itself back to its original shape after being crumpled up. This amazing metallic fabric-like material with memory was not only very strong, but a person could blow through the fabric. It certainly was not balloon material. When taken together with the testimony of top officials, the evidence clearly points to an actual flying saucer crash with extraterrestrial pilots, as astonishing as this conclusion might seem to many.

The debris from the primary field of the 1947 crash near Roswell, New Mexico, was called ULAT-1 (Unidentified Lenticular Aerodyne Technology) and it excited metallurgists with its unheard-of tensile and shear strength metals. Some of the pieces of metals were kept by officers and exhibited to others. The thin metal could be crumpled into a ball, but would snap back into its original shape. It could not be torn. The fusion nuclear engine recovered from Roswell used heavy water and deuterium with an oddly arranged series of coils, magnets, and electrodes. Back then the engine was called "neutronic" because it was discovered to run by nuclear fusion, and descriptions of it resemble the "cold fusion" studies of today.

General Arthur Exon was commanding officer of Wright-Patterson Air Force Base at the time of the Roswell crash. Dispatched immediately, he flew over and saw a football-field-size burn impact area heavily guarded by military personnel at the crash site. When General Exon was first interviewed, he flatly stated that "Roswell was the recovery of a craft from space." Among other things, he confirmed the existence of two main crash sites. Exon also said he heard that bodies were recovered and confirmed the debris was highly anomalous based on testing done by labs at Wright-Patterson. Exon added that he was aware of other crash recoveries that occurred while he was C/O at Wright-Patterson. There was scattered metal debris and radiation detected at the site. Large quantities of crash debris were hauled away in trucks bound for Wright-Patterson. General Exon also testified that he received a call from General Clements McMullin following the crash at Roswell, New Mexico, in July, 1947. McMullin's instructions to General Ramey, according to Exon, were to concoct a "cover story" to "get the press off our back."

NAZI UFO RESEARCH

Before the end of World War II, even as far back as the 1930s, scientists of the Third Reich had acquired and were backward engineering a hyper-dimensional torsion-based technology they called "The Bell." Developed at a secret base in what is today the Czech Republic, it was Nazi Germany's most highly classified and radically advanced secret weapons research project. The Bell was classified uniquely within the Third Reich, an even higher top secret classification than their atom bomb project. The Nazis regarded The Bell as a "gateway" technology to seemingly unlimited expansion of human brain potential leading to technological power and superiority. The Nazis investigated the potential application of this torsion-based technology as a means to tap into Zero Point Energy, which scientists described as the energy of the physical medium of spacetime itself. The Bell was also studied as a means to manipulate gravity, to be used as an advanced prototypical field propulsion technology. Because of the demented Nazi mentality, their scientists were also looking into the means for the ultimate, potentially planet-busting weapon. The conceptual key to the achievement of all these effects was the manipulation of rotating magnetic fields by means of the counter-rotation of plasma within the device itself.

A "culture of secrecy" is systemic within the military and government, both in Nazi Germany and in America today. Many subjects of lesser importance than UFOs are also held secret. The military has an iron-fisted control and flatly insists that secrets must be kept. After the war, many Nazi scientists were secretly brought to America under the auspices of Project Paperclip as described earlier. In the employment of the U.S. Secret Weapons Department, the Paperclip scientists continued their most-highly-classified research that characterized The Bell and other operations. They worked to understand all three avenues of its application: free energy, field propulsion, and the ultimate doomsday weapon. Dr. Hermann Oberth, who pioneered rocket design for the Third Reich during World War II and later the advanced rocket technology for the American manned space launches, cryptically stated, "We cannot take the credit for our record advancement in certain scientific fields alone; we have been helped." When asked by whom, he replied, "The people of other worlds."

REVERSE ENGINEERING ROSWELL CRAFTS

Within months of the Roswell UFO crash, the Army Air Corps became the Air Force. The National Security Act was passed, setting up the National Security Administration (NSA) partly to deal with the extraordinary secrecy authorities felt UFOs required. During this time, the CIA was also created, as described earlier. Retired U.S. Army Colonel Philip J. Corso claims he helped head a project to reverse engineer and seed all the fantastic recovered extraterrestrial technology into American industry. In his book *The Day After Roswell*, Corso summarizes all the backward engineered products gathered from the 1940s downed spacecrafts recovered in the USA:

1. *Image intensifiers, which ultimately became "night vision"*
2. *Infrared sight contact lens, able to detect waves or particles beyond the visual spectrum of light*
3. *Super tenacity fibers, or super-strong fiber cloth lasers*
4. *Molecular alignment metallic alloys*
5. *Integrated circuits and micro-miniaturization of logic boards*
6. *HARP, High Altitude Research Program*
7. *Project Horizon moon base*
8. *Portable atomic generators in the form of an ion propulsion drive*
9. *Irradiated food*
10. *"Third Brain" guidance systems, that is, extraterrestrial biological entity (EBE) head bands*
11. *Hydrogen atom particle beams used in the "Star Wars" antimissile energy weapons*
12. *Depleted uranium artillery shells*
13. *Electromagnetic propulsion systems*

Other commonly reported reverse engineered ET artifacts, claimed by Corso and others, indirectly led to the development of transistors, Kevlar and Mylar material, microwaves, fiber optics, light-emitting diodes (LED), superconductivity, the integrated computer chip, accelerated particle beam devices, and even Velcro. Although the timing is interesting, the story of a Swiss man who invented Velcro by the inspiration of pulling a burr from his dog's fur in 1948 is incorrect. The Greys were seen utilizing Velcro on their jumpsuit uniforms when the first Roswell bodies were recovered. They were also using a kind of "headdress" that interfaced directly between the brain of the Grey pilots and the craft's control mechanisms. Our scientists pioneered a mental-expansion process called "the Gateway Treatment," which "allows utilization of a vastly-increased percentage of the brain, in order for humans to mentally engage the extraterrestrials in full telepathic mental exchange." The Treatment involves "a way of opening the brain up, a way to stimulate the neurons. It allows billions of synapses to form."

In 1947, according to Corso, a covert government group named "Majestic 12" was assembled under the leadership of the first Director of Central Intelligence, Admiral Roscoe H. Hillenkoetter. Among its tasks was to collect all information on extraterrestrial spacecraft. Corso says the U.S. Administration simultaneously "officially" discounted the existence of flying saucers to influence public opinion. The U.S. was in possession of a Grey ET crash survivor dubbed "EBE" as the acronym for Extraterrestrial Biological Entity, from 1948 until the being died in 1953. Government scientists first communicated with it using pictographs. Corso further relates that the Strategic Defense Initiative (SDI), or Star Wars, was meant to achieve the capability of killing the electronic guidance systems of incoming enemy warheads and disabling enemy spacecraft, including those of extraterrestrial origin.

PRACTICAL APPLICATIONS

The U.S. Military and its subcontractors have been working on extraterrestrial anti-gravity disc prototypes for decades. These prototypes are based on the extraterrestrial crafts that can traverse the galaxy by manipulating space and time to pull their destination towards them. Time is reduced to zero and acceleration is increased to infinity. The military is also experimenting on pilots to train them to use their minds to guide advanced aircraft. Government scientists found that "some UFOs are living conveyances, and can divide and re-form." These "living conveyances" are apparently also responsive to thought commands. The Aurora SR-33A is an already-developed space plane, which operates out of Area 51. The Aurora runs on liquid methane and has anti-gravity devices on board. It carries an electromagnetic-pulse weapons system which can knock out tracking radar. The Aurora can travel to the covert bases on the Moon and Mars. The Stealth planes the public sees at air shows do not have the capacity to leave the atmosphere, but other generations of Stealth aircraft can travel into outer space.

The Department of Energy is allowed the first opportunity to acquire any back-engineered items once completed by its aerospace partners. Because it controls all of the national laboratories, the DoE has immense scientific capabilities. Unfortunately, nonpolluting free energy has never been released by any DoE program. Ever since the first nuclear explosion in nearby White Sands during the Manhattan Project tests in the 1940s, the whole region became a UFO hot spot. The Los Alamos National Laboratory in New Mexico is located a few hundred kilometers between where the twin Roswell saucer crashes were recovered. Yet the Department of Energy has nothing to say on UFOs, nor does the Federal Aviation Administration, which sends all its reports to a private civilian organization called Bigelow Aerospace Advanced Science Studies, funded by billionaire Bob Bigelow. The FAA, much like the U.S. Air Force, had no interest in UFOs and was happy to pass the reports to Bigelow and have the matter go away. Why such facile dismissal? "No merit in UFO studies" is their official cover story, but in reality the DoE and the Air Force are extremely interested in acquiring back-engineered technology.

In the early years, many raw items were taken to the Bell Labs and back-engineered to find a practical military application or commercial use for the many recovered items. Of course the golden goose was anti-gravity, grafting free energy from the atmosphere and developing the technology of interdimensional spacecraft. Such crafts would also have the ability to tap into the spacetime continuum and essentially be time machines. The spacetime continuum is a mathematical model that combines space and time into a single construct. This is usually explained with a model where space is three-dimensional and time has the role of the fourth dimension. We'll get to space and time travel in a moment.

As for practical applications, Theodore Maiman at Hughes Research Laboratories demonstrated the first working laser in May, 1960. More recently, lasers have become a multi-billion dollar industry. The most widespread use of lasers is in optical storage devices such as compact discs and DVD players, in which the laser (sometimes only a few millimeters in size) scans the surface of the disc. Other common applications of lasers are bar code readers, laser printers and laser pointers. Lasers are used by the military for range finding, target identification and illumination for weapons delivery. Lasers are used in medicine for internal surgery and cosmetic applications. The top priority for backward engineering was to keep a military and intelligence edge on our perceived enemies, namely the Soviets during the Cold War. It would be nearly impossible to think this technology would not be thoroughly examined. The potential of learning from alien crafts is astounding. Not attempting to reverse engineer this new technology would be unthinkable. But what should be made public, and when? For high technology discoveries, the secrets would last for decades. But for the sake of science and the advancement of technology, and for the positive growth of civilization, disclosure is imperative.

Imagine a visiting spacecraft from another world, or dimension, hovering over a panicked and blacked-out LA in the middle of the night, just weeks after Pearl Harbor, at the height of the fear and paranoia of W.W. II. Imagine how this huge ship, assumed to be some unknown Japanese aircraft, was then attacked. Imagine as it hung nearly stationary, over Culver City and Santa Monica, an attack by dozens of Army anti-aircraft batteries firing nearly 2,000 rounds of 5.4-kilogram, high explosive shells in full view of hundreds of thousands of residents, but not immediately being able to destroy the craft. Imagine *that* and you have an idea of what the Battle of Los Angeles was all about.

well **Daily Record**

RECORD PHONES
Business Office 2288
News Department 2287

ROSWELL, NEW MEXICO. TUESDAY, JULY 8, 1947.

RAAF Captures Flying Saucer On Ranch in Roswell Region

House Passes Tax Slash by Large Margin

Defeat Amendment By Demos to Remove Many from Rolls

Security Council Paves Way to Talks On Arms Reductions

No Details of Flying Disk Are Revealed

Roswell Hardware Man and Wife Report Disk Seen

Ex-King Carol Weds Mme. Lupescu

Former King Carol of Romania and Mme. Elena Lupescu

The astonishing news of a crashed flying saucer made the front page of the *Roswell Daily Record* on July 8, 1947. Other newspapers across the country picked up the story from the wire on the same day. But the next day the official story changed to a crashed weather balloon.

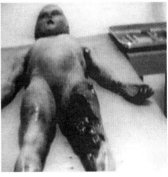

One of the supposed "Orange ET" alien victims of the Socorro UFO crash. Notice the body and burn wounds match the body lying next to the crashed disc, which was also supposedly recovered at Socorro, N.M. in early June, 1947. The film of an alien autopsy resurfaced in 1995 showing the bloated body being dissected by doctors, presumably in 1947.

The official designation for America's first announced nuclear flying saucer was the Lenticular Reentry Vehicle (LRV). It was designed by engineers at the Los Angeles Division of North American Aviation in the early 1960s under a contract with the U.S. Air Force. The project was managed out of Wright-Patterson Air Force Base in Dayton, Ohio, where former Nazi engineers had been resettled who had worked on German rocket plane and flying disc technology. During W.W. II these same scientists designed advanced aircraft and one of them was a flying disc called "The Bell." The first sightings of humanmade UFOs were seen during the Battle of Kursk in the summer of 1943 hovering in the sky, and the Battle of Berlin, with a few supposedly being shot down by the Allies. After the war this technology and the scientists were divided up between the USA, UK and the Soviets.

On December 9, 2009, a very unusual event was independently photographed from several locations around northern Norway. What has become known as the Norway Spiral has the appearance of an unknown atmospheric experiment that lasted for several minutes. This event was most likely created by the Tromsø, Norway, HAARP facility.

WEAPONS IN SPACE

"And we have vowed that we shall not see it governed by a hostile flag of conquest, but by a banner of freedom and peace. We have vowed that we shall not see space filled with weapons of mass destruction, but instruments of knowledge and understanding. Yet the vows of this nation can only be fulfilled if we in this nation are first, and we intend to be first."
–President John F. Kennedy, in his "We Choose To Go To The Moon" speech, September 12, 1962

"**IN** the Beginning," starts the famous opening line in Genesis from the Old Testament of the *Holy Bible*, setting the scene for the creation of life on Earth. The tone changes in Genesis 19:24 when it says, "Then the Lord rained down on Sodom and Gomorrah brimstone and fire from the Lord out of Heaven." This passage describes what is remarkably similar to the debate over weapons in space. Proponents of the ancient astronaut theory argue there are many references (Biblical and other sources) to high-tech warfare as waged from above in prehistory. If only we had kept true to the vision John F. Kennedy proposed "in the beginning" of the space race to the Moon.

The first *acknowledged* space weapon of the Modern Age was Nazi Germany's V-2 rocket, which terrorized the allies at the end of World War II. The V-2 was designed by the infamous rocket scientist Wernher von Braun, who would escape from Germany to America and become known as the "Father of the American Space Program."

On his deathbed in 1977, Wernher von Braun told his confidante, Dr. Carol Rosin, that when the U.S. starts placing weapons in space, it will be "based on a lie." He told her at first the reason would be to defend against the Russians who were still a threat at that time. Next, he said, the threat would be terrorists operating from third world countries, now called rogue nations. Third, there will be the threat of rogue asteroids, and this will be the strong justification for putting weapons into space. "The last card," von Braun emphasized over and over, is that the U.S. military would use invading extraterrestrial aliens as a threat. "There is going to be a spin to find some enemy against whom we have to build space-based weapons," he said, "except it's all based on a lie." These space-based weapons will be up and running before the rest of the world knows why they are there, warned Wernher von Braun. Interestingly, it is not documented whether he said explicitly that the *need* for space weapons is a lie, or that false flag enemies and events (Russians, third world terrorists, rogue asteroids, alien attacks) are the lies used to persuade the public there is a need for a secret space program, including weapons in space.

CHANGES ON THE GEOPOLITICAL CHESSBOARD

Until very recently, the United States has dominated global hegemony. However, a swiftly changing world situation is taking place while Washington's economic and political influence is declining, even as it remains the unmatched military superpower. America suffers from low growth, extreme indebtedness, imperial overreach abroad and virtual political paralysis at home. At the same time, we are spending a trillion dollars a year on wars of choice, maintaining the Pentagon military machine and initiating and expanding various other "national security" projects.

The world's four main emerging economic powers, Brazil, Russia, India and China, have been known by the acronym BRIC, and now with the inclusion of South Africa in December, 2010, refer to themselves as BRICS. This is a development of geopolitical significance and it has no doubt intensified frustrations in Washington, which has been concerned about the growing economic and political strength of the BRICS countries for several years. Given the volatile global crises with peak oil, climate change, continued U.S. imperial wars, grave poverty that will increase as world population grows from seven billion today to over nine billion in 2050, and many emerging countries seeking a rightful share of world leadership, there is a very good chance the United States could in time resort to global military aggression to sustain its dominant status, possibly even starting or provoking World War III. Considering the U.S. political system's decades-long move towards the right, the enormity of the Pentagon's arsenal, the militarism in our society, and the ability of Washington and the corporate mass media to collaborate in "selling" wars to a misinformed public, provoking a world conflict cannot be ruled out. It also cannot be ruled out that the USA has advanced space weapons and a secret space program in operation for decades that could unleash untold havoc on any perceived enemy.

Not long after von Braun passed away in 1977, the saber-rattling president Ronald Reagan, who threatened to bury the Soviet Union's communist bear, brought "Star Wars" to the world's center stage. Star Wars was actually a moniker given to the Strategic Defense Initiative (SDI). Did Reagan always want an antimissile shield in space, or was he simply following a plan set in motion long before he became president? Peace activists then and now call SDI missile defense the grand deception, the big lie, perhaps the greatest sham of all time. The true purpose of this arms program, critics believe, is to control and dominate space, because whoever controls space will control the Earth.

Ronald Reagan softened his stance against the Soviet threat during his second term. He is the only president (other than Jimmy Carter) to admit publicly that he'd seen a flying saucer. Reagan was also the only president to hypothesize, albeit metaphorically, about the possibility of hostile extraterrestrials posing a threat to Earth. In a December 4, 1985, speech at Fallston High School in Maryland, President Reagan spoke about his five-hour private discussion with General Secretary Mikhail Gorbachev the previous month in November, 1985. He relayed to the class: "How much easier his task and mine might be in these meetings that we held if suddenly there was a threat to this world from another species from another planet outside in the universe. We'd forget all the little local differences that we have between our countries and would find out once and for all that we really are all human beings here on this Earth together."

Similarly, Gorbachev said at a speech on February 16, 1987, in the Grand Kremlin Palace in Moscow: "At our meeting in Geneva, the U.S. President said that if the Earth faced an invasion by extraterrestrials, the United States and the Soviet Union would join forces to repel such an invasion. I shall not dispute the hypothesis, though I think it's early yet to worry about such an intrusion." Gorbachev also remarked, "The phenomenon of UFOs does exist, and it must be treated seriously."

PEACE IN OUTER SPACE

Is it possible for the human race to leave war out of space as Kennedy envisioned? Can space be used for peaceful purposes only? The 1967 Outer Space Treaty outlaws weapons of mass destruction to be deployed in space or on celestial bodies, but not weapons of selective destruction such as nuclear-powered "battlestats," according to Bruce Gagnon.

Bruce Gagnon directs the Global Network Against Weapons and Nuclear Power in Space from his office in Maine. The Global Network's aim is to stop any weaponization in space, along with any nuclear-powered technology ever being deployed past Earth's atmosphere and into space. He established the Global Network in 1992, and today it is considered one of the fastest-growing peace activist groups around the globe, with chapters in 170 countries.

"The U.S. has made no secret of the fact that it considers space to be the military high ground," Gagnon stated. "If you master space, you can control the world." The USA is already calling itself the "Master of Space." Indeed, the U.S. Space Command at Peterson Air Force Base in Colorado already refers to itself as such. Other nations will react by considerably increasing their arsenals, and many treaties will be broken or be at risk. How long will it be before weapons are stationed in space? Those that can be aimed at any target, anywhere on Earth? How long before the "Star Wars" fantasy becomes a grim reality? It would seem already, especially after two massive explosions in Tianjin, China in August, 2015, which alternative media outlets declared was waged with the "Rod of God," or Project Thor space weapon as an act of "kinetic retaliation" by the Pentagon, in response to China's currency war Yuan devaluation. Once given the launch command, a Thor satellite would drop a "pole," which would then speed up until going at orbital velocity, around 10 miles a second. At this speed, when it hit a ground-based target, it would have the explosive equivalent of a small-yield nuclear weapon without a radiation signature, and would also have tremendous penetrating power because of its long, thin profile. If a Thor pole was dropped on China, it would mark the first shot fired in the metaplanetary war.

What is clear is that weapons in space are considered a "global taboo" by scores of nations. This likely is because many countries will never have the know-how or the money to build such weapons to counter China, the U.S. and Russia. For several decades now, the UN has tried to help broker anti-space weapon treaties, but during the 2000s, the U.S. brushed them off. In fact, the Bush Administration unilaterally withdrew from the Anti-Ballistic Missile Treaty, originally made in 1972 with the former Soviet Union. The treaty's intention was to limit missile defense, such as deploying anti-ICBM (Intercontinental Ballistic Missile) technology, called battlestats, into space.

In the 21st century the U.S. military, especially the Air Force and the U.S. Space Command, along with their partners in the U.S. aerospace industry, have probably reached the point of no return. In 2005, the Bush Administration voted to block a UN resolution to ban actual space weapons. It was the first time the U.S. had voted that way. To the rest of the world, it certainly looked as if America was going to break one of humankind's greatest taboos.

PRE-CURSORS OF SPACE WEAPONRY

Currently, space is militarized with spy satellites, but space is not weaponized with the next generation of "battlestats," or killer satellites loaded with lasers or missiles. It is believed that there are no battlestat weapons in space now, but there are weapons on the ground that have the proven capability of destroying targets in space. Putting weapons into space, or creating weapons that can destroy targets in space, is the arms race for the 21st century, say experts. It's an arms race that was re-ignited by the Bush Administration, with huge budgets directed to the U.S. aerospace industry. Big players are also China, and, to a lesser-degree, Russia. Building constellations of battlestats, for example, could mean hundreds of billions of dollars more pumped into the aerospace industry.

What this means is that the U.S. military will someday soon be able to maneuver a satellite over a target anywhere on the Earth's surface, and then melt it with a powerful laser or particle-beam weapon. Some in the 9-11 Truth Movement, such as Dr. Judy Wood, say this is what was used to pulverize the Twin Towers. Beyond laser and particle-beam weapons in space, there is also evidence for a network of near Earth orbiting satellites to be deployed that are run by artificial intelligence, which are nano-satellites that have their own defensive capabilities.

The Pentagon insists, according to their spokespeople, that it is not researching space weapons; it is researching missile defense. Thus, according to the Pentagon, there's no need for a space weapons treaty. The 28 NATO member states are all supposed to be working together as partners in defense. But in NATO, it is well established that the USA is "first among equals." The rest follow along obediently.

Missile defense is a Trojan Horse (a hollow, deceptive program) because the Pentagon has nothing to show for all the money it has spent, said Gagnon. What it's getting for spending $120 billion is "dual use" technology, he noted. Instead of taxpayers' dollars being put into building new roads and bridges and remodeling countless schools, funding is being given to the Pentagon to create an arsenal of space weapons. Despite one in six American's living in poverty, cost cutting social programs to the bone, and even slashing PBS funding, Congress has no problem pledging to renew America's commitment to missile defense, even in opposition to nearly every other nation in the world.

Yet, officially, the U.S. military's anti-satellite program does not exist. But many experts agree the U.S. has been secretly testing anti-satellite capabilities under the mask of the Star Wars missile defense for decades. At the moment, the U.S. Missile Defense Agency is working on 12 separate programs, some of which are ready to be deployed and can take out targets in space. The Terminal High Altitude Area Defense (THAAD), on which the Pentagon has spent $120 billion, is just one of many programs, and that's just the unclassified spending. Countless man-hours have been devoted to a weapons program that has not really produced anything of value to the civilian population or the soldiers on the battlefield.

Over $120 billion dollars has been spent since 1983 when President Reagan called for the SDI program to be developed. This is only what is acknowledged. According to the Center for Defense Information (CDI), a Washington-based space weapons think tank, missile defense is the most expensive U.S. weapons program of all time.

LOBBYIST POWER

To fully grasp how the arms race got so hot during the late 2000s, it is important to understand a very familiar three-way partnership. Defense contractors, such as Lockheed Martin and Boeing, along with Congress and the Pentagon, all depend on each other in a symbiotic relationship which expands into every corner of modern technology. This relationship has come to be known as the "Eisenhower Fruition," based on Dwight D. Eisenhower's prescient plea at the end of his presidency in 1961 to beware of the "military industrial complex."

Funding for missile defense research is centered in northern Alabama. Huntsville, Alabama, is also called "Rocket City"—the city that Wernher von Braun built. The city claims to have 50 civilian companies working on missile defense, featuring all the giants, including Lockheed Martin. By 2010, over 6,000 missile defense scientists and researchers were working in and around Huntsville, a region of 380,000 people. The two senators from Alabama, Republicans Richard Shelby and Jeff Sessions, ranked first and second when it came to receiving campaign contributions. Little surprise that the largest contributions came from Boeing and Lockheed Martin. Both senators are high-ranking members of defense-related Senate committees in charge of funding missile defense research.

The aerospace industry spent millions lobbying Congress to convince office-holders that there is a need for such weapons. The Pentagon, the U.S. Space Command and the Air Force also lobby Congress, begging for funds for their new toys. It is these groups that are the driving force behind space weapons. The Rumsfeld Report (released in 2000) warned that a "Space Pearl Harbor" could cripple the nation. The report had major corporate influence. Seven of the 13 commissioners who issued the report either were currently or had worked for the aerospace industry.

SECRET SPACE PROGRAM

Another threat to peace in outer space is the advanced spacecraft of the USA black operations, advanced flying machines armed with high-tech weapons. The USA secret space program is outside the purview of Congress, and by all accounts is operating illegally, yet it remains virtually invisible under the cloak of "national security." Solar Warden is an ultra-secret project that maintains a fleet of spaceships that are operating within our solar system. Perhaps they're defending us against alien threats, or they're involved in a covert colonization of space. In order to send manned missions into the far reaches of our solar system we'd need exotic materials and propulsion systems. There are at least 12 known advanced aerospace craft currently in use: the Northrop Grumman B-2 Spirit Stealth Bomber; the F-22 Raptor advanced Stealth fighter; and its successor the F-35 Lightning II advanced Stealth fighter; the Aurora SR-33A; Lockheed Martin's X-33A; the Lockheed X-22A two-man anti-gravity disc fighter; Boeing and Airbus Industries' Nautilus; the TR3-A Pumpkinseed; the TR3-B Astra Triangle; Northrop's "Great Pumpkin" disc; Teledyne Ryan Aeronautical's XH-75D Shark anti-gravity helicopter; and the Northrop Quantum Teleportation Disc. It is now believed most of these craft operate out of a new secret airbase located near Dugway, Utah.

These craft utilize anti-gravity technology in one of three ways. The B-2 Stealth Bomber and the TR3-B Astra triangular craft both use an earlier discovered anti-gravity electrogravitic technology. This technique involves pulsating millions of volts to disrupt the ambient gravitational field. The Nautilus space faring craft uses magnetic pulsing which operates by generating high-energy toroidal fields spun at incredible RPMs, which also disrupts the ambient gravitational field using a counterforce to Earth's gravitational pull to generate power. The remaining USA secret space program craft use a more sophisticated system, a direct generation energy source that can harness the gravitational "strong force." This strong force field extends slightly beyond the atomic nucleus of Element 115.

GEOENGINEERING & WEATHER MANIPULATIONS

Another rapidly developing industry is called geoengineering, or climate engineering. The National Academy of Sciences defines geo-engineering as "options that would involve large-scale engineering of our environment in order to combat or counteract the effects of changes in atmospheric chemistry." Weather control, particularly hostile weather warfare, was addressed by the adoption of

"United Nations General Assembly Resolution 31/72, TIAS 9614 Convention on the Prohibition of Military or Any Other Hostile Use of Environmental Modification Techniques." The Convention was signed in Geneva, Switzerland on May 18, 1977, and entered into law on October 5, 1978. Ratification was by U.S. President Jimmy Carter on December 13, 1979, and the U.S. ratification was deposited at the UN in New York on January 17, 1980.

If there are laws prohibiting weather modification, then what exactly is going on in the upper atmosphere? Vigilant citizens have called attention to "chemical trails" in the skies, long white smoke-like streaks which linger for hours and then disperse into clouds. The "chemtrail" is different from the commercial aircraft "contrail," which is a condensation trail that dissipates quickly. The traditional contrails are frozen exhaust in the form of ice and fade away almost immediately. The chemtrails, on the other hand, are long lines which linger until they disperse into a fog. Chemtrail does not refer to common forms of aerial spraying such as crop dusting, cloud seeding, skywriting, or aerial firefighting. The term specifically refers to aerial trails caused by the systematic high-altitude release of chemical substances not found in ordinary contrails, resulting in the appearance of uncharacteristic sky tracks.

Chemtrails are sometimes seen sprayed into "X" formations, apparently designed for "Solar Radiation Management" in the atmosphere. Supporters of this theory speculate that the purpose of the chemical release may be for reducing global warming, weather control, biological warfare, population control, HAARP activation, or chemical warfare programs. Lab tests of rainwater falling through the chemical clouds measured amounts of aluminum particles seven times higher than federal health safety limits. Geoengineering whistleblowers claim that these trails are causing respiratory illnesses and other health problems. They are deliberately sprayed at high altitudes for purposes undisclosed to the general public in clandestine programs directed by Black Operation military officials.

Geoengineering is performed by creating clouds the upper atmosphere. Driven by scientists, corporations and governments intent on manipulating the global climate, controlling the weather, altering the chemical composition of our atmosphere, soil, and water and thereby controlling human population levels, geoengineering is touted for tcombatting global warming. Although officials insist that these programs are only in the discussion phase, evidence is abundant that they have been underway beginning around 1990. Since then the effects on crops, wildlife and human health have been drastic, and seemingly getting worse. The worldwide chemtrail spraying operation was fully on line by 1997 at the behest of Edward Teller, the brilliant and influential scientist, and a staunch advocate of SDI and aerial chemical spraying. Dr. Teller also holds the dubious distinction of being the "Father of the Hydrogen Bomb."

Right above our heads in plain sight, critics say, powders and aerosols are descending from the skies, changing the flora and fauna by altering it with poison. The practice is seemingly so weird and dangerous that chemtrailing renders the motivation open to wild speculation. Could Earth be transforming into a planet fit for some other kind of life that requires aluminum or barium? Are these developments to our benefit or perhaps for others intending to replace us? Are we and our present-day plants and animals being silently killed off by the nano-particles of aluminum, barium, strontium, and to a lesser degree, boron and arsenic? There are also Morgellons fibers erupting from people's skin that have been linked to the widespread aerosol spraying. Additional tests are also showing larger than normal amounts of titanium in trees. It's changing the pH balance of the soil, thus microscopic organisms are disappearing, organic crops are growing poorly and trees are disintegrating. Not surprisingly, food and seed monopolies like Monsanto are already using genetically modified organisms (GMOs) in their food crops, marketing such products as Aluminum-Resistant RoundUp corn and soybeans. Originally touted as one solution to world hunger, respected scientific groups, including the Union of Concerned Scientists, have conducted studies which contradict such claims, and even point to evidence that genetically modified foods cause health problems. Some people claim chemtrails have caused them to become ill. One theory suggests that chemtrail spraying could actually be part of a misguided eugenics program to reduce the population. After all, the CIA maintains a fleet of airplanes under the name Evergreen Air. With earthquakes and storm systems demonstrably proven to be manipulated or caused outright by powerful EMF manipulation, and our skies constantly being streaked with a chemical haze emitted by thousands of planes worldwide, one might think there would be cause for alarm, or perhaps a little public education. Yet the U.S. Congress refuses to discuss the chemtrail issue with its constituents.

Rising global temperatures, increasing population, and degradation of water supplies have created broad support for the various methods of weather modification. The U.S. Government has conducted weather modification experiments for over half a century, and the military industrial complex stands poised to capitalize on these discoveries. The most notorious program is HAARP, the High-Frequency Active Aural Research Program. This technology can potentially trigger floods, droughts, hurricanes and earthquakes. The scientific idea behind HAARP is to "excite" a specific area of the ionosphere and observe the physical processes in that excited area with the intention of modifying ecological conditions. HAARP can also be used as a weapon system, capable of selectively destabilizing agricultural and ecological systems of entire regions. At a recent international symposium, scientists asserted that manipulation of climate through modification of cirrus clouds is neither a hoax nor a conspiracy theory, but in fact is fully operational.

A big clue regarding barium's use in the atmosphere comes from Bernard Eastlund's patent for HAARP. The array of HAARP towers are transmitters which can be used for a variety of functions, including heating the ionosphere. It has the ability to direct a steerable electromagnetic beam at the upper atmosphere and effect rainfall patterns in a particular region. Most notably, the patent calls for large clouds of barium to be released into the atmosphere. Barium, which is an immune-system suppressant, is a soft silvery metallic alkaline Earth metal and it would never be found in rainwater under normal conditions. Yet barium is popping up in rainwater tests worldwide. Apparently it is being pumped into the atmosphere in aerosols sprayed from aircraft around the world. Is this another example of stealth warfare weapons being used in a silent war against humanity? What could possibly be gained by covertly seeding the planetary atmosphere with sprayed aerosols containing bacteria, algae, various chemicals, Morgellon nano-tube fibers and heavy metal particles? Is the intention to alter the natural atmospheric processes and Earth chemistries that have existed for millions of years? This is where the future esoteric narrative becomes downright frightening.

For decades, the military has proposed space weapon development, justified as an advantage at first strike capabilities. Yet, the challenge is deploying weapons that don't violate nuclear treaties. The answer is to create weapons that do not have a nuclear payload or any chemical signature, but can do substantial damage. This was accomplished with a space-based weapons program called Project Thor, so named after the hammer-wielding Norse god who could rain metal death down from heaven as he pleased.

The High-Frequency Active Aural Research Program, or HAARP as it's more commonly known, is owned and operated by the Air Force. It can simulate the detonation of a "heave-type" nuclear weapon. It can cause missile or satellite destruction, or modify weather patterns around the globe. HAARP can also cause worldwide brainwave pattern changes in the population with the flick of a switch. It was also developed for new weapon types: geophysical, weather and psychotropic.

"Some scientists in their laboratories are trying to devise certain types of pathogens that would be ethnic specific so that they could just eliminate certain ethnic groups and races; others are designing or engineering some sort of insects that can destroy specific crops. Others are engaging even in an ecotype of terrorism whereby they can alter the climate and set off earthquakes and volcanoes remotely through the use of electromagnetic waves." These are the words of the Secretary of Defense William S. Cohen in his April, 1997, keynote address at the Conference on Terrorism, Weapons of Mass Destruction, and U.S. Strategy at the Georgia Center, Mahler Auditorium, University of Georgia in Athens. Cohen is describing eugenic population control programs and atmospheric weapons that can alter the climate. Pictured here is the HAARP array in Gakona, Alaska.

The use of chemical and biological agents by a government against its own people is a sad historical fact. If the chemtrails being deployed in "Project Cloverleaf" contain biological agents, then people already weakened by other factors may have even died as a result of the additional strain on their systems. What could be the ultimate goal of such a diabolical plan? Eugenics on a global scale?

Dr. Leonard Horowitz on geoengineering: "I believe the chemtrails are responsible for a chemical intoxication of the public, which would then cause a general immune suppression, low grade to high grade, depending on exposure; an immune dysfunction, which would then allow people to become susceptible to opportunistic infections, such as mycoplasma and other opportunistic infections."

An artist's concept in 1984 of a ground and space-based hybrid laser weapon. The Space Preservation Act, HR2977, introduced October, 2001 by Ohio Rep. Dennis Kucinich, called for the peaceful uses of space, and a ban on "exotic weapons." Section 7 sought specifically to prohibit chemtrails. Kucinich told the *Columbus Alive* newspaper on January 24, 2002, that despite official denials, as head of the Armed Services Oversight Committee he is well-acquainted with geoengineering projects. Kucinich stated "The truth is there's an entire program in the Department of Defense, 'Vision 2020,' that's developing these weapons. Vision 2020 calls for 'dominance of space, land, sea and air.'" Under pressure, according to Kucinich, all references to chemtrails, HAARP and other weapons capable of planetary destruction were removed from HR2977. The original bill (without deletions) remains intact and on file in the congressional record.

UNDERGROUND BASES

"We seem to be moving, drifting, steadily against our will. Against the will of every race, every people, and every class, towards some hideous catastrophe. Everyone wishes to stop it, but they don't know how." –Winston Churchill

STARTING in the early 1950s, an extensive network of underground bases was begun in the USA, costing untold trillions, and comprising the largest construction project in human history. Yet few people know that these underground bases even exist. According to "anomalies-unlimited" researchers, the following are a few of the better known underground U.S. bases, many of which were started as "Continuity of Government" (CoG) facilities first built at the onset of the Cold War.

A short list of the larger, "mega-bases" include: Luke, Nevada; Roswell, New Mexico; Dayton, Ohio; Dulce, New Mexico; Nellis, Area S-51 and S-4, Nevada; MJ-12 meeting center under the Greenbriar Hotel in White Sulfur Springs, West Virginia; Mt. Weather, near Bluemont, Virginia; Mt. Pony, near Culpeper, Virginia; the Viewtree Mountain facility in Virginia; and the Manzano Mountain facility with rail-tunnels to Kirtland AFB and Sandia National Labs in New Mexico. There are over a hundred other smaller underground facilities that cannot even be mentioned by name, simply because they have no names, only nicknames and site numbers such as "Raven Rock" or "Site R-0001." And these are just in the United States! We will also examine underground military bases in other countries. This chapter will concern itself with secret military underground bases, but not before we examine other underground compounds throughout history.

Belief in a subterranean world has been handed down as myth, tale, or rumor for generations. Some of these stories date back to ancient times and tell tales of fantastic flora and fauna that can be found in the caverns of ancient races. Socrates spoke of huge hollows within the earth which were inhabited by humans, and vast caverns where rivers flowed. Medieval tradition features Saint George, the slayer of a dragon, which originated from the underworld. The Hopi Indians believed they emerged from a world below the earth through a tunnel at the base of the San Francisco Peaks near Flagstaff, Arizona. There are also legends about the mysterious city of Telos underneath Mount Shasta in northern California.

In western China, and in what today is lower Mongolia and Tibet, is a vast system of caverns below the region of the Gobi Desert. The caves allegedly link the Agharti systems of Central Asia to a "Snakeworld." This multi-leveled cavern system under the southwestern slopes of the Himalayas is the mythical location where the "Nagas" dwell, according to Hindu legend. A serpent cult of human and reptilian collaborators has supposedly coexisted for centuries, and they occasionally make contact with the above world. One recent instance was contact with the Nazi Thule Society before and during World War II.

THE BAIGONG PIPES

Not only is there a mysterious pyramid atop Mount Baigong in western China, but also dozens of upright pipe-like features can be seen protruding from various places in and around the mountain. The local legends claim the mountaintop is an alien UFO launch tower, and the pipes are airshafts to chambers below. Mount Baigong, about 40 kilometers southwest of the city of Delingha in the western province of Qinghai, also contains iron debris and unusually shaped stones scattered around this desolate area. The artifacts in the area near the pyramid structure are known as the "ET Relics."

The official travel description reads: "The pyramid has three caves with openings shaped like triangles on its façade and is filled with red-hued pipes leading into the mountain and a nearby salt water lake," according to China's state-run Xinhua agency. Two of the three caves at the foot of the mountain have collapsed and are inaccessible. The remaining middle one, which is the largest, stands with its floor about two meters above the ground, and its top about three meters above the surface. Inside the cave, there is a half-pipe about 40 centimeters in diameter tilting from the top to the inside of the cave. Another pipe of the same diameter goes into the earth with only its top visible above the ground. Dozens of strange pipes surround the opening with diameters ranging from 10 to 40 centimeters. These structures indicate a highly advanced and completely unknown construction technique. On the beach at nearby Toson Lake, which lies 80 meters from the mouth of the largest cave, are many strangely shaped iron pipes which lie scattered amid the sands and rocks. They are oriented in an east-west direction, with diameters from 2-4.5 centimeters. Further analysis of the pipes by a local smelter found that they consist of 30 percent ferric oxide (the type of iron used to make steel), large amounts of silicon dioxide (commonly found in quartz), and calcium oxide—the presence of which demonstrate that the pipes are very old. Even more bizarre is the discovery of pipes protruding within the lake itself. Some are reaching above the surface while others are buried below, with similar shapes and thickness as those found on the beach.

NEUSCHWABENLAND, ANTARCTICA

Before the onset of World War II, the Nazis began to set up a secret Antarctic research station called "Base 211" in a region they named Neuschwabenland, deep under the ice near the South Pole. This secret research facility was named "New Berlin," truly a veritable city consisting of technicians, engineers, and scientists who conducted the most advanced Nazi research. When it was certain Germany was going to lose the war, the Nazis started moving their top secret operations dealing with atomic testing, advanced weapon development, and flying discs to New Berlin. Towards the conclusion of the war, the city was fully operational and allegedly continued to operate long after the war was over. These exotic Nazi aircraft and weapons were used in the decisive defeat of Admiral Byrd during his Operation Highjump expedition in 1946-1947, including the sinking of the Navy destroyer "Murdoch."

This region of Antarctica, now called Queen Maud Land and administered by the Norwegians, contains a rift valley overflowing with geothermal activity, which was discovered by the Nazis in the late 1930s. Hot water ponds, named the Schumacher Ponds by the Germans, are teeming with algae, which is also found on surface rocks deep within Antarctica. These ponds never freeze over. Different species of algae reside in different ponds giving each pond a different color. In the same way that the Icelanders rely on geothermal energy, the Nazis started to construct a sustainable base deep within an ice crevice near the ponds. Not much more is known about the Nazi base except that in July and August of 1945, months after the German surrender, two U boats arrived in Mar del Plata, Argentina. These were no ordinary submarines, they were from the so-called "Fuhrer Convoy." Had they been to Antarctica to land Nazi treasure or high-ranking officials? Then in the southern summer of 1946–1947, the U.S. Navy appeared to "invade" Antarctica using a large naval force. The so-called scientific expedition, code-named Operation Highjump, returned just two months into their six month expedition. It is still classified as confidential. In 1958, three nuclear weapons were exploded in the region, as part of another classified U.S. operation, code-named Argus. Was this the final end to the Nazi base in Neuschwabenland?

Now the Russians have a secret military base in another location closer to the center of Antarctica at Lake Vostok, a vast underground thermal lake covered by a glacial ice dome. It is said during the long days of the Antarctic summer, the ice dome emits enough sunlight to bathe the lake in an endless twilight glow. The warm waters of Lake Vostok flow under the ice into the ocean. Another nearby base is so secret that it is run by the National Security Agency, and another by the CIA. This may be because the Nazis and Admiral Byrd found something astonishing there during their reconnaissance. There are rumors of a large UFO craft discovered in the ice, and a huge magnetic anomaly on the southwest shore of Lake Vostok, which may be due to the presence of a vast amount of metal, possibly metal of a buried lost city. Author Henry Stevens in his book, *Hitler's Suppressed and Still-Secret Weapons, Science and Technology,* maintains that the evidence points to something artificial, and moreover, something under intelligent control. Could it be something very ancient but working in conjunction with the geophysical anomalous feature? There must be something very important down there for the NSA and the CIA to be secretly running the show under the Antarctic ice. A few years ago, two Australian women were attempting to cross-country ski over Antarctica when they were captured and detained by American Navy Seal Special Forces. They were released and sent back home, but not allowed to complete their excursion.

According to esoteric UFO studies, New Berlin was constructed by Nazi ULTRA forces allied to the reptilian Draco empire. The early Nazis created treaties with the Draco-Orion forces. The U.S. Government also fell into the alien treaty trap which continues to this day. If the "Fourth Reich" of the Antarcticans were able to win control of the planet with the Dracos, they were promised 25% of the planet for their part in selling out the human race. The New World Order could only be implemented via a human and alien collaboration, namely the Fourth Reich of Bavaria. The Nazi ULTRA forces could be one and the same as the ULTRA Programmable Life Forces in the Dulce, New Mexico facility, which also maintains a strong "Bavarian" connection.

MODERN UNDERGROUND BASES

Is out of sight out of mind? Are the happenings there unseen and unknown to the rest of the world? Underground bases controlled by the militaries of the world are a known fact today as we'll see in a moment. But have they been around for eons, occupied by "subterranean super humans?" General W. Stuart Symington, appointed by President Truman to be the first Secretary of the Air Force in the 1947, believed so. He had held positions as chairman of the Surplus Property Board in 1945 and Assistant Secretary of War for Air from 1946 to 1947. Symington once formally requested a report from military sources regarding the possible existence of subterranean super humans. He may have been investigating the Nazis in Antarctica, or something completely different.

Since the 1950s, the U.S. Government has been using nuclear-powered tunneling machines called nuclear subterrenes (rhymes with submarines), which were designed at the Los Alamos National Laboratory in New Mexico. The subterrene can melt through rock at an average eight kilometers per day, creating perfectly straight tunnels to be used for high-speed trains connecting several underground cities as it burrows through the rock hundreds of meters below the surface. Nuclear subterrenes work by melting their way through the rock and soil, actually vitrifying it as they go, leaving no tailing mounds, and producing a neat, solidly glass-lined tunnel behind them. The U.S. Government at the cost of trillions of dollars of undocumented taxpayer debt is being funneled into the "black projects," which has been used to pay for these underground bases.

These vast underground facilities, some bigger than football stadiums and some buried a thousand meters below the surface, are fully stocked with food, artificial underground farms, redirected underground rivers, and thousands of kilometers of underground roads large enough for two tractor trailers traveling in opposite directions to pass each other with room to spare. These facilities have vast underground mass-transit systems connecting them to one another. The facilities are fully self-sufficient, generating their own electricity supply, their own food stocks, possessing air filtration systems, water purification systems, and vast supplies of guns and ammunition.

The government refers to these facilities as Deep Underground Military Bases & Structures (DUMBS). Wright-Patterson Air Force Base, near Dayton, Ohio, is one of the original DUMBS. This is where a multi-level underground facility houses a whole warehouse of alien hardware and cadavers taken from crash-retrieval sites over the past decades. Another original DUMB is an underground facility beneath Kirtland Air Force base in New Mexico, code named "Blue Moon" by the National Security Agency. The entrance to the base is located in the Manzano Mountains. "Blue" is the code word meaning anything extraterrestrial. The original documents of the Greada Treaty and the original ET materials from the early exchanges can be found today in this NSA facility called Blue Moon. Inside Blue Moon is the technological headquarters of the very secretive Department of Energy. The DoE at Blue Moon continues to build free energy devices back-engineered from Grey and Draco reptilian technology for use in space, and for use in the underground bases.

The private firm Wackenhut is responsible for the security of most of the underground facilities in California, New Mexico and Nevada, including the notorious Area 51. Wackenhut received multimillion-dollar contracts from the government to guard Cape Canaveral and the Nevada nuclear bomb test site, the first of many extremely lucrative federal contracts that have sustained the company to this day. The Wackenhut Board of Directors includes former CIA, NSA, FBI and Pentagon officials. Wackenhut has federal contracts to protect nuclear weapons facilities, nuclear reactors, the Alaskan oil pipeline and more than a dozen American embassies abroad. Wackenhut has long-standing ties to radical right-wing organizations and is a private militia employing 30,000 men and women under arms.

PEASEMORE, ENGLAND

In Great Britain, the primary underground military compound is called the RAF Peasemore Base, located in the Berkshire countryside, with access points at Harwell, Watchfield, and RAF Welford. There are at least six levels at Peasemore, the deepest level over a kilometer below, all interconnected and accessed from different secret locations. It is in this deep underground location where Grey aliens work with British Intelligence to genetically engineer generated life forms. These drone-like entities are used in MI-LAB abduction scenarios and in a genetic technology exchange. New Grey test tube life forms are laboratory made in three stages. First they are "born" in incubation units, kept in long racks as they develop, and indirectly programmed while being grown to maturity. They are called Programmed Genetic Life Forms (PGLF). The British project name was Puppetmaster, which became Mannequin. The UK, Canadian and U.S. governments oversee genetic engineering. The National Security Agency of the USA has been closely overseeing the manufacture of genetically engineered "super beings" in the UK underground bases. Others call these entities genetically engineered slaves, to be used by NASA for deep space operations. There are many different PGLFs, with different eye sizes, different statures, different numbers of fingers, and different degrees of programming. The Greys continue their program of abducting and using unwilling human subjects to produce more PGLFs, while the military cooperates because they want the technology. These reluctant collaborators actually seem to be stabbing each other in the back.

The main whistleblower of the Peasemore underground base is named Barry King. He worked in the early 1970s until the late 1980s as a security officer with British Intel, and had his own experience as a subject in a population control program experiment. He claims to have been chosen at an early age by secret surveys geared to genetic engineering, and reports that he has two implants. He was experimented on in the "Trip Seat," and subjected to various procedures as part of human mind control tests planned for the ultimate subjugation of humankind.

The Trip Seat connects to supercomputers; the subject wears a headband and interfaces with the computers. The goal is to make the subject susceptible to mind control. Graphic screens, electric brain link implants and various programs can make the subjects do different tasks. Due to his psi-tech abilities, he was used in a variety of roles, many of which remain classified. Barry King first published his notes called *The Voice* in 1994. He claims most human abductions in North America and in the UK, even worldwide, are performed independently by the Greys, but some abductions are carried out by our own black operations with our own PGLFs, independent of the Greys.

King says certain abductions in the UK are performed by the British Military MI-LABs for the purpose of genetic manipulation and the creation of a new human race with alien DNA, similar to the Grey clones. The military abductions of humans and subsequent crossbreeding with aliens in this underground laboratory below the Berkshire countryside marked the beginning of a new non-human race. In addition, the NSA and British Intelligence also worked in the sub-surface base, conducted abductions, and used human body parts for their own experiments, using the technology of the Greys. Much larger Draconian reptilians were also present, and King said they seemed to be running the show.

PINE GAP, AUSTRALIA

Pine Gap is the commonly used name for a satellite tracking station located only 18 kilometers southwest of the town of Alice Springs in the center of Australia. Pine Gap is operated jointly by Australia and the United States. The CIA and the NSA represent most of the government personnel from the USA. Pine Gap contains a wide range of communication devices such as HF (High Frequency) radio, underground cable, telstra telephone telex, and two satellite communication terminals. On average there are 1,200 staff working at the site, almost exclusively underground. Pine Gap is instrumental in tracking missiles with satellite imagery, or tracking the movement of troops. There are about 18 satellite control antennas, making it one of the largest satellite control stations in the world for satellites parked in fixed orbits above the equator. The most recent satellites installed are 100 meters in diameter. They intercept signals in the VHF, UHF and millimeter wave frequency bands. Within that frequency there are four categories of signals. The staff have to wear color-coded ID to match the color ribbons running along the walls. U.S. Military Airlift Command crafts and personnel carry thousands of tapes home for further study, and in return send parts and supplies twice weekly. There are direct links from Pine Gap to the U.S. bases in the Philippines, Guam, Krugerdorp, South Africa and the Amundsen-Scott base at the South Pole. For those who need instant transportation, there is a teleportation "jump room" at Pine Gap that connects to the S-4 base near Area 51 in the Nevada desert.

Pine Gap now functions as a major "control center" for the New World Order dictatorship. Pine Gap is equipped with whole levels of computer terminals tied in to the major computer mainframes of the world, which contain the intimate details of most of the inhabitants of industrialized nations. The computer room at Pine Gap is one of the largest in the world and the operators use headsets to communicate. Within the central operations building at Pine Gap, people are keeping the satellite and its antenna focused on the signals they are intercepting. Other staff members process the enormous volume of interpreted signals.

ECHELON is a highly secretive worldwide signals intelligence and analysis network run by the UK-USA Intelligence Community. ECHELON can capture radio and satellite communications, telephone calls, faxes and e-mails nearly anywhere in the world, and this includes the automated computer analysis and sorting of intercepts. ECHELON is estimated to intercept up to three billion communications every day. Along with Pine Gap, some of the known or suspected ground stations belonging to or participating in the ECHELON network include the following locations, and which country operates the facility: Fort Meade, Maryland, U.S. (headquarters of the NSA); Geraldton (Western Australia, Australia); Menwith Hill (Yorkshire, UK); Misawa Air Base (Japan); Morwenstow (Cornwall, UK); Sabana Seca (Puerto Rico, U.S.); Shoal Bay (Northern Territory, Australia); Sugar Grove (West Virginia, U.S.); Yakima (Washington, U.S.); Waihopai (New Zealand); and West Cape, Western Australia (Exmouth Gulf, Australia, & U.S.).

The Pine Gap underground base, the Dulce, New Mexico, facility and the neo-Nazi New Berlin Antarctica base are all connected to an alliance of regressive alien forces. The Dracos of Alpha Draconis, the Greys of Rigel Orion, and Aryan/Ashtar forces of Sirius B lead those "Unholy Six" of the Orion Empire on Earth. They also have a base foothold within the massive Kamagol-II facility under Giza, Egypt. The Orions infiltrated the Gnostic serpent cult, later to spawn the Grand Orient Lodge of Egyptian Freemasonry, the Gnostic Thule Society, the Bavarian Illuminati, and the Third Reich, all of which served their goals.

DULCE, NEW MEXICO

Dulce, New Mexico, is a sleepy little town of less than 4,000 inhabitants, mostly members of the Jicarilla Apache nation. Many ranchers in the nearby communities have reported hundreds of mysterious cattle mutilations and frequent sightings of military helicopters in the last few decades. It was during the mid-1980s that wild stories of an underground alien base surfaced, and continue to this day, so much so that the entire town of Dulce has become almost synonymous with an alleged underground alien bio-lab. Because Dulce is located only 160 kilometers northwest of Los Alamos National Laboratory, it provides additional fuel for conspiracy buffs. After all, Los Alamos is the leading-edge research facility on human genome and DNA research in the USA.

The Military Industrial Extraterrestrial Complex (MIEC) at Dulce is a joint government-alien biogenetic laboratory designed to carry out bizarre experiments on humans and animals. The largest section of this unseen underground base is located deep below the tangled brush of the Archuleta Mesa. Participants include the NSA, Grey aliens (Draco-controlled ETs), and a curious "Bavarian" influence. This multi-level facility is reported to have a central hub which is controlled by base security. The security level rises as one descends to lower levels. Humans, who have worked there, report at least seven sub-levels at a depth of four kilometers, but some report Dulce going as deep as 13 levels. Level 1 is general maintenance. Level 2 houses garage facilities for trains, shuttles, tunnel-boring machines and disc maintenance. Level 3 is known as the "weighing" level, since those entering are stripped naked, weighed and all information stored in the computer system and on I.D. cards checked (any change over 1.5 kilograms requires a physical exam and X-ray). Level 4 is for human paranormal research such as hypnosis, mind control, mental telepathy, remote viewing and astral traveling. Level 5 is for alien housing. It is a circular room containing an electro-magnetic generator nearly 60 meters in diameter. Security is extreme with 24/7 armed guards, weight sensitive areas and hand print and eye print stations. Housed here is a device that powers the transfer of atoms. Level 6 is known as "Nightmare Hall." It holds the genetic labs in which experiments vastly alter original animal forms. In cages and vats hold multi-armed and multi-legged humans or humanoid-bat-like creatures up to seven feet tall. Level 7 contains humans in cages, usually drugged or dazed, sometimes crying out for help. Allegedly there are rows and rows of humans (many children) and human-animal hybrid remains in cold storage, as well as embryos of humanoids in various stages of development.

The main whistleblower of the Dulce underground base was Phil Schneider, a geologist and engineer who worked on Black Operation projects. Shortly after making several public appearances discussing Dulce operations, Mr. Schneider was found brutally tortured and killed in his home. No money or other valuables were taken after the murder, later deemed a suicide, but all of his lecture materials on Dulce and his collection of "alien" metals were removed. It would appear that of all the government's dark secrets, none are as sensitive or disturbing as the Dulce underground base.

In regard to the cattle and human mutilations, most of the organic material is taken below ground through the cave openings north of the Archuleta plateau. The evidence indicates that these surgeries are performed, in most cases, while the animal or human victims are still alive. The various parts of the body are taken to various underground laboratories, the main one of which is part of the Dulce complex. This jointly occupied (CIA-alien) facility has been described as enormous, with huge tiled walls that "go on forever."

In 1978, an agreement was reached between the Ute Indians in Colorado and the Federal Government. This agreement consisted of the Ute Nation receiving all the territory now occupied along the New Mexico/Colorado border with the explicit agreement that they would strictly enforce a "No Trespassing" regulation along the border of their territory. Thus, it is not possible to cross the Ute Reservation without special permission from the Tribal Headquarters. If caught without permission, trespassers are liable to a fine, jail and expulsion. The Colorado border is only a few kilometers away from and to the north of the Archuleta plateau. The openings to the Dulce base are in caves in a steep-walled canyon to the north of the Archuleta Mesa. There is a road leading to the Archuleta area through the reservation, but the Indian Forest Service patrols it for trespassers.

Recently, a research team has gone up to Archuleta Mesa to take soundings from under the ground. Preliminary and tentative computer analysis of these soundings indicates deep cavities within the mesa. There are also above ground ventilation shafts for the base on the top of Mount Archeleta. The ducts are rectangular, horizontal, and about 10 meters wide. One researcher, cited by John Lear, did some very sophisticated frequency analysis of the area and said: "Whatever is under there puts out the energy of a city the size of New York." Presumably one huge ventilation shaft can be viewed on Google Earth, seen by traversing exactly 12.8 kilometers northeast from the Dulce Elementary School.

Inside the underground base is an elevator that leads to Level 1 of the massive facility directly beneath the Dulce area, which is also known as ULTRA or "Section-D." Proforce Security guards this level, whereas deeper and more secure levels under the Archuleta Mesa to the north contain automatic devices designed to kill intruders. Dulce is by far the most massive and most strategic of all of the underground "hubs" of the joint military-industrial-alien collaboration in North America. From Dulce, numerous tube-tunnels radiate to all parts of the continent and beyond.

The only sign in English at the tube tunnel shuttle station hallway reads "to Los Alamos." The deeper facilities under Los Alamos reportedly descend to great depths and intersect with alien sectors which constitute the largest concentration of Grey alien activity in North America, with Dulce running a close second. To minimize cattle mutilations, the U.S. Government has reportedly been transporting daily shipments of cattle to rendezvous points in the mountains southeast of Los Alamos, where some have reported sizable UFO activity on these occasions. There appears to be a vast network of tube shuttle connections under the U.S.

which extend into a global system of tunnels and sub-cities. Connections go from Dulce to a base at Page, Arizona, then onto the underground facility below Area 51 in Nevada. Tube shuttles go to and from Dulce to facilities below Taos and Los Alamos, New Mexico, and to the NORAD base at Colorado Springs, Colorado, as well as a dozen other smaller facilities throughout the Southwest.

NORAD

Both commercial and Air Force pilot UFO sightings now amount to over 10,000 reports. All U.S. Air Force pilots must report in a particular manner describing the craft and weather conditions, and then the form must be forwarded to the NORAD base. NORAD is the acronym for the North American Air Defense Command, built deep within the solid granite of Cheyenne Mountain in central Colorado. Commercial pilots, who report UFO sightings but ignore warnings not to go public and instead decide to do interviews, are routinely fired from their jobs.

The original requirement for an Operation's Center in Colorado's Cheyenne Mountain was to provide command and control in support of the air defense mission against the Soviet bomber threat; but several events and emerging technologies drove this mission to evolve beyond those initial needs. Faced with the threat of ballistic missile attack, and with the advent of larger computer processing capabilities, NORAD developed a series of warning and assessment systems. The Operations Center itself lies along one side of a main tunnel which is a kilometer long through the solid granite heart of the mountain. The center was designed to withstand up to a 30-megaton nuclear blast within two kilometers.

"Fastwalker" is a code word created by NORAD to classify UFOs which approach our Earth from outer space and then enter our atmosphere. Deep within the subterranean facility inside and below Cheyenne Mountain, the Air Force NORAD facility tracks roughly on average of 500 fastwalker incidents per year. "Slowwalkers" refer to the slow moving satellites. Fastwalkers move at incredible speeds, up to 16,000 KPH, often making a precise 90-degree turn, then disappearing.

AREA 51

Nellis Air Force Base, with its associated "restricted ranges," occupies almost 8,000 square kilometers of the southern and central Nevada desert. Nellis is a vast military reservation, home of "top gun" flight training and exotic and leading-edge R&D projects. Right in the center of the Nellis base is a place called Area 51. It is the USA's most secretive above- and below-ground military complex. There are 1,900 known people working there on any given day, and they are transported in and out by aircraft everyday, mostly from Las Vegas. One group of workers arrives in the morning and are returned about 5 o'clock in the evening. They have nothing to do with the alien flying discs. Another group of employees who work on the discs arrive later in the afternoon, and go home around midnight. The underground experimental disc facility is called Site-4 inside Papoose

Mountain. The S-4 base is located in the southwest corner of Area 51. At S-4, several human whistleblowers reported that they worked with an extraterrestrial being named "J-Rod" and described this Grey as a "telepathic translator." The entity was once said to have drawn a symbol that looked like our letter "J," followed by a straight line that looked like a rod, and the name stuck. Other Greys who assisted humans also were called J-Rod.

The first wave of Area 51 notoriety came in 1989 when a man named Bob Lazar appeared in a broadcast on Las Vegas television station KLAS, claiming to be a physicist working on backward engineered propulsion systems of various saucer-shaped aircraft. He reported that these new systems were based on recovered alien technology. The crafts he worked on were kept in a secret complex called S-4 at Papoose Lake, a dry lakebed only a few miles south of Groom Lake. Subsequent interviews with Lazar on KLAS transformed the region outside of Area 51 into a top destination for UFO watchers. The second wave of notoriety came when two mountain peaks, Freedom Ridge and White Sides Mountain, located less than 21 kilometers away from Area 51, became prime viewing platforms for nighttime aerial activity. The nearby mountains became so popular that the Air Force acquired the land from the federal Bureau of Land Management (BLM) and closed access in April, 1995, "for the public's safety." Additional Area 51 infamy involved the known testing of the Star Wars Defense Program, the Stealth Cruise Missile and hypersonic spy airplanes that can reach speeds up to Mach 7. It was also reported to be the site of the top secret training of pilots from around the world.

There have been eyewitness reports of disc-shaped crafts hovering over nearby mountains, rumors of at least 15 underground levels, and the remains of alien bodies and extraterrestrial aircraft being stored at S-4. The base does not appear on any public U.S. Governmental maps. According to modern Federal Aviation Administration pilots' charts and U.S. Geological Survey topographic maps, this air base simply does not exist.

Area 51 is as much of an enigma today as it ever was. The military still keeps the area cloaked in tight secrecy, and seeks to acquire even more BLM land to keep the curious "watchers" even farther away.

Although Area 51 is in Nellis Air Space, Edwards Air Force Base in California controls the base itself. The Nellis Bombing and Gunnery Range is the largest restricted airspace in the world and the largest restricted ground area in the United States. The entire base is 7,546 square kilometers, approximately the same size as the state of Connecticut. Although enormous in size, the Nellis Air Space is the greater whole surrounding Area 51. Even the name Area 51, a title given by the Atomic Energy Commission, remains ambiguous. The designation "Area 51" can be found on old government maps, but the base has other nicknames too. Pioneers named the dry lakebed "Groom Lake" and blazed the first dirt roads into the region long before the land was acquired by the Air Force. Another popular nickname is "Dreamland," referring to the name of the restricted airspace over Area 51. Military contractors call Area 51 "The Ranch," or "Paradise Ranch." The CIA Director of 1955 was from Watertown, New York, and CIA staffers reportedly refer to Area 51 as the "Watertown Strip." Other nicknames include the "Pig Farm" and "The Box." Rumors continue to circulate as to whether the Air Force has moved its most sensitive operations out of Area 51, or if the top secret testing continues to this day.

S-4 AND S-2 AT PAPOOSE

The wider complex at Groom Lake (one of the areas of Nellis Air Force Base) was closed for a period of about a year, sometime between about 1972 and 1974, and a huge underground facility was constructed for and with the help of certain extraterrestrial biological entities (EBEs). The "bargained for" technology was set in place but could only be operated by the EBEs themselves. Needless to say, the advanced technology could not be used against the EBE's, even if needed. There were designated areas built for their exclusive usage, and there were designated facilities for our use.

The S-4 facility inside the Papoose Mountain range near Groom Lake is said to have up to 30 levels, some designated for flying craft storage, back-engineering research laboratories, biological operations and applications to modern human technologies. Several levels are used for maintaining a variety of extraterrestrial biological entities in special environmental spheres designed to provide a different, non-Earth atmosphere for the EBEs to be kept as "captive" status. The Papoose Mountain S-4 facility at Area 51 has a special facility called YY-II to house Greys who cooperate as technical advisers, and it simulates a compatible environmental workplace for both humans and EBEs. The housed "Visitors" live within the "Bubble," officially known as "The Clean Sphere," located between Levels 2 and 3 of the 8-level S-2 facility at Area 51. The underground base is located at the south end of the S-2 facility marked "Visitor Containment." There are 12-15 compartments within the Bubble, housing the Archquloid and J-Rod Grey species in pressurized living compartments specially suited for each EBE. These entities are not allowed to leave on their own volition. There are also live aliens under human control at Los Alamos in the compartment also called YY-II.

THE UNDERGROUND WARS

A series of "wars" supposedly took place at several underground bases between humans and the Greys, although it was actually more of a massacre. The first outbreak of violence began on May 1, 1975, during a demonstration of an antimatter reactor within an underground Area 51 chamber. Two Zeta Reticulan Greys were demonstrating a 100% power-producing annihilation reaction in a relatively small antimatter reactor to two deep-cover scientists and attendant security staff, using a super-heavy element bombarded with protons. One "Ret Four" (a slang term for a resident of the fourth planet of the Zeta II Reticuli system) operating the demonstration ordered the human security officers to remove the bullets from their weapons. One security officer questioned this order, and just for having the audacity to question, one of the Greys killed the man. To the attending humans this murder exposed the fact that "they" were not allied to the American government at all, but actually an occupational invasion force that had to maintain absolute discipline among its "conquered subjects." The Greys sensed the fear of the humans and commenced to slaughter the two scientists and 41 military personnel within the tunnels below Area 51, although one human survived. This slaughter occurred apparently *only* because the colonel in charge of security questioned the Grey's orders. Only one Grey died in that initial altercation.

This was simply the initial incident in the "Groom Wars," and since then other incidents have occurred resulting in the deaths or disappearance of aliens and human scientists, workers and military personnel. All the humans who died had perished by head wounds and resultant damage of brain matter. Since no weapon was seen by the one surviving witness, it appears that the Greys are able to use their minds as weapons, in essence using their brains as bio-chemical circuit boards through which to channel electromagnetic energy via specific neural patterns or pathways. This may explain why the Greys have the ability to walk or phase through solid matter, read minds, send mental messages, and are able to lift and float themselves, as well as abductees, without observable instrumentation.

Another battle occurred below Dulce, New Mexico, four years later in 1979, after several scientists had discovered the "Horrible Truth:" that thousands of human abductees were located there in cold storage or imprisoned in cage-like enclosures in the deeper "Alien" sectors under Dulce. They were themselves captured by the aliens following this discovery. A special armed forces unit was called in to try and free a number of our people trapped in the facility, who had become aware of what was really going on. According to one source, 66 of the soldiers were killed, only two escaped, one of whom was Phil Schneider. Our scientists were not freed. These were some of the best American scientific minds, and they have never been heard from again.

The result of the Groom Wars was an end to certain exchanges between the government and the Greys. MJ-12 has never been able to fully debrief or contain a human-looking "Nordic" type alien, that is, not until the Nordics officially began working with segments of MJ-12 at Area 51, starting some time during the 1980's. Previously, they had never had an actual ET Nordic in captivity long enough to do so. It seems these beings simply said goodbye and disappeared. This may be because the Nordic type ETs also have the natural ability to phase-in and phase-out of the third dimension or, similarly, they may have been "beamed out" by their people.

ET BASES IN THE USA

Different races of ETs have been afforded their own bases within the massive Nellis complex. These are the ETs that are covertly involved with global governments and the military in an ongoing basis. The Tall Greys have two known bases. One is at the lower levels at Dulce, New Mexico, and the other is a location known as Area 55 at Nellis. Another ET race called the Tall Whites, or Nordics, who look remarkably similar to Earth humans, also have a base in the northern end of the Indian Springs Valley, located in the southern area of the sprawling Nellis Air Force Base.

Part of the enormous Nellis Air Fore Base, larger than some of the smallest U.S. states, is devoted to underground nuclear testing. Glenn T. Seaborg oversaw the Atomic Energy Commission (AEC) from 1961 until 1971 when much of the secret nuclear testing was going on, including reports of at least one nuclear space rocket meltdown. The AEC was succeeded by the Department of Energy.

Some of the deepest underground levels below Area 51, as well as Dulce, may now belong to forces not loyal to the U.S. Government or the human race. Escapees report that certain areas have been taken over by the reptoid ETs who will kill on sight any humans they deem a threat. Any humans down at these levels reportedly are under complete mental control by these malevolent ETs. It is horrifying to think that some of the scientists we presume are working for us are actually controlled by the aliens. These are the reptoid aliens who abduct people to steal eggs and sperm to create hybrids to infiltrate and influence our society for their own ends. Humans are captured mostly for their reproductive capacities. The primary reason the Grey species of non-humans need blood and tissue from animals is to absorb it, and they do so by literally painting their skin with a mix of these organic fluids. The hemoglobin used in this formula is used for nutrition.

HYBRIDS MADE UNDERGROUND

It must first be pointed out that genetic technology itself is amoral; it is neither good nor bad. It is a tool like a hammer that can either build a shelter or become a weapon. What is done with genome technology depends on who is using it, and this is especially clear with genetic manipulation.

The various reptoid species, specifically the Greys, can clone almost any living tissue into a creature via a method called "rapid-cycle cloning." J-Rod was a creature created by the Greys. Such a creature is intelligent, contains a brilliant mind and can adapt quickly to our environment. Another kind of creature, called the Archquloid, is primitive by comparison, a form of slave. It can be controlled, given orders and is safe, or at least was initially thought to be safe. The Archquloid responds to a brain chip and can be functionally controlled by a little black box. The Archquloid is an example of a Cloned Biological Entity (CBE).

Because human and reptilian beings are genetically so different in their physical make-up, a natural "hybrid" between the two is impossible. However, an unnatural genetic alteration, in essence the splicing of human and reptilian genes, has been attempted. Even if this were accomplished the offspring would not be an actual hybrid, which is half human and half reptilian, but would fall to one side or the other. Since reptilians possess no "soul-matrix" as do us humans, but instead operate on a "collective consciousness" level, the hybrid would be human or reptilian depending on whether they were born with or without a soul-energy-matrix.

In most cases one might tell the difference between a hybrid human or hybrid reptilian if the entity had round-pupils as opposed to black opaque or vertical-slit pupil eyes; or five-digit fingers as opposed to three or four; or external genitalia as opposed to none. Some of the hybrids without souls are "fed" with human soul-energy in an attempt to graft an already existing human soul-matrix into the hybrid.

Then there are the "synthetics" of several different types and varieties, some of which are very human-like and which may be used as "infiltrators," such as the Men in Black. Others apparently look more like the Grey entities, yet are not reptilian. Instead they are a type of "molded" entity form containing a "sponge-like" substance which permeates their interior. Although reptilians and humans apparently utilize "artificial intelligence" devices or organisms, the Draconians as well as some "controlled" humans have apparently developed biosynthetic or mechanical entities. This is especially true with the biosynthetic cybernetic creatures which the reptilians have created using cybernetics and biological organs stolen from animal and human mutilation victims. Interestingly, one of the biggest difficulties the reptilians faced in making these hybrids was not the technological or biological challenges, but (seemingly out of their control), having an Earth-bound spirit attach to the creature when it was "born."

TUNNELS CONNECT A NETWORK OF DUMBS

DUMBS is the acronym for Deep Underground Military Bases and Structures. The tunnels connecting each base are similar to our own Interstate highway system, except they are underground. The underground highway uses trucks, cars, and buses all powered by clean electric motors. In any case, they wouldn't want gasoline fumes polluting the tunnels. The style of transport for freight and passengers is linked together in a worldwide network called the Sub-Global System. It has checkpoints at each country entry. There are shuttle tubes that shoot the trains at incredible speed using a "mag-lev" and vacuum method. These magneto leviton trains can travel in excess of the speed of sound, at Mach 2 supersonic speeds. Massive laser boring machines can literally melt rock at the rate of up to 10 kilometers per day to form the tunnels, and the work continues to this day.

Skeptics have scoffed at claims that very long tunnels stretch from one military operation area to another. Yet, engineers have planned for tunnels to span the nation for decades. Surprisingly, skeptics are somewhat deficient in their imagination when it comes to what has already been accomplished. These same skeptics also do not believe in alien contact either. So it is even more difficult for them to accept the idea that aliens have inhabited the Earth for a long time; or to believe that they must live underground and out of sight to hide their existence at all costs; or to believe that they are manipulating key people in power to do their bidding. However, there are increasing numbers of abductees who have reported being taken to underground bases. Some of these abductees have described seeing things that really do exist in government-run underground facilities. The truth is out there, or in this case, under there.

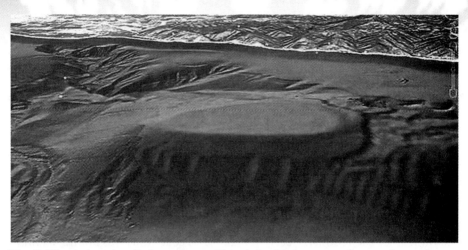

The California-based radio host Jimmy Church broke the story of a massive underwater structure off the Malibu shore in June, 2014 on the program "Fade to Black." According to Jimmy Church, this may be "the Holy Grail of UFO/USO (unidentified submerged objects) that researchers have been looking for over the last 50 years." The Malibu "anomaly" is over 600 meters deep under the surface off the Southern California coast. Image courtesy of Google Earth.

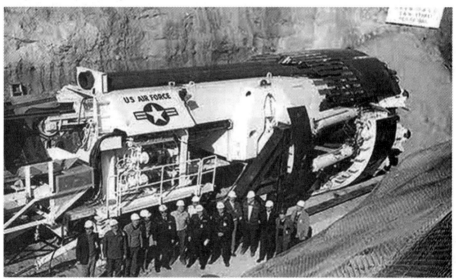

This is a $13 million tunnel boring machine (TBM) used for tunneling at the Nevada Test Site and other DUMBs. Many other types of TBMs are used by many government agencies, including the 'nuclear powered TBM' [NTBM] that melts solid rock and leaves behind glass-like walls. They are capable of tunneling up to several kilometers per day.

The U.S. Government and its contractors such as Bechtel have utilized nuclear powered tunneling machines since the 1950s. The larger models as seen here were patented in the 1970s (U.S. Patent #3,693,731). As the machine burrows through the rock hundreds of meters below the surface, the "subterrene" heats whatever stone it encounters into molten rock, or magma, which cools after the subterrene has moved on. The result is a tunnel with a smooth glazed lining, somewhat like black glass, which is apparently so strong that it doesn't require wall reinforcement. As one of the leading contractors for the black ops, Bechtel is where our tax dollars go to die. They do not need to go public for money, plus the Federal Government rebuts all inquiry by citing "national security" and "state secret privilege."

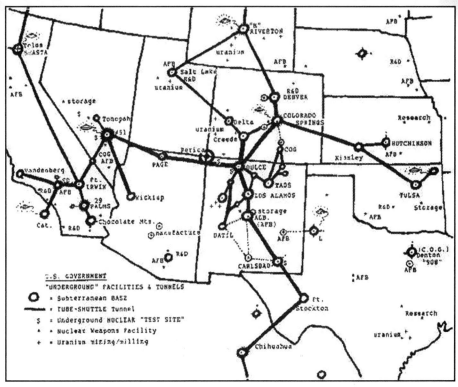

This is obviously a crude map of the "underground projects." As expected, there are no official maps of the bases or train tubes because this subject is in the politically incorrect "taboo" category of sensitive, covert black operations funded secretly without public debate. It is estimated that over 200 underground cities are now built and ready for occupation. Private security firms such as Wackenhut provide the security. The Atomic Energy Commission first oversaw the construction of military DUMBS such as Area 51, which was started in 1955. Today, Area 51 is considered the most protected base in the world. The amount of information the United States government has been willing to provide regarding Groom Lake and other DUMBs has generally been minimal due to the highly questionable happenings of these subterranean operations.

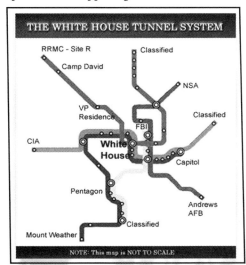

No, this is not the greater Washington D.C. subway system. It is the covert subway system connecting the White House to a network of underground bases, some of which are attached to the above ground offices of the "alphabet agencies." The underground Raven Rock Mountain Complex (RRMC) is also known as the "Second Pentagon."

COSMOS

Come oscillate through the spacetime continuum to the next dimensions with us! An essential guide to all things weird and out of this world.

"There is one spectacle grander than the sea, that is the sky; there is one spectacle grander than the sky, that is the interior of the soul." –Victor Hugo, "Fantine," *Le Misérables*

"We are members of a vast cosmic orchestra, in which each living instrument is essential to the complimentary and harmonious playing of the whole." –J. Allen Boone

"I can assure you that flying saucers, given that they are real, are not constructed by any power on Earth." –Harry S. Truman, 1950

"If I become president, I'll make every piece of information this country has about UFO sightings available to the public and scientists. I am convinced that UFOs exist because I have seen one." –Jimmy Carter, 1976

"I have not thought it hazardous to predict, that wars in the future will be waged by electrical means." –Nikola Tesla, 1915

"When the planets in evil mixture to disorder wander, what plagues and what portents! What mutiny! What raging of the sea! Shaking of Earth!" –William Shakespeare

"Behind the scenes, high-ranking Air Force officers are soberly concerned about UFOs. But through official secrecy and ridicule, many citizens are led to believe the unknown flying objects are nonsense." –Admiral Roscoe Henry Hillenkoetter, Director of the CIA, in a 1960 letter to Congress

"Reality is an illusion, albeit a persistent one." –Albert Einstein

"We are all multidimensional, omni-dimensional. Everything that exists somewhere in the world also exists in us." –Deepak Chopra

"Seek not abroad, turn back into thyself, for in the inner man dwells the truth." –Saint Augustine

"One of the penalties for refusing to participate in politics is that you end up being governed by your inferiors." –Plato

TO FLY A UFO

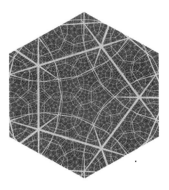

"I have an obligation to inform the public, and once that's done, I've done my job." —Navy whistleblower William Cooper, at a 1989 UFO conference

UFO sightings have been a consistently observed phenomenon for at least the last seven decades, continuing the pattern of such reports depicted throughout history. Anomalous aerial sightings have been reported by witnesses and recorded as artwork for thousands of years. Even cave drawings that date long before Christ depict alien-like figures and flying objects in the sky. Interestingly, the vast numbers of alien figures and flying disc crafts which have appeared all around the world are similar in appearance. In the modern age, humans went from Kitty Hawk to the Moon in 66 years, an amazing advance. However, our current space achievements from the first Moon walk in 1969 to the present secret space program advancements will be considered a far more remarkable technology jump, once the truth is known.

Most UFO sightings in the last 70 years are described as flying saucers. However these ships don't fly; they oscillate between dimensions. UFOs were first referred to as Identified Alien Craft (IAC) by the military, before any backward engineering began. The military now calls UFOs Alien Visitation Crafts, or AVCs for short, as opposed to ARVs, Alien Reproduction Vehicles, which are human-constructed, advanced anti-gravity craft. Since it would be difficult for anyone without a trained eye to know the difference, it's easier to continue calling any Unknown Flying Objects by their common name, "UFOs."

The consciousness that operates all the various UFO crafts is of the same energetic force within the crafts themselves. In other words, a fourth dimensional being will interact and navigate a fourth dimensional craft, and the same can be said for the more etheric fifth dimensional beings and the vehicles they would use. A resonate frequency, or a common vibration, connects machine and passenger within their co-conscious spaceship. For us Earthly third dimensional human beings, we will best relate to third dimensional spacecraft. Because of the current state on this planet, third dimensional crafts can be operated by fear-based or darker energy entities. However, there are other very human-like beings in the universe that are fourth dimensional. These fourth dimensional humans will be able to discern crafts at their level of light and consistent with their purpose. In other words, the more highly evolved the being, the higher they will connect with the higher levels of spacecraft and therefore receive higher levels of information.

VRIL ENERGY

A few years after the First World War, the ultra-secret German Vril Society was formed to study the uses of "Vril energy," or Zero Point Energy, and other speculative free energy designs. *Vril* is the German term meaning "cosmic basic energy." The Vril Society also took up the study of ancient Indian texts describing the Vimana flying craft. Using information from psychic mediums, ancient text scholars and archaeological digs, the pre-Nazi Germans called this research "psycho-physical technology." The Vril Society was known to investigate the physical properties of space and time. The Germans pushed the psychic envelope and got what they wished for, over a decade before the Nazis ascended to power.

The Vril Society wished to create a utopian new world based on alternative science. It is the first known modern organization to make contact with ETs via psychic mediums and "channeling" with the intention of acquiring advanced technology. During one such event in 1919, at an old hunting lodge in the German Alps town of Berchtesgaden, the mediums "Sigrun" and Maria Orsic made contact with a civilization (through their equivalent of mediums) in the Aldebaran Star system, 69 light years away in the constellation Taurus. The benevolent and highly advanced Aldebaran mediums reasoned that the suffering and inequalities of humans could benefit if they were given advanced technology. As a result, Maria Orsic was able to telepathically channel the plans for free energy devices and an advanced hyper-dimensional craft.

A related organization, The Thule Society, began around the same time as the Vril Society when Karl Haushofer founded the *Bruder des Lichts* ("Brothers of the Light") in December, 1919. The Vril Society is sometimes referred to as the Luminous Lodge and was eventually renamed the Vril-Gesellschaft as it rose in prominence. Whereas the Thule Society focused primarily on materialistic and political agendas, the Vril Society put its attention on the "Other Side." The predecessor to the Vril and Thule Societies was the *Ahnenerbe*, or "legacy of the ancestors."

Founded in 1935, the Ahnenerbe Society was the most mysterious organization in the Third Reich. This was the only known historical structure engaged in the study of the occult and mysticism to have state funding and support.

Some researchers believe that Nazi scientists were also preparing the first atomic blast, but the war ended before they succeeded. The subsequent series of nuclear tests by other countries also initiated the "Vril reaction," which is the driving together or collision of positive and negative charges to the annihilation of both. An electron driven into a proton will produce an overloaded neutron which will shatter into a long series of violently unstable mesons, until the whole is converted into energy. This highly-intensified energy or the majority of the quanta then are more than sufficient to drive more electrons into protons, and so on, through multiple, increasingly powerful reactions. Furthermore, scientists did not know at what point the reaction would spread to matter other than hydrogen. When the Nazis obtained these plans, they used them to create advanced wonder weapons that frightened the Allies at the end of World War II. The V-2 rocket and the first jet airplanes made a showing during the waning months of the war, but these new aircraft could not stop the Allies from advancing into the Fatherland.

NAZI UFOs

Nazi scientists were the first modern humans to experiment with backward engineering and its various strategies to achieve anti-gravity flight. In 1938, at the invitation of Benito Mussolini, German scientists were allowed to examine the remains of a UFO that was recovered in 1933 near the small town of Maderno in the Lombardy region of northern Italy. Their strategy was to combine the recovered disc designs with their Vril and Thule technology in an attempt to design their own craft. The best example of these kinds of experiments was the top secret and highly sensitive scientific technological device called *Die Glocke,* or "The Bell." The Bell was incorporated into a flying disc called the V-5 craft. Rare photos show the disc flying near the secret Nazi engineering division of the Skoda Works in Pilsen, Czechoslovakia. The Bell had a complex system of opposing turbines purported to generate a field of anti-gravity so powerful it wreaked havoc on all life in its vicinity and may have even teleported matter over vast distances.

Einstein's gravitational theorems reveal the potential for the generation of an anti-gravitational field when the equation begets a negative number. Sustaining such a system requires a continued energy input of at least 900 kilo-amperes, or the transfer of 1020 electrons per second, a huge technological jump. The Bell also would have acted as a time machine, that is, if such applications were desired. According to Nazi scientist Dr. Hermann Oberth, "Behavior of the UFOs discounts any means of propulsion and the principle of an anti-gravity device might be expected." One smaller model of craft designed by the Nazis was called the Vril, using principles of Vril energy described above. A prototype of the "Vril" disc with an engine designed by Viktor Schauberger took flight in 1939. The Vril was small enough to fit within a larger craft designed as a cigar-shaped craft, which contained extremely advanced aerodynamic and propulsion systems. It is not known if either of these crafts ever flew into the upper atmosphere or beyond.

USA PICKS UP THE SCENT

Early saucer recovery in the USA began in the 1940s and 1950s. The downed crafts that were observed contained basketball-sized chain reactor generators, some of which used water as fuel. This reactor created free energy and propelled the anti-gravity system to make the craft fly. At the time, and to most of the public today, this represents technology beyond our wildest dreams. This information is slowly making its way out to the public. In recent years both NASA and the European Space Agency (ESA) have acknowledged achieving anti-gravity and artificial gravity technologies. One would expect them to say the opposite if they have not reached those objectives.

Whistleblowers coming from the U.S. military, such as Naval Intelligence officer and UFO researcher William Cooper, say that some of the crafts they have seen are as large as an aircraft carrier. Such a craft is able to force ocean water to part before impact, utilizing some force field far beyond what is currently known. "The crafts are real," confessed William Cooper before he was murdered by police at his home in 2001. "The only question is," he added, "are ETs real?" Cooper always stressed that the important point to remember is that these sightings occurred. Not how many, what variety of craft or where, but that they occurred.

Many of the scientific principles of UFO propulsion dynamics are already known and recognized by today's physicists, and have been known for some time. *Life* magazine featured a story in 1952 which reported that "Craft can fly up to 7,000 mph. No power plant known on Earth can account for the performance of these devices."

SOVIET AIR FORCE ADMITS UFOs ARE REAL

In March, 1990, the Russian General Igor Maltsev, Chief of Staff of the Soviet Air Defense Forces, made the following statement: "Skeptics and believers both can take this as an official confirmation of the existence of UFOs." This was at a time of rare outspokenness among military brass, only a year before the dissolution of the Soviet Union. General Ivan Tretyak, who was then the Soviet Deputy Minister of Defense as well as Commander in Chief of the Air Defense Forces confirmed this position. In regard to the validity of these statements from the highest-ranking officers in the Soviet Air Force, there would be no reason to think that what they were saying was a hoax. Instead, they were reflecting *Glasnost*, the policy of maximal publicity, openness, and transparency in the activities of all government institutions in the Soviet Union. In addition, both Tretyak and Maltsev took care to note that the vast majority of cases are either misidentification of natural phenomena or hoaxes. When asked about his personal interest in UFOs, Tretyak stated it raised "moderate curiosity." Echoing the comments of his Chief of Staff, Maltsev, Tretyak further observed, "There are real phenomena of some kind which are appearing before us in the form of UFOs, the nature of which we do not know."

General Tretyak also stated that UFOs had been photographed by interceptor pilots and confirmed on both optical and thermal sensors but that they sometimes appeared to have stealth-like capabilities to evade radar. Soviet missile bases were also vexed by hovering UFOs that disabled nuclear warheads, but did not destroy them, in a seemingly determined effort to inform both the U.S. and the Soviets that their weapons would be deactivated if ever deployed. Other reports indicate that Soviet pilots actually flew over UFOs, but did not engage in combat.

General Tretyak took a page from the U.S. Air Force playbook when he also confirmed that UFOs did not appear to pose a threat, although their origin was unknown. When asked why he had not given the order to open fire on the UFOs, he stated, "It would be foolhardy to launch an unprovoked attack against an object that may possess formidable capabilities for retaliation." Both Russian and American missile defenses experienced ETs closely monitoring and even powering down their nuclear silo facilities ever since the original Trinity test. No overtly hostile actions were taken, but it seemed clear that either superpower would be prevented from actually ever using their nuclear arsenals.

Like American military observers, the Soviet Air Force had many instances in which UFOs were seen hovering and then departing at fantastic speeds. Some of the Soviet reports estimated the crafts to be between 100 and 200 meters in diameter, with speeds ranging from hovering motionless to over triple the capacity of modern fighters, with the ability to stop instantaneously. Other reports indicated that the UFOs performed "startling maneuverability," yet made no sound. Soviet investigators claimed that UFOs were "completely devoid of inertia. In other words, they had somehow 'come to terms' with gravity. At the present time, terrestrial machines can hardly have such capabilities." This means the Soviet scientists believed that the UFOs had perfect anti-gravity capability, which would represent a major technological breakthrough. In the months following the collapse of the Soviet Union, highly classified documents from the KGB became available to the highest bidder, providing UFO researchers a treasure-trove of new information.

TO FLY A SPACE CRAFT

Just as there are many levels of consciousness among various dimensional beings, there are also many varieties of UFO crafts. Some of them are made of very dense material formations, while others are very etheric (less solid) in nature. Those that are etheric can be from fourth to fifth dimension levels. The higher the dimensionality of these ships, the faster they are able to move. Many of them are constructed of light essences, or are of etheric physicality, and are very similar to a holographic construct, yet set in place and able to move at the speed of light. Most UFOs utilize the fourth dimension, which is time. Only third, fourth and fifth density beings require craft. Entities from sixth density and above can be considered light beings—those at one with the entire universe. These beings are equivalent to (or in touch with) the entire plane of consciousness in the universe and do not require spacecraft, or any material forms, for communication and connection.

Crafts from the lower dimensions that have been recovered and studied are not what we would expect either. They do not feature bunks, toilets, and leisure lounges, as one would expect on a long interstellar voyage. Instead, these UFOs are not machines as we know them, but time-travel or interdimensional travel devices. There are smaller scout craft like those recovered at Roswell, New Mexico, in 1947, as well as mother ships that are larger than an aircraft carrier. For the fourth and fifth density beings, the crafts are somehow intelligently steered, using an invisible interface between pilot and craft.

In other cases, such as the glowing orbs, there is nobody inside. The orbs, or "foo fighters" as they were called by Allied pilots during World War II, were not seen so much as a craft but as a light, pulsating with a glow. However, it is thought the orbs need mercury to function. The orbs are commonly seen as creating crop circles, and observers report seeing them chased away by black helicopters.

Both the orbs and UFOs are flown using "thought command" to guide the aerial devices. In the case of the orbs, it is presumed they are guided by a remote viewing pilot. The thought command system on UFOs is connected directly to the pilots through a sort of electrical "nervous system" on the craft, which can be controlled by their own minds. The bodies of each crew member are likewise tuned into and connected to the nervous system built into the spacecraft. In fact, the spacecraft is modeled in much the same way as the pilot's body. It is adjusted specifically to the frequency of each crew member. Therefore, the craft can be operated by collective thoughts, that is, the mental energy emitted by the pilot and crew. It is really a very simple, direct control system. Thus, there are no complicated controls or navigation equipment on board the spacecraft. They operate as an extension of the biological bodies and minds of the crew members.

The spacecraft is navigated by direct interaction between the electronic waves generated within the minds of the pilots and the craft's directional controls. The electronic brain signals are interpreted and transmitted by the headband devices, which serve as a craft interface, along with hand indentation panels. The brainwave control for navigation directs the pilot's thoughts and translates them into an electronic circuit. There is no steering wheel or conventional method of control on the spacecraft, and the headbands are designed to pick up signals from the brain. The sensors on the headbands correspond with points on the multi-lobed brain that generate low-frequency waves, so the headbands form an integral part of the circuit. The single-piece, skin-tight coveralls worn tightly by the pilots also play a role. The lengthwise atomic alignment of the fabric also allows the body of the pilots to become part of the electrical storage and generation of the craft itself. It is not just to steer or navigate the vehicle, but the pilots actually became part of the electrical circuitry of the vehicle, vectoring the craft in a way similar to the way we can voluntarily order a muscle to move. The vehicle is simply an extension of their own bodies because it is tied directly into their neurological systems.

This technology is reminiscent of homeopathy. Homeopathic doctors trace the human body down to a channel of light. So when it comes to space travel, it is advisable to know what you are getting into—to consider what kind of potential is out there. With the proper insight and star charts, along with a capable craft and crew, any place in the universe is only a moment's thought away. Interdimensional spacecraft would include a tiny cold fusion reactor in the center of a spinning disc whose center is stationary. In one model of how UFOs fly, the outside of the disc somehow is made to rotate at nearly the speed of light and then everything can scale up to infinite speeds or connections, ascending into the fourth dimension. (Basically, the fourth dimension is a realm of pure light—a higher vibrational overtone—a place where one's thoughts can instantly manifest.) After making a sharp 90° turn, only the pilot and passengers can determine the next destination, arriving as instantaneously as their collective thought. Space travel is not necessarily sending a ship from one area to another. It is more like beaming the passengers between ships from one area to another instantaneously. Theoretically, no time is involved.

CONFIGS AND SPECS

Space travel, in concept, is not very difficult. The first task is to create two counter-rotating energy fields at a very specific speed, namely, nine-tenths the speed of light. When these conditions are met, similar to stargate technology, whatever matter exists between these fields will shift up to the next dimensional level, as demonstrated by the U.S. Government in the 1943 Philadelphia Experiment. In this top secret experiment, the U.S. Navy attempted to make a battleship invisible with counter-rotating fields of energy, but stopped the experiment prematurely and created an "interdimensional crash" instead. The intense electrical fields created a rip in the fabric of spacetime before the battleship could be linked to its new destination.

What we today would call the ultimate computer can be found aboard back-engineered spacecrafts. Their computers are an electronic device that serves as an artificial "brain" or a highly complex calculating machine. It is capable of storing information, making computations, solving problems and performing mechanical functions. Computers in advanced ET societies are extremely advanced. In most of the galactic systems of the universe, very large computers are commonly used to run the routine administration, mechanical services and maintenance activities of an entire planet or even a planetary system.

According to Area 51 whistleblower Bob Lazar, propulsion of UFOs is achieved by "gravity amplifiers," three on its lowest level, independently positioned and used to emit gravitational waves. Lift is gained by gravity wave, where phase shifts the wave in a kind of opposite polarity from the force of the Earth's gravity. Liftoff is performed on one amplifier called "omecron," then transitioned to the "delta" configuration which uses all three amplifiers for space travel. The craft uses these amplifiers to distort space around the craft so it is always moving "downhill" into the zone it has created, even when it goes straight up.

Most UFO craft studied by humans have four to six layers. The upper outside layer of solid metal accounts for 25 percent, the second layer of rubber is 30 percent, the third layer of metal is also 30 percent, and the last layer has marked magnetic properties. A "diffuse layer" of electric charges occurs most effectively when the liquid "e-plasma" is moving, and the faster the e-plasma moves, the more pronounced will be the separation effect of its electric ions from the ions in the differently moving diffused layer outside. If energy is injected into the magnetic layer, spaceships can fly across the universe. Such a spacecraft would have a double hull construction with several sets of optical fiber windings between the two hulls. One set of windings is used to create a uniform surrounding force field that streamlines the spacecraft. This streamlining allows the craft to move smoothly through space itself. The other sets of windings generate the force fields that are used to propel and guide the craft on its journey. The outer body is injection molded, with no seams, cold to the touch, and made of metal. The metallic skin is also used as a translucent viewport. The display panels within UFOs appear as liquid crystal.

LET'S GO FLYING!

The first USAF pilots in the late 1950s were trained to fly these highly advanced discs in a simulator. Specifically, the flight simulator taught them how to fly "gravity field-driven" crafts. The first thing they noticed was that there were no seat belts in the simulator since there were no seat belts in the actual craft. In fact, pilots or passengers don't need seat belts, because in flight there is no upside down like in a regular aircraft. No one can feel the sensation of being upside down. That's because the craft has its own gravitational field inside, so even if the craft is flying upside down, everyone inside the craft still feels as if they are right side up.

Another interesting aspect of these crafts is that there are usually no windows. The only way the pilots have any visibility at all is done with external cameras displayed on screens or relayed to a headband device. These camera relay devices are delivered to the pilots in a mental image picture. After the craft warms up, because the disc has its own gravitational field, some pilots reported that they felt sick or disoriented for about two minutes after getting in. The earlier pilots said it takes a lot of time to become used to the sensation. Because of the very small size of the craft, there is very little room for any movement. To just raise your hand becomes complicated, so you have to be extensively trained in unconventional ways. Pilots receive rigorous mind training to learn to accept what they are seeing in their minds as an actual feeling experience. Just moving about is difficult, but after a while the pilots get used to the sensation and can become quite adept. The training taught them to become familiar with where everything was located, and to expect what was going to happen to their bodies. The early human UFO pilots said it was no different than accepting the g-forces in conventional flights, such as the strange sensations of coming out of a dive.

AS ABOVE SO BELOW

The ET crafts use a "universal grid" system in traveling from one point of space to another. Their crafts are able to travel at or near the speed of light as discussed above. This enables a craft to go into an altered space-time chamber, which allows the point of departure and the point of destination to shrink drastically in real time. It is similar to folding space, thus making the two points (departure and destination) become much closer—so close as to be virtually identical.

Although we have been given the basic blueprint for such a craft, including the propulsion mechanism and overall operating system, our scientists are still working to fully understand and backward engineer the technology. The craft utilizes minerals that we simply don't have here on Earth, such as Element 115. One particular element, similar to uranium but not as radioactive, provides the extra power for the propulsion system. These crafts also utilize a form of a space displacement system, which basically causes a vacuum in front of the propulsion that allows nothing to interfere with the created thrust. The technology uses a vacuum chamber, which consists of a mini-nuclear reactor that forces some type of matter into space which deletes the molecules and causes that very small portion of space to become a vacuum. They also utilize anti-matter in such a way as to force the propulsion system into "streams" or "waves" of energy in front of the craft. This enables it to move and flow much easier through space without any friction from the atmosphere.

There may be yet one more way to traverse the expanse of the universe. An ancient meditation practice concerns itself with astral traveling. While in this meditative state, the viewer first travels into the center of the Earth. According to the "Ascended Masters," in the middle of our planet, within the core, is a miniature universe. The remote viewer then experiences a shrinking, to the point that when getting close to the miniature universe and relative to it, the former miniature universe becomes huge and is the exact same size as the galaxy surrounding the Earth. One must be connected vibrationally to the heart of the Earth, and in this way the astral traveler may both enter and return to the universe via our solar system and, finally, return to the body externally from above. Russian scientists were the first to postulate the possibility that a navigational craft can also manipulate matter to penetrate the center of the planet, enter the miniature universe, and use this as a technique for instantly connecting to distant stars. Indeed, the Nazi's believed in the hollow Earth theory, where the poles were the entrance ways into the interior. Outside and above Earth they believed the poles could be wormhole gates to the stars, and could have been one of the reasons why they set up bases in both of the polar regions.

The "sunwheel" style swastika was first adopted by the Thule Society. The German Workers Party also used the logo when Adolph Hitler was a young and ambitious member.

During World War II, German scientists in the "Special Bureau 13" were said to be working on a top secret anti-gravity craft referred to as "The Bell." It contained two counter-rotating cylinders filled with a substance similar to mercury that glowed violet when activated, known only as "Xerun 525." Subsequent levitation-craft advances between 1941 and 1944 spawned the "Haunebu" series of the Third Reich's saucer fleet. Postwar, the USA was keenly interested in the "techno-magical" legacy of Germany. What advanced propulsion craft might exist by today's standards if the Nazi's had this technology over 70 years ago?

This is not a UFO, but a human-built and unpiloted Searl Internal Gravity Vehicle (IGV) P-11 model in flight, hovering about a half kilometer above ground. This photo was taken in 1968 from another Searl IGV model in flight. The Searl IGV craft creates a massive conversion of Zero Point Energy, which Tom Bearden calls "little pieces of vacuum." Inventor John Wheeler calls this lighting effect "quantum foam," which he conceptualizes as the foundation of the universal fabric. Vacuum (by definition in physics) when cohered by an "ether vortex" such as produced by the overloaded and superconducting Searl Effect Generator (SEG) can convert more energy than we could ever imagine. The SEGs can free the human race from poverty, pollution, and dirty energy, which produces global warming and causes greenhouse gases. Of course, the Searl Starships can also propel us to other planets and different star systems.

ANTI-GRAVITY

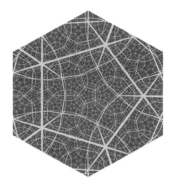

"If at first an idea does not sound absurd, then there is no hope for it." -Albert Einstein

THE scientific revolution is considered to have culminated with the publication of the *Philosophiae Naturalis Principia Mathematica* by the English physicist, mathematician, astronomer, theologian, natural philosopher, alchemist and inventor Sir Isaac Newton, who lived from 1643 until 1727. Newton published the *Principia* in 1687, detailing two comprehensive and successful physical theories. First was Newton's law of motion, from which arises classical mechanics, and Newton's law of gravitation, which describes the fundamental force of gravity. Both theories have been considered fundamental for centuries and work well independently of each other. The *Principia* also included several theories in fluid dynamics. The book is said to be the greatest single work in the history of science, describing universal gravitation and the three laws of motion. It laid the groundwork for classical mechanics which dominated the scientific view of the physical universe for the next three centuries, and remains the basis for modern engineering.

After Newton defined classical mechanics, the next great field of inquiry within physics was the nature of electricity and magnetism, both important fields of study in the harnessing of anti-gravity. Does gravity have a magnetic counterpart? Spin any electric charge and there is a magnetic field. Spin any mass and, according to Einstein, you should get a very slight effect that acts something like magnetism. This effect is expected to be so small that it is beyond practical experience and ground laboratory measurement. But is it? Let's start with what we currently know in physics and then move to the theoretical.

WHAT IS GRAVITY?

First, it is necessary to identify the two types of gravity. Gravity A and Gravity B have distinctly different properties. Within the macro scale world in which we live, Gravity B is the gravity we are all familiar with as humans on Earth; it is the gravity we experience everyday. It is what holds the planets in orbital alignments around the sun, that allowed an apple to fall on Sir Isaac Newton's head, and keeps our feet firmly planted on the ground. Yet, Gravity A is what concerns us the most in this chapter. Gravity A, or what is called the strong nuclear force, is the gravity that holds the mass of protons and neutrons together in the micro scale world. Scientists have long thought that super heavy elements could have Gravity A wave fields outside the perimeter of the atom, where they can be accessed and measured, instead of that field being strictly inside matter.

At the turn of the 20th century, it was clear that although Newton's laws and Maxwell's equations were highly successful in explaining the motion of the planets and the behavior of light, they could not explain a whole plethora of other problems, such as why gasses emit light when heated, why some materials conduct electricity at different temperatures, or why certain metals melt at certain temperatures. All of these issues require an internal understanding of atoms. In 1900, the German scientist Max Planck proposed that energy was not contiguous as Newton thought, but occurred in small discreet packets called quanta. In 1905, Einstein took this theory to the next level by stating that light consisted of these tiny discreet quanta, later dubbed "photons." The "photoelectric effect" was the label for why electrons are emitted from metal when one shines a light on it. Today, the photon and the photoelectric effect form the basis of much of modern electronics such as Thru Beam motion sensors, lasers, and solar cells.

The first law of thermodynamics in physics distinguishes between two kinds of physical processes, namely, the transfer of energy as work (or motion), and the transfer of energy as heat. It describes how the existence of a mathematical quantity called the internal energy of a system operates. The second law of thermodynamics states that every mechanism or living being within a closed system will eventually exert all of its energy and cease to function. For cars it could mean running out of gas, for a pendulum it means losing momentum, and for life forms it means old age and eventual death. Entropy is the amount of thermal energy not available to do the work, and also a measure of the disorder or randomness of the system. Equivalently, the first law of thermodynamics states that perpetual motion machines of the first kind are impossible. Of course, no machine runs perpetually since it is made of matter and all matter wears down. The way around this maxim is that the *source* of power remains virtually endless. Entropy itself can also be harnessed as energy, as in the case of auto breaks that add energy to a battery.

The internal dynamics of the atom is the new frontier of quantum science. A nearly complete picture of the atom emerged after 1925, allowing us to peer deeper into the dynamics of the atom and predict its properties. Atoms take on the composition of miniature solar systems, but this is not entirely accurate. An electron orbits in a standing wave within an electron cloud, meaning electrons are in more than one place at one time. Everything vibrates at different levels, because atoms vibrate and that is because the sub-atomic particles are in harmonic resonance. Gravity is vibration in the presence of mass and can be neutralized by changing the harmonic resonance of mass. If you generate vibrations, such as the Tibetan monks levitating boulders, you can alter gravity. This is called auditive levitation.

Another principle of physics regularly taught is that the state of matter has to do with the frequency of atoms in it and that gravity is another form of electromagnetism; but this is not the case. If we want to monumentally amplify the gravity field, there are certain conditions that need to be met. The magnetic component of gravity, which acts as a bilateral anti-gravity force along the Z-axis, sets the speed of light in the electronic structure so that it is equal to the speed of sound in the nuclear structure.

WHAT IS MATTER?

Our scientists continue to discover new elements on the periodic chart, but we do not yet have an accurate measuring system to gauge the age of matter. Scientists assume that because certain types of materials such as organic or carbon-based matter seem to deteriorate eventually, there is a deterioration of matter. It is not accurate to measure the age of stone based on the measurement of the age of wood or bone. This is a fundamental error. In fact, matter does not deteriorate. It cannot be destroyed. Matter may be altered in form, but it is never truly destroyed.

The changes in the complexion of the Earth reveal that mountain ranges rise and fall, continents change location, the poles of the planet shift, ice caps come and go, oceans appear and disappear, and rivers, valleys and canyons change. In all cases, for example, a rock breaking up in the surf, matter remains the same because it is always the same sand. Every form and substance is made of the same basic material which never deteriorates or extinguishes completely.

FORMING NEW MATTER

When Bob Lazar worked in the S-4 facility at Area 51, his task was to backward engineer the exotic propulsion engines presumably acquired from ETs. According to Lazar, the records, photos, documents, and crafts (which he actually worked on) contained anti-matter reactors run by an exotic fuel using the mysterious Element 115. At the time, this exotic fuel could not be found organically on Earth. When Lazar first spoke of Element 115 as the necessary "fuel" that was used for manipulating gravity and space in UFO propulsion engines, there were people who immediately tried to discredit him and labeled this idea as a fantasy. But in 2003, Element 115 was officially discovered and given the name

"Ununpentium" or Uup. Since then several additional super heavy elements have been discovered (113, 114, 116, 117, 118). These latest discoveries provide significant credibility to Bob Lazar's assertions. None of these super heavy elements were known to exist in 1989 when Lazar's claims were published.

Lazar claimed that Element 115 was the essential fuel used for manipulating gravity and space. He saw flying discs using amplified gravitational waves as the source of flight. He claimed Ununpentium was used in the "drive" part of the propulsion system and was in a stable form. Yet, according to Wikipedia, only 30 atoms of Ununpentium had ever been synthesized. To date, four isotopes of Element 115 have been discovered, yet none have been stable. Lazar made the claim that the U.S. Secret Government had in its possession 225 kilograms of Element 115, but how they acquired it is unknown. If this quantity is indeed in possession of the government, the only logical conclusion is that aliens gave it to them, most likely from Reticulan EBEs in the technology trade Eisenhower forged in a treaty with the Greys. Whistleblowers have reported most of the modern USA secret space program anti-gravity crafts harness the gravitational "strong force." This strong force field extends slightly beyond the atomic nucleus of Element 115. By amplifying the exposed gravitational strong force and using anti-matter reactor high energy and then directing it, it is possible to lift a craft from the Earth and then change directions by vectoring the shaped anti-gravity force field thus generated. The key is Element 115.

ELEMENT 115

According to Lazar, Element 115 is the key to manipulating gravity and producing anti-gravity devices, at least on the crafts he examined. This Gravity A wave has amplitude, wavelength, and frequency. Being able to manipulate this field has significant results, including anti-matter generators and anti-gravity devices. Lazar further explained that Element 115, inside the reactor, is bombarded with protons, transforming it into the Element 116. Element 115, when bombarded with protons and heat through a thermionic generator, provided the positive voltage to run the ship, and then the Gravity A wave was drawn off for use to power travel throughout the universe. As it works, the element decays and releases two anti-protons, also called anti-hydrogen, creating a form of anti-matter. The anti-matter is channeled down tubes where it reacts with gas and then undergoes the "total annihilation reaction" which is the 100% conversion of matter to energy. The heat created by the reaction is converted to electrical energy by a solid state, near 100% efficient thermoelectric generator. It is this energy that is used to amplify the Gravity A wave.

What makes Element 115 so truly remarkable is that it appears to have a Gravity A wave that extends outside of the atom, and it would appear that only the super heavy Elements 113 through 118 have this extended field. It should be noted that scientists have not been able to find a Gravity A wave outside of an atom from any naturally occurring element on Earth. But Element 115, which is synthetic, seems to have its own field or its own Gravity A wave. The Gravity A wave emanates from the nucleus of Element 115 and actually extends past the perimeter of the atom. Since this field protrudes outside of the atom itself, scientists can amplify that field as they are able to do with any other wave.

In most nuclear reactions scientists have worked with, they utilize fission and fusion. Fission produces energy by splitting atoms, while fusion fuses atoms, usually hydrogen, to release more energy. The total annihilation reaction that takes place in the small reactor, which Lazar observed, was the propulsion system within the disk that could amplify and focus this Gravity A wave. This would allow the craft to cause spacetime to bend, much like spacetime bends in the intense gravitational field of a black hole. This mode of travel is one of the two methods of propulsion that are used by the disc. In the first mode, the disc's gravity amplifiers are in the "delta configuration" and are pulsed sequentially in a rotational pattern. The ability to direct gravity to cause spacetime distortion allows the disc to cross vast expanses of spacetime without traveling in a linear mode at a high rate of speed.

Within the backward engineered spacecraft Lazar worked on, Element 115 had a twofold purpose. First, it is the source of a gravity wave that is currently undisclosed by Earth's scientists. Second, it is the source of the anti-matter radiation, a reaction which will provide power. Inside the reactor, Element 115 is transmutated to Element 116 which is unstable and immediately decays, releasing anti-matter. The anti-matter reacts with the gaseous matter which causes a total annihilation reaction. Bob Lazar's Element 115 flying discs, used to make the wedge for the "Sport Model" Flying Disc Anti-Matter Reactor that he worked on, would have been the isotope of Element 115 containing the magic number of 184 neutrons, therefore, having an atomic mass of 299.

SPEED OF LIGHT

Light is an electromagnetic wave. The magnetic portions are never conserved. A positive and negative charge, a proton and electron, each creates its own force field of electro-static energy, not electromagnetic energy. Once this electrical field is put into motion, it creates the magnetic portion of the field out of nothing. Thus, the magnetic components of force are never conserved. Wherever there is a force field that operates at any point in that field, it is a function of how far away it is from the source. For example, in the case of electromagnetism, the force drops off as a function of the square of the distance. This field holds information related to the force. In ideal situations this information travels at the speed of light. The speed of light is referred to as "C" for Constant, because it never changes when measured within a vacuum. As a matter of fact, the speed of light is not always the speed of light, but it is only so within a vacuum. This speed is not even related to the properties of light. Light just happens to travel at that speed within a vacuum. It's more than the speed that electromagnetic waves propagate throughout space; it is also the speed in which gravity information transfers or carries. Gravity and electromagnetism both travel at C, as this is the speed of all information propagation within a vacuum.

Light only "travels" in discreet amounts or packets. But is there a limit to how low or how small an amount of light can be emitted? The smallest amount of electro-magnetism that can possibly be emitted is a photon, or as Einstein referred to it, as light quanta, or a quantum of light. This is a *virtual* particle, not a real particle like a proton or electron, but it contains particle properties which become apparent in the photoelectric effect, which was the experiment that inspired Einstein. Light gets slowed down inside a glass or even in water. This is what causes light diffraction or a prism. Atoms are made of 99% vacuum. Atoms are able to absorb and re-emit photons, but every time they do re-emit a photon, it is in a completely random direction, not the direction from which it was absorbed. This is why only low levels of gamma rays and x-rays leave the sun. Most of it is thermal heat and light visible to the human eye.

The speed of light is actually slowed down by the electronic structure of atoms and is truly adjustable in a medium. In 2003, Harvard University physicists were able to bring light to a complete halt for a fraction of a second before sending it on its way. They could stop it permanently if it were feasible to keep the condensate so incredibly cold for a longer period. So the condition for making both anti-gravity and cold fusion work is by slowing the speed of light in the electronic structure to match the speed of sound and the speed of light within the mechanical waves of the nuclear structure. It is important to match the speed of light within the atom and the speed of sound within the nuclei. Once those conditions are met, the energy is thus able to transfer fully from one form to another, with nothing to hinder it. Points determine the quantum structure of the atom itself where the speed of light and the speed of sound are equal. Thus for the speed of wave propagation to change, because the mass stays the same, the magnitude of forces must be changing.

Doesn't that break at least one of the laws of conservation? No, because we are not dealing with the forces themselves; we are dealing with the force's magnetic counterparts. Electricity and gravity both have magnetic components, acting as an anti-gravitational force. All of the forces have underlying symmetries wherein they have similar field components even though the effect of the field component is very different. For every one of these force components, none of them are conserved, meaning it is possible to multiply the field of all of them many-fold, and it does not break any laws of conservation because it is a purely local field. After all, we are not dealing with the actual forces themselves but simply their magnetic components. A local field does not push against the whole universe like magnetism, but curves back onto itself; it is a closed system. Such a system does not break any laws of conservation, such as real magnetism itself.

It is amazing that physicists have completely neglected to look at the magnetic counterpart of most all the forces, except electricity. Consider the seemingly colossal bonus that awaits an inventor: he or she could demonstrate the ability to produce viable low energy technologies because no laws of conservation apply. In cold fusion we need to amplify the magnetic component of these forces, and when you amplify one, you amplify them all. There is a 100% energy transfer during the quantum transition.

NEUTRALIZING GRAVITY

Albert Einstein was right again. There is a spacetime vortex around the Earth and its shape precisely matches the predictions of Einstein's theory of gravity. The Gravity Probe B experiment confirms the existence of gravitomagnetism, a force originally predicted by Einstein in his general theory of relativity. Electricity and magnetism can never be truly independent; a moving electric field produces a magnetic field, and vice versa. This is the light wave, constantly switching back to and from electric to magnetic. In a bold attempt to directly measure gravitomagnetism, NASA in 2004 launched into space the smoothest spheres ever manufactured to see how they spin. These four spheres (each roughly the size of a ping-pong ball) were the key to the ultra-precise gyroscopes at the core of the Gravity Probe B experiment. The idea behind the experiment was simple: Put a spinning gyroscope into orbit around the Earth with the spin axis pointed toward some distant star as a fixed reference point. Free from external forces, the gyroscope's axis would continue pointing at the star, and in zero gravity that fixed point would be forever. But if space is twisted, the direction of the gyroscope's axis should drift over time. By noting this change in direction relative to the star, the twists of spacetime could be measured. In practice, the experiment proved to be tremendously difficult, but also tremendously successful.

By May, 2011, after accounting for persistent background signals, the results were announced, and the gyroscopes rotated at a rate consistent with the gravitational predictions of Einstein's general theory of relativity. The results, which bolster existing findings, may have untold long-term benefits, plus the short-term benefits including better clocks and global positioning trackers.

MANIPULATING GRAVITY

Finnish scientists used electromagnetic fields to levitate frogs, plants and other organic items in the 1990s. In a popular YouTube video, a frog is seen levitating using a "10 Tesla magnetic coil using diamagnetism." Biological materials containing water were the first items levitated and then scientists went on to try other objects. Another video shows a 35-kilogram cannon ball levitating.

Indeed, laboratory experiments have allowed scientists to make at least a 1% change in the weight of objects, and that goes both ways; they can make objects about 1% heavier or 1% lighter. Of course that is a long way from holding a spacecraft up because that would require a 100% change, plus the weight of crew and cargo. Scientists have understood for about 60 years that the backward engineered craft they were studying operated on this principle. Underneath the craft are three objects that people have referred to as landing gear. They are not landing gear at all, but spheres within which a charged sphere is rotating. It is spinning on magnetic bearings. They are simply ferrite bearings permanently magnetized to the north and south poles. Our scientists have built them and checked them in the lab, and they work perfectly. They are relatively simple devices. The spheres carry an electric charge and spin on this type of bearing inside these big balls. The tilt is simply produced by rotating the sphere slightly, which bends the field. The entire process, however, is much more complicated than would appear, but these are the first steps which produce the end results, with several other steps in between. In short, there are fields around the saucers in order to hold them up, in order to produce the gravity differential and the time field differentials which are necessary to operate the crafts.

Only gravitational waves can bend light. Gravitational pull theories use subatomic particles which act as a force, a form of electromagnetic waves. Gravity is a force, or a mutual attraction of matter. As we've seen, there are two forms of gravity. First, on a sub-atomic scale, particles are holding atoms together. The second is on a larger, universal scale. These are the laws holding the planets in orbit and holding us to the ground. Gravity can bend space, distort or slow down time, and can bend light. This is why we can see the stars behind the sun that are blocked by the view of the sun, because the sun has such a tremendous gravitational field it is bending light around its mass. All forces are interrelated. When you vary one, you change the other two. Space, time, and gravity are all interrelated. Altering the gravitational field is known to decrease time and shorten the distance between locations. Whenever you are around an intense gravity field, time slows down.

If scientists resonate magnetic energy through crystals and use the principles of amplifying the energy through mass densities, and then condense the speed like a transformer, it is possible to use the Earth's magnetic field as a mechanism to move mass or craft. This is similar to a reversed bumper car being repulsed, but the field of magnetism is created by the Earth.

THE KEY TO SPACE TRAVEL

With the manipulation of space, gravity, and time, a new perspective on interstellar travel comes into view. Vast distances in space can be traveled in very little time by distorting space and time, and amplifying gravity does this. Those who study UFOs say this is how the disc crafts are able to fly in outer space. Witnesses say that when a craft is hovering and viewed from directly below, it will appear invisible, that is, the light is being refracted around it, and only the sky above it can be seen. Only when stepping away from underneath the craft can it be seen. A blue misty light is also usually visible on liftoff as a corona discharge because of the high voltage.

Colonel Philip Corso, a high-ranking military official cited earlier, came clean with what he knew about the Roswell crash and other events surrounding UFOs, particularly the high technology the U.S. Secret Government was so eager to understand. Corso admitted he was no engineer or scientist, but he had done his own research and talked with experts. Based on his investigations, he made some interesting observations on how the recovered craft could fly. He stated: "The craft was able to displace gravity through the propagation of magnetic waves, controlled by shifting the magnetic poles around the craft so as to control, or vector not a propulsion system, but the repulsion force of like charges. Once they realized this, engineers at our country's primary defense contractors raced among themselves to figure out how the craft could retain its electric capacity and how the pilots who navigated it could live within the energy field of the wave." With this discovery, only a huge amount of energy was required.

After scientists learned how the propulsion system worked, next was understanding the free energy system. With this knowledge, they could activate the craft itself and the free energy system, which was found to generate an enormous amount of energy. The energy could be formed into "balls of plasma" or a steady stream of energy. The system could generate the energy equivalent to a nuclear explosion from a range of 0.1 kT up to 350 kT, yet the energy system would release no radiation at all. The system could generate this enormous amount of power while never leaving even the slightest trace of residual radiation. This puzzled scientists. They figured out that when two hydrogen atoms approach each other, their combined energy level becomes multiplied through a strange bonding principle. It makes no difference whether the ions are positive or negative as they bond together regardless of valence. It was confirmed that inside this propulsion system, something causes these strange "unnatural" phenomena to occur. Lastly, just before the gases are "mixed," there is a form of light that is focused against the outgoing energy. This light is of a lower frequency. Normally, in accepted quantum theory, a small frequency means a lower energy. However, in this system, measuring of the lower frequency of light revealed an enormous amount of energy exerted upon the outgoing energy.

TRAVEL NEAR THE SPEED OF LIGHT

The speed of light has a universal upper limit according to Albert Einstein's equations. Light travels at 299, 611 kilometers (186,170 miles) per second. Distances between stars range from our closest solar system Alpha Centauri (4.3 light years away) to a hundred thousand light years distance to other stars on the opposite side of the Milky Way galaxy, to millions of light years between distant galaxies. The speed-of-light limit only applies to motion through four-dimensional spacetime.

According to the theory of relativity, if a person climbs into a spacecraft and sets out from the Earth at a velocity close to the velocity of light and travels out to Alpha Centauri, for example, and then turns around and comes back, people on Earth would observe that the passenger has been gone for around eight and a half years. According to the clock of the traveler who left, he has only been gone for a year. This is a result of time dilation in the theory of relativity. The spacecraft in which the astronaut is traveling is moving relative to the Earth at a velocity nearly equal to the velocity of light. The paradox arises when you consider that relative to the spacecraft, the Earth is traveling away at exactly the same velocity. Therefore, to the people on the spacecraft, who are relatively stationary, 8.5 years should have passed, and by the time the Earth comes back to them, it would have only been away a year. So it is clear that the very premise upon which the theory of relativity is predicated, namely, that if A is relative to B, then B must be relative to A, leading to an impossible paradox. However, this paradox is resolved altogether if we recognize the variable nature of time. As someone moves around from one part of the universe to another, that person will encounter all sorts of values of time in certain given intervals. Thus, here on Earth, we become slaves to the clock to the extent that we believe that the intervals ticked out by the clock are time itself (rather than our spatial perspective) so we find it very difficult to readjust.

MULTI-DIMENSIONS NEAR THE SPEED OF LIGHT

Physicists state that dimensional levels are separated by 90°. Musical notes and the chakras are also both separated by 90°. It is a number that continually appears. The dimensional levels have more to do with music and harmonics than anything else. Everything in the universe can be viewed on an atomic level and can also be seen as wave forms relating to sound. Change the base wavelength of your consciousness and, in doing so, change your body pattern to a new wave length, and you can enter into another dimension.

Scientists tell us spacetime is warping and stretching around a bubble of flat spacetime, which is mathematically consistent with general relativity. This sounds promising, but the energy requirements seem to pose an impossible problem. Modern superstring and M-brane theory imply the existence of numerous additional dimensions. Recent work indicates that these additional dimensions might be much larger than the Planck scale suggests. For example, on the very dense first dimension are crystals and plants. Small animals and insects resonate in the second dimension. Humans and larger animals resonate on the third dimension. The Sirian and Hathor ET races are said to exist on the fourth dimensional wavelength. Near the top, in the ninth dimension, the wavelengths get shorter and shorter with higher and higher energy.

Our entire universe may sit on a membrane floating in a higher-dimensional space. Extra dimensions might explain why gravity is so weak and could be the key to unifying all the forces of nature. Perhaps it is possible to lift off the membrane-universe constituting our four-dimensional spacetime, move in one of the additional dimensions where speed-of-light limits may not apply, and reenter our membrane-universe very far away. All of this is speculation of course, but it is worth noting that disappearing in place, changing shape, or sometimes jumping discontinuously from location to location is frequently reported in UFO observations. Such behavior could conceivably be associated with motion into and out of a perpendicular dimension. Just before disappearing, UFOs are uniformly seen taking a quick 90° turn.

Perhaps slipping into an interdimensional wormhole is the trick to quickly traversing the universe. Astronomers have been searching for the apparent "dark matter" that is thought to be responsible for gravitational effects in the rotations of galaxies, the viral motions in clusters of galaxies, and other astrophysical anomalies. Perhaps there is no dark matter within our universe after all. Rather, the gravitational force of matter in adjacent membrane-universes is spreading out and spilling over into our universe. In other words, other universes might exist just a tiny fraction of space away from our universe in one or more extra dimensions. This possibility allows experts to speculate that if extraterrestrial visitors are indeed investigating us, they may not be coming from distant star systems light years away in our visible universe, but rather from planets in other membrane-universes that may be among us, but not visible from our limited third-dimensional perspective.

Standing is Glenn Seaborg, who was the principal or co-discoverer of ten elements: plutonium, americium, curium, berkelium, californium, einsteinium, fermium, mendelevium, nobelium and Element 106, which was named seaborgium while he was still alive in his honor. He also developed more than 100 atomic isotopes, and is credited with important contributions to the chemistry of plutonium, originally as part of the Manhattan Project. While working on the Manhattan Project he developed the extraction process used to isolate the plutonium fuel for the second atomic bomb. On the left is Ronald Reagan, President of the United States from 1981 to 1989, and on the right is Richard Nixon, President of the United States from 1969 to 1974. The picture was taken in 1957 at a meeting held at Bohemian Grove long before either man was president.

Apple Computer's first logo, drawn around 1976, was rendered by then co-founder Ronald Wayne. The logo features Sir Isaac Newton sitting under the apple tree where he supposedly discovered gravity by an apple falling on his head. The world's largest computer company was inspired by the same "apple" Sir Isaac Newton used to postulate his theories on gravity.

Can a powerful magnet bend light? This picture would seem to confirm "yes." There is a black hole in the center of our Milky Way galaxy. Black holes are known to harbor gravity so extreme that not even light can escape. In fact, astronomers are now fairly certain that these super massive black holes are at the heart of almost every galaxy in the universe. Furthermore, the mass of these black holes is somehow tied to the mass of the rest of the galaxy. They grow in tandem with each other.

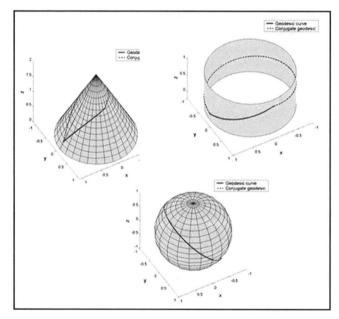

In general relativity, a geodesic generalizes the notion of a "straight line" to curved space-time. Importantly, the world line of a particle free from all external force is a particular type of geodesic. In other words, a freely moving particle always moves along a geodesic. In general relativity, gravity is not a force but is instead a curved space-time geometry where the source of curvature is the stress-energy tensor, representing matter, for instance. Thus, the path of a planet such as Earth orbiting around a star like our Sun is the projection of a geodesic of the curved 4-D spacetime geometry around the star onto 3-D space, also known as our reality.

UFOs COSMIC TOP SECRET

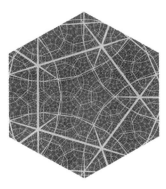

"It is a fraud for the U.S. government to pretend that it is not interested in UFOs. In fact, it has been a matter of high and probably pre-eminent interest for decades." –Paul Hellyer, former Canadian Minister of National Defense

EPPUR *si muove* is an Italian phrase meaning "And yet it moves," famously uttered by the Italian mathematician, physicist and philosopher Galileo Galilei after being forced to recant in 1633 before the Inquisition, his belief that the Earth moves around the Sun. Galileo asked the priests during his trial to look through the telescope, but they refused, because they knew they would see something that they did not want to accept. It would seem the same is true with the UFO phenomenon today.

We can offer a definition of UFOs that you may find useful when you study the subject: A UFO is the reported sighting of an object or light seen in the sky or on land, whose appearance, trajectory, actions, motions, lights, and colors do not have a logical, conventional, or natural explanation, and which cannot be explained, not only by the original witness, but by scientists or technical experts who try to make a common sense identification after examining the evidence. UFOlogists and private UFO organizations are found throughout the United States.

Since Biblical times humans have witnessed and recorded strange manifestations in the sky and speculated on the possibilities of visitors from another world. Today, the airline pilots of the world, from the skies of California to the fields of Kansas to the rice patties of the Orient, have regularly and persistently reported sightings of Unidentified Flying Objects, which are also called flying saucers. UFOs are real if you read the case reports from ordinary citizens and thousands of flight and military personnel. There are 12,000+ case files that have been reported to the U.S. Air Force from 1947 to 1968; of these, 701 are still classified as true unknowns.

While ET observation and interaction with Earth is probably an ancient phenomenon, as opposed to a purely modern occurrence, the marked increase in activity coinciding with World War II and the dawning of the "nuclear age" indicates that ETs are quite concerned about this transitional stage of human social evolution. They are particularly worried about human nuclear weapon technology and its potential for worldwide destruction, and possibly for its potential threat to ETs, although this is minimal. Some benevolent ET beings are greatly interested in our peaceful transition to a world society, international peace, and the establishment of a just, effective and representative world government.

ET technology is strictly guarded by both ETs and human governmental agencies because of its potential for military applications which would greatly threaten world security. It is imperative to the benevolent ETs that this technology not gain significant human applications until such a time as the Earth attains international peace and an effective world government free from corruption.

The U.S. Government, at least at the level of a highly compartmentalized above top secret group, has known about the reality of UFOs and their occupants since at least 1947. A strict secrecy and a worldwide cover-up of these facts has been maintained because there is a fear of public panic and social disruption if this information is known, reminiscent of the hysteria caused in 1938 when Orson Welles broadcast a phony alien invasion story. Of course there are major security issues surrounding possible military and technology applications of ET hardware, especially during the last half century of a world beset with Cold War tensions and competing interests.

MOST PEOPLE ARE TRUE BELIEVERS

According to a report by the United Nations, since 1947 over 150 million people have been witnesses to UFO sightings throughout the world. More than 20,000 of those have been documented landings. Even if we can discount 90% as misperceptions or hoaxes, that leaves far too many credible events documented many times over by high-ranking government and military officials. Consider also the careful research of countless engineers and scientists who say the evidence is irrefutable and who logically attribute to our alien counterparts the same kind of careful, sophisticated, efficient, high-tech exploration, especially those who likely are far more advanced than we. In addition, the kinds of contacts reported and objects sighted range from little floating orbs the size of a baseball to enormous lighted spacecrafts bigger than an aircraft carrier. So, there are countless manifestations of alien activity in addition to the more common flying discs.

At the beginning of the 21st century, the overwhelming majority of Americans reported they believed that UFOs are real, and that these crafts are most likely guided by intelligent beings from other worlds or dimensions. A Roper poll conducted in the USA reported that over 70% of the population believes that the government is not telling the public everything it knows about UFOs and extraterrestrials. One in 12 Americans claim to have personally seen a UFO. And this belief is formulated with no prompting whatsoever by the U.S. Government. Are that many of us unbalanced to believe this? Is this the greatest mythology of all time stirring within us? Or is this an awareness of a collective unconscious memory surfacing?

To claim, as some people still do, that there is no evidence suggestive of intelligent extraterrestrial life visiting our planet simply belies the facts. The deniers include the many branches of the U.S. military, media, and government-funded science programs such as NASA and FERMI Labs. UFO sightings are global in nature, especially since there are too many hard sensor data-points to ignore, plus literally millions of eyewitnesses. It is only through ignorance or pomposity that one can say no evidence exists.

The mainstream scientific community also remains uninterested in and scornfully dismissive of the question of the reality of UFOs, or the possibility of intelligent extraterrestrial life visiting Earth. This is in spite of scientists and astronomers discovering billions of new, potentially inhabitable, planets and never before seen solar systems; documenting new exotic life forms on Earth that thrive in extreme environments previously thought to be uninhabitable; and uncover tantalizing hints of life on at least 10 planetary bodies within our own solar system. Yet, for reasons which we shall attempt to resolve, mainstream scientists continue to mock and deride those who take the phenomenon of UFOs seriously.

Contrary to popular accounts in the mainstream media and many scholarly articles on UFOs, the phenomenon is frequently reported by scientists, military personnel, police officers, as well as commercial and private airplane pilots. There have been literally millions of sightings in over a hundred countries around the world. Jimmy Carter claims to have seen a UFO before he became president. Also contrary to popular belief, UFO reports are not limited to rural areas or confined to the United States. The phenomenon has been reported in about 150 nations and over major metropolitan areas in America, the UK, the former Soviet Union, Germany, France, Spain, all the Scandinavian countries, China, Japan, South Korea, Australia, New Zealand, throughout Africa and Central and South America, and at both the North and South Poles. In Hessdalen, Norway there are so many UFO sightings that a permanent webcam has been set up, with amazing results. UFOs have also been reported repeatedly over civilian and military nuclear facilities; at military bases in the U.S. and worldwide; above and beneath the surface of the Earth's oceans; and outside the Earth's atmosphere.

All kinds of people see UFOs. It does not matter whether you are rich or poor, educated or uneducated, young or old. In fact, most people who report seeing UFOs were not even looking for them when they had their sighting. The chances for seeing a UFO are greater for those people who live in small towns or in the country and are outside late at night. Even though most have never seen a UFO, some say that seeing one when they were children or young adults sparked their interest in UFOs. Many UFO researchers argue that UFOs have appeared throughout history. There are many myths, legends, and stories that tell of strange things seen in the sky or beings that came from above to help humans develop civilization. Because modern scholars cannot directly check the facts of these stories, it is impossible to determine if these are accurate reports of true events. Caution should be taken when evaluating many UFO news items. Readers are encouraged to investigate and research information pertaining to UFOs on an individual basis so they can draw their own conclusions.

But let's be honest. If the only strange things seen in the sky were a few oddly moving lights, or some specks glinting in the sun, there would be no UFO question. If there were no human abductions or cattle mutilations, there would be no inquiry. But there have been many close observations of these strange objects along with first-hand experiences. Plus, physical traces of various kinds have been left behind, and witnesses have experienced physical and medical effects, including injury, implants and death. If we can narrow down all of the reported sightings to between 5% and 25%, depending on the sample, then even this is enough to warrant expert examination. Even 1% would deserve attention. And the disturbing truth is that the USA and UK governments have been complicit with a certain minority group of malevolent ETs, enabling them to do harmful things to people and animals, all the while hushing up their presence in a tangled web of secret agreements run amuck.

COSMIC TOP SECRET

For those who believe there is validity in the UFO phenomenon, the study of UFOs can be broken up into four primary groups. First are those who firmly believe the phenomena involves alien beings from other star systems. The second, although declining in popularity, are those who feel UFO sightings are an effect of the human mind, perhaps summoning up deep ancestral memories—an "expression of our longing for wholeness" as Carl Jung described the phenomenon. Jung published his 1959 book *Flying Saucers,* predicting, "We are nearing the great change." There is a third camp who claim all UFOs are exclusively human-constructed, highly advanced flying crafts based on Tesla technology, produced entirely by the black operations of the secret government. Finally, there is a growing faction of those who think the "crafts" are the result of time or dimensional travel, or that they arrive from another universe which is coexisting simultaneously with ours, within the so-called "multiverse." With 200 billion known galaxies, ours is but one universe in a much wider entity encompassing millions, or billions of other universes in the multiverse, each with varying physical laws, sizes, and dimensional foundations.

The U.S. Government, and particularly CIA and NSA intelligence departments, have demonstrated time and again that they will go to extreme lengths to cover up the issue. The U.S. intelligence agencies, along with our NATO partners, classify anything UFO or ET-related as "Cosmic Top Secret." The idea that the CIA has secretly concealed its research regarding UFOs has been a major theme of researchers since the modern UFO phenomena emerged in the late 1940s.

MORE TOP SECRET THAN THE H-BOMB

Penalties for disclosing classified information concerning extraterrestrials have always been quite severe. In December 1953, the Joint Chiefs of Staff issued Army-Navy-Air Force publication #146 that made the unauthorized release of information concerning UFOs a crime under the Espionage Act, punishable by up to 10 years in prison and a $10,000 fine. A strange policy for a phenomenon the U.S. Government maintains never existed.

The following passage describes the official secrecy policy adopted in April 1954, during the time frame when President Eisenhower was making ET contact. "Any encounter with entities known to be of extraterrestrial origin is to be considered to be a matter of national security and therefore classified TOP SECRET. Under no circumstances is the general public or the public press to learn of the existence of these entities. The official government policy is that such creatures do not exist, and that no agency of the federal government is now engaged in any study of extraterrestrials or their artifacts. Any deviation from this stated policy is absolutely forbidden."

On July 11, 1934, the first treaty between the Small Greys from the Orion star system (who are approximately a meter tall with large wraparound eyes) and the U.S. federal government under President Franklin Delano Roosevelt, occurred aboard a naval ship at the port city of Balboa, Panama. This was one of the most important events in human history because it thrust us into a role we were not prepared for, namely, becoming host to a highly unpredictable (seemingly malevolent) extraterrestrial race. The intent was to renew the treaty every ten years, and in 1944 it was quickly passed because the U.S. was still fighting in World War II.

The Greys said they would provide advanced technology in exchange for being allowed to conduct genetic experiments. From the start, the Americans stated they would only agree to the terms if a list of abductees was provided to the government and the abductees returned unharmed with their memories of the event erased. The Greys provided anti-gravity devices, metals and alloys, free energy, and medical technology in return for allowing them to operate on their own terms. Unbeknownst to the Americans at the time, they would also infiltrate human society on all levels. In addition, they began to replace important world leaders with clones under their control. This information, when understood only by a select few, was kept on a strictly need-to-know basis within the government and secret services. These were the select few officials, some believe, who basically sold out the human race.

FIRST AND SECOND PRESIDENTIAL MEETINGS

About two decades later, after the first military contact in Panama during FDR's administration, a sitting U.S. president made the first known face-to-face meeting with living ETs. During the evening and early hours of February 20-21, 1954, while on a "vacation" in Palm Springs, California, President Dwight D. Eisenhower went missing and allegedly was taken to nearby Muroc Airfield (later renamed Edwards Air Force Base) for a secret meeting. When he reappeared the next morning at a church service in Los Angeles, reporters were told that he had to have emergency dental treatment the previous evening and had visited a local dentist. The dentist later appeared at a function that evening and presented himself to reporters as the doctor who had treated Eisenhower. The missing night and morning has subsequently fueled rumors that Eisenhower was using the alleged dentist visit as a cover story for an extraordinary event. The event is possibly the most significant that any American president could have conducted, an alleged "First Contact" presidential meeting with extraterrestrials at Muroc, and the beginning of a series of meetings with different extraterrestrial races.

Another important meeting had occurred a few months earlier with extraterrestrials who had a distinctive "Nordic" appearance, also called the Tall Whites. Researcher William Cooper and others note that first contact with the Tall Whites took place at Homestead Air Base in Florida, but Ike was not present. They looked so similar to us that they could have passed for humans had they been wearing heavy clothes and sunglasses. But upon closer examination they were quite different, having larger and differently colored eyes, very white skin, and platinum blonde hair. They were called the "Etherians," and allowed Air Force officials to inspect the five crafts in which they arrived for the prearranged meeting. This benevolent ET group warned us against harmful aliens that were then orbiting above the equator, plus offered to help humankind with our collective spiritual development. They demanded that we dismantle and destroy our nuclear weapons as the major condition for their assistance. They refused to exchange technology, citing that we were spiritually unable to handle the technology which we already possessed. They believed that we would use any new technology to destroy each other. This race stated that we were on a path of self destruction and we must stop killing each other, stop polluting the Earth, stop raping the Earth's natural resources, and learn to live in harmony. These terms were met with extreme suspicion, especially the major condition of nuclear disarmament. Military top brass believed that meeting the condition of disarmament would leave us helpless in the face of an obvious malevolent alien threat. We also had nothing in history to help us with the decision. Nuclear disarmament was not considered to be within the best interest of the United States. The overtures were rejected.

About a year later, on February 11, 1955, at Holloman Air Force Base in New Mexico, President Eisenhower had a "Second Contact" meeting with ETs, which lasted for about 45 minutes. What was intriguing about the incident was that the president was able to sneak away from 30 or so reporters while on a bird hunting expedition near Thomasville, Georgia, during a period of high international tension with China over Formosa (now called Taiwan). After Ike's arrival at Holloman on the Columbine III aircraft, two UFOs flew over the flight line, and one landed near the plane. Ike then went aboard a saucer-shaped craft to meet with the Greys. This led to an eventual re-signing of a technology-sharing agreement now called the "Greada Treaty," sometimes spelled the "Grenada Treaty." Under the Eisenhower Administration, a third 10-year treaty extension with the Greys and the U.S. Government was signed, now under a new name. These ETs, whom Ike met with, were the same race that crashed at Roswell seven and a half years earlier. They stated that their planet was dying and they needed a safe quarter on Earth to conduct genetic experiments which would help their race to survive. It was speculated that they reproduced by cloning themselves and this technique lacked genetic variety and had weakened them over eons of time. A secure base was to be provided for them in exchange for certain "advanced technology" that the aliens agreed to share with the military.

GREADA TREATY GONE BAD

After Eisenhower decided to ally with the Greys, a joint ET/U.S. Military underground base was started in Nevada at a remote location in the Nellis Air Force Base. The area was designated S-4, about 10 kilometers south of Area 51, known as "Dreamland." It would not be the only underground base, as a facility below Dulce, New Mexico was also constructed for their "quarters" at this time. The intent of the Greada Treaty was that alien technology was to be traded for permission to engage in human abductions and cattle mutilations for their research purposes. Before fully siding with the Greys, the motivations of each extraterrestrial race was considered by the military brass who were involved in these treaty discussions. They opted for secrecy and acquiring advanced technology over the spiritual development of the human race.

In exchange for the transfer of advanced technology, the Greys were again given permission to abduct humans on a limited basis for the purpose of medical examinations and monitoring. These living tissue samples had something vital to do with their own genetic experiments for survival of their species. Since their knowledge of biology seemed so far beyond our own comprehension, their motives were never adequately explained. The stipulation was that the humans would never be harmed, would be safely returned to their point of abduction, and that the humans would have no traumatic memories of the event. Also, the aliens would provide a detailed list of all abductees to a special group called MJ-12 who would monitor their compliance.

Although the National Security Council had an agreement with the "Big-Nosed Greys" as they were called, the reptoids would provide a periodic list of abductees to MJ-12, the original top secret panel tasked to interface with all things pertaining to UFOs and ETs. Within a short time it became obvious to the Eisenhower Administration that these Greys had broken the Greada Treaty and were abducting far more people than they reported, including large numbers of children, some never returned. Horrified by the betrayal of the Big-Nosed Greys, the government further suppressed any public knowledge of the aliens, realizing their own culpability for their betrayal of humanity. As Colonel Philip Corso revealed in his book *The Day After Roswell:* "Hide the truth and the truth becomes your enemy. Disclose the truth and it becomes your weapon." The Regressive reptoids knew their presence on Earth would be covered up at all costs, so they could treat us without accountability. An assessment was made and it was determined that the U.S. Armed Forces lacked the resources to fight them and so it was decided that the military should continue the agreement, even though it had already been violated, and to focus on exploiting the relationship with the Greys to gain even more advanced technology.

The ULTRA unit was one of the most elite and super secret programs of the National Security Council, which became the NSA faction later in time, and was originally run by Project Paperclip Nazis who were part of the NSC after 1945. All ULTRA members were cloned humans. Although there are several ET labs in America and the UK, the best-known U.S.-Grey base is underneath the Ute Indian Reservation near Dulce, New Mexico. It is supposedly devoted to inter-species genetic engineering on the lowest levels, and humans are no longer allowed to enter. If caught, they are immediately killed.

FUNDING THE BLACK OPERATIONS

A multi-billion tax-dollar secret fund was organized and maintained by the Military Office of the White House in 1957, by order of President Eisenhower, ostensibly to build secret underground bunkers for the president and Congress in case of military attacks. Later, when much more funding was needed, the appropriations were supplied by "black" projects contained in the defense budget, and not subject to review.

Justification on the part of the USA for funding these black projects was that we have gained backward engineered high technology, sometimes with major military advantage. The best example is Stealth aircraft, which utilize ET metals, skins, coatings, and residues that are also used on other aircraft and submarines. There are lasers that can melt through rock (using extreme heat vitrification) which are used to tunnel an extensive network of train tubes, and create the underground bases. We now have infrared satellites that can see through walls, Kevlar, Velcro, transistors, and titanium—all items backward engineered from alien technology.

Today, over 500 billion dollars per year must be spent to maintain the Black Ops. By some estimates, the Black Budget consists of one quarter of the GNP of the USA. Much of the Black Ops budget was used to create at least 129 deep underground bases built since the 1940s. Mach-2 electric trains connect each of these, and each base usually has multiple levels. The Dulce base for example has at least seven levels, and the lowest level is about four kilometers deep. Located here is the underground alien biogenetic base, where malevolent aliens need unseen quarters to conduct their experiments. For allowing their cover, the Greys have given the Black Ops anti-gravity propulsion technology, advanced computer technology, biological warfare technology, advanced genetic sciences, quantum technology, genome medicine, and much more.

In an ironic twist of fate, we are reminded of the 2.3-trillion dollars reported missing from the Pentagon budget by then Secretary Donald Rumsfeld on September 10, 2001, the day before two planes took out three buildings in New York City. The "ironic twist of fate" is that all of the documentation of the missing trillions was stored in the ill-fated Building 7 at the World Trade Center, and a missile struck the Pentagon where an audit was under way. After 9-11, this missing fund was never mentioned again.

TAKE THE JOHN LEAR TEST

John Lear, son of the Lear Jet founder, has an impressive resume. He is a former Lockheed L-1011 Captain who flew over 150 test aircraft and held 18 world flight speed records. During the late 1960's, 1970's and early 1980's he was a contract pilot for the CIA. John Lear developed a close relationship with CIA Director (DCI) William Colby who was in charge of covert operations in Vietnam before becoming DCI. Lear was an accomplished pilot, had inside connections with the CIA, and knew many influential politicians and high technology aerospace contractors. After he became a UFO whistleblower, he devised a test that would take on his name. The "John Lear Test" goes like this: As a world leader, you'd have a chance to make a fully truthful presentation of all the knowledge the USA has on ET technology. If fully aware of all the pros and cons, would you choose to disclose? You'd have to consider the assumption that some people would go berserk. Would it also mean the end of organized religion? Would society collapse? Maybe it would take down the government, disturb the world, or even the universe? Could you personally bear the consequences of disclosure? "Take John Lear's word as gospel if you want to take the test," suggested Art Bell, former host of *Coast to Coast*, who remarked that he personally would not disclose after taking the John Lear Test.

What is also at stake is the possibility that reality may be far more complex than our modern scientific notions of space, time and matter currently allows. Mystics might be quite pleased with the knowledge that other levels of reality exist, but for a civilization built around commerce and technology entirely grounded in physical reality, the news of other realms beyond our own comprehension, or higher intelligences who might be manipulating us, could be quite disruptive. The shock for our collective reality could lead to chaos. This justifiable fear is the primary rationale for the near century-long secrecy.

OUTSPOKEN CANADIAN

Wilbert Smith was an employee (a senior minister) at the Canadian Department of Transport. As a trusted colleague he wrote a top secret memorandum to the Controller of Communications, dated November 21, 1950, asking permission to set up a group to study the geomagnetic aspects of UFO propulsion systems. As part of his memorandum, Smith said that he had made discreet inquiries through the Canadian embassy staff in Washington D.C. where he obtained the following information:

(a) *The matter is the most highly classified subject in the United States Government, rating higher even than the H-bomb.*

(b) *Flying saucers exist.*

(c) *Their modus operandi is unknown, but a concentrated effort is being made by a small group, headed by Dr. Vannevar Bush.*

(d) *The entire matter is considered by the United States authorities to be of tremendous significance.*

He also noted that Dr. Vannevar Bush, one of America's pre-eminent scientists, along with a team of experts he had assembled, was already backward engineering UFOs by 1950. They were interested in the combined art and science of analyzing recovered objects, in this case parts of a crashed vehicle, in order to determine its characteristics for possible replication or adaptation.

OUTSPOKEN ASTRONAUT

While working with a camera crew supervising flight testing of advanced aircraft at Edwards Air Force Base, California, the camera crew filmed the landing of a strange disc object that flew in over their heads and landed on a dry lake nearby. As camera crewmen approached the saucer, it rose up above the area and flew off at a speed faster than any known aircraft. NASA Astronaut, L. Gordon Cooper was with this group and observed firsthand both UFOs in flight and extraterrestrials. In his words: "While flying with several other USAF pilots over Germany in 1957, we sighted numerous radiant flying discs above us. We couldn't tell how high they were. We couldn't get anywhere near their altitude."

Astronaut Cooper recounted the first time he encountered ETs close up:

"I was furthermore a witness to an extraordinary phenomenon, here on this planet Earth. It happened a few months ago in Florida. There I saw with my own eyes a defined area of ground being consumed by flames, with four indentations left by a flying object which had descended in the middle of a field. Beings had left the craft (there were other traces to prove this). They seemed to have studied topography, they had collected soil samples and, eventually, they returned to where they had come from, disappearing at enormous speed. I happen to know that authority did just about everything to keep this incident from the press and TV, in fear of a panicky reaction from the public."

SMALLER NATIONS USED TO BE IN LOCK-STEP

Aware of alien encounters since at least the Roswell crash, President Truman created the National Security Agency (NSA) in 1952 with the original goal of deciphering alien language and establishing communication. The NSA is even more secretive than the CIA, and both have influence over NASA and NATO. One of the conditions the U.S. Secret Service make upon other countries that receive financial aid is that any information pertaining to ETs or UFOs must remain concealed. When Ronald Reagan was president he ordered that no person or country doing any kind of business with the U.S. Government could discuss UFOs. Reagan deeply classified everything pertaining to UFOs. Nobody who did any work with the government was allowed to talk about the subject, even if they worked with unclassified material.

In recent decades, military and government officials outside the U.S. have come to the conclusion that UFO disclosure would not necessarily compromise national security, nor would it pose a threat to citizens. For this reason many countries of the world have broken from U.S. policy and have started to make surprising revelations: Official pronouncements state that UFOs are real. The governments of Belgium, France, Brazil, UK, Russia, Italy, Denmark, Sweden, Norway, New Zealand, Canada, Uruguay and Australia have opened a portion of their UFOs files to the citizens of their countries.

Unfortunately, the U.S. Government shows no sign of backing down from its position of complete denial. Even as other governments around the world are disclosing more and more information, the U.S. Government continues to cover up evidence by denying eyewitness accounts, confiscating military records and video footage, and suppressing information from people who claim to have direct contact with ETs, or compelling photographic evidence of UFOs. A common tactic is to provide alternative explanations. They frequently point to swamp gases, light aberrations, atmospheric phenomena, weather balloons, misidentified aircraft, and hoaxes. For example, in January of 2008, dozens of witnesses reported seeing a UFO in Stephenville, Texas. Despite sincere and detailed witness accounts, the military discounted the entire event, pointing to "optical illusions" and "superior mirages." A logical question is what does the U.S. Government have at stake in the UFO issue, and what it could stand to lose if there was worldwide disclosure.

HACKING COSMIC TOP SECRET

The British systems administrator Gary McKinnon, who gained access to 97 U.S. military and NASA websites in the early 2000s, has become a UFO folk hero of sorts. He intended to find top-secret files regarding free energy but stumbled upon something much bigger. McKinnon claimed to have uncovered a spreadsheet containing names and information about "non-terrestrial officers" and transfers between fleets. He cross-referenced these names with a database of all U.S. Navy and military personnel but was unable to find any of the officers. McKinnon therefore concluded they were not of this world and labeled them as "Space Marines." It was not long before he was caught. After admitting his actions, McKinnon was originally given a six-month community service penalty in his home country. This ballooned into a 60-70 year prison sentence and millions of dollars in fines if he would be extradited to the USA, but extradition was eventually denied by the UK. Musical artists Sir Bob Geldof, David Gilmour and Chrissie Hynde have recorded music to prevent the extradition of McKinnon to the USA. An undisclosed military source reportedly said that they were concerned about what else McKinnon might have seen in his wanderings around the world's worst kept secret, but maybe has not yet disclosed or divulged to WikiLeaks. This begs the question. Why pursue this man with such a heavy hand who fell for a "hoax," set up for some reason on unsecured military computers, if there are no such things as UFOs?

McKinnon had heard that the Johnson Space Center Building 8 had people erasing, airbrushing, and manipulating evidence of UFOs from high-resolution satellite images. He found his way into the computers at Building 8 and located the file folders. They were named "raw" and "edited," and he was able to download large images in NASA's proprietary graphic format. He saw a huge cigar-shaped object with geodesic domes at its ends, with no sign of riveting or other manufacturing. The photo was apparently taken from a satellite looking down onto the alien object. Was it ours or theirs? He was disconnected before he could save the image, and Gary was subsequently tracked down and arrested by the British High Tech Crime Unit. Although threatened with extradition, in reality he did them a favor by showing how pitiful their "security" systems were. He also did the rest of us a favor. He exposed U.S. Navy Space Command's Solar Warden program. It is clear now that NASA can be seen as merely a cover for the real space program.

STILL PAYING THE PRICE OF SECRECY

The extent of the "treaty" mistake was greatly underestimated. Not only do the disturbing abductions and the hybrid program continue to this day, but the "research and development" of alien technology has been exploited almost exclusively for defense contractors and kept secret. Some in the military have expressed an uncertainty and mistrust regarding ET motives and their ultimate intentions. There is already embarrassment and consternation over the human military inability to secure world air space from repeated UFO penetrations; add to this the embarrassment resulting from disclosures concerning how this matter has been handled, such as the harassment and ridicule of whistleblowing civilians or military personnel, and the withholding of vital information from the public and Congress.

With each continuation treaty with the Greys, the secret government within the Military Industrial Extraterrestrial Complex (MEIC) is becoming more and more advanced and insidious. There are now select groups of humans who are living lives literally thousands of years more advanced than the Earth's civilian population. These people are described as a "breakaway civilization." For every one year that goes by since the start of these treaties in 1934, military technology advances by 44 years. Every now and then, the public gets a new computer or some other piece of technology from the MIEC, but these are just little trinkets comparable to when the early white American settlers gave beads to the Indians. Nothing of real importance, such as interstellar craft or free energy, is divulged.

Granted, we were given microcircuits, semiconductors and exotic elements, but the real technological benefits were seized by defense contractors to make miniaturized atomic bombs and other weapons of mass destruction. The advances in biology were applied to biological warfare and may have resulted in some of the retroviruses or Morgellons that are currently perplexing biologists. But the main benefits, namely the technology associated with the UFO propulsion systems and free energy generators, are the real "gifts" that the people of Earth are denied knowledge of and not allowed to utilize. The Powers That Be know that the benevolent technologies would transform our civilization almost overnight, particularly related to energy sources. Free energy alone would shuffle the balance of resources and power, with more directed to the Earth's population.

In the last few decades there have been a few brave whistleblowers, and some have made the ultimate sacrifice. Dulce underground base whistleblower Phil Schneider was first tortured then strangled to death by catheter tubing in his Portland, Oregon apartment in January, 1996. William Cooper was shot to death by deputies outside his Arizona house in November, 2001. There are many others who have revealed their secrets and then have disappeared without a trace. Others retracted their stories and never spoke out again. And on it goes.

Newly declassified government files on UFOs seen in the UK from 1985 to 2007 reveal that the Ministry of Defense (MoD), the UK equivalent to the Pentagon, did not make much effort over the years to investigate these strange sightings that continued to be reported. BBC News quotes National Archives consultant David Clarke as saying, "One of the most interesting documents in the files is a piece from an intelligence officer, who basically says that despite thousands of reports that they've received since the Second World War, they've never done any study or spent any money or time on the subject, and they say that people just won't believe that when they find out." The people in charge, those who have the responsibility for disclosure, apparently do not care to share any of this information on UFOs with anyone, for their own reasons. And on it goes.

BACKED INTO A CORNER

How would U.S. citizens react to the knowledge that tens of trillions of dollars have been spent on unauthorized, secret and unconstitutional projects over the decades? And that these taxpayer dollars have been used by corporate partners in total secrecy to develop spin-off technologies based on the study of ET objects which were later patented and used in highly profitable technologies? Not only have the taxpayers been defrauded, they have also paid a premium for such breakthroughs which were the result of research funded by their tax dollars.

Advanced technologies which have been identified from the study of these anti-gravity vehicles, once disclosed, will replace the currently used forms of energy generation and propulsion. Fossil fuels, nuclear energy, and airplane transportation will become obsolete. Free energy technologies will enable the Earth to attain a sustainable civilization without pollution, energy shortages, or global warming. These technologies are already fully operational. They have been developed within super-secret, unacknowledged special access projects. In short, the definitive solution to the world's energy, pollution, and poverty problems exists within compartmentalized projects that need a planned disclosure and relevant legislation.

The program controlling these issues continue to operate outside of legally required Congressional oversight. Even recent presidents have been left out of the loop, deliberately deceived, and denied full access. Therefore, urgent action is needed on the part of Congress, the White House, and other institutions to obtain the necessary oversight and control of these operations to ensure that these now-classified technologies are announced for world cooperative energy generation and propulsion.

The secrecy is about much more than an exotic propulsion system back-engineered from a flying saucer. It is about the control of energy production. Fuel is something that just about everyone in the world needs. Because the Military Industrial Extraterrestrial Complex controls these discoveries, and because of their error that resulted in abductions and potential displacement of humanity by hybrids, this remains the most secret information on the planet.

This controller elite includes terrestrial governments, including members of the executive, legislative, and judicial branches in the USA, media organizations, influential international organizations, and military and intelligence organizations that may be populated by hybrid clones, or implanted humans under the command and control of the reptilian faction whose intent may be to take over the Earth. And they know we the people are powerless to stop them, or they believe that we are. The sheer audacity of making these unreal claims is their greatest protection. Who could possibly believe this most esoteric of all claims? And what is it that they possess that the controllers want more than anything? We'll see in the next chapter.

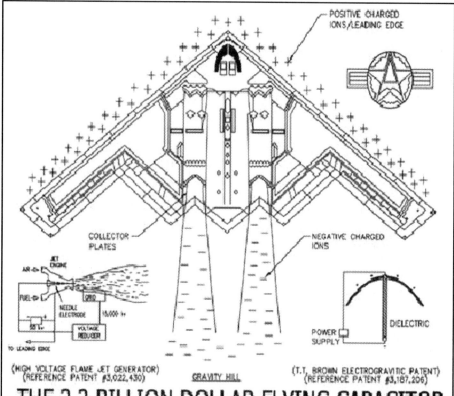

THE 2.3 BILLION DOLLAR FLYING CAPACITOR

AVIATION WEEK AND SPACE TECHNOLOGY (MARCH 9, 1992) REPORTED THAT THE NORTHROP B-2 ATB STEALTH BOMBER UTILIZES A NUMBER OF CLASSIFIED "BLACK" TECHNOLOGIES DESIGNED TO ENHANCE IT'S "STEALTH" CAPABILITIES. ONE TECHNIQUE REPORTED IN THE AVIATION WEEK ARTICLE INDICATED THAT THE B-2 ELECTRICALLY CHARGES IT'S WING LEADING EDGE TO REDUCE THE RCS (RADAR CROSS SECTION). THE ARTICLE WENT ON TO SAY THAT THE EXHAUST GASSES OF THE B-2 ARE NEGATIVELY CHARGED TO REDUCE IT'S INFRARED SIGNATURE (IR). THIS PROCESS OF POSITIVELY CHARGING THE LEADING EDGE, AND NEGATIVELY CHARGING THE EXHAUST GASSES IS VIRTUALLY IDENTICAL TO THE ELECTROGRAVITIC PROPULSION SYSTEM DEVELOPED BY THOMAS TOWNSEND BROWN IN 1965. THIS SYSTEM PRODUCES A GRAVITY "WELL" IN FRONT OF THE CRAFT, AND A GRAVITY "HILL" BEHIND THE CRAFT, WHICH ALLOWS THE B-2 TO RIDE ON A "GRAVITY WAVE", SIMILAR TO A SURFER RIDING A WAVE ON THE OCEAN. THE FOUR F-118-GE-100 ENGINES INSIDE THE B-2 SERVE AS "FLAME JET GENERATORS", PRODUCING UP TO 100 MEGAWATTS OF ELECTRICAL POWER. THIS ELECTRICAL POWER CAN BE STORED DIRECTLY INSIDE THE STRUCTURE OF THE B-2 WHICH IS PRIMARILY MADE UP OF AN ADVANCED DIELECTRIC CERAMIC MATERIAL, AND ESSENTUALLY TURNS THE B-2 INTO ONE LARGE CAPACITOR. ONCE THE "GRAVITY WAVE" IS ESTABLISHED, THE ENGINES ON THE B-2 CAN BE SHUT DOWN, TURNING THE CRAFT INTO AN "OVERUNITY DEVICE", THAT CAN FLY AT SUPERSONIC SPEED, WITH AN UNLIMITED RANGE.

Whistleblowing engineers revealed that ET technology has been utilized on many crafts, including the B-2 Stealth Bomber. One of them referenced Townsend Brown's Electrogravitic (U.S. Patent #3,187,206), which specifically describes how the B-2 electrically charges the leading edge of the wing to reduce the radar cross section. Then it negatively charges the exhaust gases to reduce the infrared signature. The B-2 is essentially a flying capacitor.

Project Paperclip rocket scientist Dr. Wernher von Braun is seen working alongside the seated American astronaut L. Gordon Cooper.

COLD WAR ERA ROCKET?

TRIDENT II (D5) MISSILE
SAID LAUNCHED BY NAVY

BLUE LIGHT OVER CALIFORNIA
NOVEMBER 7, 2015

...OR EXOTIC ENERGY WEAPONS?

YOU DECIDE.

NORWAY SPIRAL ON DECEMBER 9, 2009

LIGHT OVER HANGZHOU, CHINA, ON JULY 9, 2010
CCCPUBLISHING.COM/FUTURESOTERIC

A Chinese airport was closed in July, 2010, after the mysterious object on the bottom right was seen streaking across the sky. Arcing over Zhejiang's provincial capital Hangzhou, the streaking light appeared to glow with a white light and left a bright trail in its wake. Xiaoshan Airport was closed after the UFO was detected at around 9 p.m. and dozens of flights had to be diverted. A very similar incident occured on November 7, 2015 over five western states and two countries. The bright erergy weapon, or as the Navy called a "missile launch," was witnessed by thousands of people from northern Mexico to San Francisco, CA, and as far east as Nevada and western Texas.

The WAR of the WORLD
By H. G. Wells

The novel *War of the Worlds* by H. G. Wells was published in 1898. The storyline would take on infamous proportions when Orson Welles presented the novel as a series of simulated radio "news bulletins" on Sunday, October 30, 1938, which suggested to many listeners that an actual alien invasion by Martians was currently in progress. In the days following the adaptation, the "panic broadcast" led to widespread insecurity, outrage and even suicides by some listeners who believed the events described in the radio program were real. It was such public hysteria over an alien invasion that was used as a justification to keep all information regarding UFOs classified as top secret for decades.

SPACE AND TIME

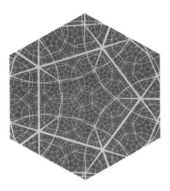

"Give up worrying about the past. Give up dreaming of the future. The past no longer exists. The future has not been born. But deeply observe the present moment, just as it is, and you shall attain the peace and unity of the ancient masters."
–Buddha, Bheda Karata Sutta

THE concept of spacetime in cosmology is a construct which combines space and time to a single abstract universe. Mathematically it is a manifold consisting of "events" which are described by some type of coordinate system. Typically, the three spatial dimensions of length, width, height, and the temporal dimension of time are required. Time is simply an arbitrary measurement of the motion of objects through space. For us on Earth, time is based on the 365.25 days it takes for the planet to make a complete orbit around the Sun, and the 24 hours it takes the planet to complete a rotation is called a day. Besides the day of 24 hours, or 86,400 seconds, the word "day" can be used for several different spans of time based on the rotation of the Earth around its axis.

Yet space is non-linear. Space is determined by the point of view of an observer when looking at an object. The distance between the observer and the object being viewed is called "space." Dimensions are independent components of a coordinate grid needed to locate a point in a certain defined space. Objects in space, or even masses of energy, do not necessarily move in a linear fashion. In this universe, objects tend to move randomly or in a curving or cyclical pattern, or as determined by the agreed upon rules in physics. Now physicists have demonstrated the existence of higher dimensions, with hyperspace well grounded in scientific principles.

Today's theoretical physicists have clearly defined hyperspace, introduced the existence of "wormholes" or tunnels between dimensions, parallel universes, and theoretically have postulated access to both the past and the future. Most of these physicists are searching for ways to access hyperspace by a mechanical, third dimensional means. Stargates or wormholes are cosmic gateways that theoretically link regions of the universe millions of light years apart and allow nearly instantaneous communication or travel between these regions.

HISTORY AND TIME

History is not merely a linear record of events, as many authors of Earth history books imply. Because history is not a string that can be stretched out and marked like a measuring tool, our concept of time needs to be reexamined. History is a subjective observation of the movement of objects through space, recorded from the point of view of a survivor, rather than those who have perished in battle, for example. Although time seems to run consecutively, events do not happen in an independent, linear stream. Rather, all of these interactions are concurrent and simultaneous. In order to view and understand the history or reality of the past, one must view all events as part of an interactive whole, the holographic perspective as described below. Time can also be sensed as a vibration which is uniform throughout the entire physical universe.

Linear time is more accurately described as an intentional fabrication. The true nature of time is cyclical. Time is a difficult factor to measure as it depends on the subjective memory of the observer and there has been no uniform record of events throughout the physical universe since the beginning. As on Earth, there are many different time measurement systems defined by various cultures, which use cycles of motion and points of origin to establish age and duration.

The "paradox" of time travel often references the example of a man traveling back in time and killing his grandfather. What would happen? How could this be possible? If the man's grandfather died, then the man would have never been born to kill him. What apparently happens in this case is that the timeline the person left (when he began time travel) continues as is, with no changes except that the person no longer exists, thereby generating this new timeline. The person then forfeits his chance to return to his own timeline. When this person killed his grandfather, a new timeline starts, minus his grandfather, and he must then remain in this altered timeline.

TIME TRAVELERS

Fantastic as it sounds, one of the main reasons the Extraterrestrial Biological Entities (EBEs) are here now is to attempt to alter our timelines, that of our future. The reason for this is that they have the ability to time travel in both directions, so they already know, or they know as a memory, what happened here in our potential future. In "Timeline Two" there is a catastrophe arising in our near future that drastically reduces the population of the Earth and splits humans into two population groups. These two populations will develop in the classic stages of evolution when a single species becomes isolated from another and the two adapt to different environments. What we know of as Homo sapiens today might develop into two distinctly different species over many thousands of years after a possible catastrophe, which will send many people underground while some will survive on the surface.

If we do have one of these catastrophes, it would mean that the benevolent EBEs did not succeed in altering the timeline. Yet if it does not occur, we can say either the information was false, which skeptics will claim without delay, or we can say they did succeed in a covert program of altering the timelines and averted a major catastrophe.

According to the "Doctrine of the Convergent Time Lines," a certain species of Greys evolved from humans in our future. In other words, one species of Greys come from our future and they have traveled backwards to our past, which is now in our current present. This would explain why the Greys and the Tall Whites have been allowed to operate for decades at Area 51 and other secure bases around the world. It would also suggest that there is no such thing as "evil" aliens, just a priority of service to self rather than a service to others.

Apparently, whatever genetic traits the future EBEs inherited, they are suffering from some kind of defective gene which has caused neural degeneration in their system, or a "peripheral neuropathy." Some human scientists at Area 51 have worked alongside the Orion Grey ETs they called "J-Rod." They were given the task of looking into the possibility of genetic reverse engineering to repair the Tall Grey's degenerate system. These Greys claimed they are an altered form of us, a new species that branched off from Homo sapiens as Homo evolutis, beginning as manufactured hybrids. These are the same as the Programmable Life Forms (PLFs) which are currently being developed at several secret underground bases.

ANOTHER MOTIVE FOR BEING HERE

These Greys are entities that will continue to evolve in our future, according to the Doctrine of the Convergent Time Lines. They come from many thousands of years in our future and have traveled backwards to our past, in other words, our current present. Eventually the two Homo sapiens sub-species from the future moved to the planets of Zeta Reticuli 1 and 2, Gliese 876-c, and Epsilon Orionis. The Tall Whites are just another branch that has evolved from Homo sapiens, but they follow more of a spiritual evolutionary path. It is as if there are all these threads woven, as we would think of a braid with multiple pieces of hair, each being a timeline. More significant to the near future on Earth is the convergence of both Timelines One and Two.

Timeline One: With the first future scenario, we work out our differences, avert disaster, and evolve quickly as an advanced sentient species.

Timeline Two: Here we have a catastrophe where more than half the humans on Earth will perish. Those who live will eek out a harsh living on the mostly destroyed surface, while other survivors will exist for many generations underground.

The Nordic Blonds and the Greys had independently decided they were going to attempt to change their history because they had learned how to travel backwards in time to some point from our distant past. Again, we're talking about this fantastic subject of time travel and how it can manipulate our reality. Of course, it is very complicated. A stargate can either be a natural subspace wormhole, or it can be artificially created. A stargate is a portal device that allows practical, rapid travel between two distant locations in the universe, as well as time travel. A lot of scientists have toyed with these ideas and the many paradoxes it presents. There are stories of those who have found themselves somehow displaced into the past, and/or dropped into the future. This has been something never explored by classical scientists because essentially we are speaking about practical applications of the theory of relativity still thought to be impossible or far into the future: traveling faster than light, through wormholes, stargates, and using a time machine or holographic history device which can access the timeline of future and past events.

UNDERSTANDING TIME DEVICES

In 1995, the Los Alamos Laboratory reported in a highly classified document that both crashed Roswell discs recovered in July, 1947, contained time devices that our scientists were able to translate into our time periods. However, the time devices found in both Roswell crafts were not known to be time devices until 1995. Scientists at Los Alamos used a supercomputer to analyze the device and discovered that the display on the device was a recording of a time period just prior to the craft crashing.

Using the alien "Energy Device," code-named "Crystal Rectangle" or the PV-EED-1 that was also found in the craft, they were able to turn on the time device and view different displays or readouts in the EBE language. The Crystal Rectangle could provide "unlimited power," also referred to as the "Particle Vacuum Enhanced Device." Based on what they already knew of the language, they were able to determine each time display sequence as being a set date under the EBE calendar. It took them many more months using cutting-edge supercomputers to translate those time frames within our own calendar dates. They then determined that the twin crashes occurred in the middle of June 1947, only to be discovered by humans about three weeks later. It was an important discovery by our scientists. Since then, new time peering devices have been developed and utilized.

LOOKING GLASS TECHNOLOGY

The time devices described here are part of what has come to be called "Looking Glass" technology. Earth's future is not set. It is constantly being altered by us, and does not always evolve into what was seen in the past by devices that can peer into the future. According to Timeline Two, the Nordics are the more positive of the two future species of humans who will stay above ground and become spiritually unified after the catastrophe, and in the future they become space travelers. They as a species will leave the Earth for several thousand years in the future after the Earth surface is mostly destroyed, and upwards of two-thirds of the population is eliminated. The Nordics will then remain on the Moon and Mars in our solar system, and return again to the Earth farther into the future. Their contemporaries, the Tall Greys, will stay underground on Earth, and develop as a hybrid species through genetics, which is already developing. They too are visitors from our future, who become our future offspring, but after many generations of continuous genetic manipulation they change dramatically.

The Looking Glass technology was provided to us from visitors of the future. It was original technology derived from ancient cylinder seals and backward engineered. The Looking Glass is a tool to help access the wormholes and stargates for a view of probable future outcomes. Two looking glass devices were required to operate simultaneously to gain both visual and audio reception. Originally the cylinder seals were a series of instructions for accessing the wormholes passing through hyperspace. Saddam Hussein had a stargate in Iraq but the U.S. removed it immediately in 2003 after the second Iraq War invasion. The Americans, Iraqis and possibly others built the devices from the instructions, and tweaked their operation as a method where the future and the past could be studied. The future is always muddled, but viewing the past is crystal clear.

Some researchers believe the Looking Glass technology must be disabled or destroyed, as it is providing powerful and dangerous people a vision of the Timeline Two probability, which could assist in prompting a major human catastrophe. It is a form of cheating at a game by already knowing the outcome. Natural stargates can remain open; however, the Looking Glass technology has the unfair advantage of knowing future probabilities which could be used to facilitate this disaster. The calculated odds are 19%, or a one in five chance, that over four billion people could die from natural catastrophes triggered by the activation of the human-made stargates such as CERN, when mixed with the wormholes which began to pass the Earth starting in 2012 and continue for the decade beyond. The galactic energy is related to natural stargate amplifications in our solar system. This will possibly be precipitated by the presence of some artificial stargates on Earth. This configuration could trigger massive Earth changes in a similar way that a pole shift would devastate civilization as we know it around the world. Some of the future alien visitors are in a race to close down the Looking Glass technology and secure the human-made stargates, while other malevolent ETs wish to facilitate the disaster. The twists and turns of the convergent timeline paradox also affect the aliens of the future as much as they do ourselves.

WORMHOLES

Wormholes are the microscopic equivalent of the so-called Einstein-Rosen bridges located in the vicinity of black holes, currently believed to be left behind by burned-out stars. These are tunnel connections between entirely different areas in the universe through which information can be transmitted outside of space and time.

In a hyperspace environment, using a shipboard generation of amplified gravity waves, it isn't speed that increases, but relative to time and space. When acted upon by a force such as gravity waves, timespace reduces itself within the hyperspace field generated around the hull of the craft, where spacetime becomes "warped." An Einstein-Rosen bridge wormhole created by a gravity-exerting craft in space is just one example. The *Star Trek* scenario may be based on actual reality principles. Artificially created gravity waves can theoretically reduce time to near zero and acceleration to near infinity. Einstein only had a problem with gravity in his unified field theory because, in the limited understanding of this force at the time, its properties did not seem to fit. However, he did come to the conclusion that gravity and acceleration were somehow connected. With a more advanced understanding of spacetime and time travel, it becomes clear that it is not space itself which is physically traversed, because space folds in on itself, as gravity waves act upon time.

The impossibility of faster-than-light relative speed only applies locally. Wormholes allow superluminal, or faster-than-light travel, by ensuring that the speed of light is not exceeded locally at any time. While traveling through a wormhole the subliminal, or the slower-than-light speed, is employed. If two points are connected by a wormhole, the time taken to traverse it would be less than the time it would take a light beam to make the journey if it took a path through the space outside the wormhole. However, a light beam traveling through the wormhole would always triumph over the traveler. For example, a runner going around to the opposite side of a mountain at maximum speed will take longer than walking through a tunnel straight through the mountain.

The theory of general relativity states that if traversable wormholes exist, they could allow for time travel. Accelerating one end of the wormhole to a high velocity relative to the other, and then sometime later bringing it back would accomplish this. Relativistic time dilation would result in the accelerated wormhole mouth aging less than the stationary one, as seen by an external observer, similar to what is seen in the twin paradox. However, time connects differently through the wormhole than outside it, so that synchronized clocks at each mouth will remain synchronized to someone traveling through the wormhole itself, no matter how the mouths move around. This means that anything which entered the accelerated wormhole mouth would exit the stationary one at a point in time prior to its entry.

As for humans, it appears our DNA is the key for the physical body to travel through wormholes. DNA apparently is also an organic superconductor that can work at normal body temperatures. Artificial superconductors require extremely low temperatures of between 200°C and 140°C to function. All superconductors are able to store light, and thus, information. This is a further explanation of how the DNA can store information. This is another phenomenon that links to DNA and wormholes. Normally, these super small wormholes are highly unstable and are maintained only for the tiniest fractions of a second. Under certain conditions stable wormholes can organize themselves which then form distinctive vacuum domains in which gravity can transform into electricity.

PROJECT SERPO

The first manned mission to another planet, assisted by the U.S. secret space program, was called Project Serpo, named for the planet where the astronauts resided for over a decade. This program was initiated under President Kennedy. The first step was selecting and training a team of U.S. military personnel for a planned 10-year stay on the home planet of the Greys in the Zeta Reticuli I and II star system, 38.42 light years away. During the planning and implementation of the program, the effort was code-named Project Crystal Knight. Upon the return of the remainder of the team 13 years later, the code name was changed to Project Serpo, named for the inhabited planet in the Zeta Reticuli binary star system. Three members of the 2044th were trained in the technical means to work within the ET spacecraft system. The system was complicated and required a special power system that was found inside the crashed alien spacecraft they called the Crystal Rectangle. Once the 2044th technicians learned the system, the communication was ready to function. Researchers also deciphered certain "spots" which were the space travel tunnels. Our astronomers compared the different star charts and found that they were not consecutive, meaning that one star chart was from one part of the universe and the next was a chart closer to their home system. Our scientists concluded that the spots on the chart were a form of short cuts from one point of space to another.

After Kennedy died, President Johnson ordered the top-secret program to continue. The 12 team members left the sprawling Groom Lake complex in Nevada on July 16, 1965, and returned in August 1978 to the exact same location. Due to delays and some differences of time on the host planet, the mission was extended by three years. Eight members returned. Two died on the planet and their bodies were returned. Two others decided to remain on the alien planet. The eight members were isolated for one complete year at a special facility located at Los Alamos.

When the exchange began, the human team members were taken to an "enormous" mothership in orbit between the Moon and Mars, where they proceeded to travel through a form of "space tunnels" that allowed the mothership to travel from our solar system to theirs extremely fast, without having to exceed the speed of light. In total, it took the various spaceships nine of our months to travel to their planet Serpo. By using wormholes, the crafts could travel faster than the speed of light, but then needed to slow down and establish an orbit over the planet, whereupon the crew was escorted down to colonies on the planet's desert-like surface.

Project Serpo researchers say the 1977 science fiction film *Close Encounters of the Third Kind*, written and directed by Steven Spielberg, was loosely based on the real life ET-human Serpo exchange. At the end of the film, a single alien disembarks and is escorted away, presumably to a secret site. The Richard Dreyfuss character joins the 12-person human exchange team, met by a group of small Grey ETs, who escort the human volunteers to board their Mother Ship, and presumably return to their home planet. Many suspect that Spielberg had an inside track on classified information, and that the ambassadorial exchange with an alien race was indeed a real event. Once again, art imitates life!

YELLOW BOOK AND RED BOOK

The "Yellow Book," also called the "Orion Cube," or the "Bible," was provided by the Greys and presented to the U.S. military at the famous Holloman AFB New Mexico landing in April 1964. The Yellow Book is not exactly a book. It is a block of material, approximately 6.35 centimeters thick, and is transparent in appearance. It is a 20 x 28 centimeter object that is constructed of a clear, heavy fiberglass-type material. The border of the book is a bright yellow color, hence the name. When the reader looks at the transparent surface, words and pictures suddenly appear. The Yellow Book is said to be a sort of holographic image generator, which can project 3-D pictures of the information it contains. When the "reader" places the book close to their eyes, they will begin seeing words and images flashing on the "screen." Depending on the particular language the viewer is thinking, that particular language will appear. So far, scientists have identified 80 different languages. It contains references to Biblical events, including a holographic depiction of the crucifixion of Christ. It contains an endless series of historical stories and images of our galaxy, diaries of other inhabited planets, and other interesting stories from just about anywhere in the universe. It also contains a complete storyline of Earth's most recent history, as well as our distant past. It is the true and correct complete history of humankind as relayed by the EBEs.

The Orion Cube was the core of the Montauk chair, and was "Saurian Man" technology. It utilized a device to navigate 3-D time called a Temporal Vector Generator (TVG), which could target a temporal coordinate. With the coordinates of where the subject was located, it was possible to plot a course to another temporal location using Zero Time Reference (ZTR). This reference was used for the Phoenix III Project during the Philadelphia Experiment.

The "Red Book" is a very lengthy, very detailed summary account written and compiled by the U.S. Government on UFO investigations dating from 1947 to the present. This orange-brownish book is updated every five years and also includes some crossover information from the Yellow Book. It contains volumes of information that agents have gathered regarding our interactions with a dozen or more Extraterrestrial Biological Entities. The first volume begins in 1947 with the acquisition of ET craft and the first captured Grey entity known as "Ebe." Other volumes cover all the decades since then. It includes an intelligence analysis of any trends, types of sightings, human contacts with the EBEs, or any national security concerns our government or the planet might have. The Red Book is presented to the sitting president of the United States every five years. It is a summary of alien visitations that have occurred in the U.S. and other countries.

Looking Glass, portal, stargate and Yellow Book are all essentially the same because they each utilize the same spacetime technology. One of the biggest threats to the Powers That Be is that anyone who can take a factual look into the past, plus foresee future events, has gained far more access to clandestine operations than they can allow. This is their core secret, even more important than UFO technology. Indeed, devices that can demonstrate the past clearly, and peer into future events, have to be some of the weirdest esoteric studies in this book! But wait, it still gets "weirder."

THE HOLOGRAPHIC UNIVERSE

What if our entire material existence is nothing more than a holographic projection of another? In other words, what if the flat version of the life you are living is a two-dimensional "surface" at the edge of the universe? Are we real, or are we quantum interactions on the edges of the universe? To proponents of the holographic universe, it is now becoming clear that observing phenomena through a holographic lens could be the key to solving some of the most perplexing problems in physics, including what reigned before the universe started to expand, what gives particles mass, and an understanding of quantum gravity. It would also explain how under certain circumstances subatomic particles such as electrons are able to instantaneously communicate with each other, regardless of the distance between them, whether separated by a few millimeters or the vast expanse of the universe. Even the human brain appears to operate in a manner similar to a hologram.

The Yellow Book is essentially a holographic image generator. The Greys demonstrated this technology in 1964 to an assembled group of U.S. generals who filmed the incident. They were shown the actual crucifixion of Christ in a detailed three-dimensional light video laser projection. The generals commented that what they viewed was a hologram history video of the events surrounding the last days of Jesus Christ. This technology can somehow access the true and real history of all events from all time. *It also suggests that objective reality as we perceive it does not really exist.* Despite its apparent solidity, the universe is at heart a phantasm, a gigantic and splendidly detailed hologram.

Once you accept the holographic universe theory, it is logical to reason that our third dimensional (3-D) realm would exist within a higher dimensional spacetime of many more dimensions. From our perceived third dimensional realm, there are higher dimensional projections all the way "up" to the eleven or twelve dimensions suggested via string theory. With proper training, or if one were a higher dimensional being, that individual could conceivably observe all 3-D worlds currently undetected. A viewer could reach down or through the "dimensional membrane," which is the edge of the 3-D space-time universe. It is not the surface of a 3-D sphere, but a pervading and co-existing oneness that is everywhere tangential to all 3-D surfaces and separated by a Planck scale distance. A good way to visualize this is to imagine that we humans go about our lives within our 3-D realm akin to ants on a tabletop. Like ants on a tabletop, we would be surrounded by a higher dimensional realm that we cannot see, but could probably detect indirectly if we were able to peer "upwards" into the higher dimensions.

A higher dimensional being would be able to "retrieve" the holographic memories from any human's subconscious mind. The Grey ETs use their technology and mental powers to monitor or read the mental energy of their subjects. They can create "halo effects" or impose post-hypnotic dream-like sequences that seem real, but really are not. They can potentially create their own holographic virtual reality sequences via combined technology and collective consciousness to display images in real time. Such would explain the seemingly super mental powers of the Greys as described by the unsuspecting victims they abduct.

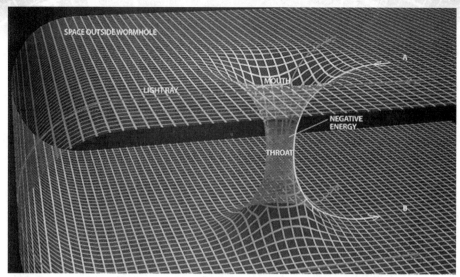

In fiction, but also in physics, a wormhole is a hypothetical topological feature of space-time that would be fundamentally a "shortcut" through spacetime. This is a simple visual explanation of a wormhole depicting spacetime visualized as a two-dimensional surface. If this surface is folded along a third dimension, it allows one to picture a wormhole "bridge." This is supposedly how the Project Serpo team were able to travel many light years away to an inhabited planet in the Zeta Reticuli binary star system. At a close distance to Earth, located above both of the poles are two presumed wormholes. When harnessed, they can be used for intergalactic or interstellar travel.

In the late 1980s, a scientific sensation was created by American astrophysicist Kip Thorne and his colleagues' work. Other scientists suggest their work has significant practical characteristics, such as building time travel devices and ensuring intergalactic travel. Kip Thorne concluded that near Earth, there's an entrance into a wormhole leading to the star Vega. What's more, There is a relationship between electromagnetic waves and interstellar travel, wherein electric waves are 90° away and perpendicular to magnetic waves. This fits into the construct of how a parallel universe works.

General relativity describes the possibility of wormholes forming when two black holes become connected to each other. Hypothetically, wormholes could enable almost instantaneous time travel over long distances. The thermodynamics of black holes allows one to deduce limits on the density of entropy in various circumstances. The holographic bound defines how much information can be contained in a specified region of space. Conversely, a white hole is the opposite of a black hole. A white hole, in general relativity, is a hypothetical region of spacetime which cannot be entered from the outside, but from which matter and light may escape. It is theoretically possible for a traveler to enter a rotating black hole, avoid the singularity, and travel into a rotating white hole which allows the traveler to escape into another universe via wormholes.

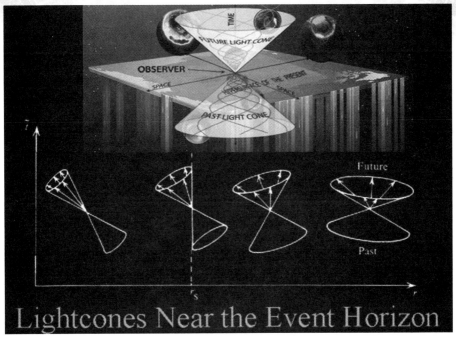

Lightcones Near the Event Horizon

Far from the black hole, lightcones are as they appear in flat spacetime, or our linear world. Time and space, according to Einstein's theories of relativity, are woven together, forming a four-dimensional fabric called "spacetime." The mass of Earth creates a "dimple" on this fabric, much like a heavy person sitting in the middle of a trampoline. Gravity, says Einstein, is simply the motion of objects following the curvaceous lines of the dimple. Thus, a UFO entering a black hole would need to match the direction and the velocity (speed) of the black hole's rotation. In doing this, it would be possible to "swirl" around the singularity and exit the black hole in a different part of spacetime. It may seem impossible that a UFO could exit the black hole itself, because it would require faster than light speed. However, the rotating black hole distorts spacetime so that the singularity can be avoided and the UFO can exit the black hole at reasonable speeds. This would imply that a UFO going through a rotating black hole would exit out of the white hole in a different region of spacetime. Such a technological development would also enable time travel.

The "Baltic Sea anomaly" is 60 meters in diameter, 85 meters deep, and appears to be a underwater crash site of a circular craft on the floor of the northern Baltic Sea, between Sweden and Finland. It was discovered by the Swedish "Ocean X" diving team in June, 2011.

How many star systems are within 20 light years of Earth? There are at least 83 known star systems within this relatively short distance, containing a minimum of 109 stars and eight brown dwarfs. Our Milky Way galaxy is a barred spiral galaxy that is a part of the billions of galaxies in the observable universe. Most galaxies are believed to have a super massive black hole at their center.

Military personnel inspect the lightweight metal and exotic debris in the days following a newspaper in Roswell, NM reported a nearby downed "flying saucer" craft in July, 1947.

EBEs

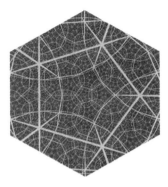

"To think of these stars that you see overhead at night, these vast worlds which we can never reach. I would annex the planets if I could; I often think of that. It makes me sad to see them so clear and yet so far." –Cecil Rhodes

WHEN most people think of aliens, they think of foreigners residing in a country illegally, or those "little green men" with big eyes. These latter entities are commonly referred to as the Greys because of the color of their skin, which is not green at all, but greyish in tone as the name implies. The Greys are the most widely reported alien species encountered worldwide, and the full spectrum study of all ET relations with Earth humans is called exopolitics.

There are many species of Greys, varying in size and skin tone, but they all belong to the same "hive" mentality of the reptoid species of ETs, which also include the tall reptilian Alpha Draconians. There are many other alien life forms reported to be interacting with Earth humans, some who look much like we do, many with helping us in mind, while others are out to exploit us and consider us livestock.

What is rarely touched by the major news outlets is any reporting on UFOs, let alone intelligent alien life forms, called Extraterrestrial Biological Entities by the military, shortened to EBEs. What follows is a synthesis of the most commonly reported data points about EBEs, when they were first discovered, what they look like, and what their motives might be here on Earth.

The most commonly discussed EBE is the reptoid species called the Greys, which have been captured and studied since the rash of UFO crash recoveries beginning in the late 1940s. Most of the Greys report they come from two planets rotating around the binary star system of Zeta Reticuli, located in the constellation Reticulum when seen from our southern sky. Since a live Grey was found in the 1947 Roswell crash, it has been observed that captured Greys must be kept in an electromagnetic shielded environment so they cannot escape. They can literally walk through walls. A few years later, the Greys made a formal agreement with the USA to exchange high technology for permission to work here on genetic engineering. The Grey aliens were given permission under the Greada Treaty (originally signed by President Eisenhower) to operate clandestinely in their specially designed underground bases. The most renowned is below the Jicarilla Apache Reservation at the Four Corners region in northern New Mexico, another is located at the vast Nellis Air Force Base in Nevada, and there are likely many others, including the Los Alamos National Laboratory. What is known is that the physical system of the Greys is chlorophyll based, and all are essentially synthetic "test-tube" entities with incredible cognitive abilities. The body of a Grey alien processes food in a similar way that plants do, and their excretions are also the same as plants. Greys are known to deceive and lie to humans. Some claim to come from a red planet revolving around a star in Orion called Betelgeuse. Some Greys say they are from the star system Rigel, and others claim they are from two planets revolving around the binary star system Zeta Reticuli, one of those is planet Serpo.

PANSPERMIA

Let's back up a little bit. In 1996, a NASA researcher named David McKay reported he had found traces of Martian life inside a meteorite recovered in 1984 from the Allan Hills in Antarctica. The origins and continuation of microscopic life spreading throughout the universe became known as the phenomenon called "panspermia." McKay is not the only researcher from NASA to claim a discovery of alien life inside meteorites. In March, 2011, another NASA scientist reinvigorated the debate over life elsewhere in the cosmos after claiming to have found tiny fossils of "alien bugs" inside meteorites that landed on Earth. Richard Hoover, an astrobiologist at the U.S. space agency's Marshall Space Flight Center in Alabama, said filaments and other structures in rare meteorites appear to be microscopic fossils of extraterrestrial beings that resemble algae known as cyanobacteria. Hoover, an expert on life in extreme environments, has reported similar structures in meteorites several times before. After a balloon came back from a high altitude flight in 2015, it was covered with microscopic life forms that originated from space, suggesting the ancient remains of alien life, or directed panspermia.

The co-discoverer of DNA, Francis Crick of Cambridge University, believed human genes could not have evolved on Earth by chance, given only 500-600 million years of evolution from the primeval soup to modern humans. This conventional belief in human evolution is extremely unlikely. Francis Crick was a proponent of the directed panspermia theory. An interesting aspect of these stories is that although they each were distributed by the major news outlets, little or no follow-up occurred, much less exploring EBE life forms or the implications of the panspermia theory.

The biologic unit of material life is the protoplasmic cell, the communal association of chemical, electrical, and other basic energies. The chemical formulas differ in each system, and the technique of living cell reproduction is slightly different in each local universe, but the life carriers are always the living catalysts who initiate the primordial reactions of material life. They are the instigators of the energy circuits of living matter directed throughout the universe.

THE PRIME DIRECTIVE

The Law of Planetary Free Will, or the Prime Directive as popularized by the *Star Trek* franchise, is a real cosmic law. Benevolent ETs have not been allowed to intervene on Earth beyond a minimal level, due to what has been called a "Quarantine" that is imposed by the Confederation of Planets to protect Earth humanity's free will from undue influence. In the case of *Star Trek*, sometimes art does imitate life. But this is not by accident. *Star Trek* creator Gene Roddenberry was said to have been allowed to take notes during several Council of Nine channeled sessions with ETs when he was scriptwriting for the popular television series.

Direct intervention with people on primitive and spiritually evolving planets, Earth being a good example, is not allowed. Other beings are permitted only to observe emerging civilizations. A long-standing edict prohibits the unauthorized or forcible colonization of planets. However, in some cases, benevolent ETs have chosen to intervene in certain affairs in order to ensure the longevity of an observed planet and civilization. Although the ETs seem to have no interest in conquering Earth, or in controlling the population of this planet, it does serve their interests to ensure that the resources of Earth are not destroyed or spoiled. To that end, certain ETs have been sent to Earth on reconnaissance missions from time to time to gather information.

Nuclear war was a very real threat in the 1950s, and so it remains today. We do not hear about this threat as urgently any longer, but the largest nations of the world are armed to the teeth with planet-killing weapons. This problem has apparently caused the ETs to intervene much more directly in our planet's affairs than they normally would have, but this is strictly in order to prevent the possibility of a nuclear exchange. ETs have been systematically deactivating nuclear sites ever since Earth humans began building them, regardless in which country they were found. This includes China, India and Russia.

The Quarantine, or Prime Directive, led to a false complacency within the ranks of the reptoid "Dark Forces," who came to think they were manipulating the right humans to covertly direct the course of civilization on Earth. They believed the benevolent ETs were totally powerless to do anything to stop them, via universal law, and could only stand back and cry in horror as they enslaved the planet. They justified their human experiments based on the cruelty that humans exhibit to farm animals, for example, and the ongoing exploitation of Earth's natural resources. If humans were treating the living organisms of the world that way, they could do the same to us. Unfortunately, our government under Eisenhower made a pseudo-legally binding agreement with certain negative extraterrestrial groups, disallowing the good ETs to interfere with our free choice, unless humans would endanger our planet, solar system or anywhere in the galaxy. Only in this capacity the "good" ETs have been systematically deactivating nuclear missiles in restricted areas for decades. The Confederation ETs would not usually destroy the missile sites. They merely deactivated the warheads in what appeared to be their telling us that they have the capabilities to completely shut down our weapon systems in the event that any significant nuclear exchange is executed.

The Prime Directive, regarding Earth, seems to have diminished once we entered the nuclear age. There are now much greater consequences. The ability for some militaries of the world to create massive destruction radiates outward and adversely affects our solar system, our galaxy, and even our universe. We are not an isolated planet. What we do here really does affect the universe. Therefore, we incorporate the universe into our affairs with the continued explosions of our nuclear bombs. This escalation in the proliferation of weaponry has caused the Prime Directive to virtually no longer be in effect.

In 2011, the UFO blogosphere was alight with news that the Andromeda Council won a series of battles within our solar system, ridding almost all of the malevolent entities on behalf of the people of Earth. The Andromeda Council had to persuade others within the Confederation of Planets to intercede on Earth's behalf. Extensive discussions were held and a new law was passed overriding what is ubiquitously known as the Prime Directive of non-interference. A conscious, collective decision was made by the Council to break precedent and do this simply because Earth's people were at a distinct disadvantage living a third dimensional life. The humans simply did not have the fourth dimensional physiology, knowledge, tools, or technology to win against the Draconians and Greys.

WHY ARE THE GREYS HERE ON EARTH?

In appearance, the most commonly viewed Grey alien is about a meter tall, a hominoid in appearance, with grayish "skin," and usually three spindly fingers and a thumb on each hand. Their feet also have four digits. On the end of each of the four fingers are little pads resembling suction cups. Their heads are very large in proportion to their frail-looking bodies. Their large almond-shaped eyes appear even bigger, and they never blink. On their disproportionately large heads, the eyes are uniformly reported as deeply set, the skulls are soft and flexible, the nose is concave with only two orifices, the mouth is a fine slit, and inside the mouth there is heavy cartilage instead of teeth. The ears are only small orifices with flaps. They have no hair, and the skin is a greyish hue in color with some variation. Their mannerisms have been compared to insects.

There are several different varieties of Greys, as their height, weight, and digits on their hands and feet can vary depending on what task they were developed to perform. Sex organs no longer function and all Greys are genetically manufactured entities. Their hominoid bodies appear to move more like insects than mammals, especially their hands. Amongst all Greys, communication is strictly telepathic, as their mouths can no longer speak. Since they have lost their capacity for love and natural sexual reproduction, their genetic strength is breaking down. They need fresh human DNA and animal reproductive tissues to ensure the survival of their species.

True or not, the Greys known as the Arcturians claim to be partly responsible for much of the life that exists on Earth. This is how they justify avoiding the Prime Directive and have remained here for eons. The Arcturians are one of the oldest alien species in our galaxy, yet other species of malevolent Greys arrived more recently. The fact that certain Greys continue to harvest cattle and abduct humans attests to their prowess as master genetic scientists. Indeed, without love as a way to organically reproduce, certain strains of Greys are dying breeds. They are no longer able to reproduce naturally by having sex. The Grey's genetic structure is deteriorating, and they are abducting humans for genetic experiments to strengthen their own DNA strain. In addition to human experiments, bovine organic material allows the Greys to feed and create their own test-tube entities right here on Earth.

MASTER GENETIC SCIENTISTS

As extremely adept genetic scientists, who even manufacture themselves as their own life forms, the Greys have stated that evolution is untrue. They deny the notion that the creation of any life form could have resulted from a coincidental chemical interaction moldering up from some primordial ooze. To them, highly complex mammal evolution is beyond absurdity. Certainly, some organisms on Earth, such as Proteobacteria, are modifications of a Phylum designed primarily for planets similar to Earth, where they have been terra-forming this planet from the earliest time millions of years ago. In other words, according to "The Domain," a kind of authority with which the Greys identify, they have bio-engineered every single organism on this planet. After all, ours holds a designation for a planet with an anaerobic atmosphere nearest a large, intensely hot blue star, such as those in the constellation of Orion's Belt in this galaxy, which are ideal for terra-forming. The cloning of sheep and monkeys is a documented fact in our society, so it is not beyond the limits of possibility to suggest that a high tech alien culture might, unfortunately, succeed in cloning human hybrids.

In fact, we are already cloning ourselves. In July, 2011, several articles announced that scientists have created more than 150 human-animal hybrid embryos in British laboratories. These "above-ground" hybrids have been produced secretively over the past three years by researchers looking into possible cures for a wide range of diseases. The revelation comes just a day after a committee of scientists warned of a nightmare "Planet of the Apes" scenario in which work on human-animal creations goes too far.

Creating life forms is very complex, highly technical work for human scientists who specialize in this field, but seemingly simple for the Greys. They claim genetic anomalies which are very baffling to Earth biologists because Earth humans have had their memories erased between lifetimes. Unfortunately, the false memory implantations prevent Earth scientists from observing obvious anomalies. In recent decades, Earth research physicians have begun to develop advanced biological engineering technology, including heart bypasses, cloning, test tube babies, organ transplants, stem cell regeneration, plastic surgery, genes, chromosomes, and various artificial organs.

For the Greys, the greatest technical challenge of creating Earth-bound biological organisms was the invention of self-regeneration, or sexual reproduction. It was invented as the solution to the problem of having to continually manufacture replacement creatures for those that had been destroyed and eaten by other creatures. They claim to have introduced the "reproductive trigger" used for lesser life forms, such as cattle and other mammals, which is initiated by chemicals emitted from the scent glands, combined with reproductive chemical-electrical impulses stimulated by testosterone, or estrogen. These are also interactive with nutrition levels which cause the life form to reproduce more when deprived of food sources. Starvation also promoted reproductive activity as a means of perpetuating survival through future regenerations, when the current organism fails to survive. These fundamental principles have been applied throughout all species of life.

In regard to their own manufactured bodies, nearly all Greys, especially the space officers and crewmembers, need container-like bodies to interact on third dimensional levels. These are the Greys who occupy the spacecraft required to travel through intergalactic space, and who have interactions with humans. The Greys are each equipped with a body manufactured from lightweight and durable organic materials. Various body types have been designed to facilitate specialized functions. Some bodies have accessories, such as interchangeable tools or apparatus for activities such as maintenance, mining, chemical management, navigation, and so on. There are many variations of this body type which also serve as an insignia of rank, including those of a drone soldier or the obedient worker class. Therefore, the appearance, features, composition and functionality of the different body types of the Greys are highly specialized, and limited to the requirements of their duties.

Since human abduction experiments began in earnest a half century ago, about 5,000 crossbreed hybrid Grey/human life forms have been created, and some still live on Earth. These hybrids have been programmed since birth with the agenda of the Greys. They will all eventually need to be removed from Earth and deprogrammed so that they may evolve on their own into free thinking, free willed beings. And, since they are a new sentient life form, they will eventually need to be relocated to their own third dimension planet. Because they have been operating so long in our solar system, the Greys consider themselves endemic, and believe they have a right to remain here and harvest organic tissues that they deem necessary. Since they are masters of time and space, the Greys may never fully be eliminated and could very well remain a part of Earth's future. Humanity may even split into two races. There will be those who resemble humans as we look today who remain on the surface, and those who go to live underground, either by choice or by force, and eventually become an Earth variety of the Tall Greys.

ON HUMAN ABDUCTIONS & CATTLE MUTILATIONS

We'll examine each of these famous phenomena separately, as they are both rather complicated subjects. Suffice it to say, the Greys are behind both issues. The cattle mutilation phenomenon began to be recorded in the late 1960s, which included genital removal, rectums cored out to the colon, eyes, tongue, and throat tissue all surgically removed with extreme precision. In some cases the incisions were made by cutting between the cells, a process we are not yet capable of performing. In many of the mutilations there was no blood found at all within the carcass, and there was no vascular collapse of the internal organs.

The Greys from Rigel were empowered after Eisenhower signed the Greada Treaty, which allowed the reptoids limited harvesting in exchange for high technology. They would furnish us advanced technology, and in return be allowed to work in underground bases and conduct abductions on a limited basis. Among the most famous abductees is Barney Hill who along with his wife Betty was abducted by "Zeta Reticulan Greys" in 1961. Many others were to follow. The Greys are mainly working on hybrid humans, clones, and genetic strengthening of their own DNA. They also work alongside a small permanent population of reptilian Alpha Draconians who are in charge of all the malevolent beings on this planet. Strangely, there are times when the Greys have shown signs of benevolence or compassion and extreme intelligence when dealing with their human subjects. Portions of the U.S. military, in the service of the black space operations, is said to be monitoring the Greys in their abduction and mutilation agenda, hybridizing their species using bovine hemoglobin to culture egg cells to fertilize alien DNA in their labs, and possibly to produce hybrid warriors for the secret space program. The Greys have a major base of operations located underneath Dulce, New Mexico, which is so vast it also extends under the Ute Reservation in southwestern Colorado.

NORDICS

The human-like "Nordic" ETs look very similar to northern European Scandinavians, hence their association with the Nordic people. The Lyrans are the oldest ancestors of the Nordics ETs, and four known sub-species are actively interacting with Earth. The Nordic's height can be extremely tall or very short in human terms. A full grown adult can range in height from a meter to 2.5 meters tall. Although one race comes from the Pleiades star system, they have had an interaction with Earth for a very long time and even shared with us some of the suffering we now experience. "Project Plato" was the original government diplomatic effort with all ETs. The Pleiadians, sometimes spelled Plejarens, are here for our evolution into a Golden Age. It was the Pleiadians who met with Air Force officers at Homestead, Florida, in 1954 and offered assistance in ridding our planet of the Greys. They demanded that Earthlings advance in our spiritual development before any technology could be traded. This notion was shunned by the administration, essentially because of its myopic focus on weapons to be used for "defense." While it is often believed that most aliens are an unfriendly bunch, there are a few species that have been on Earth for centuries who serve to disprove this claim.

The most important European base for the Nordics was in Italy. One of its entryways was at the Rocca Pia Castle. Interestingly, the Rocca Pia Castle belongs to the Orsini and Colonna families who are very important in Italian history. Both families belong to the Black Aristocracy, basically the papal families, and both sired more than one pope. The main portion of the Nordic base in Europe was actually under the seabed. It was located deep under the Adriatic Sea, and it stretched from Ortona to Rimini in eastern Italy. The larger underwater base was almost in contact with the continental shelf. Italy was one of the first countries to study UFOs. Original documents with Benito Mussolini's signature and other paper watermarks prove the Italians have observed an ET presence since at least the 1930s. "Project Grudge" is the MJ-12 study of any and all ET contact globally, which is tasked to document everything we know about them or any interactions. Indeed, we're not the only tenants in the building.

For thousands of years indigenous Nordic ETs, also called the Telosians, were concentrated in the mythical mountains of Tibet. They also have bases in the Americas, at one of the highest areas of the Andes, an underground city at Mount Shasta called Telos, and another in the Canadian Yukon Territory. Another longstanding base is under Lake Titicaca because it is situated in a high place, at 3,800 meters above sea level. An uninhabited island in Lake Titicaca is the closest physical point to both a lodge of the Great White Brotherhood and a Galactic Confederation base here on Earth. Mount Shasta had been an important underground base to the Great White Brotherhood, but provocations from the U.S. prompted them to move most of their North American operations to the Yukon. Thousands of years of scientific advancement have given the Telosians the ability to circumvent disease and aging. The Telosians are widely known for their longevity and could help us with our own. They are also true protectors of the Earth's environment and keepers of knowledge about our planet's past.

Body types of the "Tall Blondes" are predetermined largely by the type and size of the star around which their planet revolves, the distance from the star, and the geological as well as atmospheric components of the planet. On average, these stars and planets fall into gradients of classification which are fairly standard throughout the universe. For example, Earth is identified as a "Sun Type 12, Class 7 planet." That is a heavy gravity, nitrogen/oxygen rich atmosphere planet, with biological life forms, in proximity to a single, yellow, medium-size, low radiation sun or "Type 12 Star." Biological human flesh bodies live for only a very short time—only 60 to 150 years, at most—whereas the manufactured "doll bodies" of the Greys can be reused and repaired almost indefinitely. The Greys of course are not part of the Confederation, but then neither are Earth humans. We need to develop more as a conscious species first. The human form is the predominant life form in the universe, and currently Earth is the most populated planet. There are upwards of 30 billion human-like beings in the Milky Way galaxy.

EBE BASES ON EARTH

It has been observed for some time that the ETs operate their bases underground and below the seas. Over time, an Earth-bound ET race known as the Alpha Centaurians evolved into an aquatic species with gills and webbed limbs. Some researchers believe they are responsible for most of the underwater and the USO phenomena. But in general, ETs can construct an underground base by opening a hole, then compressing the material of the earth into hard walls. The bases do not need to have an entrance. The ETs just open up a hole in the ground and can access their artificial chambers. The base requires a force field to remain in use. The ETs utilize technology to displace the atoms of the rock and soil into a parallel reality known as "time-space," liquefying the atoms, and then pushing them into walls while they are in that configuration. Once the fields are turned off, the earth naturally re-assumes its original shape.

In 1953, contact was made with benevolent human-looking EBEs, who warned us of the dangerous EBEs, and offered to help us with our spiritual development, but they refused our request for advanced technology. Unless we disarmed our nuclear arsenal, the Nordics said, they would not give us advanced technology. They reasoned that we'd use it against ourselves. First, the Nordics said, we must stop killing each other, second we must stop exploiting the Earth and having little regard for animals. We must stop raping the Earth's resources and learn to live in harmony. These overtures were rejected because nuclear disarmament was deemed unrealistic. This decision could have been made because some of the generals were abducted, implanted, and working for the reptilians already, possibly unknowingly.

On April 15, 1964, two U.S. intelligence personnel met under Project Plato with the Greys in the New Mexico desert to arrange for a formal meeting on April 25 at Holloman Air Force Base. This meeting was to renew the 10-year treaty that had started in 1934 and was renewed consistently every decade. It was a psychological bid to buy time in order to solve the problem of the Greys and Draco reptilians. The covert treaty stated that in return for the Greys providing high technology, the U.S. federal government would allow the Greys to proceed, unhindered, with human abductions for use in an ongoing ET genetic program. By 1964, the upper levels of U.S. intelligence believed that the Greys and Dracos had this planet time-tabled for invasion and takeover between the years 2000 and 2030. This would take place under the auspices of an alien false flag invasion event. The Andromeda Council also knew this and stepped in during the first decade of the 21st century and began to clear out reptilian underground and undersea bases using highly accurate and highly focused sonic beams to destroy the bases and tunnel systems. The ground underneath the United States had the highest concentration of these malevolent beings. The moderate 2011 earthquakes felt in Virginia, Colorado, New Mexico, Nevada, and other states were the effects of clearing out the Dracos and Greys from their protected underground bases. The effort is ongoing and for the most part successful, but there are still some remaining underground and undersea Reptilian operational bases.

THE VARIOUS FEDERATIONS AND COUNCILS

Most of the Nordic races belong to the Confederation of Planets, also called the Galactic Confederation, which has operational bases on both Venus and one of the moons of Jupiter named Ganymede. This confederation was responsible for the Prime Directive discussed earlier. Some of the ETs in the Confederation of Planets are very different looking from Earth-like Nordics, including those who form the Great White Brotherhood, originally from Venus in our solar system. One common trait of all the advanced extraterrestrial visitors within the Confederation is their complete dedication to nonviolent ethics. This is how they communicate, operate missions together, and even love one another.

The Galactic Confederation is closely monitoring Earth and has been establishing a bridge of communication with receptive humans for several decades. For their part, it's a program of assistance in a very non-direct way. It is a mission of contact because the evolved worlds that occupy our Milky Way galaxy, those who form the Confederation of Planets, have seen that not only are great changes in consciousness taking place on Earth, but also within the whole galaxy. They claim our planet, as we know it, has not finished evolving and is about to make a huge shift. It is still transforming itself on a consciousness level. Within this transformation, it is up to willing individuals to take a part and assume a role regarding the planetary changes that are happening. When we finally do reach a critical mass of aligned humans, we will be welcomed into the galactic community. When that happens we will sit around the table with our benevolent galactic governing body, the Confederation of Planets.

The Confederation of Planets was founded over 4.5 million years ago to prevent interdimensional dark forces from dominating and exploiting the Milky Way and other galaxies. At present, there are over 200,000 member star nations, confederations, or unions. Approximately 40% are humanoids and the remaining 60% are varied forms of sentient beings. Most members of the Confederation of Planets are fully conscious beings. Another member star nation with close ties to Earth are the Andromedans, founders of the Andromeda Council, who are humanoids similar in appearance to Earth humans. The benevolent Sirius A is part of the Confederation, but they are not to be confused with Sirius B, who are malevolent and at odds with their Sirius A neighbors. The Sirians have waged war in the past with the Draco-Orion forces, or the "Unholy Six" reptilian star systems located in the Orion open cluster.

Conversely, the group going by the name "Galactic Federation of Light" is co-opting the name to trick us. They are using the name to confuse us and are actually from the Orion Group. Although they can alter themselves to look very human-like, they are in fact reptilian species by their genetic makeup. Also, there appears to be more than one "Blond" human society involved in the UFO scenarios, and subterranean human societies may have developed "blond" hair due to lack of sunlight. There does not seem to be anything more than a peripheral connection between the "Blonde" Telosians who live below Mount Shasta, the

Pleiadean and other benevolent off-planet "Nordics," or the newly created Antarctican "Aryans" born since the founding of New Berlin. The Antarcticans may consist largely of "batch consigned" pure-bred blue-eyed, blond Aryans who became victims of Hitler's obsession to create a super race. Most of these may be controlled through mind manipulation and implants, being "human drones" who are used to keep this hidden society functioning. An easy way to differentiate the many agendas and races is to simply determine if an ET group is "service to self" oriented, or in "service to others."

There are several other affiliated councils throughout the universe, some formal members of the Andromeda Council, some not, some willing to help the people of Earth in its process of evolution, and some who only wish to exploit. The Andromeda Council is an intergalactic governance body of affiliated star systems and planets. It is made up of worlds, people, and beings that are third dimensional, but primarily fourth, plus some fifth and sixth dimensional beings. They are of varying skin colors, sizes and races, and many of these entities are very human looking, although each is in a different stage of evolution.

One of the affiliated councils is the Galactic Federation which is a federation of star systems and planets of benevolent beings based in the Tau Ceti star system. The Galactic Federation is comprised of approximately 140 star systems and at present 300 planets. It has its own sitting council representing its own star systems and planets. It is lead by a Chairman from the Tau Ceti star system. The Galactic Federation itself is the tenth senior chaired member of the Andromeda Council. The Federation's lead planet is called Xeta. There are 12 senior chaired members of the Andromeda Council.

The Andromeda Council maintains that the Earth's people have a right to a fresh, clean, new beginning, free from the serious residual, psychological and emotional effects brought on by the Greys, the Draco Reptilians, and all their technology. The Andromedan Council appealed to the galactic governance council that they have a special affinity with the humans of Earth and are extremely concerned about the impact of the centuries-old Orion Grey and Draco Reptilian occupations of Earth, our Moon and Mars. Through time travel, the Andromedans were able to figure out where a significant shift in energy occurred that will cause extreme tyranny around the year 2368. This will also affect the Andromedans adversely 353 years in our future. They traced it back to our solar system and have been able to track it down further to Earth, our Moon and Mars. Hence, their proactive intervention at this time to ensure humanity enters the Golden Age.

OPPOSITE POLARITY

We live in a world and universe of duality. There are many extraterrestrial civilizations throughout the galaxy, universe, and omni-universe that have come to Earth to collect commodities and perform experiments for their own selfish purposes. They are not here to be of service. Some of these extraterrestrials are of what might be termed a neutral nature, and some are serving the

Dark Forces. The number of negative extraterrestrials is small compared to the vast number of positive extraterrestrials; however, the negative ones are quite dangerous if not controlled.

There is also a malevolent ET confederation, known variously as the Draconian Empire, the Corporate Collective, or the Old World Order forces. They consist primarily of reptilian ETs from the star systems of Alpha Draconis and Hydra, Greys from the Orion Group, and the Greys from Zeta Reticuli. Other malevolent ETs include those from Sirius B, Rigel, and elsewhere. The most odious for humans on Earth are the Alpha Draconian reptilian ETs who have been manipulating humanity for a long time. For the last 5,700 years, they have always found a way to manipulate the right humans to achieve their goals. Recently under their direction, the Old World Order has funneled billions of dollars making propaganda movies to prepare humanity for the ultimate 9-11-style false flag operation, using Project Blue Beam holograms, they will hoax a massive and totally fake "alien invasion." This is the point when the reptoids will assert themselves as overt masters of the planet. This Timeline Two scenario is called the Orion Conspiracy. There are many hidden agendas present here on Earth.

Reptilians are described as being very aggressive and arrogant and they perceive humans to be nothing more than cattle. The Reptilians are operating under a "locust" mentality. Because the collectivist mind-set automatically opposes sovereign philosophy, which advocates personal freedom, the Draconian/Grey collective of its own initiative will not, and cannot, cease from its violations and abuses of human cultures throughout the galaxy. The reptilian Dracos are the masters of the "Dark Forces," or all of those species whose philosophy is service to self. They are psychic, adept builders, very smart, very strong physically and rather tall. They can live hundreds of years, sometimes in seemingly impossible conditions. Not only are they of reptile origin from a far away galaxy, but they are of an opposite polarity. They have chosen to ignore love and unity with other races. Their main stronghold in the Milky Way galaxy is called the Orion Group, which are a series of neighboring stars in the Orion constellation, those being Betelgeuse, Bellatrix, and Rigel.

There are actually six planets in the Orion system, occupied by a group called the Deros, from inner space, that have had to be cordoned off by the good EBEs, and are thus cautious about having any relations with the Orion Nebula. Most EBEs from the Orion Group are genetically manipulated and controlled by the Draconians, just as the Zeta Reticulan Greys are manipulated by higher malevolent races, namely the Draconians, in a very rigid hierarchy. The Draconians will not cease their abusive practices unless forced to do so by humanoid cultures that have succeeded in taming their own base, or lower predatory instincts. This could only be accomplished by those possessing a higher than the base predatory-physical nature, that is, by those capable of utilizing and exercising the power of their higher spiritual selves. This, too, is how humans can defend themselves from any malevolent ET influence. *The reptoids cannot manipulate individuals who have lost fear and anger to a place of love and compassion.*

Even while space craft of the Greys and other advanced entities can travel trillions of "light years" in a single day, the time required to traverse the space between galaxies is still significant, not to mention the length of time to complete just one set of mission orders, which may require thousands of years.

The Orion Empire, the "Dark Forces," are fourth Density Negative. They are "lost" in the sense that they have drifted so far from their true nature that (despite many attempts) the various councils have been unable to reach them or help them to develop. They exist within their "Group Soul Complex," mostly as a group of discarnate entities within the astral planes of the planets they visit. They have no intention of "returning home," and instead seek to feed off of negative energy to keep themselves going. According to the benevolent ETs they are disconnected from their inherent natural life force by refusing to abide by the One Infinite Creator's incarnation principles. They are essentially "imprisoned" within the fourth Density Negative cycle, as there is no "Negative Harvest" beyond the fourth Density. So they spend their time traveling the galaxy, fundamentally using the dark side of the "Force" (in this case negativity) to achieve their means. They will eventually be brought back before the Infinite Creator and dissolved back into the intelligent infinity, the source of all, though they are being given every chance, for as long as possible, to learn the error of their ways, return to seeking the positive, and begin their journey back home. The problem is, they do not want to go home. They see themselves as being "gods," and do not intend to submit to the authority of "The One."

THE DRACONIANS

Alpha Draconian reptilian ETs, or Dracos for short, are omnivores who move across planets like locusts seeking natural resources, including food, which in this case are humans and certain animals on Earth. When they on occasion use people for food, they prefer adolescents who have yet to be poisoned by Earth toxins. As shocking as this may seem, it suggests an answer to where thousands of missing children have gone, especially those who vanished from New Mexico. The Dracos have two hearts, are between two and four meters tall, and have the strength of a dozen men. They are hard to kill, have psychic and technological skills in battle that are thousands of years ahead of ours, and they're cold-blooded. They show no remorse or compassion for an enemy.

The Dracos have been manipulating humanity into a nearly invisible system of servitude for thousands of years, feeding off of our labor, energy and our bodies through the wars that they instigate, and the hostile belief systems that they foster in the form of religious and social institutions. They do not wish to be seen, only to direct their control orders to the Greys or certain influential people on Earth they have under their control. These people on Earth have sold out the human race, and in most cases, for their own greed and empowerment.

If the Dracos and Greys can hold us back from evolving to the fourth dimension, they can stay in control indefinitely. There is no guarantee we will break the bonds of our current heavy third dimensional reality, and their intention is to hold humans back from evolving to the fourth density at all costs. The reptoids did not evolve here; they were created elsewhere in the universe and migrated here to exploit our planet. Other UFOlogists believe that a sentient Saurian Race naturally evolved during the last stage of Earth's Cretaceous Period of the Mesozoic Era, departed the planet, then returned 5,700 years ago. Perhaps they left because of the asteroid Extinction Level Event that created a hostile living environment for the dinosaurs. It would explain how they have lived underground for so long and avoided the requirements of the Prime Directive.

Like the Greys, the Alpha Draconians claim to have genetically seeded our planet thousands of years ago, a reason they use to "justify" their attempt to retake Earth for their own purposes. They are apparently a major part of a planned "invasion" which is eventually turning from a covert infiltration mode, to an overt invasion mode as the "window of opportunity" begins to close. They are currently up against the Confederation of Planets decree to allow the Andromedans to rid them from our solar system. Earth is currently "quarantined," with Solar Warden assisting in enforcement. The Draconians are in a race against time between keeping us ignorant, or until our human society can make an interplanetary alliance with other human-like benevolent ETs. In such an alliance, humans could accept interstellar power allegiances that could rid the Earth of all reptoid species, similar to the choice Eisenhower was given when first contact was made with the Nordics.

Earthlings can still accept the offer of interplanetary alliance with all beings, but we have to come together as a planetary species. Ike didn't know that his agreement with the Greys would be a trick to trade technology for a treaty to experiment upon and exploit the Earth. The Draconians and Greys are attempting to implement their own imperialistic agenda by secretly withholding advanced technology for the betterment of humanity. If we were all made aware of the tremendous technology now available to humans, it would lead to eventual colonization of other planets by Earth and an eventual solution to the population, pollution, food and other environmental problems. But we are at an extreme disadvantage while still under the reptoid spell.

CAN WE ASCEND WITHOUT INTERFERENCE?

The first meeting of the Andromedan Council concerning Earth was to decide whether or not to directly intervene. According to an Andromedan contactee named Morenae, there were only 78 systems from the Confederation of Planets which originally took up the issue. Of those 78, just short of half decided that they wanted nothing at all to do with Earth, regardless of our disadvantages. These are star systems that are hundreds of millions of light years away from Earth, even some who have never observed us. They were aware that the vibration of the planet was negative and reflected the general attitude of Earth people. From their perspective they wanted to have no connection with Earth because humans did not respect themselves, wild or captive animals, or the planet as a whole. What could possibly be the value of Earth humans to the other higher entities? Fortunately, the majority of the Council gave the opinion that because

Earth has been heavily manipulated for over 5,700 years, we deserve an opportunity to ascend on our own. We should at least have a chance to prove the other part of the Council wrong.

Hence, they ordered everything extraterrestrial on the planet, on Earth's Moon, and on Mars to leave the solar system. The motive of the Council majority is to see how we will act when we are no longer being manipulated. This control will continue for a while longer because the human elite Powers That Be had worked in concert with the malevolent ETs, and it looked as if they were winning. However, now the human controllers won't have fourth dimensional back up, and that is leading to a much more level playing field. They still sanitize the masses with their agenda through television, religion and government. They are still teaching people what to think, but not how to think. If you take what they dish out, you become one of their robots. You become "sheeple." This is why there may never be an official government disclosure about UFOs or EBEs.

The big picture is of a well-populated universe of space-faring beings of very diverse physical attributes. For a number of reasons some of these ETs have taken an interest in Earth affairs, both out of service to others and of service to self. Their motives depend on whether it is profitable for them to interface with humans in their own self-interest, or a cooperative interest for the benefit of planetary evolution. We live in a galaxy that is teeming with life, including higher intelligence entities in every direction. We're just one of a series of evolutionary products, and by no means the leading one.

STAR SEEDS

Those who do not believe any of this will begin to open their minds as Earth consciousness expands, and we will start to see fantastic changes taking effect. Most people will be terrified and will have no idea what is happening, because elite power brokers have concealed vital information from the mass population, and will continue to do so as long as they can cling to power. One vital bit of information being withheld is that some of us are "travelers" or what has been termed "star seeds," incarnated on Earth in the last half century to help on the civilization and society level, willingly born into human bodies during this period of tremendous transformation to be the "ground crew" in humanity's great awakening.

Many of these star seeds have not yet "awakened." The Confederation stands by ready to help, if necessary. Individuals who have yet to awaken are those who have felt all their lives that they are somehow different, those who have a deep sense that they somehow do not belong here. Many of them will also have peculiar dreams and even visions of their lives on their home planets. The late past life regression hypnotherapist Delores Cannon had identified and helped many star seeds understand their role, and to adjust to their sometimes-confusing experience as incarnated humans on Earth. Many of these star seeds are in fact Pleiadians. This is why the Tall Blondes keep "showing up." They have voluntarily come to help their families awaken to their assignments here on Earth.

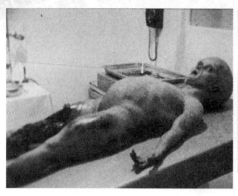
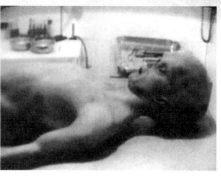

The above two images are still-frames from the famous 1995-released Ray Santilli Alien Autopsy video, purportedly showing an "Orange ET" from the June, 1947 Socorro, NM crash. This humanoid does not have a navel. There are several variously known extraterrestrial races interacting on Earth. One race has orange-grey skin, very big heads and large dark eyes with no irises or whites, and six-fingered hands as seen here. During dissection their brains have been found to have four brain lobes, different optic orbs and nerves, and a sponge-like digestive system. These ET brains are more developed and connected, and have no corpus callosum.

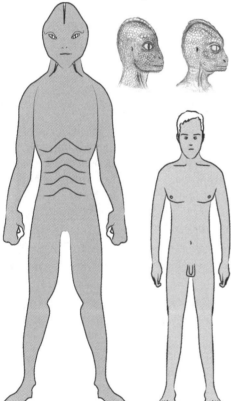

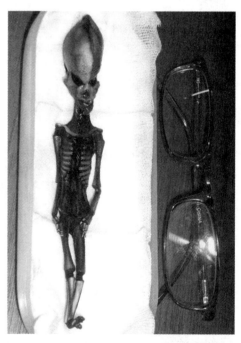

The size of bipedal and sentient EBEs seem to run the gamut from many meters tall to only a few centimeters in height. This supposed tiny extraterrestrial was examined in Steven Greer's film *SIrius*.

Two artist interpretations of the Alpha Draconian reptilian ETs. The human is shown for relative size.

CATTLE MUTILATIONS & HUMAN ABDUCTIONS

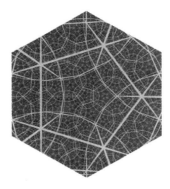

"The next war will be an interplanetary war. The nations must someday make a common front against attack by people from other planets."—Five Star General Douglas MacArthur, 1955

IN the realm of UFO-related mysteries, the cattle mutilations and human abduction phenomena are among the strangest reported. Thousands of farm animals have been surgically mutilated across North America, mainly in the Great Plains and the southern Rocky Mountain states, especially Colorado and New Mexico. Most of the mutilations have been done on cattle, although other farm animals have also been used. A common explanation is that the mutilations are associated with "occult" religious behavior, yet no group has come forward and no arrests have ever been made. The federal government shows absolutely no interest in investigating, and the Department of Justice dismisses it all as "performed by persons as part of a ritual or ceremony." However, Lou Girodo, Chief Investigator for the District Attorney's Office in Trinidad, Colorado, had been assigned to investigate the mysterious, bloodless, trackless animal deaths in southern Colorado. He concluded the perpetrators were "creatures not from this planet."

Here again we have a clear division between those who report something "high strange" regarding the cattle mutilations, and in a related category, the alien abduction phenomenon. The issue is very black and white. There is no grey zone. It is either so far out there that it is simply unbelievable, or an experience that has utterly changed a witness's life. It should be noted that it is a form of gullibility to believe the "official line" as much as it is to accuse believers of the same. If there were not overwhelming proof, a logical motive, and plausibility, there would be no discussion. Yet there is little doubt that an alien-related phenomenon exists for the many thousands of people who have witnessed mutilation remains, or who claim to have been abducted. The big question about cattle mutilations and human abduction is where could these stories be coming from? Do they originate up there, down here, or a combination of both? Or are we again dealing with mass hallucinations?

PHANTOM CATTLE SURGEONS OF THE GREAT PLAINS

What is a typical animal mutilation? Commonly the lips are gone, jaw flesh muscle is stripped to the bone, and the tongue removed. On other occasions one eye is surgically extracted, the ear cord gone, small centimeter skin patch areas are sliced off, the rectum cored out in an oval cone shape, utters taken from females, male or female sex reproductive systems extracted, and if it is a pregnant female, the fetus is removed; however, the fetal bag is not cut.

These are common medical observations by eyewitness reports from reputable sources such as veterinarians, the sheriff who was called out to investigate, or the rancher who lost his valuable livestock. But it gets even more high strange. All the blood is drained with no collapse of the vascular system, with not a drop of blood spilled anywhere. Tongues are cut far back in the mouth, yet not torn. Several mutilations can happen on successive nights, but there is no evidence of human tracks either. Apart from occult explanations, the Federal Government also blames "coyotes," yet there is no blood remaining in any of the wounds. There are always two holes and not a drop of blood within the carcass. The sex organs show specific parts missing. The carcasses appear to be dropped from above and left dead on the ground. What's more, the cattle mutilation phenomenon has been occurring regularly for a half century.

It is quite apparent that the party responsible is harvesting blood, eyes, tongues, hemoglobin, and removing specific body parts in a very precise manner. In some cases the incisions were made by cutting between the cells, a process we are not yet capable of performing in temporary field hospitals. Many thousands of individual cases have been reported with not a single arrest to date. It appears nothing can be done to stop the mutilations, along with no plausible explanation as to why they are occurring. There is no government explanation for the carcasses dropped into snow with no surrounding footprints. Yet, some of these animals weigh up to 6,350 kilograms! Since the phenomenon started in the mid-1960s, there have been over 50,000 reported animal mutilations.

Cows and humans are genetically similar. In the event of a national disaster, humans could use a cow's blood. Incidentally, there have also been human mutilations. One of the first was Sgt. Jonathan P. Louette at the New Mexico White Sands

Missile Test Range who went missing in 1956. He was found three days after an Air Force Major had witnessed his abduction by a "disk shaped" object at three in the morning while searching for missile debris down range. His genitals had been removed and his rectum cored out in a surgically precise manner. His eyes were extracted and all the blood in the body was removed, again with no vascular collapse.

THE MYSTERIOUS VALLEY

No other region in North America features more variety, intensity, and unusual animal mutilation phenomena than are found at the world's largest alpine valley, the San Luis Valley of Colorado and New Mexico. The world's first reported animal mutilation case called "Snippy the Horse," occurred in September, 1967, on the King Ranch near the Great Sand Dunes. As a result of this case, the San Luis Valley is regarded as the publicized birthplace of the highly unusual livestock mutilation phenomenon. Since then hundreds of animals, mostly open-range cattle, have been found bizarrely slaughtered around the valley. Thousands more have been discovered elsewhere in the Midwest and Southwest. Nearly all of the mutilated animals are found devoid of blood, eyes or other facial features, and signs indicate these body parts have been dismembered by precise heat laser incisions. Almost every mutilated animal has its "soft tissue" anal passage cored out and the genitals surgically removed. The fetus is routinely taken from pregnant cows, and it appears they are specifically targeted.

There are never tracks found near "authentic" mutilation sites, neither predatory animal nor human, but many have been found near burned ground with detectable levels of radiation. Some of the dead animals appear to be dropped from above, with evidence such as broken branches directly above the carcass and cracked animal bones from the fall impact. There are very few, if any, additional clues available at an animal mutilation site. As a result, no one has ever been officially charged or convicted of perpetrating an animal mutilation. As the largest alpine valley in the world, the San Luis Valley sits like an altar at the apex of the continent. At least one researcher has compared the valley to the high altars atop MesoAmerican pyramids, describing the valley as "North America's sacrificial altar" because of the multitude of animal mutilations.

The San Luis Valley is also a location of frequent UFO and paranormal encounters, especially above and around the Great Sand Dunes and Blanca Peak. The UFO sightings include unidentifiable aerial craft, flying metallic orbs, and mysterious floating lights, or "cheap fireworks" as the locals call them. Thousands of documented highly strange accounts of UFOs, crypto-creatures, human abductions, skinwalkers, Native American lore describing sorcerers, along with portal areas, secret underground bases, and covert military activity including the notorious black helicopters have been reported in and around the valley. The San Luis Valley is considered America's premiere unsolved mysterious "hot spot" because no other region in North America features the variety or intensity of unusual phenomenon that can be found here.

A common feature of the other primary North American paranormal hot spots, such as Area 51 in Nevada and White Sands in New Mexico, have a top-secret military presence nearby. On the eastern slopes of the Sangre de Cristo range in Colorado is the NORAD base located deep within Cheyenne Mountain. It is one of the most secretive and defensively secured military bases in the world. Reports of a clandestine underground base used by extraterrestrials, or an inter-dimensional portal within the Sangre de Cristo range and the Great Sand Dunes have also been claimed. Even Native American legends speak of a "doorway" in the Sangres that implicitly leads to another world or dimension. From the ancient past until today, strange phenomena have been a constant feature in the valley. The San Luis Valley town of Crestone has hosted several UFO and mysterious phenomenon conferences. This mysterious region at the top of North America has a higher incidence of UFO reports than any other area on the continent.

MEET BETTY AND BARNEY HILL

Anyone familiar with the alien abduction phenomenon likely has heard of an interracial couple named Betty and Barney Hill. On the night of September 19, 1961, Betty and Barney Hill, a married couple from New Hampshire, were driving home from Canada when they were subjected to a terrifying experience. Initially, however, it was a lost memory. They arrived home several hours later than expected, and there was little to indicate that anything unusual had happened during their return trip.

After some months of unexplained emotional distress, the couple could take no more, and they sought assistance from Benjamin Simon, a Boston-based psychiatrist and neurologist. Subjected to rigorous time-regression hypnosis, both Betty and Barney recalled precisely what had taken place during those missing two hours. Astonishingly, they provided a very close account of their encounters with alien beings who had taken the pair on-board a very advanced aircraft, and who had subjected them to a variety of distressing physical examinations.

Since the Betty and Barney Hill case, thousands of similar accounts have been reported around the world. A turning point came in 1981 with the publication of the late Budd Hopkins' book, *Missing Time*. Hopkins describes several abduction accounts, advancing a theory proposing that at least one extraterrestrial species was involved in the routine abduction of human beings. Hopkins' later work revealed a potentially far more sinister link to the abductions, namely, that the aliens were kidnapping people as part of some genetic operation, the goal of which was the production of a half-alien, half-human hybrid race.

HUMAN ABDUCTIONS

At least thousands, perhaps millions, of people (some reports say close to 1% of the entire human population) have claimed they were abducted by advanced alien life forms. Such large numbers are staggering and deserve serious attention devoted to this matter, yet none is forthcoming. The abductees are not crazed lunatics. Indeed, most are the opposite. When these people are profiled, they exhibit above average intelligence, rarely have any prior psychiatric history, and clearly were subjected to some kind of trauma. They often try to hide their experience for the backlash of incredulity the story might create.

Another commonality of abduction confessions is they all experienced nearly the same circumstances. At the M.I.T. Abduction Conference, Harvard abduction researcher John Mack said "If what these abductees are saying is happening to them *isn't* happening, then what is?" In summarizing his observations of the abduction experience, Dr. Mack wrote:

> *"I was faced with the choice of either trying to fit these individuals' reports in a framework that fit my worldview—they were having fantasies, strange dreams, delusions or some other distortion of reality—or of modifying my worldview to include the possibility that entities, beings, energies—something—could be reaching my clients from another realm. The first choice was compatible with my worldview, but it did not fit the clinical data. The second was inconsistent with my philosophical grounding, and with conventional assumptions about reality, but appeared to fit better what I was finding. It seemed to be more logical, and intellectually more honest to modify my cosmology than to continue trying to force my clients into molds that did not suit them."*

The patterns or common elements that Dr. Mack observed in his patients' abduction memories can be described as: (1) medical and surgical procedures, often including an introduction of the abductees to alien/human hybrids; (2) the relaying of an ecological warning about the survival of the planet and the human species; (3) the initiation of a transforming, consciousness expanding phenomenon; (4) the eventual development of relationships with these beings. Subjects who claim they were abducted have in many cases discovered they were given implants in the nose, within the skullcap, in the ear or in arm locations. Is the idea of implanted people who have been abducted really so farfetched? Animal pets are regularly chipped, and sometimes implants are found in mutilated cattle carcasses. There are ex-cons now receiving RFID chip implants upon being released from prison. RFID chips are being introduced to corporate employees, and the overall roll-out will be made to appear as beneficial to the implanted person. Fundamental Christians look at any form of implanted RFID chip as "666," or a "Mark of the Beast."

WHO IS DOING THIS?

Almost all of the human abductions and animal mutilations on Earth are done by the Greys, small neo-saurian hominoids with several sub-species. The Greys, or the best-understood Zeta Reticulans, appear to be divided into two different groups. There is one group that appears to be a little more tolerant towards human beings. The other group is interested in colonization and conquest of planet Earth. Certain Greys seem to have influence over the Reticulan and the Beeletrax species of Greys, where all Grey species are in turn under control of the Draconians. It should also be noted that black helicopters have been connected to the dropping of carcasses. It could be that implanted and controlled humans are also under control of the reptoids and also play a role in the mutilation mystery.

The abducting Greys are described as having a crystalline translator wand that allows telepathic communication with humans. This device can also completely subdue the victim. Crystals are known transmitters and receivers with incredible storage possibilities. Crystals, when programmed, hold certain frequencies and can counteract opposites, plus utilize tone and sound. Crystals can naturally absorb nature's information. Upon abduction, most subjects are inserted with a tiny, three-millimeter spherical device through the nasal cavity into the brain of the abductee. The device is used for the biological monitoring, tracking, and continued mind control of the abductee. The Greys also have an energetic presence that can mesmerize an abductee, described as radiating at a higher frequency, associated with all ET contactees.

The Greys are highly telepathic, intelligent scientists, and are prolific across the universe. The Greys are logic-based and operate on base animal survival or predatory instincts and in most cases are emotionally insensitive to humans. The Greys range from 1 to .3 meters in height on average, with skin colors ranging from gray-white to grey-brown to gray-green to grey-blue. They have been cloning themselves instead of the practice of natural reproduction we use on Earth. Each time they re-clone, however, the genetic copy becomes weaker, which is part of their problem. Their attitude towards humans is tolerance towards inferiors. They are technologically superior but spiritually and socially backward.

It would appear their brains, or their intellect, belong to a serpent race, whereas the larger reptoids allegedly act as the physical overlords, and thus are of a higher "ranking" than the Greys. Aside from feeding off of human and animal proteins and fluids, they also allegedly feed off the chi or "life energy," the "vital essence" or "soul energy" of humans, as do other reptilian species. Their basic program is service to self rather than sharing or service to others. Our world is not the only world they have tried to conquer.

Similar to other reptilian entities, they feed off of human and animal vital fluids by rubbing a "liquid protein" formula on their bodies, which is then absorbed through their skin. Like typical reptiles that shed their skin, the "waste" is excreted back through the skin. These Greys have no stomach and digest their food by absorption through the skin or under their tongue. They are using this planet as a supply depot for biological materials, and are responsible for nearly all of the human abductions and cattle mutilations. But just as the Draconians do not wish to do the dirty work of abductions, neither do the Greys. They leave that to the Programmed Life Forms (PLFs) or humans under their control.

The Draconians are a subspecies of the Greys, or more precisely, masters of the Greys. The command hierarchy in this reptilian society are the Dracos on top, with the winged sub-species first in command. Secondly, the non-winged Dracos are next in charge. Then there are the Greys in their multitude of species and varieties. Lowest on the pecking order are the PLF cloned hybrids being produced underground here on Earth. This group, which include genetically spliced aspects of the Greys, pose the greatest danger to Earth humans at this time.

HYBRIDS

Dr. Steven Greer of the Disclosure Project reveals compelling insider testimony that most of the UFO abductions are now being carried out by the so-called PLFs, or Programmable Life Forms, developed in conjunction with the human shadow government or cabal. Therefore, according to Greer, once we defeat the cabal we can stop the abductions, and end the UFO cover-up. Greer's contacts confirmed that the PLF technology was acquired from the Greys and involves advanced cloning principles to create a "biological robot," which is part human, part alien.

To do this, a human fetus is grown in an artificial test tube environment. Without the pressure of growing in the womb, it retains fetal proportions and features—including the large eyes, big head and thin body—on into adulthood. PLFs could easily be mistaken as Greys, as they look very similar, but are genetic hybrids with some distinct human aspects. The PLF technology was first perfected in the early 1960s and soon put into wider use. This may be why there are no reports of alien abductions prior to the infamous Betty and Barney Hill case.

Having studied the abduction phenomenon for over 45 years, Temple University professor David Jacobs, Ph.D., the author of the highly regarded books *The UFO Controversy In America* and *Secret Life*, has come to regard the abductions as a means to breed hybrids in an attempt to replace our human population on Earth. He is somewhat apologetic about his conclusion and realizes how outrageous it sounds—especially to those with little or no knowledge about the aliens or the abduction phenomenon. According to Dr. Jacobs, the program is huge and spans a tremendous amount of time. It's done slowly and carefully to remain clandestine. However, the duration only seems long to humans, who have an average lifespan of about 80 years. Aliens presumably live much longer and have more patience and time to reach their eventual goal. And that goal, according to abduction experts, is to take over our planet, replacing Homo sapiens with a hybrid race. Dr. Jacobs feels certain that the intentions of the aliens is to build a critical mass of hybrids and then, when they are ready, a "trigger event" will disable our infrastructure and culture, allowing the hybrids to overtly initiate their planned takeover of the planet.

HOW DO THEY GET AWAY WITH IT?

The Greys, and by extension the PLFs, have the ability to magnify their mental field in order to maintain control over humans. Sometimes humans are seen working with the Greys. These humans "drones" have been implanted and programmed. It is not known whether they work with the Greys willingly or unwillingly. The human assistants have appeared "lifeless" and "emotionless" to the witnesses who observed them during human abductions. Similarly, as far as the Greys are concerned, the PLFs are not a species themselves, but they have been created to work for someone else. There are several different levels to the PLFs, and there are many instances that indicate they do not function independently. There are many different types of Greys and PLFs and they operate from higher orders. They are all programmed cybernetic organisms.

In his blind quest to acquire high technology for military purposes, President Eisenhower met with the Greys and signed the "Greada Treaty." But this was never passed by the Congress or made known to the people of Earth; therefore, there is no valid treaty. Unfortunately, there is still a "curtain of ridicule" promoted by corporate-controlled mass media, NASA, and the U.S. Military, which keep many abductees silent and all reputable scientific researchers sidelined from the subject. The subject is simply too fantastic to be believed.

The Greys are extremely deceitful to humans, and although they act on "logic" (to them abductions are "logical"), they use extremely complex forms of deception to bring about their goals. They are the most commonly observed alien entities encountered during UFO events. They use skillful telepathic communication. All the different species of reptilians are regressive members of a network which is a type of loose alliance in which all have common aims; but it is the Greys and PLFs who perform the direct work on people and animals.

TO SERVE MAN (IT'S A COOKBOOK!)

The Greys are impregnating human females on a massive scale, and later extracting the fetuses. Most of their biological materials come from cattle mutilations. However, it is known that at times they have done human mutilations and killed the subject. The human body parts found on the Grey's crashed UFOs was especially shocking to the U.S. Military and science personnel in the late 1940s, reinforcing their belief that the whole phenomenon must be kept secret until a plan is developed for how to deal with the multiple and increasingly bizarre implications.

It appears the Tall Greys have been on Earth for many centuries, along with their reptilian Draco masters, with a legacy base operating near the Aleutian Islands. Another older base tied to ET abductions and human disappearances is about 70 kilometers west of the capital Honiara, in the range of Mount Poporion on Guadalcanal in the Solomon Islands. Also in the Solomon Islands, on mainland Malaita, about five kilometers directly inland from that circular reef entrance, is a lake which has two connected entrances and exits. It appears the reptoids are mining a very rare type of gemstone with a far higher specific gravity than diamonds under this volcanic rock island.

Back in America, the latest estimate is that over 1,000 Greys are currently working in the underground base at Dulce, New Mexico, doing genetic experiments. There are some books on the market which say that the Greys are our friends, and that we agreed to these abductions. This is completely untrue. These are very disturbed entities and are here to exploit whatever they want on this planet for their own selfish purposes. They view humans in a similar way that the majority of people in society regard industrialized farm animals: to be harvested and exploited.

It appears that the Greys are trying to regenerate their own species at our expense. They have apparently suffered either some kind of nuclear holocaust, or they may be on the backside of a bell-shaped evolutionary curve where in essence they are "devolving" instead of evolving because they lost their capacity to reproduce naturally. In any case, according to several autopsies of aliens that have been leaked, the Greys have an atrophied digestive system and many other physical problems. This would account for their attempts to crossbreed with humans as outlined in *Intruders* by Budd Hopkins. The book is a detailed study of an Indianapolis woman who, over the course of a decade, has produced seven crossbreed alien children unwillingly, none of whom she was allowed to keep. She has been coming to terms with these traumatic events ever since.

HELPING US BETTER UNDERSTAND ABDUCTIONS

It would appear that human abductions have been taking place for quite some time, but their frequency has accelerated in recent decades. For several thousand years there have been reports of alien abduction for sexual purposes. Because of the number of reports coming from early church members, much attention was given to the phenomenon during the 11th and 12th centuries. Thomas Aquinas wrote in his 13th century book *Summa Theologica*: "If sometimes children are born from intercourse with demons, this is not because of the semen emitted by them, or from the bodies they have assumed, but through the semen taken from some man for this purpose, seeing that the same demon who acts as a succubus for a man becomes an incubus for a woman." Another writer from this era named Bonaventura wrote: "Devils in the form of women yield to males and receive their semen; by cunning skill, the demons preserve its potency, and afterwards, they become incubi and pour it into female repositories."

Karla Turner, Ph.D. was a dedicated and compassionate woman who helped many abductees come to terms with their abusive alien experiences, as she herself was an abduction survivor. Part of the trauma that most abduction victims experience, she noted, is the lack of support from the government or help from any official survivor's group. Dr. Turner began doing independent abduction research objectively, cutting through the ridicule and denial offered by virtually every other channel. She was not afraid to tell the truth, no matter how bizarre it sounded. One such remark was: "Personally, I believe one could control political leaders more easily with implants." Dr. Turner has appeared on the *Montel Williams Show* and other programs to discuss her research. She passed away at age 48 from a particularly deadly form of terminal cancer. She died rather suddenly in early 1996, after multiple death threats demanding she stop her work. Since Dr. Turner's passing, several other people involved in UFO investigations have also experienced threats, followed by contracting various forms of highly unusual cancer. The fast-moving cancer has been the cause of death for other researchers, and would seem a way to eliminate a whistleblower without causing much suspicion. Some suspect that Dr. Turner's cancer was induced via radiation received from earlier abductions, but this cannot be confirmed. She did alert the public to the reptilian atrocities, which she called "Draconicide." One of her most remarkable statements was: "Aliens can take us—our consciousness—out of our physical bodies, disable our control of our bodies, install one of their own entities, and use our bodies as vehicles for their own activities before returning our consciousness to our bodies."

Whitley Strieber, one of the most popular abductees to write about his experiences, reportedly was abducted in 1985 from his cabin in upstate New York by non-human beings. He wrote about these experiences two years later in his first nonfiction book, *Communion*, with several more to follow. There is a pet theory among ET researchers which states that aliens, whether objectively real or not, serve as "mirrors" of our spiritual nature, on an individual or a species-wide basis. Streiber has voiced this theory in his book *Majestic*, where he says, "In the eyes of the others (the aliens), we who met them saw ourselves. And there were demons there." The idea, spiritual or otherwise, that there is no objective reality apart from our perceptions or projections of an internal state is an ancient cornerstone of many mystical thought systems. In that sense, what we see or experience at the behest of aliens—or our next-door neighbors—is a product of our minds. This belief reduces fear since changing our minds undoes the sense of threat. Throughout this book, this first-order solution is mentioned as internal work from which appropriate action can emanate. That said, missing people is a documented phenomenon, especially children who often vanish without a trace. Since 1980, at least 20,000 children have been reported missing each year in the U.S. alone.

IMPLANTED HUMANS

The Andromeda Council has recognized that a sizeable percentage of Earth's population was unknowingly implanted and negatively affected by Grey etheric and physical implant technology. To briefly revisit the Andromeda Council, this is an intergalactic governance body of third to sixth dimensional beings, with a particular affinity to humans and who believe Earth's inhabitants have the right to be free of the reptoid manipulations. The manipulative techniques are meant to keep humans in a state of anxiety, fear, subservience, manipulation and control. Though some physical implants have been found and removed by Earth physicians over the years, at our current stage of spiritual evolution and technology we do not yet have the means to detect, measure, or eliminate the Greys' use of physical and etheric implants.

On behalf of Earth's freedom, the Andromeda Council is helping to clean up the mess, but there is still much to do. Especially vexing are the microscopic implants within thousands, maybe millions of Earth humans, which are still in place and operational. The resulting spiritual, psychological, emotional impact, and multiplicity of problems the Greys have inflicted on humans will take some time to fully resolve. They have unlawfully sought to enslave an unaware human population on this planet. As long as their presence is kept secret by the Powers That Be, while the people of Earth remain unaware of the many ways in which we are being manipulated, can our true human evolutionary advancement and spiritual freedom be fully achieved. Their influence has been strong and it will take time for humans, especially those under the spell of implants, to break free. But first we have to know what we are truly up against.

Betty and Barney Hill alleged that they were abducted by extraterrestrials around 10:30 PM while traveling through rural New Hampshire. According to the reports the couple has provided over the years, they first spotted a bright light at a distance which they did not think could possibly be an aircraft. When the craft approached them, they stopped in the middle of the road and could see the craft was saucer-shaped with humanoid figures inside. When it approached too close they became frightened and sped off. At some point they believe they were abducted because later they discovered that they had traveled 56 kilometers with only spotty memories of this portion of the trip. Their watches no longer worked correctly, and Barney Hill noticed that the strap for his binoculars was ripped, even though he cannot remember tearing the strap.

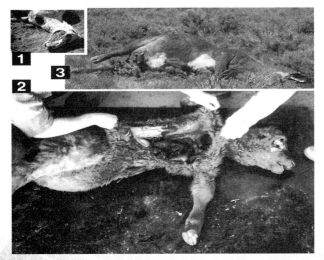

These images are from famed cattle mutilation researcher Christopher O'Brien. They were all taken in and around the San Luis Valley. In the first image, Mr. O'Brien is investigating the Hooper, CO mutilation in January, 1999. The second is a calf from Del Norte, CO taken in March, 1996, which he says was his "weirdest case." Finally, the third image is the San Antonio Mountain, NM case, which was discovered in July, 2010.

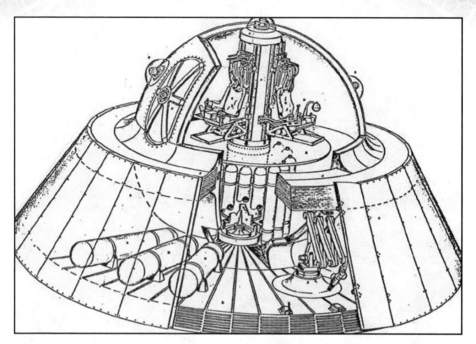

This is a cutaway illustration of the backward engineered "Alien Reproduction Vehicle," or "flux liner," as it is sometimes called. The crew compartment is a composite sphere surrounded by a large coil of copper-colored wire embedded in a greenish, glass-like material. The central column holds the secondary windings of this very large Tesla Coil device. The base of the vehicle is about 7.3 meters in diameter and is made up of 48 individual asymmetric plate capacitor sections, each having eight plates. By varying the amount of electricity pulsed at each section from the central column, and exploiting the Biefield-Brown effect, maneuvering control can be achieved.

Area 51, near Nevada State Route 375, otherwise known as the "Extraterrestrial Highway," is a small section within the vast Nellis Air Force Base. But Area 51 receives the king's share of attention because this is where the military has for decades stored frozen ETs, harbored living ETs, and keeps various models of recovered alien spacecraft used for backward engineering science by certain aerospace contractors.

MEN IN BLACK

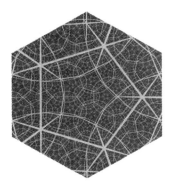

"The truth may be puzzling. It may take some work to grapple with. It may be counterintuitive. It may contradict deeply held prejudices. It may not be consonant with what we desperately want to be true. But our preferences do not determine what's true." –Carl Sagan

MENTION the term "Men in Black" and most people will probably roll their eyes, or refer to the 1997 motion-picture sci-fi hit starring Tommy Lee Jones and Will Smith. But what many people may not realize is that the origin of the movie is based on hundreds of real-life encounters with the proverbial "MiB." Paranormal witness encounters with intimidating agent-like men in black suits who are thought to belong to a secret organization with a secret agenda have been occurring for decades. There have been many anomalous and supernatural reports, throughout the years, of a group of men wearing trench coats and fedora hats, wrap-around glasses, and stern expressions with the sole purpose of harassing UFO witnesses. They appear the way they do, not for effect, but as camouflage. Most Men in Black encounters are by night. The MiB are eerily elusive with very few confirmed photos or any evidence of their visitations.

The legend of the Men in Black first emerged in the late-1940s around the time of the first UFO crash recoveries, but they became more ubiquitous in the 1950s when covert organization began to control all operations surrounding paranormal activities. Knowledge about the MiB started gaining popularity in the 1950s with books such as Gray Barker's *They Knew Too Much About Flying Saucers*. Their presence is still in the mainstream today with the *Men in Black* franchise of movies, which are originally based on a comic book theme inspired by the phenomenon. At the height of the MiB sightings in the 1950s, J. Edgar Hoover ordered a copy of Barker's book, and was using the FBI to actively investigate the mystery.

WHO ARE THESE GUYS?

Initially, the first reports of Men in Black involved witnesses of UFOs or extraterrestrial encounters. One of the first reports of MiB was in 1947 when Harold Dahl reported that he saw six UFOs when he and several friends were boating. After the encounter, Dahl said an intimidating muscular man wearing a nondescript black suit took him out to breakfast and threatened him and his family if he ever spoke of the encounter. Dahl later recanted this meeting, but it may be that he was intimidated again and decided to simply deny that he saw anything rather than have his family meet the Men in Black.

Since the first reports of MiB, many have tried to discover the true identity and agenda of these dark agents, with little success. And for those who do know their true identity, either by association or as a "subject" of one of their operations, it has been strongly suggested that the means they utilize to maintain total suppression of all paranormal information is disturbingly successful.

According to the accounts of people contacted by them, the Men In Black always seem to have detailed information on the persons they contact, as if the individual has been under surveillance for a long period of time. This can be shocking to the witnesses, who maintain they have never done anything wrong and have no police record. The MiBs have been described as seeming confused by the nature of everyday items such as pens, eating utensils, or food, as well as using outdated slang, although accounts of their behavior vary widely. They often claim to be from an agency collecting information on the unexplained phenomenon their subject has encountered. The MiBs are associated with almost all paranormal and anomalous phenomena, not just UFOs. They have spoken to witnesses of poltergeists, spacetime disturbances, telepathy and psychokinesis, along with sightings of Bigfoot and the Loch Ness Monster, just to name a few. They are suspected to be the shadow organization and the workhorse team behind countless above top secret projects around the world. In all cases, agents in black appear to collect information and silence those specific witnesses who claim to have experienced weird or unusual phenomena.

MiB ARE HUMANS IN THE BLACK OPS

The U.S. top secret projects associated with MiB include Majestic-12, stargate technology and Area 51. To this day, they continue to infiltrate the governments around the world, seeking out, analyzing, and concealing (at all costs) extraordinary phenomena of every type for their own ultra top secret agenda. Sometimes the Men in Black have claimed to come from the U.S. Air Force or the CIA. Those who have encountered them say they produce identification, but when verification is later sought, the people described either do not exist, have been dead for some time, or do exist but have a different rank.

Shortly after the 1947 Roswell crash, several strangers came to the air base dressed in plainclothes and flashed ID cards for an unknown project, perhaps part of the special CIC-team, then called the Army Counter-Intelligence Corp. Many reports confirm a special CIC-team was placed in charge of the Roswell recovery operation. Also in attendance at the base were Secret Service agents representing President Truman.

The presence of MiB may have heightened Eisenhower's concern over losing control of the UFO technology situation. He felt betrayed by the end of his term when he saw enormous power falling into the hands of private corporations who were given access to the recovered materials. This would explain his damning condemnation of the military industrial complex power grab in his final speech before leaving office.

Another possible explanation of ongoing MiB activities is that the newest MiBs are trained cyborg assassins (a cybernetic organism being with both biological and artificial parts), gleaned from test tube babies developed in the early 1970s.

In a March, 2011 interview, Michael Prince revealed that between 1976 and 1979 he was one of a group of 42 children who were subjected to trauma-based mind control and implanted as future cyborg super soldiers. He claims he was trained at a secret Nazi SS and MI-6 U.K. intelligence networks trauma mind control training facility at Fort Nelson, British Columbia, Canada. The super secret base was officially called the Nazi SS Q552 base, not far from the tourist town of Nelson. The 42 children (including himself) were all test tube babies, each bearing sought-after human-extraterrestrial DNA. They were adopted into human families that were part of multi-generational trauma-based mind control families. The children were being trained to be future assassins and continue to operate in that capacity today. This information collaborates with abundant independent evidence of a threatened takeover of human society by the controlling elite, who are in turn following the agenda of a hostile reptilian faction leading the efforts.

OFFICE OF SCIENTIFIC INVESTIGATION & RESEARCH

The Men In Black, acting as secret governmental agents, are commonly identified as working clandestinely with the Black Arts. They were created under the alias of a non-descript organization called the Office of Scientific Investigation and Research (O.S.I.R.). Created in the early 1940s as a byproduct of a top secret government program, the O.S.I.R. is an ultra top secret organization whose far-reaching operations can be found in every corner of the world. Their secret officers are dispatched to throw people off the Black Ops trail, spread disinformation, or intimidate paranormal witnesses to keep quiet.

The O.S.I.R., among other things, is known to conduct scientific research and investigations surrounding anomalous phenomena. This is also known as paranormal, parapsychological, supernatural and metaphysical phenomena. The organization is said to have significant power, utilizing their far-reaching authority to suppress and maintain their operations and very existence. They operate independently of all governments and private organizations, and while their true agenda is unknown, it is believed that the study of anomalous phenomena and its potential applications might be their primary focus.

With significant funding and resources, as well as rumored advanced technology and influence with various powerful officials, the O.S.I.R. infiltrates many aspects of society and government, scanning for phenomena and conducting their scientific operations. Aspects of science, law, medicine, religion, government, and business applications in the corporate world are permeated with their operatives.

For anyone who might be involved in any of their clandestine operations, be it a person who experiences a phenomenon, or an individual recruited to partially assist their operations, the O.S.I.R. utilizes disturbingly unorthodox all-encompassing means of intimidation, coupled with techniques to suppress or cover-up any and all information. It is the peculiar *modus operandi* of the O.S.I.R. that suggests they are indeed the notorious MIBs. In order to conduct their clandestine operations, the organization takes on various aliases and "cover identities," choosing to hide in plain sight.

The O.S.I.R. came into the public eye in 1990 when the organization opened a public affairs department. For a decade, by means of this department, the O.S.I.R. interacted with the general public and the media, openly stating that their primary focus is "anomalous phenomena." In 2000, the O.S.I.R. closed its public affairs department and terminated all contacts with the outside world. Nothing important has been heard from them since.

NON-HUMAN OR INTERDIMENSIONAL MiB

Some MiB reports describe them as being eerily inhuman, taking on characteristics of an unearthly nature. Some theorists propose that many of these reports of MiB were allowed to be disseminated in order to create an air of unbelievability among those who reported them, who will more readily dismiss their own paranormal encounter. The only constant is their apparent objective to track down true paranormal encounters and control the situation to suit their own agenda.

However, if they are of strictly human origin, this does not explain many of the "high strange" aspects of the MiB encounters. Also referred to as "Horlocks," several theories claim they are apparently humans, but act strangely because they are controlled by Draconian influences. An extension of this theory suggests the MiB are the hybrid human and Grey mix being developed on Earth for decades and paranormal witness intimidation is one of their programmed tasks. The most bizarre of encounters reveal the MiB as non-emotional and non-expressive, with no visible response, almost as if they know nothing of human culture. Logic, surprise, or human emotions do not seem to apply to these biosynthetic MiB forms. Most MiB do not seem to act or talk like government agents or policemen either. Their behavior seems more reptilian or synthetic than human. Most humanoid MiB have probably been implanted by the Draconians, and are essentially their telepathic "slaves."

Over the decades, MiB have taken on somewhat different forms. Some are reported as exceptionally tall, while others are much shorter than average, but their similarities are undeniable. Stiff black suits, sunglasses and traveling in big black Cadillacs are all associated with their appearances. The MiB are often, though not always, associated with large black automobiles, some of which have been seen disappearing into mountainsides. Although appearing new, the old model black cars seem weirdly out of date, especially in the more modern MiB encounters. On rare occasions, the MiB have been reported walking through walls to confront paranormal witnesses. They have been seen driving off into canyons or tunnels, or in some cases appearing or disappearing into thin air.

The MiB, as the malevolent ET theory suggests, come from external societies existing underground. They are said to reside in ancient antediluvian or "Atlantean" underground complexes which have been re-established beneath the Eastern U.S. seaboard, on the West Coast, and elsewhere. In the case of one subterranean base located between Hopland and Lakeport, California, their cars are last seen driving into the side of a mountain and disappearing! Another suspected MiB base location is near the Dugway airfield in Utah, called the "New Area 51," where backward engineered crafts are being actively tested. Their black cars seem to be cloaked or treated with an advanced electromagnetic technique (a capability discussed recently by physicists) or have interdimensional aspects, because they can be gone in an instant, seemingly having the ability to materialize and dematerialize at will. While something similar to this invisibility phenomenon has been demonstrated in our modern laboratories, interdimensional phenomena is barely at the theoretical stage. The possibility of multiple dimensions is suggested by mathematics and vigorously discussed by theoretical physicists, but its implications are scarcely touched upon.

SHAPESHIFTING

The term "shapeshifting" refers to a change in the shape or form (visible to the naked eye) of a person or an alien creature. It is also called transformation, transmogrification, homeomorphism or metamorphosis. Although MiB possess human shape, form, and basic anatomy, strictly speaking, they are not human beings. While they can morph to look like us, the only thing that cannot change are their pupils, which they hide behind contact lenses, or heavy sunglasses, and they always have vertical slits instead of circles. Their actual normal or "real" appearance is that of a hideous-looking creature that would most certainly alarm or terrify any Earth human.

These entities are known to have infiltrated our military industrial complex, with a particular interest in our planetary missile defense network called Star Wars. Many scientific researchers in the USA and the UK working on the Strategic Defense Initiative (SDI) have died of mysterious causes. At least one shapeshifter was discovered working inside the SDI program. Apparently the entity had been stealing documents and transmitting their contents to some point beyond the planet. Rumor has it that the entity was physically examined and it was discovered that its internal organs were not human. Another way the shapeshifters can be detected is by the strangeness of their auras.

Some UFO witnesses report being terrorized by apparent quasi-human infiltrators who look like the Men In Black, although many of the MiB who have been reported were obviously humans working for some obscure operation such as a subterranean intelligence or an off-world planetary agency. Other entities could be either cyborgs or clones or even paraphysical manifestations. There was a branch of the so-called MiB that exhibited definite reptilian characteristics. Among their own kind, they use thought only, but they have learned to speak English and other languages fluently. In essence, these are reptilian humanoids with a full-blown (although at times not-too-convincing) "reconstructive surgery" job, apparently intended to allow them to operate in human society undetected. Some of the early infiltrators betrayed themselves with their "plastic" or artificial appearance, whereas in more recent years, the disguise has become far more sophisticated. With the advent of molecular shapeshifting occult technology, techno-hypnotic transmitters and portable laser-hologram technology, artificially created entities are much more difficult to detect.

Besides changing their own physical attributes, shapeshifting entities are also reported to attach to humans by two of the lower chakras. The entity itself stays hidden in the lower fourth dimension, while the human is manipulated to do the entity's bidding. The reptoids overshadow a human while not actually occupying the body.

The shapeshifting ability is not a "natural" phenomenon in the same sense that the creature we know as a chameleon can change its skin color. Those creatures capable of shapeshifting do not exist as a separate race. However, they engage in rituals and utilize certain technologies that enable them to alter their particular physical appearances. It has to do with the fact that the body, as is true of all physical things, is not really solid. It looks and feels as if it is, but in actuality, all matter is composed of atomic and sub-atomic particles of light interacting as molecules and compounds chemically joined together. There are certain rituals which, when undertaken, allow for a range of "manipulations" of the so-called "solid" bodily mass to arrange itself into different appearances.

UFO CONNECTION

Throughout their history, MiB have been primarily associated with UFOs and extraterrestrial phenomena because of the simple fact that these phenomena are primarily aerial events in the atmosphere and widely viewed by many witnesses. Therefore, when reports of MiB follow reports of UFOs or extraterrestrial encounters, they are given more credence and attract a wider audience. The MiB have been encountered most often after UFO sightings, usually intimidating witnesses into keeping silent about what they've seen. Some of the witnesses may be abductees with suppressed memories of the event.

Some UFO witnesses did not report their sightings, had not yet spoken to anyone, but had an impossibly fast visit from the MiB, sometimes within hours. It is as if the MiB have precognition of the best and most efficient location to confront a fresh witness. One theory is they are space travelers, coming back at the right time, and fitting into society with their strange mode of dress and outdated cars. Maybe some UFOs are time machine crafts, rather than interstellar craft, and the MiB are tasked with making these objects seemingly invisible.

Apparently instilling fear is the goal of the MiB; a form of psychic intimidation, but not necessarily direct physical threats. They have an air of intimidation, described as the feeling one gets before a dog barks and then bites. There are lots of psychological dramas playing out during the high strange MiB witness encounters. Their threats appear to be motivated by telepathic attempts to utilize terror and fear as a psychological weapon against witnesses. But make no mistake, say researchers, MiBs have been monitoring, analyzing and researching every type of anomalous and paranormal phenomena imaginable for decades. It is very likely the MiB are associated with the rogue J-Rod Greys, who are against disclosure of the situation in any manner that could promote our present-day human species enlightenment, since this enlightenment would provide human conscious souls the freedom from their devious plan of mass manipulation. Thus, they must continue to control the greater human consciousness to be an expedient resource for their own "service to self" means and ends.

DOCTRINE OF THE CONVERGENT TIMELINE PARADOX

According to the "Doctrine of the Convergent Time Lines" as proposed by Area 51 microbiologist Dan Burisch, the rogue J-Rods are really future humans who have deployed a population of human-Grey clones in this current era. These entities are early products of prior accomplished future-human/past-human genetic hybridization work. These Programmable Life Forms (PLF) are the most likely candidates of the MiB identity, whose core mission is to enforce their own timeline operations. This causality control and containment operational force of MiB, instigated by the Tall Greys, is intended to accomplish the ends of preventing the population from becoming aware of their devious genetic and abduction activity. They have a vested interest in preventing the kind of scientific progress which would develop technologies that could be used against them. Their present era manipulating presence is also to prevent any mass human enlightenment breakthroughs that could impair their capacity to manipulate present day humans toward a future of servitude to their own future evolutionary ends. From the rogue ET view, any widespread consensus acknowledgement and awareness of their manipulating presence would produce unpredictable responses among the genetic resource stock, and thereby hinder their regressive usage agenda.

If benevolent ETs contribute to averting an Earth catastrophe, this will help balance the "karmic effect" they have made of the present era as an evolutionary pit stop for their journey into a new future from this looping back point. During the next decade, present era humans will experience an optimum evolutionary boost from the natural stargate activation, and the massive wave of cosmic energy called Wave X, which started to arrive on Earth at the end of September 2015. This will feed forward to produce new evolutionary and future spiritual factors that will again feed back to support our new course into an even deeper positive participant quantum energetic karmic loop. If successful, there is no turning back. The Men in Black and all malevolent forces will find it nearly impossible to exist on the newly awakened planet Earth.

This is an image from a video of two Men in Black entering a hotel lobby, as reported on the *Coast to Coast* radio program in April, 2012. The MiB were described as looking exactly alike, without eyelashes, eyebrows, and hair that looked like a wig attached to their hats. Their eyes were so big and their pupils so blue that they were described as almost hypnotizing. For the entire extent of their conversation their eyes were unblinking. The witness also sensed that the Men in Black were telepathic.

An approximate caricature of a Man in Black. It is possible they are "Programmable Life Forms," created by malevolent ETs interacting with Earth. If so, they would hold tremendous power and advanced abilities over humans. Author George Kavassilas postulated an interface between human chakras and alien implants.

CRYPTOZOOLOGY

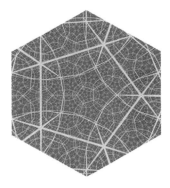

"The first peace, which is the most important, is that which comes within the souls of people when they realize their relationship, their oneness, with the universe and all its powers, and when they realize at the center of the universe dwells the Great Spirit, and that this center is really everywhere, it is within each one of us."
–Black Elk, Sioux holy man

CRYPTOZOOLOGY is a term coined in the 1950s by a French zoologist named Bernard Heuvelmans. It means, literally, the study of hidden or unknown animals. It is the study of such obscure creatures as the Australian bunyip, or the more popularly recognized Bigfoot, chupacabra, or the Loch Ness Monster. In the early 20th century, American writer Charles Fort started compiling great quantities of exhaustively documented and "puzzling evidence." This is data which science is unable or unwilling to explain, such as rainstorms which dropped fish, frogs, mysterious animals, blood, or the discovery of manufactured artifacts in the deep strata. Fort collected numerous accounts of aerial phenomena prior to the invention of aviation, including descriptions of huge cylinders and spheres in the sky. Many of these today would be considered UFOs. Cryptozoology, or Fortean Zoology, is the study of any kind of unexplained animal or "monster." Such creatures or "cryptids" are unrecognized by mainstream scientific consensus and thus their existence is considered unlikely. As such, cryptozoology is not a recognized scientific branch of zoology.

Even in the 21st century, many assume there's nothing really new to discover on this large, diverse planet of ours. This assumption couldn't be further from the truth! There have been numerous sightings and encounters over the centuries of creatures that were either thought to have been extinct, or were never properly identified. There are over 700 distinct species of butterflies on the island of New Guinea alone. Overlooked new creatures are identified all the time, or are hypothesized to be living in the untamed vastness of areas such as the Amazon and other dense jungle regions, not to mention the deepest realms of the world's oceans.

The Weiser Field Guide to Cryptozoology is a book that includes information, interviews, and stories about 40 different cryptids seen in various locations all over the world. Credible eyewitnesses include policemen, rangers, and doctors. Such creatures are known as Anomalous Biological Entities (ABEs). Readers will learn where and how to find flying mothmen, hairy humanoids, and odd creatures of all kinds including giant rabbits, bats and spiders. The guide also tells the reader where to find the perennial favorites such as goblins, vampires, werewolves, demons, and even aliens. The author Deena West Budd surveys the still-emerging field of cryptozoology, always on the lookout for animals not recognized in standard zoology. The list includes traditional cryptids like Bigfoot, the Abominable Snowman and Nessie; mythical cryptids like unicorns, vampires, dragons, and werewolves; lesser-known cryptids like bunyips, the *Encantado* or Dolphin Men of Brazil, thunderbirds, and chupacabra. These creatures are very much alive, declares Budd, even if they exist beyond the realm of normal perception.

According to Jorge Martin, a Puerto Rican journalist who describes himself as a leading UFO researcher, the Anomalous Biological Entity phenomenon can also be the product of highly sophisticated genetic manipulations by ET or human agencies. Martin cites a Chinese-Russian scientist, Dr. Tsian Kanchen, who has produced genetic manipulations which have created new species of electronically crossed plant and animal organisms. Kanchen developed an electronic system whereby he can pick up the bioenergetic field of the DNA of living organisms and transfer it electronically to other living organisms. By this method he has created incredible new breeds of ducks crossed with chickens, which include physical characteristics of both species. Goats and rabbits have been developed, along with new breeds of plants such as corn and wheat, peanut mixed with sunflower seeds and a cucumber cross with watermelons. These are produced by linking the genetic data of different living organisms contained in their bioenergetic fields by means of ultra-high frequency biological DNA cross connecting. If the Russians have created this technology, then without doubt the U.S. (led by biochemical engineering giant Monsanto) and other industrialized nations can do this as well. Therefore, according to Martin, it is quite possible that humans could have developed the "chupacabras" or other ABEs.

Finally, it is important to note that legendary creatures played an important role in many ancient texts. The mythology of dragons, werewolves, unicorns, mermaids, giants and other elusive creatures fall in the cryptozoology category. Sometimes they were symbols of the hermetic processes of alchemy. In other cases they crop up in ancient accounts of natural history. There is little doubt that aspects of these creatures haunt our collective consciousness to this day. Out of hundreds of cryptozoology creatures reported and cataloged, the following are some of the most popularly spotted worldwide.

BIGFOOT

For decades across North America, eyewitnesses have occasionally sighted large, hairy, bipedal humanoids most commonly called Bigfoot because of the massive footprints they leave behind. The beast has been reported as far south as the Swamp Ape of the Louisiana bayou and as far north as the smelly Sasquatch in the Yukon Territory. This phantom creature is known by many names worldwide, depending on the region of the world where there are frequent sightings. In the Himalayas it is called the Abominable Snowman, Yeti, hairy ghost, or ancient devil. This massive beast is known as Mapinguari to certain Amazonian tribes, where descriptions match that of a giant sloth thought to be extinct. The walking ape-man is called Yowie in Australia. For the Pacific Northwest Native Americans, *Sasquatch* means "Wild Man of the Woods." In the redwood empire of northern California, especially near Hoopa California, legends of Bigfoot are abundant alongside souvenir shops sharing the same name.

The myth has it that the Yeti, or the Abominable Snowman, is a massive creature which inhabits the Himalayan regions of Nepal and Tibet, where tales about Yetis have been passed down through generations. Despite the thousands of Yeti that would seemingly need to exist for a breeding population, not a single body has been recovered. Not one beast has been killed by a hunter, struck dead by a speeding car, or found dead from natural causes. Only in some Himalaya monasteries do the monks claim they have Yeti skullcaps. In the absence of hard evidence, like teeth or bones, support comes down to eyewitness sightings and ambiguous photos and films. Fossil remains found in the Himalayan region from the Pleistocene age of 2,500,000 to 11,700 years ago, reveal skeletons of a creature called the Gigantopithecus, or great ape, which became extinct 300,000 years ago.

Bigfoot is described as an ape-like cryptid that inhabits alpine forest regions, and prefers complete solitude. These creatures are described as larger than humans, hairy from head to toe humanoids who can also be cavern dwellers, or live in inhospitable mountain environments. They are known to forage through mountainous or wooded areas in search of roots, berries, grasses and nuts which make up their vegetarian diet. They are believed to possess a heightened "sensing" ability which allows them to steer clear of any human activities. They are more human than animal looking according to some reports, although they are usually mistaken for animals, which has forced them to take up a largely nocturnal lifestyle. They have often been described as having a human face on an "ape-like" body.

They are usually described as being up to three meters tall, while others may be smaller. "Hairy humanoids," both large and smaller "dwarf-like" entities, have on some occasions been observed in connection with UFO encounters, or trips into subterranean regions. Most Sasquatch apparently possess a human soul-matrix.

Sasquatch beasts have been known to attack humans only in self-defense, such as throwing large boulders to frighten away intruders. Sasquatch apparently have the ability to spontaneously induce invisibility through producing an electromagnetic psychic shield around themselves, and are said to commute between our dimension and a 5th dimensional realm.

BIG CATS OF OZ

Big cats, such as cougars or black leopards, are said to be roaming the Western Australian outback killing wildlife, pets and livestock. However, there are no native big cats indigenous to Australia. Once again, no evidence has emerged that they exist in the outback, but there are many eyewitnesses. Attempted explanations include zoo or circus animals that have escaped, or possibly World War II-era big cat mascots that arrived on American warships and escaped.

BUNYIPS

Another Australian mystery is the "bunyip," a legendary spirit or creature identified by the Australian Aboriginal people as "waterhorses." Bunyips haunt rivers, swamps, creeks and billabongs. They cause nocturnal terror by eating people or animals that wander into their vicinity. They are renowned for their terrifying bellowing cries in the night and have been known to frighten Aborigines to the point where they would not approach any water source where a bunyip might be waiting to devour them. The bunyip is considered an evil or punishing spirit from the Aboriginal Dreamtime.

CHUPACABRAS

The *chupacabra*, which literally means the "goat sucker" in Spanish, is an animal unrecognized by science. Another variation on the name *chupacabra* means "goat stalker," as this is one of its favorite meals. It is known to systematically slaughter animals in places like Puerto Rico, southern Florida, Nicaragua, Chile, and Mexico. A YouTube video emerged in April, 2015 depicting a captured bald animal with massive claws biting to get out of a cage near Sarawak, on the island of Borneo. The creature's name originated with the discovery of some dead goats in Puerto Rico with puncture wounds in their necks, their blood allegedly drained. According to *UFO Magazine*, there have been more than 2,000 reported cases of animal mutilations in Puerto Rico attributed to the chupacabra.

There is no consensus about what chupacabras might be, mainly because descriptions vary widely. According to eyewitness reports, those that do not look like conventional animals usually have no hair and are seen on two legs instead of four. In addition, it appears to run on two hind legs with the knees bent backward, not forward like on a human. It has the body of a slim small child (not like a fat kangaroo) and is about 1 to .5 meters tall. In motion, the arms can be seen chugging back and forth like a person running. The head has a pointed chin and a pointed top at the back, like a rooster's comb. The hairless body looks gray or some other dark color.

MONSTERS OF THE SEA

In June, 2011, a giant 22-meter "sea monster" was found washed up on a beach in Guangdong, China. According to local reports from the southeast of the country, the fish weighed an astonishing 4.5 tons. The beast from the deep was so badly decayed that it could not be identified. People have flocked from all over China to see the creature, despite the rotting corpse's foul stench. It was found tangled in ropes, and one theory is that a fisherman caught it but could not haul it aboard because it was too big.

LOCH NESS MONSTER

The Loch Ness "Monster," affectionately known as "Nessie," is the most famous aquatic lake monster in the world. It is said to inhabit an extremely deep Scottish lake near Inverness. Many sightings of the monster have been recorded, going back at least to Saint Columba, the Irish monk who converted most of Scotland to Christianity in the 6th century. The modern legend of the Loch Ness Monster reignited in 1933 when its "existence" was first brought to the world's attention by George Spicer and his wife. They said they saw an unusual animal cross the road in front of them, then descend into the lake.

In 1934, Dr. Robert Kenneth Wilson, a London physician, allegedly photographed a plesiosaur-like beast with a long neck emerging out of the murky waters. The legendary beast of the deep is said to stalk the atmospheric Scottish Highlands, not only deep within the loch, but sometimes on land. The most frequent speculation surrounding the mythical creature asserts that it could be one of a surviving clan of aquatic plesiosaurs, though this has never been proven. Countless subsequent searches of Loch Ness over the years, using sonar, submarines and other high tech approaches, have failed to conclusively prove that the monster exists. As a result, the Loch Ness Monster remains a modern-day myth and sightings are often dismissed by the scientific community as wishful thinking.

MOKELE-MBEMBE

The Mokele-mbembe is an alleged surviving sauropod dinosaur now living in the Likoula swamp region of the Republic of the Congo. Local pygmies, who have given the creature its name, reportedly have encountered it for centuries. *Mokele-mbembe* means (depending on your source) "rainbow," the "one who stops the flow of rivers," or "monstrous animal." The Mokele-mbembe is allegedly the size of an elephant with a very long reptilian neck, and a thick tapered body with thick legs that leave distinctive footprints. The creature is said to be hairless and reddish-brown, dark brown, or a dull gray, with a long whip-like tail 1.5 to 3 meters long. The creature apparently spends most of its time in the water, but the pygmies claim they have seen prints left on land of a three-clawed foot. Reports of this creature have been circulating for the past two hundred years, yet no one has photographed the creature or produced any physical evidence of its existence.

THUNDERBIRDS

The thunderbird is a part of Native American mythology in the pre-contact tribes of the Pacific Northwest, Southwest and Great Lakes region. These giant birdlike creatures were capable of generating lightning from their eyes, and could cause thunderclaps by flapping their massive wings in the sky. There are countless sightings on record of the revered supernatural entity, or a huge bird fitting its description, both by Native Americans and the "white man" after contact. It is considered a "supernatural" bird of power and strength. It is especially important, and richly depicted, in the art, songs and oral histories of many Pacific Northwest coast cultures, and is found depicted in various forms among the peoples of the American Southwest and the Great Plains. A recurring story among Native Americans features water spirits who lived in deep lakes doing battle with powerful thunderbirds in the sky, and in so doing threw up the boulders and cliffs. The destruction was caused by the lightning bolts of aerial thunderbirds versus the spouts of the water spirits while fighting each other. The result of their squabbles are the many mythical and sacred landforms found across North America. More recently, a dozen or so black and white images on the internet depict 19th century hunters surrounding recently killed pterosaurs, the flying dinosaur thought to have become extinct at the end of the Cretaceous Period.

MOTHMEN

Mothmen are largely subterranean, pterodactyloid-like hominoids with bat-like wings. Sometimes describes as possessing "horns," they are thus considered very similar to the traditional depiction of the "devil," according to certain eyewitnesses who have encountered them. These human-like creatures with wings have also been referred to as the Ciakars, Pteroids, Birdmen and Winged Draco. They have been called very intelligent and extremely malignant. Although often referred to as mothmen, this label might be a little misleading because the insects we know of as moths are docile. Interestingly, in most primitive traditions around the world, snakes and dragons are ruthless killers, but also the creators of life, and beings who impart power and knowledge. Mothmen have been most commonly encountered near known cave systems or underground bases. The most common locations for sightings have occurred near Montauk Point, Long Island; Point Pleasant, West Virginia; and Dulce, New Mexico.

Beings matching the description of the Winged Draco have been seen flying, using their wings. This was reported in the multiple sightings of Draco-like creatures in the town of Point Pleasant, WV, on which the Richard Gere film *The Mothman Prophecies* was based. The Alpha Draconian reptilian entity is an extraterrestrial race that is the most negative, destructive, and evil in their intent. These Draco extraterrestrials are human in shape and have reptile-like faces. They also have scales which make their skin waterproof. They have three fingers with an opposing thumb. The mouth is more like a slit. They average about two meters tall, but can reach three meters in height. They are well-suited for space travel because they are able to hibernate. They are cold blooded biologically, so they require a balanced environment to maintain their body temperature.

Less is known about the mothmen than their similar-appearing brother race, Alpha Draconians. Among the latter, the soldier class (which do not have wings), can bury themselves in the ground and wait long periods of time in order to ambush an enemy. In an emergency they can survive on one very large meal every few weeks. These reptilians have been interacting with Earth for a very long time. In their home system they apparently also live underground, where they seem very well-adapted to survive on nearly any planet in the universe. This reptilian species directs the efforts of the various working class Grey species, which are only about a meter tall. The leaders of this species are called the Draco Prime. They are white in color and are the royalty or elite of the group. They are seen far less by humans in underground facilities during abduction experiences. The various colored Draco have wings, while the other Draco reptilians lower on the hierarchy, seen more often by humans, do not. The wings are made of long, tiny bone spines or ribs that protrude out of their backs. The ribs are adjoined by flaps of leathery, blackish-brown skin, and the wings are usually in a retracted position. The soldier class and the scientists of their race do not have wings.

DRAGONS

Dragons are found in Greek mythology, as well as in documented historical accounts from ancient to medieval times. Legends and myths of dragons can be found in ancient Sumer, Babylon, Egypt, and especially in Far Eastern countries, most notably China. In his memoirs, Alexander the Great mentioned a dragon about 30 meters long that his soldiers witnessed while on their campaign inside India. The hissing creature was described as living in a cave and not friendly to people. Alexander was begged by the local residents not to kill the creature, and the soldiers obliged. The Macedonia army reported several other dragon encounters while on their historic campaign, but the men chose to leave the ferocious beasts alone as to not arouse their anger.

In the foreword of famed cryptologist Dr. Karl Shuker's 1995 book, *Dragons: A Natural History*, he wrote:

> *"In the world of fantastic animals, the dragon is unique. No other imaginary creature has appeared in such a rich variety of forms. It is as though there was once a whole family of different dragon species that really existed, before they mysteriously became extinct. Indeed, as recently as the 17th century, scholars wrote of dragons as though they were scientific fact, their anatomy and natural history being recorded in painstaking detail. The naturalist Edward Topsell, for instance, writing in 1608, considered them to be reptilian and closely related to serpents: 'There are diverse sorts of Dragons, distinguished partly by their Countries, partly by their quantity and magnitude, and partly by the different form of their external parties.' Unlike Shakespeare, who spoke of 'the dragon more feared than seen,' Topsell was convinced that (dragons) had been observed by many people."*

In many ways the above descriptions suggest that the dragons of lore were quite possibly the various colored Draco reptilian species, both with and without wings, which have been living underground here on Earth for the past 5,700 years. This would explain the popularity of dragon stories worldwide, living in caves, and being slain by brave warrior humans over the centuries. The most popular account is Saint George slaying the dragon, depicted in literally thousands of artistic renderings. Given the rumored Draco taste for animal or human flesh, it would stand to reason that they would come above ground on occasion to hunt for new victims, and occasionally clash with humans.

SKINWALKER RANCH

Another possible explanation for the creatures in the cryptozoology catalog may involve some kind of a gateway through various dimensions of the universe or through spacetime. The most famous location for unusual sightings in the U.S. is the Sherman Ranch, also called Skinwalker Ranch, located on an approximately 1.9 square kilometer property southeast of Ballard, Utah. It is the site of frequent paranormal and UFO-related activities. Its name is taken from the skinwalker of Native American legend, which is an entity with supernatural abilities that can turn itself into any animal form it desires. Native American shaman also said they could do this, but they had to be wearing an animal pelt in order to transform into that animal form. Similar lore can be found in cultures throughout the world and anthropologists often refer it to as shapeshifting. Both the Apache and the Hopi tribes in the Southwestern states have folk traditions involving travel between different dimensions. The Skinwalker Ranch is off-limits to the neighboring Ute tribe, who say "the ranch is in the path of the skinwalker."

The Skinwalker Ranch, located in west Uintah County bordering the Ute Indian Reservation, is popularly dubbed as the "UFO Ranch" due to its verifiable 50-year history of odd events reported at the site. According to researchers, over 100 incidents have been documented, including vanishing and mutilated cattle, sightings of unidentified flying objects or orbs, large animals with piercing yellow eyes that were not injured when struck by bullets, and invisible objects emitting destructive magnetic fields. The ranch has been acquired by billionaire Robert Bigelow for the National Institute for Discovery Science (NIDS) to study anecdotal sightings of UFOs, Bigfoot-like creatures, crop circles, glowing orbs and poltergeist activity reported by its former owners.

Among the strangest of all the phenomena is an occasionally seen large orange portal in the sky, which appears to open into another dimension. At night, blue sky can be seen through it, and black vehicles have been seen entering and leaving the portal. Huge humanoid creatures are seen using their arms to pull themselves out of a "tunnel of light." The creatures deposit themselves on the ground and walk off into the darkness, and then the tunnel of light recedes and disappears. In addition to teleportation and magnetic anomalies, there also appears to be an intrusion of alternate realities. These parallel universes, or gateways to the higher dimensions, are connected to the orange portal. This portal, among a select few others reported worldwide, might be the pathway for cryptozoology creatures coming and going into our third dimensional reality.

The "Tatzelwurm" is from an era 32,000 years ago, when "visitors" attempted to genetically cross-breed a variety of species. Remains of this remarkable creature have been uncovered in the Swiss Alps, predominately in the vicinity of Austria in higher elevation mountain valleys, or at locations in southern Czech Republic. Supposedly this creature would hatch from a spherical egg and could live thousands of years if not killed. This skeleton is still in the toddler stage, but later, bat-like wings will form, and still later, this creature will turn into a "dragon." The right-side image (from medieval times) shows a Tatzelwurm confronting a frightened person.

This preserved skull and hand, said to be that of a Yeti or Abominable Snowman, is on display at Pangboche Monastery near Mount Everest. Sightings of the Bigfoot cryptid are reported worldwide, but the humanoid is most commonly spotted in the Pacific Northwest region of North America, or anywhere around the Himalaya mountain range in Asia.

A movie still image shows what former rodeo rider Roger Patterson said is the American version of the Abominable Snowman. He said his film of the creature, estimated at 2.5 meters in height, was taken northeast of Eureka, California, in October 1967.

Locals gather around the rotting corpse of a mysterious 22-meter long "sea monster" that washed up June, 2011, on a Guangdong beach in southeastern China.

An approximate caricature of a chupacabra.

Despite numerous testimonies about the existence of a monster from the 6th century to the present, the legend of the Loch Ness Monster really began with this blurred photo in 1933. Since then, scientific experts have explored the deep lake in Scotland with submarines and sonar scans, but have yet come up with any conclusive evidence supporting the plesiosaur theory.

In 1890, two cowboys encountered a giant flying creature out in the desert of the Arizona Territory. They shot and killed the beast. The body was then taken to nearby Tombstone. The April 26, 1890, *Tombstone Epitaph* listed the creature's wingspan as 4.9 meters wide, about 130 cm around the middle torso, and had a head about 2.5 meters long. The beast was said to have no feathers, but a smooth skin and wing flaps "composed of a thick and nearly transparent membrane ... easily penetrated by a bullet." Could this animal have been the legendary thunderbird of the Southwest?

CROP CIRCLES

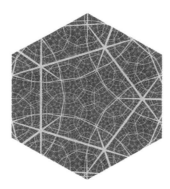

"There is truly an astounding phenomenon unfolding in England and elsewhere in the world. It's very unfortunate that the unscientific thinking, and perhaps deliberate disinformation, of a few individuals have been picked up and accepted by a naive press worldwide. As a result, millions of people have been deprived of the opportunity to experience a consciousness expanding phenomena. It is our civilization's loss; but fortunately the apparently successful attempt to ridicule or 'debunk' crop circles will do nothing to stop what may be a major transformation ahead for humanity."
–Alan Holt, project manager for NASA's International Space Station

W E are in a curious situation when the theories of our top modern physicists and astrophysicists arguably predict that we should be experiencing extraterrestrial visitation, yet any possible evidence of such lurking in the crop circle phenomenon is scoffed at within the scientific community, despite crop circles appearing with greater frequency all over the world for the past thirty years.

At least 5,000 "authentic" crop circles have appeared in over 30 countries, the majority in the United Kingdom. They are most often found in southern England, usually located near ancient sacred sites, but they have also appeared in random crop fields in countries such as the United States, China, Canada, Japan, Australia, Germany, Italy, Belgium, Holland, Russia, and Israel. Branded as a hoax by some, the intelligence of the formations, the energy they emanate, and the unique phenomena surrounding their appearance are unmistakably conscious.

Despite decades of research and inquiry, the origin and purpose of genuine crop circles remains completely unknown. Although mainstream scientists have tried to come up with logical explanations for the phenomena—including random atmospheric whirlwinds or teams of hoaxers, who somehow defy gravity and leave behind no footprints—the fact is that crop circles remain a modern day unsolved mystery. While some crop circles are clearly hoaxes, many others are remarkably intricate geometric patterns that appear in the middle of the night and are virtually impossible to replicate without taking a great deal of time, and inexplicably, leaving no traces behind of performing the task.

After years of meticulous research, many who study the phenomena find themselves stymied over the esoteric geometric communications. The very fact that some sort of energy creates the crop circles, alters the cellular structure of the crop itself, and also fashions them as two-dimensional images using three-dimensional energy whirlwinds suggest that deeper meanings may be hidden within the otherworldly transmissions from another reality.

Unfortunately, the groups who should be giving us answers, namely government researchers and scientists from the USA and UK, spend more resources debunking crop circles than investigating them with unbiased intent. Having mainstream media ignore the phenomenon or report every crop circle as a hoax simply does not account for the facts. It is hoped that the leaders of world governments and major media outlets will soon realize that humanity does not need to be protected from the knowledge of this mysterious phenomenon. Just as with sacred geometry and other esoteric principles, crop circles have been marginalized by practically the entire scientific community. Certainly their unmistakable presence and mind-boggling characteristics challenge the current worldview, rendering conventional science incapable of explaining their origins. According to top officials within government agencies, scientific circles and the mass media, crop circles simply can not exist unless they are all hoaxes.

DESIGNS IN THE CROP FIELDS

The worldwide phenomenon known as crop circles first came to the world's attention sometime in the mid-1980s. Although a pair of British hoaxers named Doug Bower and Dave Chorley claimed to have started the phenomenon in 1978, the circles have been around much longer. Their origins were first recorded in the 17th century and have appeared in dozens of countries, but it is in southern England where they occur most frequently, and most spectacularly. Beginning in the spring of 1990, the patterns of English crop circles changed dramatically. From simple geometric shapes they have evolved into elaborate and complex designs. The patterns commonly feature multiple circles with key-shaped, or otherwise abstract-shaped objects, protruding from a center point. Crop circles take on ancient sacred design patterns such as Celtic crosses, pentagrams, plus more modern symbols, such as the Mandelbrot, Julia set, and star set fractals. Some of the newer crop circles measure over 125 meters across, much larger than a football field.

England is not the only country to receive this natural phenomenon, nor is it only a contemporary occurrence. Taken together, over 10,000 formations have been cataloged worldwide in nearly 50 countries. Some are obviously hoaxed, but others defy explanation. The large geometric designs appear mostly in mature fields of planted crops; over 100 have been reported in Japanese rice fields alone. An English journal entry from 1678 reports the first known crop circle. Many UK farmers recall simple circles appearing on their farmland for generations. Dozens of English eyewitnesses describe crop circles forming in a matter of seconds as far back as 1890. Other word-of-mouth testimonies spanning several centuries acknowledge similar phenomena occurring in various locations on mainland Europe.

LOOK AT THE PLANTS FOR CLUES

Hoaxed crop circles are easy to recognize because the stalks get trampled and broken. Genuine crop circles appear flattened in a near instant, are intricately interwoven, yet none of the stalks are bruised or broken. The anomalous features of genuine crop circles continue to defy human explanation or replication. Some of the best clues are within the plants themselves, suggesting a higher intelligence at work. The plant stems are lightly burned around the base, the bend is about a few centimeters above the soil, and their cellular structure is altered. What's more, the electrical discharge that creates genuine crop circles escapes through the plant via small "explosion cavities" in the stem joints, leaving behind yet more tantalizing clues. The plants are bent in some peculiar way at a 45- to 90-degree angle at the node junction near the base of the stalk, woven in a spiraling pattern in such a way that the plants remain alive. If left untouched the plants within crop circles will have longer nodes than those in undisturbed surrounding crops. Reproductive capacities of plants in crop circles are severely altered. Immature crops will often be incapable of producing seeds or produce stunted seedlings, while mature crops will often experience a significant increase in growth and yield rates. Holes are often blown out of the nodes on crop circle plants, also referred to as the expulsion cavities. This has only been replicated in a lab by heating plants in a commercial microwave for 20-30 seconds. Groundwater evaporates immediately following a crop circle formation, and the local electromagnetic field of the surrounding area is discernibly altered. Geomancers and dowsers detect long-lasting energy patterns, not to mention the measured effects on the human biological field. Crop circle formations often appear in corn, barley, or rapeseed fields. The rapeseed plant has a consistency like celery. If the stalk is bent more than about 45-degrees, it snaps apart. Yet, in a genuine crop circle formation the stalks are often bent flat at 90-degrees. No botanist or natural scientist has been able to explain this, nor has it ever been duplicated by a human being outside a laboratory.

The electromagnetic field over the crop area where the image has been laid is often electro-statically charged. Plasma release is known to emit microwave bursts and electromagnetic energy. Crop circles have the capacity to alter the local electromagnetic field so that compasses cannot locate north, cameras, cellular phones and batteries cease to operate, and aircraft equipment fails while flying over formations. The electromagnetic field is one of the hallmarks of an authentic crop circle. Magnetic fluctuations can be detected between the center and outside the formations. Geiger counters record levels of background radiation up to 300% above normal, radio frequencies fall dramatically within their perimeters. Hours before a crop circle materializes, animals in local farms avoid that particular area of the field or simply act agitated. Car batteries in entire villages fail to operate the morning after a crop circle is located nearby. On some occasions, local power outages are reported. Sometimes the areas in the immediate vicinity of a circle are littered with strange magnetic particles. These particles were first discovered in the early 1990s while experts were studying a crop circle in England. Plants in the formation were coated with tiny fused particles of iron oxides, which turned out to be hematite and magnetite. Since this discovery, soil sampling is regularly undertaken at crop circle sites. Traces of melted magnetic material, adhered to soil grains, have regularly been identified.

MORE ELECTROMAGNETIC EFFECTS

Eyewitness accounts describe the formations materializing within minutes, usually accompanied by strange lights, crackling sounds, and debilitating or enhancing energy fields. Farmers usually report hearing a low humming noise on the nights the formations materialize. Some researchers who encounter a circle shortly after it has appeared report feeling weak, faint, or light-headed within the formation. Others report phenomena such as strange sounds, buzzes, and whines. Some have observed insects and animals that turn away at the perimeter of a crop circle and refuse to enter the area.

The military has become involved as observers. When clues suggest a new crop circle may appear, its appearance is usually accompanied by military helicopters that can track electromagnetic movements on radar. Some circles appear in a matter of hours during the pouring rain in violent thunderstorms. Some have appeared in fields near highly secured observatories and scientific installations. Videotaped footage shot in broad daylight shows small, metallic-like balls of bright white light quickly maneuvering in and around the crop fields just before a pattern emerges. The weightless objects clearly move with purpose and intelligence. Many people report malfunctioning of electrical equipment within or around crop circles including photographers, pilots, and nearby residents. It has even been reported that cell phones will sometimes stop functioning within the boundaries of crop circles, but work perfectly fine just outside of the patterns. This suggests that crop circles may be produced by orbs emitting electromagnetic radiation that leaves behind concentrated energy fields.

Dr. W. C. Levengood, a U.S. biophysicist and retired researcher at the Pinelandia Biophysical Laboratory in Michigan, is a leading crop circle researcher. He measured both magnetic and microwave energy effects involved in the circle-making process. Shortly after a formation occurs, compasses placed in the center of a circle will spin randomly. Levengood noted that the stalks of crops are warped in certain directions, often appearing woven, and whatever force is creating them can "warp the nodes." After intense investigation, Levengood believes that microwave energy, or rapidly rotating plasma vortexes, create the phenomena. His theory, however, doesn't explain the obvious intelligence behind the process and its cryptic messages.

DECODING THE PATTERNS

Interestingly, the whole pattern process seems to interact with the human mind. Some of the symbols reflect ancient patterns derived from the Celtic religion, Hopi culture, hieroglyphics, Eskimo petroglyphs, and Tibetan Thanka art. Patterns featuring modern science depict recent DNA discoveries, musical ratio scales, elaborate faces that appear extraterrestrial, and the ever-popular fractals of chaos theory, which display a mathematical precision only recently developed by humans.

A revolutionary new 3-D approach to looking at crop circles is called the "Fractal Resolution Imaging" (FRI) process that can detect other subtle changes to the plants never before seen. The FRI process reveals amazing hidden messages within authentic crop circles which can be analyzed from photos taken shortly after a pattern appears. The FRI process is discovering many new messages hidden from the naked eye, yet existing within the circles, adding new dimensionality and new meanings. For example, within the arcs and delineation of the Yin Yang formation, FRI reveals a Grey alien image hidden in the message. Meanwhile, when processing the Waden Hill crop circle image, FRI uncovered a human figure in the pattern holding a globe, depicting lungs, and glowing with an aura. For the very first time, the FRI process allows the often enigmatic, supplemental, and important new alien communications to be seen, interpreted in an entirely original way and, most importantly, beginning to be understood by astonished humans. Some underscore the original message, while others seem to be revealing hidden warnings.

Using sound waves may be one of the energy sources capable of creating genuine crop circles. It may seem preposterous to think sound waves are rendering plants flexible enough to bend, intertwine, and then lie down by applying firm and gentle pressure. Combine this process with the complexity of enormous patterns precisely arranged by sound, or more exactly ultrasound, and one part of the puzzle begins to emerge. Scientists know that ultrasound applied at very high frequencies can be directed at physical elements and make their molecules move. This requires frequencies in the high MHz range, such as those detected for decades inside crop circles. If sound is one of the formative principles behind these formations, it is not surprising that crop circles leave such a profound impression on those who are receptive to their tune. Thousands of people who have come into contact with crop circles have taken away with them a more positive view of the world and the cosmos above.

EARTH GRID ENERGY

A first step in understanding crop circles, as well as the placement of sacred sites worldwide, is to understand that the Earth has a precise energy grid emanating from the planet. This network of invisible lines completely encompasses the planet with flowing potency. The Earth grid intersects the planet much in the same way veins cover plants and animals. In this sense, the ancient Greeks devised the "Gaia hypothesis," the concept that the Earth is a living and spirited "mega-organism" on which all other life depends.

In the early 1900s, Sir Alfred Watkins discovered that many different sacred sites in England, from the Neolithic period right through to more modern abbeys and cathedrals, were built upon straight energy paths he called "ley lines." Similarly, most crop circles manifest at key intersection points on the Earth grid. We can conclude that whatever is causing these formations has an acute awareness of this energy network, and is attracted to the same sacred sites where early humans built their ancient monuments.

Shamans long ago discovered the art of dowsing, which is the use of rods and pendulums to locate where these energy lines, or ley lines, exist. Early colonial farmers used to "witch" for water when the landscape was not yet obstructed by expressways and strip malls. Dousing can also be used to detect underground caves or hidden minerals. Interestingly, most stone circles, pyramids, temples, cathedrals and significant shrines appear where these energy lines cross. The most prominent ley line on the planet is the Fibonacci, or logarithmic spiral, which emanates from the three Great Pyramids at Giza, and mathematically points exactly to the right shoulder of the Sphinx. It is directly underneath this point of immense Earth energy where the yet-to-be-revealed Hall of Records exists.

According to Romanian physicist Lonel Dinu, magnetic field lines cannot be just fictitious geometric lines, but something exists where these lines travel. In his view, the field lines are a manifestation of the flow of the pervasive ether. A source-free magnetic structure is just what it says, quite literally, a finite structure of static magnetic field lines in empty space with no sources in it, and the field going zero towards infinite distances in all directions. It is obtained as a solution to Maxwell's equations. These ramifications suggest an entire world of Trans-Maxwellian physics—of which Maxwell's equations may represent only a limit.

If it were possible to activate the certain types of energy grids or tracks, these ley lines could become time-space grids that spacecraft could use as a type of highway. These energies are magnetic in nature. Energetic beams from one portal to another construct them. These energies can be collected and relayed from a smaller spacecraft to a larger mothership, or reversed from a mothership to an anchor point on a planet. They can also work from one planet to another planet, utilizing a series of relay stations. These great magnetic grids can be set up utilizing Earth energy. The spacecraft that use the magnetic grids can disembark from that particular system and then proceed into their own system, having stored internally a certain magnetic energy field that will sustain their batteries for some time. The oldest pyramids on the planet may have been built in part to utilize this system of transferring Earth energy.

Researcher Ivan T. Sanderson rigorously charted where all the ships and planes were disappearing on Earth and found ten different "vortex points," with the most prominent being the Bermuda Triangle. Strangely, these points were equidistant, and by adding the North and South Poles as well, Russian scientists then found the points assembled into a geometric pattern. NASA and NOAA scientist Hanshou Liu and doctor Athelstan Spilhaus independently discovered this same geometric pattern in the structure of undersea volcanic ridges and mountain ranges world-wide when they charted the geodesic Earth grid.

BERMUDA TRIANGLE

Another strange phenomenon related to UFOs, the Earth grid and electro-magnetic activity is a region in the Atlantic Ocean about a thousand kilome-ters southwest of England. The Bermuda Triangle is a vast region off the coast of Florida between Puerto Rico, Miami, and Bermuda, where planes have been lost, as well as ships. Enigmatic disappearances have decreased since the 1970s, but there were many mystifying events before then. The mystery is not only about marine vessels that vanish, with the obvious conclusion that these disappearing ships merely sank, or the planes had crashed. The Bermuda Triangle also enve-lopes commercial airliners that were on radar with radio contact, and then simply vanished without contact, including the loss of wreckage or no bodies recovered.

In certain cases there were people who disappeared and then reappeared. There was a case in late 1969 where a National Airlines 727 passenger plane flying into Miami had lost all radar and radio contact for 10 minutes. Of course, air traf-fic controllers were alarmed. Ten minutes went by and communication suddenly came back on. After landing, the air traffic controllers asked them where they had been, and they had no idea what the controllers were talking about. They had no perception that anything had happened, nor had the passengers. After closer in-spection it was discovered that every timepiece in the entire aircraft—every clock, all the passengers' watches, every chronometer—had inexplicably lost 10 minutes of time! It was as if they blinked out of existence for 10 minutes, then came back.

Trace evidence of the fabled sunken continent of Atlantis can be found within the infamous Bermuda Triangle. The official confines of the triangle run from Melbourne, Florida, to the British overseas territory of Bermuda, to the island of Puerto Rico, while encapsulating most of the Bahamas, including the island of Bimini where several unexplained sunken ruins are located. The most famous are the underwater megalithic blocks called the "Bimini Roads." Strange mani-festations, UFO sightings, and time warps are just a few of the unexplained phe-nomena said to take place within the Bermuda Triangle. One theory suggests that damaged 12,000-year-old Atlantean "fire-stone" crystals on the sea floor have been left generating power out of control, thus having an effect on some of the airplanes and ships passing through the region. Announcements in 1990 and 2012 by American oceanographers confirm the existence of two giant "perfectly smooth" underwater pyramids located in the direct center of the Bermuda Trian-gle at the incredible depth of 2,000 meters. Whatever phenomenon the Bermuda Triangle may represent, these finds only enhance the legacy of Atlantis, and may someday vindicate Edgar Cayce's prophecy about a portion of the fabled sunken continent being located off the shores of Bimini.

POLICE CONFRONT ALIEN AT CROP CIRCLE

A police officer contacted British UFO and crop circle experts after seeing three aliens examining a freshly made crop circle near Avebury, Wiltshire, in July of 2009. The sergeant, who has not been named, was off-duty when he saw the figures standing in a field near Silbury Hill, and stopped his car to investigate. When he approached the "men," all standing close to two meters in height with blond hair, he could see they were all involved with looking at something and did not notice him approaching. He also heard "the sound of static electricity," and when he shouted at them, the trio ran away "faster than any man I had ever seen." The officer returned to his home in Marlborough, Wiltshire, and contacted paranormal experts and told them he had spotted a UFO. Wiltshire Police have refused to comment on the incident, saying it is a "'personal matter" for the officer involved.

Crop circle researcher Andrew Russell co-investigated the bizarre sighting on behalf of the officer and described the circumstances of the sergeant's story: "At first he thought they were forensic officers as they were dressed in white coveralls. He stopped his car and approached the field. The figures were all over six feet tall and had blond hair. They seemed to be inspecting the crop. ... This crackling noise seemed to be running through the field and the crop was moving gently, close to where the noise was."

The sergeant shouted to the figures who at first ignored him, not glancing at him. When he tried to enter the field they looked up and began running away. The officer said: "They ran faster than any man I have ever seen. I'm no slouch, but they were moving so fast. I looked away for a second and when I looked back they were gone. I then got scared. The noise was still around but I got an uneasy feeling and headed for the car. For the rest of the day I had a pounding headache I couldn't shift."

The bizarre incident occurred on the morning of July 6 as the police officer was driving past the ancient earthen mound called Silbury Hill. Since he had witnessed other paranormal activity previously, the officer contacted crop circle expert Colin Andrews, who investigated the incident and said he is "convinced" by the police officer's story. Andrews concludes, "I am quite convinced the officer had an experience that day and one that we have not fully explored. I think with the unusual movement of the beings, and the poltergeist experience, there is too much additional information to say that (nothing significant occurred)."

A DEEPER MEANING IN THE PATTERNS

If not of Earthly origin, who or what might be creating these amazing geometric formations? And what are they trying to tell us? Crop circles appear to be communications from advanced civilizations beyond our third dimensional perception on this planet. The designers are seemingly making contact with us by delivering key information about the way energy works in the universe. What other critically important messages could we receive as we continue to pollute the air we breathe, fight to take the oil under other people's land, and risk nuclear annihilation of life as we know it on this planet? This corresponds with high-level testimony that UFOs have disarmed nuclear warheads while in flight, or stationary missiles in the silos. It appears there is a higher power that seeks to protect us from the dangers of our own nuclear weapons, and usher in a Golden Age of humanity, with access to unlimited free energy, and living peacefully on a healthy and sustainable planet.

The fundamental patterns of the torus and the vector equilibrium (as discussed so eloquently by Foster Gamble in his movie, *Thrive*) appear to be central concepts in the organization of the universe. These shapes depicting the primary flow and structure of energy show up in hundreds of crop circles. Could they be showing us a way to access clean, abundant and completely free energy? Or a possible key to traveling through spacetime? Another interesting feature is the proximity of crop circles to Neolithic stone circles. Some "croppies" ask, what came first? Perhaps the crop circles appeared thousands of years ago and ancient people erected the stones to hold the energy or the message, or vice versa.

The entities responsible for the genuine patterns are sometimes even more explicit in their communication. In 2001, a crop circle appeared next to the Chilbolton Radio Telescope in England. It was designed to be a response to the 1974 transmission message sent out from the Arecibo Radio Telescope in Puerto Rico. The original pictorial message sent from Earth described basic human features such as our number system, important biological elements, DNA structure, shape of the human figure, world population, location of Earth within our solar system, and an image of the Arecibo dish transmitter that was used to send the transmission into space. "They" responded with a similarly designed crop formation in 2001. By using the exact same code pattern and design, the ETs returned similar information by depicting themselves as aliens with larger heads, a different DNA structure, and other enticing information.

VISITING CROP CIRCLES

Genuine crop circles often manifest within short distances from known sacred sites in England, especially Neolithic sites. Most crop circles appear in the southwestern Wiltshire and Hampshire regions, with Stonehenge as the apparent center of activity. Follow travel directions to Stonehenge and the Salisbury Plain, or Avebury. The Silent Circle information center and cafe at Cherhill in Wiltshire, close to the megalithic village of Avebury, is a good place to start. Crop circle season starts in late spring and ends in the autumn just at the time when farmers harvest the fields.

Some believe genuine crop circles materialize in order to direct information into the Earth's subtle energy grid. Thus, the patterns inspire people who visit them to feel enabled to pursue and achieve their highest potential. Conversely, other people experience splitting headaches or other painful physical ailments. Those visiting a genuine crop circle, especially a fresh one, should walk away immediately if feeling uncomfortable in any way. Otherwise, visiting genuine crop circles is perfectly safe, however some may require permission to enter.

The circle from 1678 was dubbed the "Mowing-Devil" by the author of the pamphlet and a portion of it states: "Being a True Relation of a Farmer, who Bargaining with a Poor Mower, about the Cutting down Three Half Acres of Oats, upon the Mower's asking too much, the Farmer swore 'That the 'Devil should Mow it, rather than He.' And so it fell out, that that very Night, the Crop of Oats shew'd as if it had been all of a Flame, but next Morning appear'd so neatly Mow'd by the Devil, or some Infernal Spirit, that no Mortal Man was able to do the like."

Obviously there are faked crop circles, or those made by people to throw others off the trail. But the proof is in the plant stalks. Hoaxed crop circles are trampled down and the stalks are broken, when in authentic crop circles the stalks are interwoven and the plants are not damaged. Authentic crop circles also interfere with aircraft instrumentation when flown directly over newly-created formations, plus other measured disturbances.

Sacred geometry is the key to understanding the building blocks of our planet and our universe. Crop circles share visual and mathematical similarities with space and our planets, as well as ancient Egyptian architecture and other curious designs. The real ones seem to contain important messages.

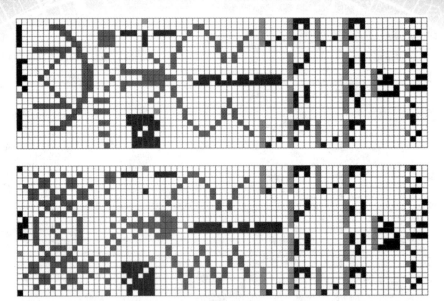

The Arecibo message (top) was sent into outer space in 1974, and in 2001 the Chilbolton reply (below) came back in the form of a crop circle.

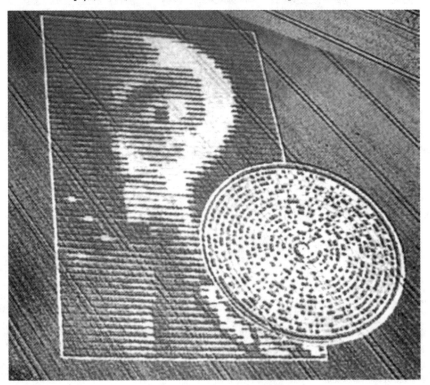

Only 339 days after the attacks on 9-11, this 180-meter long crop circle appeared in Crabwood, England. The disc contains an 8-bit binary code. When deciphered it reads: "Beware the bearers of FALSE gifts & BROKEN PROMISES. Much PAIN but still time. BELIEVE. There is GOOD out there. We oppose DECEPTION. Conduit CLOSING."

OTHER PLANET STRUCTURES

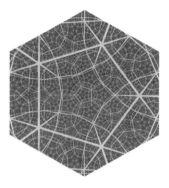

"These 'babies' are huge, sir! Enormous! Oh My God! You wouldn't believe it! I'm telling you there are other spacecraft out there, lined up on the far side of the crater edge! They're on the Moon watching us!" -Apollo 11 astronaut Neil Armstrong reporting to Mission Control

THE above exchange between Neil Armstrong and NASA was picked up and recorded by Ham radio operators, bypassing frequencies used by TV and radio stations during the historic 1969 Moon landing. The first man on the Moon described other spacecraft lining the rim of the crater where the Eagle module had landed, and commented later: "Their ships were far superior to ours, both in size and technology—Boy, were they big! And menacing!" Neil Armstrong also remarked that NASA was not the first to reach the Moon. In 1979 Maurice Chatelain, former chief of NASA Communications Systems, confirmed that Neil Armstrong had indeed reported seeing two UFOs on the rim of a crater. "The encounter was common knowledge at NASA," he revealed, "but nobody has talked about it until now." Unfortunately, NASA has never talked publicly about the existence of UFOs.

Edgar Mitchell, the sixth man to walk on the Moon, and Mercury 7 pilot L. Gordon Cooper are two of the most outspoken astronauts. Edgar Mitchell claimed to have seen UFOs, and although he has never seen an ET, has described the Greys and the Roswell recovery. "Aliens are among us," says Mitchell, adding "I don't know how many, or where, or how they're doing it, but they've been observing us, and here, for quite some time. And we see these crafts all the time." Astronaut Cooper once said in front of the United Nations: "ETs are real and they're here." Before he entered the Space Program, Cooper says his fighter squadron witnessed a disc-shaped craft in flight on a mission over Europe. In 1958, he was working at Edwards Air Force Base when he witnessed a small saucer land on the dry lakebed and then fly off at an incredible speed.

Astronauts and ranking military personnel must keep quiet about seeing UFOs because if not they risk 10 years in prison, a $10,000 fine, their status as heroes, public ridicule, and they may lose pay in allowances due, or pay ever to become due. Suffice it to say, those who do speak out are risking a great deal when they go public. These are America's true heroes.

APOLLO ASTRONAUTS SPEAK OF ET ENCOUNTERS

Apollo 11 astronauts Neil Armstrong and Edwin "Buzz" Aldrin both said they saw glowing orbs shortly after their historic July 21, 1969, landing on the Moon. Armstrong confirmed that the story was true but refused to go into further detail, beyond admitting that the CIA was behind the cover-up. The Apollo 11 astronauts landing on the Moon noticed traces of activity, a surprise to them, and made comments which were instantly broadcast to the rapt audience participating in this historic landing worldwide, and the general populace. Upon return the astronauts were silenced in the usual manner, and all forthcoming broadcasts have never again been broadcast live. The astronauts continue to be under strict orders not to discuss their sightings.

Apollo 11 astronaut Buzz Aldrin also commented they had seen a spacecraft during their historic flight to land the first man on the Moon. "There was something out there, close enough to be observed, and what could it be? Now, obviously the three of us weren't going to blurt out, 'Hey, Houston, we've got something moving alongside of us and we don't know what it is, you know? Can you tell us what it is?'"

Soviet scientists were allegedly the first to confirm the Moon ET incident. "According to our information, the encounter was reported immediately after the landing of the module," said Dr. Vladimir Azhazha, a physicist and Professor of Mathematics at Moscow University. "Neil Armstrong relayed the message to Mission Control that two large, mysterious objects were watching them after having landed near the moon module. But his message was never heard by the public, because NASA censored it." But if there was no secrecy surrounding the mission, why has this sighting not been made public? A certain professor, who wished to remain anonymous, was engaged in a discussion with Neil Armstrong during a NASA symposium. He asked what really happened out there with Apollo 11? Armstrong replied, "It was incredible, of course we had always known there was a possibility, the fact is, we were warned off! (by the aliens). There was never any question then of a space station or a Moon city." The professor inquired into Armstrong's meaning of "warned off." Armstrong replied, "I can't go into details, except to say that their ships were far superior to ours both in size and technology—Boy, were they big! And menacing! No, there is no question of a space station. ... NASA was committed at that time, and couldn't risk panic on Earth." Years later, astronaut L. Gordon Cooper testified to a United Nations committee that one of the Apollo 11 astronauts actually witnessed a UFO on the ground. Astronaut Mitchell on the Apollo 14 answered the question about his feelings after a successful return from the Moon in 1971: "My neck still aches as I had to constantly turn my head around because we felt we were not alone there. We had no choice but pray."

THE MOON

Before we get into the structures on the Moon we should examine several lunar enigmas that still pose big problems for scientists. For starters, why is there a dark side that never faces the Earth? Or, how did the Moon come to appear in Earth's orbit? What are the principles of its revolving around the Earth? Why does it not rotate around like all the other planets? Why is it shrinking? How to explain the "bottomless" craters? And why do the *mascons*, or higher concentrations of mass, found in the *marias* cause fluctuations in gravity that have never been satisfactorily explained? The Moon is not the dead planet we've been led to believe. There is also the nagging evidence that the Moon has an atmosphere, and contains pockets of water. What's going on up there?

The Moon is unlike any other planetary satellite in our solar system. Our Moon is older than the Earth by nearly 800,000 years according to scientific dating. The Earth is thought to be around 4.6 billion years old, while rocks from the Moon were found to be around 5.3 billion years old, and the dust the rocks were found in are thought to be about a billion years older than that. This information conflicts with the theory that the Moon was produced by a collision the Earth had with another body early in its history. Also unusual is that our moon is the only moon in the solar system that has a stationary, near-perfect circular orbit. From any point on the surface of Earth, only one side of the Moon is visible. Towers two kilometers high and uniform banding suggest that the Moon was somehow constructed as an artificial satellite. Similar to irrigation canals on Mars, there is also evidence of terraforming and terraces on the Moon.

One of the biggest academic enigmas about the Moon is how it is apparently in the wrong orbit for its size. Such a claim would presumably be based on its assumed density. Technical reports claim that the Moon has a density of 3.3, as compared with 5.5 for Earth. Astronomical data indicates that the internal regions of the Moon are less dense than the outer, giving rise to the inevitable speculation that it could be partly hollow. An interesting fact suggesting the Moon is a "hollow object" is confirmed when a meteor strikes the Moon, it then rings like a bell. Astronomers knew this, and when the Apollo 12 crew landed on the Moon for the second mission, they intentionally crashed the lunar module ascent stage into the surface of the Moon. After returning to the orbiter, the module impact with the Moon caused their seismic equipment to register a continuous reverberation for over an hour.

These results were repeated during the Apollo 13 mission during the third stage impact, which caused the Moon to reverberate for over three hours. This leads to the speculation that maybe the Moon is not hollow from natural causes, but was cored out as a result of an extensive mining operation. Hollow Moon researchers say this is proof that the interior of the Moon was extracted using artificial means. They note the Moon has a surface shell of only about 30 kilometers thick, composed mostly of metal. This would also explain the extreme difficulty astronauts had when drilling down a few inches into the Moon's *marias,* and that when the drill bit was pulled out, metal shavings were visible. Moon rocks were found to contain brass, mica, titanium, and elements uranium 236 and neptunium 237, an element not previously found in nature.

MOON BASES

Whistleblower William Cooper, a former Naval Intelligence Officer, reported that not only do alien Moon bases exist, but the U.S. Naval Intelligence Community refers to the largest Moon base as "Luna." He also reports the U.S. secret space program has bases on the Moon and Mars called "Adam and Eve," respectively. NASA and other space-related agencies know that there is a huge mining operation going on there, and the back side is where the aliens keep their huge motherships. Cooper claims the trips to Earth are made in smaller "flying saucers." The alien base Luna is located on the far side, or dark side of the Moon, that never faces Earth. A base, a mining operation using very large machines, and the very large alien craft described in sighting reported as motherships exist there, according to Cooper. These were also seen, reported on, and even filmed by the Apollo astronauts, but of course this information has never been made public.

The NASA Clementine Mission was launched in 1994 to map the Moon. When the images were released, some objects were clearly masked out. What can be seen are mushroom shaped buildings, tall objects, towers and extensive mining operations. There are dozens of known bases on the Moon, especially on Crater Kepler where there are four domes, mining machines, pyramids, tanks, towers, a Christian cross, and even a W. W. II-era bomber plane called the B-24 liberator! The secret human base on the Moon has been operating since 1954, according to Cooper. Our human base on the Moon is a combined effort between the USA, UK, and Russia. This base was built using technology given to us by the Greys.

ET MOON BASES

In the mid-1970s, the CIA-funded Stanford Research Institute (SRI) tasked some of their psychic remote viewers to investigate specific Moon coordinates. What they discovered were major ET bases on the back side of the Moon containing structures, spherical buildings, towers, and massive structures, some a half kilometer in size. Other locations, such as Ocular Luna, revealed major mineral mining operations. The crater named Darwin has changed in appearance several times over the decades, as if huge amounts of soil are being pushed around. There also appears to be an atmosphere on the far side of the Moon. Astronauts have even reported seeing clouds in the atmosphere of the Moon.

Elsewhere on the surface of the Moon are active lunar city bases, along with some that are abandoned, which stretch along for many kilometers. Huge transparent domes are presumed to be covering massive basements with numerous tunnels and other constructions. A transparent dome that rises above the crater edge was discovered near the crater Copernicus. The dome is unusual in that it glows white and blue from inside. Another rather unusual object, which is strange even for the Moon, was discovered in the upper part of the "Factory" area in Copernicus: a disk of about 50 meters in diameter stands on a square basement surrounded with walls. In the picture, close to the *rhombi*, there can also be seen a dark round embrasure in the ground that resembles an entry into an underground bunker. There is a regular rectangular area between the Factory and the crater Copernicus that is 300 meters wide and 400 meters long. Crater Copernicus is 3.8 kilometers deep and 93 kilometers in diameter. According to researcher David Hatcher Childress, the crater Gassendi and dozens of others have been observed with light emanating from the crater floor, called transient lunar light phenomenon. He also reports pyramids and obelisks rising from the Moon surface. A double beam of lunar transient phenomenon can also be seen in a crater of Ceres, located in the asteroid belt between Mars and Jupiter.

Some partially destroyed objects on the lunar surface cannot be placed among natural geological formations, as Mother Nature never creates perfect 90° angles, straight lines, or perfect dome shapes. Out of the ordinary objects are of complex organization and geometrical structure. In the upper part of Rima hadley, not far from the location where the Apollo 15 module had landed near Hadley rille, a construction surrounded with a tall D-shaped wall was discovered. Mysterious terrace-shaped excavations of the rock have been discovered near the Tiho crater. The concentric hexahedral excavations and the tunnel entry at the terrace side cannot be results of natural geological processes. Instead, they look very much like open cast mines. Curiously, no high powered nationally-funded telescope is allowed to photograph the near surface of the Moon.

Apollo 10 astronauts took a unique picture (AS10-32-4822) of several anomalous objects on the lunar landscape, including one called the "Castle," which rises to the height of 14 kilometers, and casts a distinct shadow on the lunar surface. The object seems to be consisting of several cylindrical units and a large conjunctive unit. An internal porous structure of the Castle is clearly seen in one of the pictures, leaving an impression that some parts of the object are transparent. It is located in the lunar region between Rima hyginus and Boskovic, but the image currently on the NASA website has been retouched and does not show the original features. In all, uniquely different base structure artifacts have been discovered in at least 44 regions of the Moon. From these photos and reports, it appears that the Earth's moon, along with the asteroid belt, is used as a permanent base of operations for the "Domain Forces" of the Grey and Draconian aliens. The Apollo astronauts and other humans have spotted their structures.

THE ASTEROID BELT

The asteroid belt is composed of small and large smashed pieces of a planet that once existed between Mars and Jupiter. Numerous irregularly shaped bodies called asteroids or minor planets occupy the orbit where a planet existed before being destroyed billions of years ago. The asteroid belt serves as a good low-gravity jumping-off point for incoming space craft traveling toward the center of our galaxy. There appear to be artificial satellites in the asteroid belt that act as platforms for the take off and landing of spacecraft. It is used as a "galactic jump" between the Milky Way and adjoining galaxies. There are not any other useful planets at this end of the galaxy that can serve as a good galactic entering spot for incoming transport and other ships.

The asteroid belt beyond Mars is very small, but is an important location for the Grey aliens in this part of space. Actually, some of the orbiting objects in our solar system are very valuable for use as low-gravity space stations. Interstellar travelers are interested primarily in the low-gravity satellites in this solar system which consist mainly of the side of the Moon facing away from Earth, and the asteroid belt, and to a lesser degree, Mars and Venus. Dome structures synthesized from gypsum or underground bases covered by electromagnetic force screens are constructed to house the Greys.

VENUS

Venus and Earth are often called twins because they are similar in size, mass, density, composition and gravity. Venus has a dense atmosphere, consisting mainly of carbon dioxide with clouds of sulfuric acid, and scientists have only detected trace amounts of water in the atmosphere. The atmosphere is heavier than that of any other planet, leading to a surface pressure over 90 times that of Earth. Not only are conditions on Venus infernal, but an ancient name for Venus was "Lucifer." This name did not carry any fiendish connotations, however—Lucifer means "light-bringer," and when seen from Earth, Venus is brighter than any other planet, or even any star in the night sky because of its highly reflective clouds and its closeness to our planet and the Sun.

The atmosphere of Venus, the second planet from the Sun, is much denser and hotter than that of Earth. The Venusian atmosphere supports thick persistent clouds made of sulfuric acid, which make optical observations of the surface very difficult. Venus is roughly the same size as Earth, but it has a thick atmosphere dominated by carbon dioxide. With an atmospheric pressure 92 times that of Earth, a waterless and volcano-riddled surface, and a surface temperature of 740°K degrees, Venus has never been considered a serious target of research into the possibility of extraterrestrial life, but our view of extraterrestrial holds to the kind of life we are familiar with in our third dimensional reality.

The atmosphere of Venus is in a state of vigorous circulation and super-rotation. The whole atmosphere circles the planet in just four days (super-rotation), which is a short time compared with the sidereal rotational period of 243 days. However, this atmospheric state is incapable of preventing the loss of water, which is continuously blown away by the solar wind through the induced magneto tail. The winds supporting super-rotation blow as fast as 100 meters per second. Only the ionosphere and a thin induced magnetosphere separate Venusian atmosphere from outer space, and serve to shield it from the solar wind, which usually does not penetrate very deeply. Venus' anticyclonic structures, called polar vortexes, are located near the poles, and in them the air moves downward. Each vortex is double-eyed and shows a characteristic S-shaped pattern of clouds. Venus has an opposite rotation to the other planets, suggesting it is an interloper planet that entered the solar system independently.

Despite the harsh conditions on the surface, at about a 50- to 65-kilometer level above the surface of the planet, the atmospheric pressure and temperature is nearly the same as that of the Earth. This makes its upper atmosphere the most Earth-like area in the solar system, even more so than the atmosphere of Mars. Venus is considered Earth-like due to the similarity in pressure, temperature, and the fact that breathable air is a lifting gas on Venus, much in the same way that helium is a lifting gas on Earth. The information about the surface features on Venus has been obtained exclusively by radar imaging conducted from the ground and Venera 15-16 and the Magellan space probes. The main atmosphere gases on Venus are carbon dioxide and nitrogen, which make up 96.5% and 3.5% of all molecules. Other chemical compounds are present only in trace amounts.

Venus has a very dense, hot and heavy atmosphere of sulfuric acid clouds. Although deadly to most Earth creatures, there are a few life forms on Earth that could endure an atmospheric environment like Venus. The Greys and other advanced races reportedly use the planet Venus as a defensive position against other space forces. Also, the Nordic-looking benevolent ETs that repeatedly contacted George Adamski claimed they too lived on Venus. His Venusian visitors stated they lived in underground cities, thus not being exposed to hostile conditions on the surface. John Lear also believes advanced civilizations exist on Venus.

Supporting the claim of intelligent ET life, Leonid Ksanfomaliti, an astronomer based at the Space Research Institute of Russia's Academy of Sciences, analyzed Venus photographs taken by a Russian landing probe during a 1982 mission to explore the heavily acid-clouded planet. Ksanfomaliti announced in January, 2012, that Russian photographs depict objects resembling a "disk," a "black flap" and a "scorpion." He also cautioned that the objects seem to "emerge, fluctuate and disappear" in different photographs taken from a variety of vantage points.

THE RED PLANET

Mars has fascinated humanity since pre-historic times with notions of canals and cities on the Red Planet. The notion of little green men and Martian Society really got its start in the 19th century with Italian astronomer Giovani Schiaparelli. He noted *canali* on the visible surface of Mars. American Percival Lowell took the idea much farther from 1885 to 1898 with a series of three books detailing his observations of the Martian surface and the intelligent civilization that he believed existed there.

The atmosphere of Mars is relatively thin, and the atmospheric pressure on the surface varies from around 0.03 kPa on the peak of *Olympus Mons* to over 1.155 kPa in the depths of *Hellas Planitia*, with a mean surface level pressure of 0.6 kPa, compared to Earth's 101.3 kPa. The atmosphere on Mars consists of 95% carbon dioxide, 3% nitrogen, 1.6% argon, and contains traces of oxygen, water, and methane. Curiously, methane is emitted more frequently in the hemisphere of Mars when experiencing its summer. The atmosphere is quite dusty, giving the Martian sky a tawny color during windstorms. But if calm, the Mars atmosphere looks clear and blue, much like the Earth's sky when seen from the surface.

MARS IS MUCH LIKE EARTH

According to tentative astrophysical theories and reports of alien communications, life once thrived on Mars in a similar way to that on Earth, and quite possibly even seeded life on Earth via crashed meteorites. There is so much we have not been told about Mars and the other objects in our solar system. However, in its long history, Mars experienced two major catastrophes. One by ice, from which life did re-emerge, and one by fire, from which it did not. One of the unexplained discoveries about Mars is the presence of a xenon isotope in the atmosphere and an abundance of uranium and thorium on the surface. Experts posit that these elements are the products of a natural fission reaction. The ore bodies containing these oxides were infiltrated by water, causing a thermal neutron reaction with fallout that rained down and caused the end of life on Mars. Debris patterns can be seen radiating from a site in the northwest of *Mare Acidalium*. One hypothesis states that the event was probably triggered by a change in groundwater distribution related to a global cooling event, and that it would have produced an energy release equal to the impact of a 70 kilometer-diameter asteroid.

There is considerable evidence suggested by mainstream astronomers that Mars was once just like Earth, but something catastrophic happened that wiped out its life long ago. Clouds on Mars show that an atmosphere still exists. On Mars there are forests, scrub brushes, water reservoirs, lakes, ice caps, and evidence of an ancient civilization, originally secretly named by NASA a Martian "Inca City" from the images that came back from Mariner 9. There are dried-up oceans, irrigated farms, fossil evidence, skulls and more modern structures. There appears to be a transportation system of tubes that circle the planet above ground and beneath. For years NASA released photos of Mars with a reddish tinged sky and rusty red landscape. This view prevailed until independent researchers and Mars missions undertaken by the European Space Agency (ESA) revealed that the Martian sky actually looks very similar to Earth's sky—and the Martian landscape pretty much resembles the pale reddish colored terrain of the American Southwest.

ARMCHAIR ASTRONAUT DISCOVERS A MARS SPACE STATION

An armchair astronaut discovered a "space station" on Mars using Google Mars as reported by *MailOnline* on June 7, 2011, but the video he posted was removed a week later. The video has since resurfaced. David Martines claims to have found evidence of intelligent life on Mars and has posted a video showing a long cylindrical base he named "BioStation Alpha." He did not discover it with a telescope; instead he claims to have randomly uncovered the picture while scanning the surface of the planet one day using Mars surface imagery available via Google Mars. Describing the "structure" as living quarters with red and blue stripes on it, to the untrained eye it looks like nothing more than a white cylinder with what appear to be connected domes on an otherwise unblemished red landscape. He even lists the co-ordinates 49'19.73"N 29 33'06.53"W so others can view the anomaly for themselves.

Martines' YouTube video of the BioStation Alpha went viral with over a million hits since he first posted it in May, 2011. According to his calculations, "It's very unusual in that it's quite large, over 700 feet long and 150 feet wide; it looks like it's a cylinder or made up of cylinders." He goes on to speculate, "It could be a power station or it could be a biological containment or it could be a glorified garage—hope it's not a weapon. Whoever put it up there had a purpose I'm sure. I couldn't imagine what the purpose was. I couldn't imagine why anybody would want to live on Mars. It could be a way station for weary space travelers. It could also belong to NASA; I don't know that they would admit that. I don't know if they could pull off such a project without all the people seeing all the material going up there. I sort of doubt NASA has anything to do with this," he concludes.

MARS BASES

The infamous "Face on Mars," appearing to show eyes and teeth, was discovered by the Viking 1 probe in 1976. It was quickly debunked as a quirk of geography which threw shadows over a small hill in the Cydonia region of Mars, making the inanimate rock look like a carved face. The large "Face" covers an area about 3.6 kilometers on a side. The picture was heralded as proof of an alien civilization by some, but was dismissed as a mere trick of the light by scientists at NASA. Cydonia lies in the planet's northern hemisphere in a transitional zone between the heavily cratered regions to the south and relatively smooth plains to the north. Some planetologists believe that the northern plains may once have been ocean beds and that Cydonia could have been a coastal zone. Also located in the Cydonia region next to the infamous face are several pyramids (four times the size of Cheops' Pyramid in Egypt), city structures and agricultural terracing.

According to alien contactees, the Dracos once had a large underground base on Mars, used as their primary control center within our solar system. Their base on Mars is over a million years old, and was last active over 300,000 years ago. The base is over a hundred square kilometers in size and is located beneath the surface location on Mars known as Tempe Terra. Supposedly Mars currently supports a population of 600 million entities, most of whom are human looking in appearance. An intelligent civilization lives under the surface of Mars, and this civilization is involved in on-going secret liaison programs with agencies of the U.S. Government, including the CIA.

An active base on Mars contains Earth humans and human-looking ETs working side by side. There are at least 43 different types of human-like beings operating jointly, each of whom has evolved on different worlds. The vast majority of them look quite similar to Earth humans, though they could range from one meter tall up to four meters in height. Of the 270,000 "personnel" who work at one base, only 10,000 were born on or descended from people on Earth. This base is located underneath Mars' expansive *Utopia Planitia*, which is an ancient seabed. Transport from the Earth is by two means: portal "stargates" for personnel and small items; or spacecraft for larger items of freight. The secret U.S. space fleet that transports items and personnel back and forth is codenamed Solar Warden.

Other Earth travelers arrive on Mars via "portal technology" that allows them to step into an elevator-like room on Earth, and step out at the base on Mars. Teleportation trips are made via a "jump room" once located at a CIA and Hughes Aircraft facility in El Segundo, California. The most famous person alleged to have used the jump room to Mars was yet-to-be President Barack Obama in the early 1980s when he was a student at Occidental College in Los Angeles. Thousands of others have passed back and forth since then, and now some who were once part of a Mars training program in the 1980s are recounting their Red Planet experiences with "Barry Soetoro." Readers can access internet sites on these issues and draw their own conclusions.

Orbiting Mars, the moon Phobos has an "unusual monolith," as described by astronaut Buzz Aldrin. He described it once in an interview: "We should go boldly where man has not gone before. Fly by the comets, visit asteroids, visit the moon of Mars. There's a monolith there, which is a very unusual structure on this potato shaped object that goes around Mars once every seven hours. When people find out about that they're going to say 'who put that there?' The universe put it there. If you choose, God put it there." Astrophysicist Dr. Iosif Samuilovich Shklovsky calculated the orbital motion of Martian satellite Phobos. "Considering the extremely rarefied Martian atmosphere at this altitude," he said, "Phobos should have ... very low average density ... less than an Earth cloud." That could not be, however, or it would have dispersed long ago. Therefore, the only way its carefully calculated attributes could be reconciled is that it "is a hollow, empty body, resembling an empty tin can ... It must have an artificial origin ... (some kind of) spaceship." Another Russian astronomer, Dr. Cherman Struve, agreed that its shape and behavior could not be due to natural causes. He also observed Phobos as changing its speed from time to time.

AMNESIA MECHANISMS

Some of the structures on Venus, Mars and the Earth's moon are known to be electronic monitoring points and force screens designed to detect and capture wandering spirits, as when the human spirit departs the body at death. These sentient spirits are captured, then brainwashed using extreme electronic force, in order to maintain the Earth's population in a state of perpetual amnesia. Further population controls are installed through the use of long-range electronic devices via thought control mechanisms. These stations are still in operation and they are extremely difficult to attack or destroy. The Black Knight satellite is an ancient alien artifact in Earth's orbit that may also play a role in the amnesia of Earthlings.

Theoretically, if the amnesia mechanisms being used against Earth could be broken entirely, humans could potentially regain all of their memory over a long period of time, including past life recalls. Some esoteric scholars speculate that our spirits have been deposited on Earth from all over the galaxy, adjoining galaxies, and from planetary systems including Sirius, Aldebaran, the Pleiades, Orion, Draconis, and countless others. There are spirits on Earth from unnamed races, civilizations, cultural backgrounds, and planetary environments. Each of the various populations once had their own languages, belief systems, moral values, religious beliefs, training and unknown and untold histories. These newer entities are mixed together with earlier inhabitants of Earth who came from another star system more than 400,000 years ago to establish the civilizations of Atlantis and Lemuria. Those civilizations vanished beneath the tidal waves caused by a planetary polar shift, many thousands of years before the current "prison" population started to arrive. The early humans from those star systems were the source of the original races of Earth, beginning in Australia and the Far East. The force that put these devices into place long ago does not want the humans of Earth to suspect that they have been captured, transplanted to Earth, and brainwashed.

But don't expect NASA or any other space agency to confess the existence of structures on other planets any time soon. Richard Hoagland, a specialist for lunar and Mars artifacts, says that NASA continues to veil photo materials before they are published in public catalogues and files. NASA also fabricates digital retouching, or can partially refocus images while in the process of copying. Some investigators, Hoagland among them, suppose an extraterrestrial race has used the Moon and other planets as a terminal station during their activity on the Earth. These suggestions are confirmed by the legends and myths invented independently by different cultures on Earth for millennia.

THE SUN AND OTHER PLANETS

Although not a planet and with no known structures, the Sun has many fascinating features. The Sun is not a series of thermonuclear explosions as we have been led to believe. The Sun is an electromagnetic sphere that reacts with the electromagnetic fields of certain planets, that is, virtually all the planets in our solar system. In the early 21st century, something weird happened to the Sun. Normally, our star, like the Earth itself, has a north and a south magnetic pole. But for nearly a month, beginning in March 2000, the Sun's south magnetic pole faded, and a north pole emerged to take its place. The Sun had two north poles. NASA has released a wealth of information proving that climate change is occurring on every planet in our solar system, including the Sun. They simply never put all the pieces together at once, and invariably blame it on "seasons" in each individual case. When we survey the data itself, we clearly see that the Sun and all the planets are becoming brighter, hotter and more magnetic.

Our Sun is also a portal, a stargate, and as such can be used for inter-dimensional space travel. Physicist Nassim Haramein contends that NASA Stereo data of giant solar UFOs prove that extraterrestrial civilizations access our solar system via a stargate within the Sun when using large vehicle spacecraft, with some ships arriving as large as small planets. According to Mr. Haramein, every Sun contains a "black hole singularity." All other distant suns of the same classification as our Sun are also "natural" stargates. In order for a space ship to enter into our Sun as a portal or stargate, each ship must do a few things. The craft must change its frequency to match the vibratory rate of the Sun, it must be attuned to a 4th dimensional vibratory frequency and rate, and it must also input into their ship's navigation system the Sun's unique signature code. Each major celestial body has one, and this signature identification code is much like a GPS location device.

Other features of our solar system are also fascinating. Firstly, all planets are not orbs but instead are spheres. Not only the Earth, but also the Moon, Saturn, Jupiter, and the Sun itself are spherical. Gaseous planetary bodies like the largest planets of our solar system and the Sun cannot generate a magnetic field, yet they all have one. All the solar system's outer planets emit more energy than they receive from the Sun, especially the most geologically active moon Io, rotating around Jupiter. Neptune, one of the farthest planets away from the Sun, has an atmosphere remarkably similar to the Earth's atmosphere.

A spinning planetary body in formation has zero gravity in its center. Therefore, mass accumulates where gravitational and centrifugal forces are balanced within the area of the spinning matter, and that form would be a sphere with openings at the top and bottom, like a hurricane of matter in space—not as a solid body with a solid center. The center has zero gravity.

If planets were formed from cosmic dust which began to condense into a body like the Earth, then the angular momentum would still continue to increase, but it does not. Instead, the Earth's spin is steady, not slowing down or speeding up. Larger planets with more mass should spin more slowly than smaller planets with less mass, yet they do not. The largest planet Jupiter spins faster, once every 10 hours, a lot faster than Mercury, which is just a tiny fraction of the size of Jupiter and needs 58 Earth days for one spin around its axis. Mercury is very similar to the Moon, with seemingly anomalous objects found in its craters.

THE MILKY WAY

The spiral arms of our Milky Way galaxy contain interstellar matter, diffuse nebulae, young stars, and open star clusters emerging from this matter. The bulge component of our galaxy consists of old stars and contains the globular star clusters. Our galaxy has probably about 200 globulars, of which we know of about 150. These globular clusters are strongly concentrated toward the Galactic Center. Our solar system is thus situated within the outer regions of this galaxy, well within the disk and only about 20 light years "above" the equatorial symmetry plane, towards the direction of the Galactic North Pole. The Milky Way is about 28,000 light years from The Galactic Center.

Three studies released in January, 2012, in the journal *Nature* and at the American Astronomical Society's conference in Austin, Texas, project about 1.6 planets per star systems on average. That would be 160 billion planets in the Milky Way galaxy alone. This estimate would represent approximately 1.6 billion planets in life zone orbits, or the "Goldilocks Zone," which is considered not too hot and not too cold for life to exist. Only Earth and Mars are situated within our Sun's life zone orbit. Another estimate puts the figure at 200 billion stars in the Milky Way galaxy. And with about 500 billion galaxies in the observable universe, the estimated number of inhabitable planets is bound to go up. Way up.

With the odds so high in its favor, it would now seem that any argument which states that there is no other intelligent life in the Milky Way galaxy (let alone the universe) is about as substantive as arguing the Earth is flat. If there is other life out there, then it is reasonable that there are other intelligent and highly advanced life forms. This would lead directly to a fundamental question: Has intelligent life from elsewhere visited Earth? To determine that, we would need to look for any evidence on Earth or in our solar system for such visitations. When we do this, as we've just done, we find that the evidence is everywhere, both in the present and the past, both on Earth and off planet. What we don't have is a government in the USA willing to discuss the matter. Thus, it is time for us to mature as a species and demand that government leaders take their heads out of the sand, and reveal what they already know about these visitations, and the agendas involved. If they will not do this, they must be replaced by leaders who will.

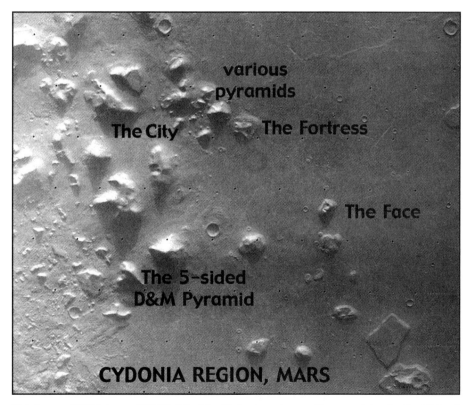

This famous NASA image (#F035a72) of the Cydonia region on Mars was taken by the Viking 1 Orbiter on July 25, 1976. Cydonia is an odd collection of landforms, with many different shapes and sizes. For instance, there are pyramidal mountains, impact craters, flat looking slabs of rock, possible islands, possible shorelines and beach remnants. Except for several pyramidal landforms, nothing seems to look quite like anything else, especially the notorious "Face."

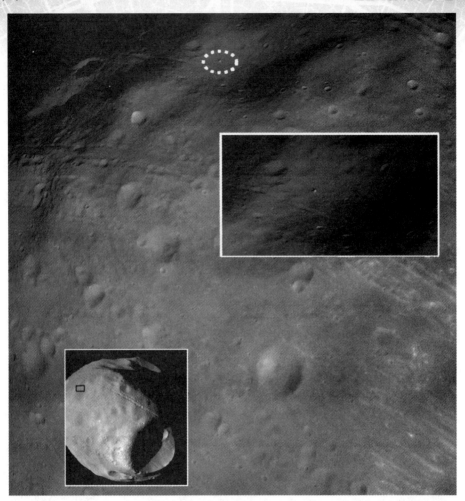

Buzz Aldrin, the second man to walk on the Moon, spoke of a monolith detected on the Mars moon of Phobos. He said in an interview: "We should visit the moons of Mars. There's a monolith there. A very unusual structure on this little potato shaped object that goes around Mars once every seven hours."

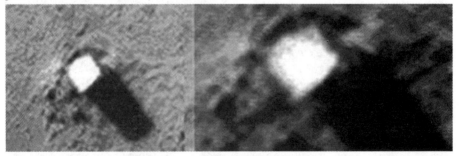

Another "monolith" was also discovered in 2009 on the surface of Mars. This monolith was snapped from 265 kilometers away using a special high resolution camera (HiRISE) on board the Mars Reconnaissance Orbiter, a NASA space probe. So why doesn't NASA promote this to the world? Largely because of the 1959 Brookings Institute report which recommended that the NASA administration "rigorously suppress" any evidence of ET life, particularly advanced sentient life, to keep society from collapsing.

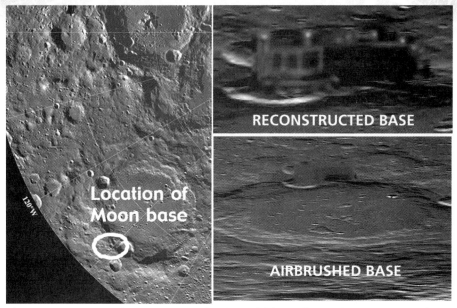

RECONSTRUCTED BASE

Location of Moon base

AIRBRUSHED BASE

The NASA image on the bottom right has been deliberately smudged to omit evidence. This massive Moon base building called the "Zeeman Crater Anomaly" appears to be several stories tall. The fact that this structure can clearly be seen from orbit indicates just how enormous it is. Above right is a reconstruction of the Zeeman Crater Moon Base by Bret C. Sheppard using all available evidence.

Evidence of "mining activity" on the Moon and elsewhere in our solar system is quite abundant. Unfortunately, no high powered observatory in the world is allowed to look closely at the Moon or take images of where (according to officials) the Apollo missions landed. No professional astronomer may photograph the Moon by law. Why? The Moon was discovered to harbor a multitude of alien bases decades ago.

This original image of the crater Copernicus was taken by NASA to prepare for the Apollo landings. Five Lunar Orbiter spacecraft were launched during 1966 and 1967 to gather detailed images of the Moon, including this image. This photo seems to show some type of mining operation because the surface appears lighter, as if it had been excavated recently. Cylinders, plus perfect 90-degree corners, suggest buildings or artificial construction of some type when this image is magnified.

UTOPÎA

Envisioning free energy for all and an end to money is only the beginning. The Golden Age for humanity is just around the corner.

"It was the best of times, it was the worst of times, it was the age of wisdom, it was the age of foolishness, it was the epoch of belief, it was the epoch of incredulity, it was the season of Light, it was the season of Darkness, it was the spring of hope, it was the winter of despair, we had everything before us, we had nothing before us, we were all going direct to Heaven, we were all going direct the other way." –Charles Dickens, *A Tale of Two Cities*

"Happiness depends upon ourselves." –Aristotle

"By choosing your thoughts, and by selecting which emotional currents you will release and which you will reinforce, you determine the quality of your Light. You determine the effects that you will have upon others, and the nature of the experience of your life." –Gary Zukav

"Energy, power and vibration, is in every human being, animal and mineral. What moves more has more of it. The Earth and our solar system, all the galaxies, the cosmos itself has energy, power and vibration." –Shaman Mancoluto, *Stepping Into The Fire*

"The spiritual journey is individual, highly personal. It can't be organized or regulated. It isn't true that everyone should follow one path. Listen to your own truth." –Ram Dass

"Each of us is a God. Each of us knows all. We need only to open our minds to hear our own wisdom." –Buddha

"All matter originates and exists only by virtue of a force which brings the particle of an atom to vibration and holds this most minute solar system of the atom together. We must assume behind this force the existence of a conscious and intelligent mind. This mind is the matrix of all matter." –Max Planck, in a speech as he accepts the 1919 Nobel Prize

"The doorsteps to the temple of wisdom, is the knowledge of our ignorance." –Benjamin Franklin

"If you want to find the secrets of the universe, think in terms of energy, frequency and vibration." –Nikola Tesla

"Your task is not to seek love, but merely to seek and find all the barriers within yourself that you have built against it." –Rumi

"There will come a time when the Earth grows sick, and when it does, a tribe will gather from all cultures of the world, who believe in deeds and not words, they will work to heal it. They will be known as warriors of the rainbow." –Cree Indian Mother

"May you be alive at the end of the world." –Irish prayer

UTOPIA

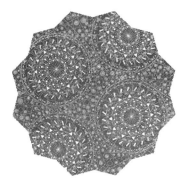

"Utopia or bust." –Robert Anton Wilson

SPEAK of a utopian society and most people will dismiss the notion as a wishful vision of a world filled with only good, well-intended optimists where everything always works out perfectly for everyone. Unfortunately, we share the Earth with mentally sick individuals who exhibit skewed psyches with destructive intent. In our society it is possible for ambitious individuals with antisocial behavior to become empowered as decision makers. A study in 2012 suggested that one out of every ten Wall Street employees exhibits the characteristics of a clinical psychopath. This is ten percent, whereas the average in the general population is one percent. Given the high percentage of dangerous and corrupt people, what could be more risky than having a privately-owned Federal Reserve system with a monopoly on making money, backed up by a monopoly on military and private mercenary forces, in which such individuals can rise to the top of a highly centralized power pyramid?

There goes our utopia. Humankind is caught in the cycle of fear, greed, apathy and hatred. These human instincts drive hierarchical political systems and bureaucracies that often limit the basic human right of the pursuit of happiness. To begin looking into a utopian scenario, it will be necessary to dismantle the current plutocracy, ruled as it is by a few extremely rich people. A country or society governed by the wealthy will never care for all individuals, but instead will focus on its own self-interests.

The dream of a "Golden Age," first expressed by Hesiod, and various philosophical writings such as Plato's *Republic*, has become a reoccurring theme in literature. Many have attempted to define the ideal society. For some, the dream has turned into a nightmare, a dystopia, which will also be covered in this section. Such dichotomies between the two possibilities come exactly at a time when we find ourselves at a critical turning point in human history. The path we are on is veering towards a global police state, the markers being the erosion of more and more human rights. We must change direction away from tyranny, but how? What are the guiding principles that would lead from war to peace, from hunger to abundance, from domination to liberation, and from total oppression to the freedom of an enlightened Golden Age? How can we work toward a world where no one is violated or coerced in any way?

Within our lifetime, we have the potential to create a peaceful and healthy civilization, one free of conflict and honoring the rights of every human on the planet. A world based on equality, integrity, freedom, and compassion. A world where everyone is able not only to survive, but to excel and pursue happiness. In a thriving society, no one is allowed to violate anyone else, except in genuine self-defense, which is redirected to peaceful resolution. And for the oppressive Powers That Be, let's refer to them now as the Powers That Were, because their time is up. If enough of us withdraw our support, the global domination agenda simply cannot work. We have the power of nonviolence and non-participation, along with the position of moral authority, a force which Mahatmas Gandhi called the "simple power of truth."

The very notion of utopia is static. Yet the survival of any social system ultimately depends upon its ability to allow for appropriate change to improve society as a whole. The paths that we choose have enormous consequences in the future. Our choices in the next few decades will ultimately determine whether or not there will remain intelligent life on Earth. The future does not depend on our present-day beliefs or social customs, but will continue to evolve as a set of values unique to its own time. Maybe there is no such thing as a "utopia" for all people, but we can surely do better than where we are headed. Think about not having to use gas anymore, or not having to pay taxes. Think about the poorest people in the world no longer worrying about having enough food to eat.

WHO'S UTOPIA?

Throughout the history of civilization, few national leaders or politicians have attempted to articulate a comprehensive plan to improve the lives of all people under their jurisdiction. Although individuals such as Plato, Edward Bellamy, H. G. Wells, Karl Marx, and Howard Scott made some attempts to present a new civilization available to all, the established social order considered these individuals impractical dreamers with utopian designs that ran contrary to the innate elements of human nature. Arrayed against these social pioneers was a formidable status quo composed of vested interests that were comfortable with the way things were, and a populace at large that, out of years of indoctrination and conditioning, wanted no radical change. These became the millions of non-appointed guardians of the status quo. The outlook and philosophy of the leaders were consistent with their positions of differential advantage.

In 1898, Edward Bellamy wrote the book *Looking Backward.* He conceived of an ideal egalitarian social system with many advanced ideas for its time. This best-seller generated a great deal of interest, and many people inquired as to how this type of cooperative utopian society could be developed. But Bellamy answered that he was just a writer and did not know how to create such a society.

The proposals he presented, similar to those of Plato's *Republic*, the writings of Karl Marx, H. G. Wells in his book *The Shape of Things to Come*, and many others all represent attempts to find workable solutions to the many problems that earlier civilizations were unable to resolve. There is little doubt that at the time of Bellamy's book these social conditions were abominable, which made a utopian ideal extremely appealing. What appeared to be lacking in most of these concepts, however, has been an overall plan, and the necessary methods for a transitional system to enable the idea to become a reality. Most of the early visions of a better world did not allow for changes in either technology or human values, tending to arrest innovative efforts. Additionally, all have lacked a comprehensive set of blueprints, models, and a methodology for implementation. Finally, they lacked competent and determined individuals who could actually bring about such a transition.

The answers do not lie in debate or philosophical discussion of values, but rather in methodology. Thus, what is needed is an operational definition of a better world. That operational definition in our age would be to constantly maximize existing and future benevolent technologies with the sole purpose of enhancing all human life and protecting the environment. It would by definition eliminate all human suffering.

Today we have developed the necessary technology to surpass the fondest of hopes and visions that any social innovator could have dreamed of in the past. The fact that previous attempts at social change have failed is no justification for us to ever stop trying. It is merely the current leadership structure that has failed all the people of the world. The real danger lies in apathy and complacence. The only limitations to the future of humankind are those that we impose upon ourselves. It is now possible to relieve humanity of many of its unresolved problems through the humane application of technology that is already available. Our goal, if we are to accept the challenge, is to identify the impediments of reaching utopia, and remove the guilty parties from power.

COMBATING THE ILLUSION

The greatest advantage of our adversaries is how absurd the truth really seems to the mass population. How can we stand up against something that is not agreed upon or understood? The technique of divide and conquer works remarkably well. Our would-be masters are also masters at manipulation. They know if they can keep using the "FUD Factor," that is, applying Fear, Uncertainty, and Doubt, to any subject they find threatening, the Powers That Were will continue winning. They own the mass media and control the message. Remember, as the John Mayer song lyrics suggest, when you own the information you can bend it all you want.

It is interesting to see the manner in which certain seemingly universal human experiences—telepathic communication, out-of-body flight, secret forms of identity, magical influence, altered states of energy or consciousness—occupy a rather curious place in our present Western culture. Whereas such marvels are vociferously denied or simply ignored in the halls of academic respectability, they are enthusiastically embraced in popular culture such as fiction, film, and fantasy. People are obviously fascinated by such subjects and shell out billions of dollars per year for their special display, yet our society will not discuss these subjects, at least not in a serious and sustained professional way. Popular culture has become our new mysticism. The public realm is our esoteric realm. And the paranormal is our biggest secret, hidden in plain sight.

Each of us has the choice to create our lives so that we may participate in the utopian world that will manifest on Earth after this ascension process has completed. Let's never forget the end goal is a world without poverty, hunger or suffering. Developing new human abilities are also in the realm of possibilities. A new world where full-body levitation, spontaneous healings, instant telepathic communication, and other super human abilities become possible. It is an age where abundant love and sharing is the only currency, and declared the new law of the land. The only thing that ever mattered was how much love you were willing to share while you were incarnated on Earth. But of course we are told none of this. We need to figure it out for ourselves. But never forget that the truth will always stand on its own for all time. Truth is a constant in the universe.

BRAVING A NEW WORLD

It's pretty amazing that our society has reached a point where the effort necessary to extract oil from the ground, ship it to a refinery, turn it into plastic, shape it appropriately, truck it to a store, buy it, and bring it back home is considered to be less effort than what it takes to just wash the spoon when you're done using it. Let's rethink what we consume and what we create as waste. Engineers and technology have made our lives easier, and with a plan to move forward, we already have the technology to create a utopia where everyone on Earth has clean air, pure water, green energy, plentiful food, adequate shelter, a college education, advanced health care, the liberty to live our lives in peace, and the freedom to become whomever we choose according to our abilities. What would life be like in a cleaner, greener utopia where greed, ignorance, and slavery have no place?

Star Trek series creator Gene Roddenberry was connected to a number of individuals who were basically foretelling future events. Some of the technology was featured on the show, including transporters which are referred to today as star-gates. This technology has been used on Earth for years. Another *Star Trek* concept is a food replicator, also called the materializer, which has also been around for decades. The latest versions can literally visualize what someone wants to eat, and it will then scan and produce the best possible reproduction of what the person visualized. Side innovations include the food acting as a mouth cleanser as it is being eaten, and it actually turns the synthetic food into pure nutrition when digested. If someone wants a steak, this device can make it out of matter, and the texture and taste will seem just like the real thing. We will not have to slaughter animals any longer. These extraordinary, major and fantastic changes are available if we can break the bonds of secrecy.

To re-conceptualize a new world without the oppressive "Order," let's start with the basics. All of the 6,000 free energy patents currently being suppressed need to be re-tested, and if they work, released to the world. Let's begin by re-examining all Tesla technology, and if it stands the scrutiny of the scientific method, it needs to be released. The oil cartel and military-industrial billionaires have been holding back human technological development for their own monopoly. This must end, because with unlimited free energy we can completely transform society, re-establish natural ecosystems, clean-up polluted regions, reverse global warming, and provide fresh water to all people with desalinization stations.

When energy is no longer an expensive obstacle, we could pump the nutrients from the deep parts of the ocean to increase fish stocks near the surface by ten times. We can reverse planetary degradation, save endangered species, create more wildlife habitats, and provide for everyone. We're all one planet, we're all one people. No one should be born with a price tag just to remain alive. We ultimately need to do away with money. End poverty and we'll also end much of the current rate of deforestation. When energy no longer has a price tag, we can have a world of abundance, but there must be cooperation, fairness and consensus among all people.

THE PARADOX OF OUR TIME

While it would seem that we are naturally heading towards an era of unprecedented peace through technology and other means, we still have wars and tremendous human suffering. We live in a world of paradox, of great duality. We have taller buildings but shorter tempers. Wider freeways but narrower viewpoints. We retain more information but have less wisdom. We have more options for leisure and less fun. More conveniences, yet less time. We have more medicine and medical options, yet less wellness. More kinds of food available, but less nutrition. We have more media outlets but less communication. More acquaintances, but fewer friends. We have increased our possessions, but reduced our values. We have conquered outer space, but neglected inner space. We have smashed the atom, but not our prejudices.

"When I was five years old," remembered Beatles musician John Lennon, "my mother always told me that happiness was the key to life. When I went to school, they asked me what I wanted to be when I grew up. I wrote down 'happy.' They told me I didn't understand the assignment, and I told them they didn't understand life." Later in his life, when John Lennon became a crusader for peace, he noted how difficult it was to struggle against a society seemingly indifferent to the pursuit of happiness and focused on violence. "When it gets down to having to use violence, then you are playing the system's game," Lennon said. "The establishment will irritate you—pull your beard, flick your face—to make you fight. Because once they've got you violent, then they know how to handle you. The only thing they don't know how to handle is nonviolence and humor." In our pursuit for a utopian society, or even a utopia within ourselves, we need to transcend the meaningless distractions and the temptation to become angry or fearful. "Imagine all the people sharing all the world," as the lyrics to *Imagine* suggest, "You may say I'm a dreamer, but I'm not the only one. I hope someday you'll join us, and the world will live as one." John Lennon got it right again when he sang *All You Need is Love.* No one is the solution for your own happiness but yourself.

A GOVERNMENT OF PEACE

A sustainable future for the Earth must be made a top priority. The economic impact of total military disarmament, to name only the most obvious consequence of peace, would revise the production and distribution patterns of the globe to a degree that would make the changes in the past 50 years seem insignificant. We can plan in advance the whole transition to make it go as smoothly as possible. Political, technological, sociological, cultural, and ecological changes would be equally far-reaching.

The governing and relations between nations after total disarmament are basically judicial in nature. We will need to plan for institutions similar to a World Court or a United Nations, but vested with real authority. The United Nations Security Council needs to be re-zoned. The most populous landmasses should be divided into the eight general regions of the world. One vote should go to each region, which includes: South America and the Caribbean; North America; China; Japan and Southeast Asia; Europe; the Muslim Middle East; India; and Africa. Each of the eight zones could only veto an item that is directly within their boundary, which would lead to a much more effective government that prioritizes the sharing of resources and governance equally among all people.

We need a whole new social contract, and it will be up to each of us to create such a system when the Powers That Were are finally gone. In the future we will only want to use energy sources which are 100% clean, cheap, decentralized, and safe. Energy must become strictly zero-emission, have minimal life-cycle environmental impact, and be completely renewable. Energy must be provided free or very affordable to everyone, with an end to the energy monopolies. It will become a crime to manufacture devices that emit noxious gases. Energy must also be decentralized, with no more power grids or power plants. And lastly, let's make energy a benevolent technology that is completely safe and publicly accountable. No weapons use, no secrecy, and no greed.

Without a social system based on money, greed can be eliminated. Without greed there is no envy or desire for material items. And without desire, according to the Buddha, there is no longer any suffering. We have been relentlessly conditioned to think that money will buy our happiness, where just the opposite is true. Money is simply a way to transform our efforts into a way where we can get what we need in life. For example, the television show *Star Trek* was a utopian view of a peaceful human race set several hundred years into the future, charting out the unknown regions of the universe in the name of exploration. There was never a single scene where humans were seen using a currency of any kind to get what they needed. They would tell the computer what they wanted, and out it would come. Simple as that. Money will have no place in a utopian world, at least not one that has found a lasting peace, free from destruction and where all people are created equal. But as we shall see, there are several hurdles to jump before we can get there.

The Russian artist Konstantin Yuon depicted his vision of "Utopia" in the Magazine *Zolotoe Runo*, published at the end of 1907. This image was drawn shortly after the 1905 Russian Revolution and the creation of the Russian Constitution. A feeling of optimism had begun to spread across vast expanses of Russia, led by intellectual agitation for more political democracy and limits to Czarist absolutism.

This sculpture of Plato is found in the modern Academy of Athens. The ancient Greek philosopher Plato was among the first to outline the earliest recorded proposal to create a utopian society in his book, the *Republic*. Part conversation, part fictional depiction, and part policy proposal, the book offers a categorization of citizens into socioeconomic classes in order to determine who can become the best leaders. The top-tier "golden citizens" are trained in a rigorous 50-year long educational program to become benign oligarchs. The wisdom of the "philosopher-kings" would eliminate poverty and deprivation through fairly distributed resources.

AGE OF TRANSPARENCY

"There are only two mistakes one can make along the road to truth; not going all the way, and not starting."

–Gautama Buddha

MEMBERS of the so-called New World Order have been positioning themselves for an American power grab since 1913 when the Federal Reserve was established in the United States. In 1933, President Franklin D. Roosevelt ordered the all-seeing eye to be placed upon one dollar bills, along with the motto *Novus Ordo Seclorum*, which is Latin for "A New Order of the Ages." The power base that would have us controlled by their agenda from the cradle to the grave is for the first time in history feeling the pressure of a new game changer called the Internet. Now ordinary citizens can discuss the diabolical agenda of the cabal, comment on websites, and share images. The Internet is only a starting point for an Age of Transparency, a new dawn when lies and secrets cannot be covered-up any longer.

The seismic impact that the Internet and social media have had on established power structures worldwide is nothing short of remarkable. For the first time in history, ordinary citizens can communicate in times of adversity, gather during martial law, and post their own ideas, photos and videos. Social media has become a new avenue for the collection and distribution of the news. Unless governments become more accountable to their citizens and more transparent in their operations, they will face eventual downfall. This is part of a larger movement seeking greater governmental and corporate transparency. With the combination of Internet connectivity and transparency, a new oversight by citizens is emerging. Social media allows the opportunity for more people to see, share and shape what is going on around them. Suddenly the Powers That Were will find themselves more exposed than they have ever been. The result is a huge increase in social energy, which is being channeled in all different directions, and may even lead to the downfall of once powerful Western governments.

THE POLICY OF TRUTH

After the tumultuous "Arab Spring," when online protesters and social media played a crucial role in overthrowing unpopular leaders in northern African countries, and at a time when WikiLeaks' military source Bradley Manning was put on trial, keeping the Internet free, or Net Neutrality, has never been under greater assault than it is now. The clash between power, truth, access, transparency and a "small-d" democracy is unfolding in our newly hyper-networked world. Inspired by WikiLeaks and the urgent debates that have been ignited by that phenomenon and its founder, the Internet is changing the status quo and may never be the same.

Author and lecturer David Icke warned a few years back that anti-pirating laws will be used as an excuse to shut down the Internet. Under closer examination we learn the same entertainment companies leading the Stop Online Piracy Act (SOPA) charge against copyright piracy and suing students and single moms for thousands of dollars, are the very same companies who originally designed and distributed pirating software. CBS Viacom co-branded with C/net and other media sites to release the file sharing software BitTorrent; Time/Warner and MSN supported Kazaa; Disney supported and then sued the Scour search engine; and there are also other examples of big media companies inducing users to piracy. SOPA was one big bait and hook scam perpetrated by big media to control the Internet in order to have us watch their content exclusively.

The U.S. Government is diligent and obsessive in defending its borders against invaders. We are now told that a small international band of renegades, armed with nothing more than laptops, will present the greatest threat to the U.S. regime since the close of the Cold War. The National Defense Authorization Act, almost unanimously backed by the Senate and passed in the House of Representatives, contains language that allows the Pentagon to effectively wage a cyberwar on any domestic enemies of the state. Yet, in 2015 it was declared that if China engages in cyberattacks against USA interests that will be considered an act of war. The NDAA was largely in response to the WikiLeaks release of a massive trove of secret official documents which embarrassed and riled politicians. They seek to limit the true extent in which the Internet can be used as a tool to make the governments more accountable for its policies, judgments, and actions. However, this argument cuts both ways. The government cautions that if we are not doing anything wrong, we have no reason to fear government censorship. Yet citizens can counter that if their government were not doing anything improper, it would have no reason to fear free speech.

A true democracy with a capital "D" would require government officials to be accountable to the citizens who elected them to office; in all circumstances, they would remain beholden to the wishes of the people. A true democracy would consider it treasonous, for example, if elected officials in any way undermined the people's right to free speech, their right to a fair trial, or their right to protection from indefinite detention. A true democracy would aggressively protect the open and free forum provided by the Internet. Instead, the National Defense Authorization Act (S. 1867), signed into law on the eve of 2012, which authorized the president to detain U.S. citizens indefinitely without trial, reverses these assumptions. Fortunately, the SOPA and PIPA Internet censorship bills were shelved after a major backlash of protest from Internet users. In fact, some of the largest websites went "black" for a day on January 18, 2012, in protest. As soon as citizens fight back, another arcane law is created. On May 1, 2012, with little or no mass media coverage, President Obama signed Executive Order 13563 declaring International Law to apply to the United States. This order can be used to institute gun confiscation laws without any consent by our Congress or Judicial oversight. And once these foreign laws are brought to the United States under the various security agreements, foreign troops could be brought in to enforce these foreign laws upon citizens of the United States. Suddenly, our once-grand democracy is looking like no democracy at all.

COUNTERING PROPAGANDA

"**If** we understand the mechanism and motives of the group mind, is it not possible to control and regiment the masses according to our will without them knowing about it?" These are inquires by Edward Bernays, a former U.S. Presidential Advisor, from his book *Propaganda*. "The conscious and intelligent manipulation of the organized habits and opinions of the masses is an important element in democratic society. Those who manipulate this unseen mechanism of society constitute an invisible government which is the true ruling power of our government. We are governed, our minds molded, our tastes formed, our ideas suggested, largely by men we have never heard of."

You have to ask yourself, do we *really* learn anything about politics from TV announcers? Or are we simply repeating what we've been programmed to say by clever TV propaganda? It seems that most of the mainstream media has stopped investigating "news" stories a while ago. Our journalists have been replaced with tele-prompt scripted readers. The "lame-stream media" only works for unthinking people who do not know the truth, who ignore history, and especially for those who do not do their own independent research. It only works for those who naively believe everything they hear. President Richard Nixon knew the power of propaganda when he stated: "The American people don't believe anything until they see it on television."

The modern human is utterly saturated by advertising and political messaging every day. Few realize the pervasive powers of propaganda or how to possibly counter it. One way is to go live in the woods and shut oneself off from any media messages. Another way is to recognize propaganda by understanding its programming effect so it is then rendered transparent. To be effective, propaganda must constantly short-circuit all logical reasoning. Ideally, it must operate on the individual at the unconscious level. This kind of "subliminal seduction" works best when people do not even realize that they are being manipulated by outside forces, and operates below the threshold of consciousness.

With the emergence of the visual media (primarily television), it became possible to use propaganda techniques to saturate the entire culture and to shape thoughts and opinions of the masses. The orchestration of press, radio, film, and television created a continuous, lasting and all-pervasive environment that is hard to escape. Mass media provides the essential link between the individual and the demands of our technological society. But what we think we know is not always the way things really are. The first step to countering propaganda is to recognize that there is a very organized perception-shaping apparatus called the controlled mass media, which is the real "silent weapon for a quiet war."

THE BATTLE FOR TRANSPARENCY

WikiLeaks has announced that their ongoing "battle" will be to ensure that the Internet does not turn into a vast surveillance tool for governments and corporations. According to Julian Assange, the Internet itself has become "the most significant surveillance machine that we have ever seen." He was referring to the unethical use of the detailed information people give about themselves online. "It's not an Age of Transparency at all," he said; in fact, "the amount of secret information is more than ever before," adding that information flows in, but does not flow outward from governments and other powerful organizations. "I see that really is our big battle. The technology gives and the technology takes away," he concluded.

Although information disseminated by the Wikileaks website is often bothersome to governments, there is sometimes no other way to tackle the problem in light of the oppressive atmosphere which characterizes the flow of information. Wikileaks believes that since people are now living at a time when freedom of information is under assault, we all must remain vigilant, and in a way, all become watchdogs.

Political analyst and author Micah Sifry argues that WikiLeaks is not the entire story involved with protecting freedom of information. Wikileaks is one example of calling attention to a problem and taking action; it is one indicator of an ongoing generational and philosophical struggle between older, closed systems, and the new open culture of the Internet. Despite Assange's house arrest, the publication of secret documents endures. Just as the closure of Napster failed to stop unauthorized music file sharing, the U.S. government's draconian crackdown on WikiLeaks will also be futile. Even if the website is forced to shut down, many new whistleblower sites are erupting to follow its model.

The annual Reporters Without Borders report in 2014 showed the United States dropping 14 points on the "freest media" list to 46th place, due to the pursuit of NSA leaker Edward Snowden and the Justice Department's seizure of AP phone records in an effort to find the source of a CIA leak. Other countries in the Middle East that cracked down on journalists also took big falls in the rankings. Reporters Without Borders use a simple equation for their rankings: the absence or suppression of civil liberties which leads to the suppression of media freedom. Dictatorships fear free speech and ban information, especially when it may undermine their rule. "Never has freedom of information been so closely associated with democracy. Never have journalists, through their reporting, vexed the enemies of freedom so much," the group said in a statement accompanying its report.

HUMAN INTUITION

Deception is at an all time high, although intuition is slightly in the lead. In these confusing times we could all use an effective perception meter to separate the "wheat from the chaff." For those of us who seek to hone our intuition, first it is important to believe we can attain enhanced human capabilities, and one of these is the ability to distinguish between truth and lies. As these perceptual abilities become developed, nothing but the truth will hold meaning. Lies and deception will appear as a telltale aura field surrounding the perpetrator. Those who would do us harm, either physically or with their words and actions, will become exposed until they themselves feel self-conscious. Sooner or later every liar will become aware of their "appearance" to others, and decide to change their ways. Until then, it is up to us to be the best possible individuals we can be, and this will increase our own intuition abilities. This is absolutely essential. We must each adopt a policy of no lying, cheating, stealing, or any other dishonest action. Nothing works except a complete personal devotion to honesty and truth.

Once developed, the personal ability to detect dishonesty will also allow people to finally know themselves at their core, their spiritual selves. As soon as we can realize that we are truly one with everyone, indeed with everything on the planet and the cosmos beyond, suddenly we allow the cleansing away of that which has enslaved us in the false illusion we now face in the world. The visionary mystic and poet William Blake said it best: "If the doors of perception were cleansed, everything would appear as it is, infinite."

The idea of attuning to a greater human perception is nothing new and is usually achieved through some kind of meditation practice. Originally used in Hinduism and Buddhism, a mantra is a word or sound repeated to aid concentration in meditation. A mantra is also a Vedic hymn and in Sanskrit literally means "instrument of thought." A yantra is a geometric diagram, or any object, used as an aid to meditation in tantric worship. In Sanskrit, a yantra is literally a "device for holding or fastening." Tantra refers to a mystical or ritual text involving mantras, meditation, yoga, and ritual. Adapting these Eastern techniques to the West, the New Thought movement (originating in the 19th century) has at its core a belief that a higher power pervades all existence. Auras around people and other life forms appear subtly to the trained eye. Individuals can create their own reality (more accurately, their experience here) via affirmations, meditation, and prayer. Early New Thought groups emerged from a Christian Science background and some New Thought writers refer back to selected portions of the Bible as their foundation text. Other New Thought groups dismiss any Biblical connection.

Developing greater human intuition is also in our best interests, as it will help each of us obtain a healthy, happy and more meaningful life experience. Eventually all lies will be known and forgotten, and only truth will hold up to the test of time. Meanwhile, orient yourself to the highest standards of ethics today, and live by them with no exceptions. Your personal credo must remain a directive that never wavers. It is a deal made only between you and You. Orient yourself to humbly being in service to others, make nonviolence your unwavering conviction for conflict resolution, lose your ego, and surrender to a force greater than yourself in the universe. Call it by any name "God" has ever been called, or call it nothing at all. Even an atheist can recognize a life force pervading within every creature struggling to survive. Humble yourself before a larger conscious universe inhabiting everything, be aware that what you are hearing in your mind can be of assistance to your growth, and reinforce your devotion to upholding the truth. This is how human intuition can be dramatically enhanced. We can voluntarily orient our thoughts to the negative or positive. Once we identify our negative judgments and attitudes and let them go, we can be positive at all times in order to evolve spiritually and prepare ourselves to ascend into the next dimension.

A MATTER OF DIMENSIONS

Honing our intuition is only one of the enhanced abilities we'll be experiencing as we advance into the next dimension. But what exactly is a fourth or fifth dimensional being? First, let's remember that we live in third dimensional space. How do we know? Simply because we have three directions of free movement all around us. Those are left-right, back-forth, and up-down. Each dimension above third is a different degree of light and density.

There are eleven levels of density. The ultimate goal is evolution on an individual basis, and together as a species. Since humans are living in the third dimension, some of us might fear fourth dimensional beings because we do not understand them. We fear what we do not know, and fear is another of the negative emotions which will recede in the Age of Transparency. We will lose all negative emotions in the process, and become truly happy people.

Higher dimensional beings can read the auras of human beings and intuitively sense our energy fields, and they can literally see through our bodies. They are highly telepathic and are invisible to third dimensional beings. They possess more of a group mind. No one can possibly have a hidden agenda because they can see right through you. There are no secrets, no deceptions, no mystery whatsoever surrounding any conspiracy theory. Everything that has ever happened from all time becomes apparent in the Age of Transparency. Just like a sunbeam cannot separate itself from the sun and a wave cannot separate itself from the sea, we cannot separate ourselves from one another. In the grand scheme of things we are all part of a vast sea of love, one indivisible and transparent divine mind. But to arrive at this awareness is the biggest challenge for most freewill individuals on Earth.

READING ENERGY FIELDS

All living things, including humans, and even solid objects such as crystals, manifest an aura in a very subtle way. Often reading energy fields is held to be perceptible, spontaneous and painless for some, and for others it is a lifetime of devotion to training and practice. Such perceptions have been compared to the third eye of Hindu spirituality. Each color of the aura has a meaning, indicating a precise emotional state. Auras are not actual light, but a sensory reading or perception added to the reader's visual processing. Auras cannot be seen in complete darkness and cannot be seen unless some portion of the person or object emitting the aura can also be seen. Auras are connected with clairvoyance, the individual's spirit and their etheric body, or the lowest layer in the "human energy field." The etheric body is in immediate contact with the physical body, to sustain it and connect it with "higher" bodies. Auras are mental and emotional emanations.

As we move into the fourth density, the ability to read each other's minds will become feasible. We will become clairvoyant and we will communicate telepathically. Near instantaneous manifestations will occur at the speed of thought. You might begin to already notice your abilities as you walk past a stranger and can seemingly read everything about that person, immediately. We will also gain increasingly acute glimpses into our future, more déjà vu experiences, and situations where we can knowingly alter future events. As a bumper sticker recommends: "Do something today that your future self will thank you for."

In the Age of Transparency a new kind of court system will become necessary, where all of the evidence will be apparent to everyone. The judge and jury will be clairvoyant and able to read the energy field of the accused. If we try to hide something, everyone nevertheless will see it. When humans are able to develop telepathy on a species level, we will have an exceptionally clear way of communicating with each other. All of the different languages on Earth will not matter as every member and group of society will communicate telepathically. As a result, there will no longer be any hidden agendas. Everyone will know what the truth of any agenda might be, so it will become easier to solve problems.

The New World Order wishes to keep the ordinary person locked into a state of third dimensional fear and anger. What the Powers That Were dread the most, and will stop at nothing to prevent, is when people develop their higher dimensional abilities and can then see the world in a whole new light. At that time, our thoughts will create our own experience of reality. When the full range of history can be uncritically examined for all to see, the guilty parties who are still alive will become known for their crimes. Instead of inflicting violence on them, a truth and reconciliation panel should be established to determine a prison sentence, and allow the rest of us to move on from the illusion they imposed upon us for so long.

The Flammarion print by an unknown artist is a wood engraving that first appeared in Camille Flammarion's book *L'atmosphère: météorologie populaire* in 1888. The image shows a man crawling under the edge of the sky, which is depicted as if it were a solid hemisphere, and the man is astonished to see the mysterious heavenly world beyond.

The "Milk Hill Galaxy" crop circle manifested during a single night and was first reported on August 13, 2001. Experts who study the formation of crop circles attribute the creation process to a multitude of dimensions. Crop circles are created by tubes of light or orbs of light that are generated on fields of grain, most commonly in England. Metaphysical interpretations of dimensions as they relate to the formation of crop circles are as follows: The eighth dimension (8D) is a form in the mind of God; the seventh dimension (7D) is sacred sound that can manifest form; the sixth dimension (6D) is the geometrical field that creates forms; the fifth dimension (5D) is unconditional love, an energy that comes when creation happens; the fourth dimension (4D) is where energy polarizes so that things can manifest; the third dimension (3D) is the field where the crop circle formation takes place. Excerpted from *Alchemy of Nine Dimensions: The 2011/2012 Prophecies and Nine Dimensions of Consciousness* by Barbara Hand Clow with Gerry Clow, Hampton Roads Publishing, Inc., Charlottesville, VA (2010).

SUPER HUMAN ABILITIES

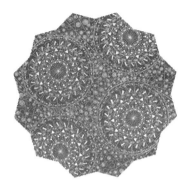

"All speech, action, and behavior are fluctuations of consciousness. All life emerges from, and is sustained in, consciousness. The whole universe is the expression of consciousness. The reality of the universe is one unbounded ocean of consciousness in motion." –Maharishi Mahesh Yogi

FOR many centuries, an essential claim of the occultists was that mental processes can be independent of the human body. Consciousness is not bound to the brain or the body, or so contended the yogis and esotericists. It has taken a long professional quest into the history of psychical research, Cold War remote viewing, and quantum physics in order for experts to arrive at a tentative conclusion, and a gross understatement: Practitioners with demonstrable psychic abilities have "extraordinary knowing." Those in the business call it the Intuitive Arts. A modern organization, The Institute of Noetic Sciences, studies this extraordinary knowing scientifically. Noetic is from the Greek term, *nous*, a kind of inner knowing which transcends intellect.

It has been said that a question is not asked until the answer is known. Such is true for tapping into the full potential of a human being. Harnessing a mastery of consciousness has been an eternal quest. Countless spiritual, religious, and secret societies have attempted to master the human mind. Spiritual gurus contend that just about anything is possible with the proper training. How much can we possibly accomplish? For starters, we can make speed mental computations, become a human calculator device, have a super power memory, develop a photographic speed-reading capacity, or obtain excellent mental or physical athletic abilities are all in the realm of possible. The key is to exercise your brain and train your mind.

Super human mental abilities have been researched by the KGB, British Intelligence and various American spy agencies for about a century as a way to manipulate each other. These human experiments reached a fevered pitch during the Cold War. Telepathy, telekinesis, and other important experiments of the mind were recorded and sometimes utilized for nefarious purposes. But the findings never resulted in much strategic benefit, and were ultimately stopped. It is very difficult to manipulate someone with advanced mental capabilities without a pure heart.

Some extraordinary human abilities used to control others are considered the dark sciences, largely because a person being manipulated typically loses their free will. Mind control is one example: a phenomenon encompassing all the ways in which personal, social and institutional forces are exerted to induce compliance, conformity, belief, attitude, and value change in others. Mind control techniques, however, are never ethical without the full consent of the individual.

SAGAN SPEAKS

Dr. Carl Sagan was a noted astronomer, scientist, author, and paranormal skeptic. Sagan was a founding member of a group that set out to debunk unscientific claims, but he surprisingly found merit in certain paranormal categories. He wrote the book *The Demon Haunted World* in which he remarked that there are several areas in parapsychology which deserve serious study. This statement by Sagan admirers is largely ignored. Sagan wrote: "At the time of writing there are three claims in the ESP field which, in my opinion, deserve serious study: (1) that by thought alone humans can (barely) affect random number generators in computers; (2) that people under mild sensory deprivation can receive thoughts or images 'projected' at them; and (3) that young children sometimes report the details of a previous life, which upon checking turn out to be accurate and which they could not have known about in any way other than reincarnation. I pick these claims not because I think they're likely to be valid (I don't), but as examples of contentions that might be true."

Carl Sagan also commented on mirror organisms, or the possibility of life existing in the higher dimensions. "If a fourth-dimensional creature existed it could, in our three-dimensional universe, appear and dematerialize at will, change shape remarkably, pluck us out of locked rooms and make us appear from nowhere. It could also turn us inside out." These are interesting observations from a known skeptic. If we take Sagan's research to the next level, perhaps the ultimate result will be for us to become multi-dimensional, psychic, astral voyaging, and time traveling super humans.

RECEIVING THOUGHTS AND IMAGES

There have been, and remain, many dubious sciences of the mind bent on controlling or conditioning other people. Mind control, or "brainwashing," refers to a broad range of psychological tactics that are able to subvert an individual's control of his or her own thinking, behavior, emotions, actions, or decisions. This concept is closely related to hypnosis, but differs in practical approach. Hypnosis is the most basic of these control mechanisms. It has been considered a dark science since before Moses' time. The concepts of "hypnotic suggestion," or "pointing the bone" in voodoo traditions, speaking in tongues, or even demonic possession all relate to mind control sometimes with, but usually without, the subject's permission. Current theories of hypnosis, however, hold that it is impossible (using hypnosis) to induce individuals to behave in ways that are contrary to their wishes or ethics.

A contemporary view of mind control explains it as an intensified and persistent use of well-researched social psychology principles like compliance, conformity, persuasion, dissonance, reactance, framing or emotional manipulation. Mind control is the process by which the individual or collective freedom of choice and action is compromised by agents that can modify or distort perception, motivation, affect cognition, or dictate behavioral outcomes. It is neither magical nor mystical, but is a process that involves a set of basic socio-psychological principles.

PAVLOV'S DOGS

An insight into the conditioning of mammals was performed in 1927 by the Russian researcher Ivan Pavlov, who experimented on stimulus-response mechanism with dogs. The typical procedure for inducing classical conditioning involved presentations of a neutral stimulus along with a stimulus of some significance, called the "unconditional stimulus." The original and most famous example of classical conditioning involved the salivary conditioning of Pavlov's dogs. During his research on the physiology of digestion in dogs, Pavlov noticed that, rather than simply salivating in the presence of food, the dogs began to salivate in the presence of the lab technician who was feeding them regularly. Pavlov called these "psychic secretions." From this observation he predicted that if a particular stimulus in the dog's surroundings were present when the dog was presented with meat, then this stimulus would become associated with food and cause salivation on its own. In his initial experiment, Pavlov used a bell to call the dogs to their meal and, after a few repetitions, the dogs started to salivate in response to the bell, whether food was presented or not.

In 1957, British psychiatrist William Sargant published one of the first books on the psychology of brainwashing entitled *Battle for the Mind*. Sargant connected Pavlov's findings to the ways people learn and internalize their own belief systems. Conditioned behavior patterns could be changed by stimulus stresses beyond a dog's or a person's capacity for response, in essence causing a breakdown. These stresses could include longer than normal waiting periods, rotating positive and negative signals, and changing a creature's physical condition, as through illness. Depending on the creature's initial personality, these techniques could cause a new belief system to be held tenaciously. Sargant also connected Pavlov's findings to the mechanisms of brainwashing in religion and politics. Under severe or prolonged stress, the mind can change radically, profoundly, and with lasting results. In all cases, Sargant concluded, it's a manifestation of a "normal" psychological process by the brain of accommodation to circumstances, which under severely abnormal circumstances can result in very surprising and strange accommodations indeed.

When the mind is in such a "wiped" state, it can be reconstructed in many ways. Brainwashers, Sargant shows, use this compromised mental state to get people to do things they normally would never even consider. Sargant concluded: "Though men are not dogs, they should humbly try to remember how much they resemble dogs in their brain functions, and not boast themselves as demigods. They are gifted with religious and social apprehensions, and they are gifted with the power of reason; but all these faculties are physiologically entailed to the brain. Therefore the brain should not be abused by having forced upon it any religious or political mystique that stunts the reason, or any form of crude rationalism that stunts the religious sense."

MIND CONTROL

William Sargant and Dr. Ewen Cameron of Project MK-ULTRA notoriety were friends and colleagues. The two exchanged views and information on brainwashing and "de-patterning" techniques, along with their mutual research in these areas. Both men had extensive CIA and British Secret Intelligence Service connections.

One aim of Cameron, Sargant, and the CIA's research programs during the Cold War was to find ways to obliterate the memories of allied spies, called de-patterning, and then implant false memories at a deep level so that if a spy were captured in his adoptive country, he would be incapable under duress or even torture of revealing his true American or British allegiance; he would only be able to reveal the falsely implanted memories that supported his assumed persona. This concept was dubbed *The Manchurian Candidate* after the popular novel and film. The extensive use of "heroic" doses of Electron Convulsive Shock Treatment combined with the narcosis Deep Sleep Treatment, anti-depressants, tape-loops, insulin coma therapy, and other drugs in this context, were designed to induce catastrophic memory loss which then would be replaced with false memories and ideas. These "ideas" were given to the subject via tape loops, hypnosis, LSD or conversations with the person while they were drugged.

Different forms of mind manipulation continue to the present day. The space between our ears may be the newest battleground in the conflict between privacy and technology. A new technique called hypersonic sound (HSS) projection enables sound to be directed precisely to one individual without any spillover. A person only needs to be standing in the path of an HSS beam in order to hear the sound. The sensation to those hearing the sound is that of its being projected from inside their skull. If HSS can already be used on Earth, which has been using electricity for only 150 years, imagine a technology that has been refined over thousands of years or more. This advanced technology could conceivably transmit thoughts that are precisely targeted to an individual person across vast expanses of outer space.

TELEPATHY

According to Wikipedia, telepathy derives from the Greek word *tele*, meaning "remote" and *patheia*, meaning "to be affected by." The definition describes the purported transfer of information on thoughts or feelings between individuals by means other than the five classical senses. The term was coined in 1882 by the classical scholar Fredric W. H. Myers, a founder of the Society for Psychical Research, specifically to replace the earlier expression "thought-transference." Telepathy is a common theme in science fiction, with many super heroes and super villains utilizing telepathic abilities. Such abilities include both sensing the thoughts of people and controlling the minds of others.

A person who is able to make use of telepathy is said to be able to see into the minds of others, and communicate without words being spoken. We already possess some form of telepathy in the form of facial expressions and recognizing patterns in others. But taken to its limit, telepathy can create a close mental link where it is possible to overshadow entirely, or even "possess" the personality of another. Without the permission of another person, this is a form of mental manipulation called "psychic parasite" control.

Telepathy as a form of communication already occurs in humans and animals. Most people are aware of facial cues, grunts, partial words, or reading the looks they get from other people. Trans-humanists believe that technologically enabled telepathy, called "techlepathy," will be the inevitable future of humanity. Proponents seek to develop practical, safe devices for directly connecting one human nervous system to another.

Teleportation and force fields should not be confused with telepathy, although they all work under similar principles. Teleportation is used to dematerialize and materialize various sorts of objects. A force field relies on the behavior of electromagnetic fields, and this has been accomplished in laboratory tests. The term force field refers to the lines of force that one object, the "source object," exerts on another object or a collection of other objects. An object might be a particle of mass, or an electric or magnetic charge, for example.

REMOTE VIEWING

A famous hypnosis experiment by Dr. Thomas Garrett in the 1930s was among the first to document the mental ability of a subject being hypnotized, in this case the son of a famous Broadway playwright. The subject was able to leave his body and view a situation that was deeply troubling to him. The young man had a falling out with his fiancée from a Wellesley sorority. Under hypnosis he was instructed to visit her sorority room and fly through her door, which he did while remote viewing. He found the girl at her desk, writing him a letter at that moment. He copied down the letter she was writing to him, attempting to reconcile their relationship. He dictated the letter to Dr. Garrett, who wrote it all down precisely. When the telegram came the next day, the two letters were almost identical. He was literally able to recite the letter remotely and provide proof to skeptics in the form of the two letters.

Once remote viewing became accepted in the medical profession, the next extension of this technique was used for military applications. If they could train people to master these techniques and send agents remotely to spy on their enemies, there could be a big tactical advantage. Subjects were trained to soar above their own bodies and immediately realize that they were "outside" of their body, looking down from the ceiling at the top of the body's head. They soared higher and higher above until they arrived at the room they were going to study. Spy agencies around the world, as well as police detectives, now employ those with remote viewing abilities to successfully gather information or solve crimes. It works just often enough to have become one of their tools for solving crimes.

A Chinese remote viewing experiment using "Extra High Functioning" (EHF) psychics was developed in a laboratory. In these experiments, subjects were able to remotely view a complex Chinese letter character in a completely dark, light-shielded room. While the target was being correctly viewed, the study scientists also reported 15,000 photons which also appeared in the room. When the subject was accurately remote viewing the target, photons were sent into a particular area they were viewing and could then be measured. The Chinese concluded that there is a measurable energy that the astral body gives off when remote viewing.

We all have the ability to access information this way, including the transmitting of visible photons. Our minds are the gateway, or access point, to consciousness, and the entire universe. What if thoughts not only occur in the mind, but are broadcasting outwards like a satellite? Could the mind somehow tune into the "source field" (as described by author David Wilcock), that which is space, time, energy, matter and biology, all created by a universal consciousness? Do we share consciousness with other forms of life on Earth? How about sentient beings beyond Earth? How about with the alleged source of life itself?

REMOTE INFLUENCING

The goal of remote influencing is to suggest thoughts to other people using the subject's mind. In test studies, the ability of remote influencers to concentrate was improved, physiological calming effects were reported, and those with chronic anxiety even felt calmer. This technique only seems to work with loving consciousness. It is not effective in trying to suggest other people do harm, although there seems to be some examples to the contrary.

As is sometimes common in scientific discoveries, simultaneous developments can occur, as evidenced by a number of inventors who conceive the same idea simultaneously. The concept of "multiple discovery" is when several people invent the same item or make the same discovery at the same time. Calculus, the telephone, the theory of evolution, the oxygen molecule, color photography, logarithms, identification of sunspots in the 1600s, the conservation of energy, and decimal fractions were all discovered simultaneously around the world by different independent researchers. The thermometer had six different claims of invention at the same time. The telescope had nine different claims, the steamboat had five different claims, and the typewriter had multiple claims. At least 148 examples were cataloged by 1922. As we are working on problems, and we gain new insights, this somehow unconsciously projects out as remote influencing. It is as if those thoughts go into the global mind, and others can access the information. The British biologist Rupert Sheldrake dubs this phenomenon "morphic resonance" or "morphic fields." His research has documented this effect in animals, birds and crossword puzzle enthusiasts.

Over 500 scientifically controlled studies have proven that consciousness affects biology and electrical systems. Perhaps this is the explanation for people cursing at their computer or devices, and then those machines suddenly breaking down. With odds like this, there is less than one chance in a trillion that any other explanation exists. Yet this is not a new concept at all. The Native Americans called this force *manitou*, a way that humans can interact with the natural world and affect change. It is a term used to designate the spirit beings among the various Algonquian language groups. It refers to the concept of one aspect of the interconnection and balance of nature and life, similar to the East Asian concept of *chi*, or the Hindu concept of Brahman. The modern metaphysical document, *A Course in Miracles*, uses the term "mind" to represent the "activating agent of spirit, supplying its creative energy." Furthermore, its definition of "miracles" is not that of amazing feats such as raising the dead or moving objects at a distance, but rather changing your mind, such as a shift from ego perception to seeing with spiritual vision. This deep inner shift might or might not manifest as physical changes to the eye, or even as extended human capacities, but nevertheless opens up one's spiritual or "all-encompassing" healing abilities at the deepest levels.

ASTRAL PROJECTION

People who were near death and revived, or actually pronounced dead and brought back to life, have reported various mystical experiences. These sensations are commonly reported as going into a tunnel and emerging in a region of light, being reunited with loved ones, or a profound sense of peace. All of which may suggest an existence beyond the grave.

It would seem we all have an "astral body" floating around, living in the source field. The ancient Egyptians called this light body the "Ka" and some could willingly leave their body and come back at their choosing. Astral projection is the ability to access the gravity wave instantaneously and consciously leave the body. When someone goes from the waking state to an out-of-body state, there is always a cord connected back to the body. This "silver cord" is the lifeline between the astral body and the living body. Those with astral projection abilities can go forward or backwards or sideways in time, or go wherever they wish to go if their minds are properly trained. Astral projection is also known as the lucid dreaming state while asleep, also called the near death experience, or the out of body experience (OBE). The trick is to be conscious of the experience. Spontaneous OBE can occur at any time, sometimes not by a person's choice, such as in a fatal accident when the spirit leaves the body, and then returns.

The astral experience gives us the opportunity to consciously explore beyond our limited physical senses. We can learn more about ourselves by recalling our past life experiences, and remember the purpose of coming to this lifetime on Earth in the first place. It is also an opportunity to meet with your non-physical guides, or guardian angels, in person. Astral projection also allows the adept the sensation of flight. Other benefits include an overall feeling of well-being, reduction in hostility, amplified psychic abilities, accelerated personal development, inner calmness, a heightened quest for answers, increased respect for life, revitalized zest for life, meeting deceased loved ones, increased intelligence, memory recall, and most importantly, a personal understanding of life after death. Fear of death is simply the fear of the unknown. Once a person can astral project, they have the solid belief that their soul will live beyond the physical body.

THE PINEAL GLAND

The pineal gland is a small endocrine gland located between the two hemispheres of the vertebrate brain. It was named after the pinecone because its shape and texture literally resemble a miniature pinecone. The pineal gland is found in the brain of all humans and animals with a spinal cord. It is located in the geometric center of the brain, a region long associated with attainment and restriction of knowledge. While the human pineal gland is only about the size of a single grain of rice (5-8 mm), it performs several functions that are extremely important to the human body. An entire chapter is devoted to the pineal gland in the companion book *Modern Esoteric: Beyond Our Senses* by Brad Olsen. The information contained here is primarily related to how the pineal gland interfaces with the potential to assist us in activating our super human abilities.

The pineal gland produces the serotonin derivative melatonin, a hormone that affects the modulation of wake and sleep patterns and seasonal functions. Melatonin is the natural sleep hormone that plays a vital role in every person's normal sleep function. Melatonin is not only necessary for proper sleep, but it also regulates the onset of puberty and fights against harmful free radicals. Melatonin can be taken as a supplement, or it can be found in food and drinks such as cherries, bananas, grapes, rice, herbs, olive oil, wine, certain cereals, and even beer.

The pineal gland is activated by light. It works with the natural biorhythm of the body. One function of this mysterious gland is to work in harmony with the hypothalamus gland in directing the body's thirst, hunger, sexual desire and biological clock that determines the body's aging. It is also called the pineal body, epiphysis cerebri, epiphysis, or the "third eye," due to its resemblance to the human retina. It even has the internal connections of an eye within the brain. By being so uniquely situated in the brain, the pineal gland does appear to be a functioning third eye, complete with retinal tissue, and is directly wired into the visual cortex. The interior tissue has "pinealocytes," just like rods and cones in the retina, wired into the visual cortex of the brain exactly like eyeballs. It is located near the center of the brain, between the two hemispheres, tucked in a groove where the two rounded thalamic bodies join. The pineal gland contains a complete map of the visual field of the eyes.

Mystical traditions have long realized that activating the pineal gland is a way to initiate supernatural powers or develop psychic talents. The image of a pinecone and the power of the pineal gland is featured in nearly all mystical traditions worldwide. Egyptian, Greek, Roman, Hindu, Maya and even the Vatican have statues and imagery of a pinecone, representing the pineal gland. This third eye produces our inner vision, or as Descartes described, the "seat of the soul." Ancient Greeks thought it was the connection into all realms of thought, or a connecting link between the physical and spiritual realms. "If thy eye be single thy whole body shall be full of light" according to Matthew in the Biblical verse 6:22. It is also a symbol of the all Seeing Eye of Horus, the Babylon mystery school, and the spiritual third eye represented in many other traditions. Advanced mystical teachings of Sufi Islam, the Vatican, and Freemasonry all identify with the image of the third eye. It represents a lifting of the veil, or the raising of the curtain, and thus the adherent attaining enlightened consciousness. All are metaphors for the awakening of the pineal gland.

The pineal gland appears to be the main access-point between the astral body and the physical body. It seemingly collects impressions from the astral body, which we experience while dreaming, having an out of body experience, remote viewing or in a near death experience. Located in the exact center of the brain, the pineal gland is the physiological center that determines how psychic information is processed. This is likely how independent inventors could pick up direct information that other people were also thinking of, collectively working on the problem together, activating the multiple discovery effect.

When a mystic has an out of body experience, he or she activates the pineal gland. The astral body is picking up on this in the source field, giving off photons when remote viewing, and tapping into a universal data bank. Crystals in the water around the pineal gland are stimulated in darkness, activating an electromagnetic (EM) shield around the water that can then open itself to the source field. EM activity feels like pressure, a buzzing sound, a cracking sound tone or an acceleration feeling inside the mind. EM activity shields water inside the pineal gland from all electromagnetic effects in space and time. Water is then the direct conduit to space and time, or our parallel reality. Time is no longer linear in a local environment, and adherents can jump around in time. The situation is similar to remembering vivid or lucid REM dream states. The inner retina records visual imagery. This is also how remote viewing or lucid dreaming is done, in a half conscious state.

HYPER-COMMUNICATION

In nature, hyper-communication has been utilized by animal species for millions of years. The organized flow of life in insects proves this point dramatically. Hyper-communication is a form of telepathy. As an example from nature, when a queen ant is separated from her colony, the remaining worker ants will continue building fervently, according to their plan. However, if the queen is killed, even far away from the hive, all work in the colony stops. No ant will know what to do. Apparently, the queen transmits the "building plans," even when she is far away. She can dictate the group consciousness with her subjects. She can be as far away as she wants, as long as she is alive. Such is the case with honey bees, which are also hyper-sensitive to odors, pheromones, tastes, and specific colors, including ultraviolet.

Modern humans know hyper-communication on a much more subtle level called "intuition." But we, too, can regain full use of it if we wish. Human DNA naturally attracts bits of information and passes them on to our consciousness. This process of hyper-communication, which is really telepathy and channeling, is most effective in a calm state of relaxation. Stress, worry, or a hyperactive intellect can prevent successful hyper-communication. In a state of agitation, the information transferred will be totally distorted and useless.

Human DNA has been described as a biological Internet, and superior in many aspects to the artificial one. Russian scientific research has been investigating the scientific basis for phenomena such as hyper-communication, clairvoyance, intuition, spontaneous and remote acts of healing, self-healing, affirmation techniques, unusual lights or auras around people (namely spiritual masters), the mind's influence on weather patterns and much more. Russian biophysicist Pjotr Garjajev claims that this communication, used with conscious intention, is not something that is triggered only inside the individual cells or between one cell and another. He claims organisms use this "light" to "talk" to other organisms and suggests that this could explain telepathy and ESP. It is like human beings already have their own wireless Internet based on our DNA.

In addition, there is evidence for a whole new type of medicine connected to this hyper-communication ability in which DNA can be influenced and reprogrammed by words and frequencies without cutting out and replacing single genes. This influence appears to have something to do with electromagnetic fields, because the side effect encountered most often in hyper-communication is mysterious electromagnetic fields in the vicinity of the persons concerned. Russian scientists irradiated DNA samples with laser light. On screen, a typical wave pattern was formed. When they removed the DNA sample, the wave pattern did not disappear; it remained. Numerous replicating experiments showed that the pattern still came from the removed sample, whose energy field apparently remained by itself. This is now called the phantom DNA effect. It is surmised that energy from outside of spacetime still flows through the activated wormholes after the DNA is removed.

On the practical level, these inexplicable electromagnetic fields appear to operate around electronic devices such as MP3 players, computers and digital recorders, rendering them inoperable for minutes or hours. Many healers and psychics know this effect from their work. The better the atmosphere and the energy, the more frustrating it is that the recording device stops functioning exactly at that moment. Often, repeated switching on and off after the session does not restore function, but the next morning all is back to normal. Perhaps this is reassuring for many, as it has nothing to do with being technically inept, but it simply means one is good at hyper-communication.

INDIGO CHILDREN

In one of many similar studies, New Zealand's James Flynn substantiates that raw IQ scores have been going up three points a decade, all around the globe, for over a century. Advances in literacy cannot explain this, as it is occurring in illiterate countries as well. This does not mean that we have "better brains," just a different brain, with rerouted neural circuits. It means every generation is becoming smarter than previous generations, mutating as it were, leading to a restructuring of our DNA and our brains. Human DNA evolution is now moving 100 times faster than it has in the last 5,000 years, according to Dr. John Hawks. He reports the human DNA molecule is now fully seven percent different than it was in 3000 BCE, worldwide.

The term "Indigo Children" was conceived by parapsychologist Nancy Ann Tappe who began noticing that many children were being born with "indigo" auras, or as she described, their "life colors." These life colors are carried in their auras and associated with the third eye chakra, which represent intuition and psychic ability. These gifted children may be the next stage in human evolution, and two new DNA blocks called Microcephalin and ASPM are triggered in these adolescents. These genes regulate brain growth and provide a broader spectrum of thinking and a newer way of learning. Some of these children are being born smarter, more than twice the IQ of an average person who is the same age, and close to adult genius status. Some Indigo Children are known to possess paranormal abilities such as telepathy, telekinesis, and remote viewing. These results came from studies on young Chinese children, who are called "China's Super Psychics." Indigo Children are described as more empathic and creative than their peers, and often promote the concept of "unity and oneness."

The first wave of Indigo Children began in the early 1970s and even more are being born today. The label Attention Deficit Disorder (ADD) describes either a very empathic and compassionate child, or a very cold and callous one. Some child psychologists see a parallel between this new generation of gifted kids and the increase of autism, ADD and ADHD diagnoses in American children. These children are sometimes rebellious to authority, nonconformist, impulsive and extremely emotional. They can be physically sensitive or fragile, highly talented or academically gifted. Still others are metaphysically gifted, usually highly intuitive, and are wise beyond their years. They can see, hear or know things that seem unexplainable.

Something within the Indigo Children seems to be striving more and more towards a new kind of group consciousness, one that can no longer be suppressed. As a rule, for example, the weather is rather difficult to influence by a single individual, but it may be influenced by group consciousness. If this seems shocking, think of aboriginal or Native American tribes performing their rain dances. Weather is strongly influenced by Earth resonance frequencies, the so-called Schumann frequencies. But those same frequencies are also produced in our brains, and when many people synchronize their thinking as individuals, change can occur. For instance, spiritual masters can focus their thoughts in a laser-like fashion, and then, scientifically speaking, it is not at all surprising that they can thus influence objects or even the weather. Wilhelm Reich created a weather control device, alternative cancer treatment, and much more based on the science of Orgone energy.

BIONIC HUMANS

The brain is the most complex organ in the human body. We take it for granted how easy it is to think a command for our body to move a limb for example, and how quickly it responds. Of course this is an easy task if you have legs, but what about making thought control real if you do not have legs? The answer is that bionic limbs can now be controlled by the human brain. For an amputee, when they think the thought "leg move," their artificial leg can move in the desired way. An amputee's brain interacts with a computer, connected to sensors in the body, which enables the bionic limb to respond. This is the fusion of biology with technology. Thoughts can now move artificial limbs.

The next step is to eliminate the body sensors altogether and replace them with brain neuron implants. We'll soon bypass robotics entirely, allowing brain signals to power limbs in the future. This will also allow the blind to see. Bionic eyesight is a camera download to a computer wirelessly, then back to the brain where it stimulates the retina. Brain signals will soon be implanted in the body. Implants on the retina will then detect neurons firing, sending feedback robotically to the brain. For the blind, it then sends visual images back to the brain.

This technology will not just replace what is lost, it will make all of our body parts superior. The *Six Million Dollar Man* would more realistically cost six billion dollars today. Mind merging with a mechanical body part is becoming a two-way street. Targeted Muscle Reintegration carries a motor arm signal, arm signals recorded by EMT signals, which are attached to chest muscles. These tap directly into the brain in the form of wavelengths and thoughts understood by a computer, including a sense of touch. Soon and without difficulty these inventions will replace any body part and even perform much better that their natural counterparts.

A MAN WHO DOES NOT EAT FOOD
OR DRINK WATER

An Indian yogi named Prahlad Jahni shocked the medical community in 2009 when he announced that he has not eaten for seven decades. For two years, until the summer of 2011, he was placed in rigorous testing until a conclusion was reached. The media in Asia announced that the ascetic had passed all medical tests that they could subject him to, and there was no doubt that Jahni did not eat any food or drink any liquids for 70 years. His case is a true human phenomenon. One of the main regrets of the scientists who studied him is that they discovered him at such an advanced age. "It's incredible," said one doctor. "Dozens of machines kept him under close surveillance. It seems that the biological processes taking place in his body are unprecedented, never before in the history of modern medicine being recorded such anomalies."

How does he do it? For one, it is observed that he hydrates through a hole in the palate. The old yogi does not need to drink water; he can hydrate by keeping water in his mouth for several minutes. According to his doctors, any man who does not eat or drink for five days usually enters a coma and dies. For him, the situation is the other way around. "If he would be forced to eat, food could kill him," said one of the 32 doctors who have examined him. The doctors are convinced that the old man is a true "fountain of cures" for many of the current diseases. It appears there are many super human abilities we can learn from the masters of India, as masterfully illustrated in *The Autobiography of a Yogi* by Paramahansa Yogananda, where each chapter describes a different master with their own unique individual human power.

LEVITATION

Scientists in the laboratory have levitated frogs, grasshoppers, and mice by means of powerful electromagnets utilizing superconductors, producing diamagnetic repulsion of body water. The mice became confused at first, but adapted to the levitation after approximately four hours, suffering no immediate ill effects. A number of different techniques have been developed to levitate matter, including the aerodynamic, magnetic, acoustic, electromagnetic, electrostatic, gas film, and optical levitation methods, but what about the human mental ability to levitate objects, or one's own body? Levitation is an aspect of psychokinesis. Yogic masters claim that mystical levitation can occur as a *siddhi*, a Sanskrit term that can be translated as "perfection," "accomplishment," "attainment," or "success." Levitation can occur during higher levels of consciousness, such as mystical rapture, euphoria, or astral projection. In Buddhism, it is believed a master can levitate his body through intense spiritual meditation, which involves a completely focused state of mind.

Psychokinesis and telekinesis are terms given to the ability to move or manipulate objects with the power of the mind. All of us already have these abilities and use them, at least unconsciously, because our thoughts and emotions influence and interact with everything in our environment. Our thoughts and emotions can have the real affect of manipulating energy, which is at the core of everything. To understand the object that we desire to move, we must first establish a rapport with the object. We must "tune into" it as the Tibetan monks did to levitate boulders, that is, synchronize our own energy with the object. In this way the object becomes an extension of ourselves, and moving it or affecting it in any way then equals moving a part of one's self.

TELEKINESIS

Telepathy, along with telekinesis, comprises the main branches of parapsychological research. Many studies seeking to detect and understand telepathy have been done within this field. In 1977, the CIA-funded Stanford Research Institute (SRI) paranormal research team investigated remote perturbation, commonly called psychokinesis, or mind over matter. The research was employed with the aim to sabotage an enemy, or as a nuclear missile deterrent. Of the individuals tested at SRI, at least one person had allegedly perturbed sensitive test equipment, and remote viewed the interior of a sensitive device. Two individuals, Uri Geller and Ingo Swann, have demonstrated some of these paraphysical effect abilities under controlled laboratory conditions. The abilities of these individuals were submitted to rigorous scientific investigation.

An anonymous source, working in the alternative energy and transportation industry, commented that, "actually, they (U.S. Government security personnel) became interested in Swann when he psychically remote viewed some of their well-hidden deep underground vaults, and the contents thereof. This was when they approached SRI because they were finally truly scared about the reality of psychic remote viewing as a tool in the hands of the Soviets." SRI harbored concerns that the Soviet KGB might be interested in the work they were doing, and always held it in the back of their minds that they could someday be kidnapped, or worse. Cold War paranoia (not unfounded as this book suggests) was still in full bloom during the early days of psychic-spy research.

Uri Geller is famous for his public displays of using his amazing telekinesis powers. He has bent spoons from a distance for the scientific community and in front of live audiences. The fact that he was a showman should not lead to the assumption that he was faking his abilities. In April 2000, Arthur C. Clarke announced that he keeps his own door key that was bent by Geller. Furthermore, he indicated that he does not rule out the possibility of all sorts of remarkable mental powers. Clarke went on to say that there are even things like telekinesis and other psychic phenomena that we do not know about.

The American psychoanalyst Jules Eisenbud studied Ted Serios who could mentally imprint detailed images on photographic film under carefully controlled conditions. Dr. Eisenbud came to the conclusion through his studies of Serios' abilities that, "man has in fact within him vast untapped powers that hitherto have been accorded him only in the magic world of the primitive, in the secret fantasies of childhood, and in fairy tales and legend." Some of the younger generation, specifically the Indigo Children, appear to have developed telekinesis quite naturally, along with the ability to "see dead people." Some of these children often find that their bodies will no longer tolerate foods of lower vibration, and they are impelled to eat diets high in fresh organic fruits and vegetables.

LET'S ASSUME THERE ARE HUMAN-TYPES OUTSIDE OF EARTH

Human biological bodies, on most planets such as Earth, are usually engineered to live for an average of about 150 to 200 years. Yet the average human lifespan is barely half of that. Earth is classified as a "Sun Type 12, Class 7" planet within a solar system favorable to life, especially humans. Astronomers are now finding "Earth-like" planets in vast quantities all over the galaxy. If the numbers of planets with human life potential hold up, one estimate puts the Milky Way galaxy with 30 billion humans, with Earth home to seven billion. No wonder there is such intense ET interest in Earth's development at this crucial moment in our evolution, that is if, considering the age of the universe, humanoid bodies have existed in various forms throughout the universe for upwards of a trillion years. If other entities are nearly exact replicas of us, yet are far more advanced, wouldn't we all be hard wired the same way? Couldn't they have something very important to teach us, especially in the realm of mind expansion, and all the advanced human abilities that might come with it?

Could it be possible to communicate with other humans from other eons or dimensions by using "mental images," or "telepathic thought," which can project directly into the mind of another being? This is called channeling and can extend over vast distances. Such super human abilities could mark the end to spoken language, but more importantly, open a huge amount of potential for what can be done with the power of our minds.

CHANNELED INFORMATION VIA ETs

If properly developed, channeling can be a natural form of communication between humans and beings of a higher intelligence. If your mind were continually filled with pictures, colors and sounds, which is what it might be like to connect telepathically with another, you'd be able to "see" what they see. Telepathy is a dynamic means of interaction, much more precise than any spoken language on Earth. We've all heard the expression "a picture speaks a thousand words." Well, therein lies the answer to the ultimate form of communication. With the transference of a dozen pictures or diagrams in as many seconds, huge amounts of information can be passed on to one another in a very short period of time. Channeling must always be completely voluntary between two or more parties, never forced or coerced, utilizing communication through emotion and thought, rather than the spoken word.

But the "alien language" has an extra dimension to it beyond the visual imagery, and that is sound. By adding color codes and a corresponding, almost musical, resonance to match and back up the pictures or icons, the ETs prevent their communications from being misread. It is worth mentioning here that this "sound" has a definite resemblance to some of our more melodic languages and musical tones of the Far East. Developing telepathy in all its various forms on a global scale with all people will become the macro super human ability of the future.

Another form of ET communication appears to be the enigmatic crop circle phenomenon. Cutting edge authentic crop circle research called Fractal Resolution Imaging reveals that the designs are advanced pictogram and mathematical communications from another reality. As we've seen, some circles appear in a matter of minutes, sometimes during the pouring rain at night. Some have appeared in fields near space observatories or highly secured scientific installations. Many crop circle researchers are now convinced that they are indeed ET communications, in some way interacting telepathically with human imagery.

Given such new ways of looking at ourselves, and looking at higher intelligences in the universe interacting with Earth, it now becomes necessary to make an attempt to unify all the theories.

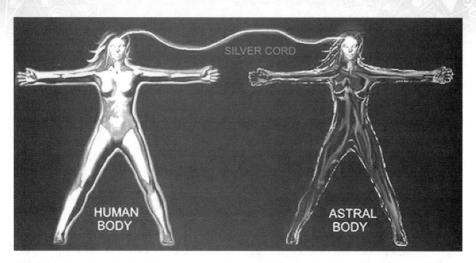

The "silver cord" is the bond between the physical body and the astral body. It is called the silver cord because it is formed by an assembly of high vibrational particles which rotate very rapidly and can be perceived as a shiny ray of silver, gray, or whitish-blue florescent light. It has been described as being smooth, very long, and very bright, like an elastic cable made of light. Its higher vibrational field allows it to be stretched infinitely, except at the moment of death. It appears to be about an inch wide, sparkling like tinsel on a Christmas tree, and attached to one of several possible locations on the physical body. The existence of this connection can be seen as a mystery, as this is the vehicle of transmission for all our "spiritual food," that is, our ideas and discoveries.

How many trees do you think hate each other in the same forest? In order to activate your own super human abilities, it is absolutely necessary to eliminate hate from your mind. Live and let live with all others in your "forest."

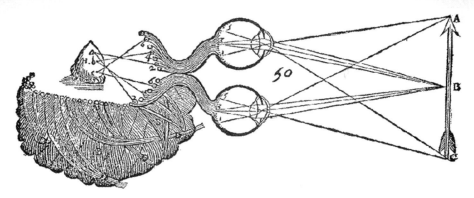

Diagram from Rene Descartes' *Treatise of Man* (1664) showing the formation of inverted retinal images in the eyes, and the transmission of these images via the nerves so as to form a single, re-inverted image (an idea) on the surface of the pineal gland. Descartes wrote in 1640: "My view is that this (pineal) gland is the principal seat of the soul, and the place in which all our thoughts are formed. The reason I believe this is that I cannot find any part of the brain, except this, which is not double. Since we see only one thing with two eyes, and hear only one voice with two ears, and in short have never more than one thought at a time, it must necessarily be the case that the impressions which enter by the two eyes or by the two ears, and so on, unite with each other in some part of the body before being considered by the soul. Now it is impossible to find any such place in the whole head except this gland; moreover, it is situated in the most suitable possible place for this purpose, in the middle of all the concavities; and it is supported and surrounded by the little branches of the carotid arteries which bring the spirits into the brain."

The aura, or etheric human bioenergy field, is an essential component of the human energetic matrix. The aura is an energetic sphere that encapsulates and intersects the physical body and is controlled by how we feel. It is often regarded as a "bubble of light" that emanates from the physical body. In historical times it was described as a "halo."

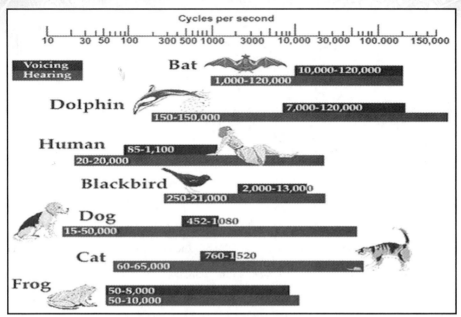

The human ear can hear between frequencies of about 20 Hz to 20,000 Hz. Thus, "sound" as we can hear it is just vibration in this frequency range. Just because humans cannot hear the sounds made by elephants or bats to communicate does not mean that their vibrations do not exist. The upper frequency limit in humans is due to limitations of the middle ear, which acts as a low-pass filter. Many animals—such as dogs, cats, dolphins, bats, and mice—have an upper frequency limit that is greater than that of the human ear and thus can hear ultrasound. This is why a dog whistle can be heard by a dog. A vibrating object causes the surrounding air to oscillate, creating a longitudinal compression wave which moves away from the source at the speed of sound.

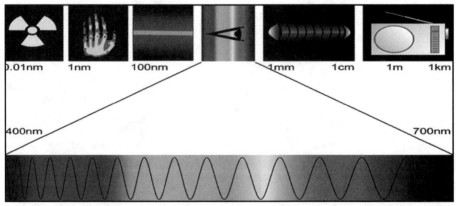

Only the narrow middle part of the electromagnetic spectrum is actually visible to humans. Everything in creation, both animate and inanimate, is made up of moving energy. The electromagnetic spectrum extends from low frequencies used for modern radio to gamma radiation at the short-wavelength end, covering wavelengths from thousands of kilometers down to a fraction of the size of an atom. The long wavelength limit is the size of the universe itself, while it is thought that the short wavelength limit is in the vicinity of the Planck length, although in principle the spectrum is infinite and continuous. Just because we cannot see the atoms that make up our body doesn't mean they don't exist!

GRAND UNIFIED FIELD THEORY

"There is another way, whether it's wormholes or warping space, there's got to be a way to generate energy so that you can pull it out of the vacuum, and the fact that they're here shows us that they found a way." –Jack Kasher, Ph.D, Professor Emeritus of physics, University of Nebraska

IT has been said that mathematics is the language of God. But until now, it seems that no one has been speaking God's language. The first half of this chapter is largely based on a Charlotte, North Carolina, 2010 TED talk by Randy Powell called "Vortex Based Math." A previously unknown mathematical language, one inherent to nature, called vortex based math, is putting the language of God all together now. All matter is spun into creation in the form of a double torus shape with a black hole, or infinite density, in the center, creating a feedback loop with the infinite energy field. When there is massive energy or information in a feedback loop with itself, there is a conscious energy field. Randy Powell calls this feedback loop the definition of consciousness. He explains that when scientists follow what these numbers are doing, they get doubling. A connection of all the sciences is doubling. The cells in our body multiply and double, the binary code of computers double, musical scales are doubling, nuclear reactions, squares and square roots all are doubling. Doubling is motion at an angle, or what is called angular momentum. It's the whirlwind in the treadmill of creation. It spins the atoms in our bodies, the Earth on its axis, the movement of the solar system, entire galaxies and the whole universe. What is it that causes this doubling, and what is it that is being transmitted and received?

According to the current understanding of physics, forces are not transmitted directly between objects, but instead are described by intermediary entities called fields. The term "Unified Field Theory" was coined by Albert Einstein, who attempted to unify the general theory of relativity with electromagnetism, hoping to recover an approximation for quantum theory. The so-called "theory of everything" proposed here is closely related to Einstein's Unified Field Theory, but differs by not requiring the basis of nature to be fields, and also attempts to explain all physical constants of nature.

A universal theory cannot be realized with our current understanding of physics. Researchers will first have to take a different, more esoteric approach. What is emerging now with vortex based math is the true and verifiable Grand Unified Field Theory. The implications that emerge from an understanding of it are nothing short of revolutionary. With it we can create inexhaustible free energy, end all diseases, produce unlimited food, travel anywhere in the universe, build the ultimate supercomputer, create artificial intelligence far beyond our own, and introduce absolutely awe-inspiring technology.

How is it possible to make such outrageous claims? With vortex based math we have the secret that links all technologies together. And that secret is numbers. Mathematics is a living language. A jigsaw puzzle that when pieced together no longer creates a rendition or an approximation of reality. Numbers *are* reality. Neither flat, nor arbitrary, nor imaginary, nor irrational. Mathematical points can define space and time, literally.

Nature likes to repeat itself. As above, so below. Six numbers forming a hexagon, for example, can frequently be seen in nature on any scale. A snowflake, light polarizing, the pattern of beehives and Saturn's north pole are all hexagon shaped. These shapes form pathways for any matter in motion, which is never straight, but always at an angle. Nothing in the physical world ever moves in a straight line; not a bullet shooting, not a lightning bolt. Not a beam of light. Everything is a coil, even a photon coming from a distant star, proving relativity exists. Our body has a DNA coil. Thus, we are a vortex "machine," which sucks materials in at the top and shoots them out at the bottom. This is the basic flying principle of disc-shaped crafts. They pulsate energy out, then draw it back in, and by doing so a craft regulates its own temperature and gravity field. Everything is connected. All bits of energy in the universe and beyond are all connected. They just appear spread apart by the illusion called "space."

THE GOD PARTICLE

The discovery of the Higgs boson particle, the so-called "God particle," is, in theory, a tiny never before seen sub-atomic particle. The Standard Model (SM) of physics in the sub-atomic world allows for other particles to have mass. Finding evidence of the Higgs boson for the first time was somewhat like finding the Holy Grail for physicists. Its "existence" represents the elimination of all other basic elements in the fabric of the universe. More specifically, the

Higgs boson is a hypothetical massive elementary particle predicted to exist by the Standard Model of particle physics. Its existence is postulated to resolve inconsistencies in theoretical physics. Many scientists do not like the nickname God particle because they think it overstates the particle's importance in the grand scheme of things.

We have electricity, and at the center of electricity is magnetism, and at the center of magnetism is a flux. A flux field is a higher dimensional energy known by many names such as dark energy, tachyons, monopoles, greaveons, or etheron energy. It is the energy that keeps us conscious and alive. It is not static or stationary energy. It is a pulse, or a surge, a beating heart of all existence. Thus, the God particle is the ultimate fundamental particle in the universe. This energy is the source of all time, motion and vibration. It is the only thing that comes from the whole, or the zero. An example would be the center of a cyclone. It emanates linearly in all directions, penetrating everything, without any resistance. It cannot be shielded. As the cyclone penetrates, it leaves a grain. It shows how things move, stick together or come apart. It animates everything. It is the source of the non-decaying spin of the electron. Combine it with a coil and what appears is a perfect mathematical vortex, consisting of a positive electromagnetic energy radiating out, and a negative back draft counter space, essentially the same as gravity, which allows for contraction. This perfect mathematical vortex can be read as timeless geometric codes out of which emerge all life forms we know including the strands of our DNA, the cornea of our eye, snow flakes, pine cones, flower petals, diamond crystals, the branching of trees, a nautilus shell, the star we spin around, the galaxy we spiral within, and the air we breathe.

Etheron energy, one name for the flux field of higher dimensional energy, is literally the glue holding the universe together. Einstein called it an inertia ether. The Big Bang theory was just one of the reactions giving birth to this expanding universe which appears only to be expanding because we are on the southern half. The northern half is contracting. As space expands, time contracts. A black hole turns into a white hole. Compression to decompression. An etheron forms the shape of a donut, or a "torus," which is what everything becomes at its maximum acceleration. The DNA is a torus, blood cells are a torus, also magnetic fields and galaxies. Nature appears to rely on this one core recurring pattern to evolve life at every scale. It is an energy vortex where everything, everywhere, from atoms to galaxies and beyond, share this common characteristic. This is why a tornado is more powerful than an atomic bomb. It is a one-way living systemic machine. Thus, a tornado is a self-sustaining jet.

Using a mathematical hologram, the torus can be scaled up and down to infinity. By any other name, it is possible to create a localized spacetime implosion. Think of it as a controlled desktop black hole. This is the final technology. It is the Philosopher's Stone. It becomes a reactionless drive, because it is unaffected by any wave that it carries. It is the true model of an atom, and with it comes the key to the periodic table. For the first time we can cross over from one science to another, unbroken. Whether the subject is subatomic physics, the periodic table, computer science, or DNA, this torus does it all. It is also a surgical tool, a spaceship, a supercomputer, and even a high fidelity speaker, all in one. We now have the potential to cure all diseases, create artificial intelligence far in excess of the human brain capacity, and all of these breakthroughs are a result of etheron flux fields. Here we have a blueprint for a perfectly efficient magnetic field generating coil.

REVERSING THE TORUS

Einstein discovered that space and time are part of a single unified "fabric." This leads to the conclusion that an atom is simply a "displacement," also known as a vortex, that is, in space and time. Then all that's left is a flow within spacetime, an aperture through which the flow may occur.

Spacetime starts out "flat," without curvature, but as it accelerates towards the speed of light, the curvature increases. This curvature bends gravity along with it, though on the quantum level it is far too small to be appreciated as part of the same basic force, so we would refer to it as the "weak force." At the speed of light a torus is created. Space could now be thought of as the outside surface of the torus, and time as the inside.

Ultimately, to understand this in terms of physics, we have to see all atoms and molecules as almost like "portals," that is, as having a great source of energy flowing into and through them. All matter is constantly taking in this energy to replenish itself each and every moment, and if the flow were cut off, the object would disintegrate. This suggests that the universe is alive and its infinite energy can be tapped by aligning harmoniously with nature.

What happens when you accelerate the curvature past the speed of light? The torus unrolls again, but now it is inside out. Time, which was on the inside of the torus, has now moved to the outside of the torus, on the surface. What was once time has now become space. This suggests that everything inverts. As velocity of an object further increases or decreases, the torus again flattens out, becoming a stable, inhabitable plane. This is the gateway into "timespace," a parallel reality in which there are three dimensions of time and one dimension of space. On the other side, the three dimensions of time become the space we move through, and experience as space, and the one dimension of space becomes the steady flow of time.

THE TORUS IS LIFE

The torus is the form of the flow of energy throughout the universe. The universe inherently "grows" a torus in every dynamic system. It can scale up or down to any size. Scientist and philosopher Arthur Young explained that a torus is the only energy pattern or dynamic that can sustain itself. The torus is made out of the same substance as its surroundings, similar to a tornado, a smoke ring in the air, or a whirlpool in water. The essence of torus dynamics contain two toruses—called "tori"—like the male and female aspects of the whole. As one half is spiraling towards the North Pole, its opposite is spinning towards the South Pole. This is also referred to as the "Coriolis effect." Examples are the weather on the Earth and the plasma flow of the Sun. The torus also defines the shape of the Earth's magnetic field. It has a truly universal ubiquity.

At the human level, every person is not only an energy torus, but each one of us is surrounded by our own toroidal electromagnetic field. To understand this, consider that our bodies are a continuous surface, that being our skin, with a hole through the middle, that being our intestinal tract. Each individual's torus is distinct, but at the same time it is open and connected to every other living organism in a continuous sea of infinite energy. It is the same energy field that we can feel with a magnet. It is usually invisible, but by scattering iron filings loosely around a magnet we can actually observe the toroidal shape of energy. The torus in a human is the energy field around the heart when it is coherent with the frequencies of love, consistent with a violet aura, which is a golden ratio algorithm of the 3/4 rhythm of the heart. In other words, the aura torus field around the body is centered in the heart, the strongest electromagnetic field in the body.

UNIVERSAL PATTERN OF ENERGY FLOW

Torus formations, also known as "donut-on-a-stick," have been studied in plasma labs for decades, in part, by generating tremendous electric discharges. A high-energy electric discharge will generate magnetic forces many times stronger than gravity. In the lab, scientists can pull plasma into threadlike channels and spin it. The researchers use the Electron Beam Ion Trap (EBIT) to reconstruct processes in the laboratory as they occur in the matter around black holes. Instabilities compress the plasma into hot, spinning balls and generate ring currents around them, forming in the shape of the torus. Once again, "as above, so below" proves completely true in the laboratory with the recurring shape of the torus. The world according to quantum scientists is a holographic universal illusion (every speck or wave is present everywhere and in everything, but maddeningly elusive), because energetically we are all light. The substance of the universe is consciousness, although this is not the typical terminology of quantum scientists, because it is not something one can easily get a hold of in a laboratory setting.

If we look through the lens of the torus as the fundamental and universal pattern of energy flow, the in and out waves could just be the enfolding and unfolding aspects, the inhale and exhale that maintain the toroidal wholeness. Another further vital concept is to imagine that at the same time as waves spiral infinitely out from a point of "singularity," its complementary wave spirals infinitely in, just like the dark spirals between the light bands of a galaxy. If a device could access the boundless power of that inward pressure wave there would never again be an "energy crisis." It could then be accessed anywhere in the universe, and suddenly fuel-less propulsion becomes a possibility. Such a "drive" would be creating its own gravitational field, so theoretically it could do maneuvers independent of the Earth's field, and by aiming its pressure differential it could be pulled through spacetime like a helium balloon rising in the air, only much faster.

IN SPACE THERE IS NO GRAVITY

The terms gravitation and gravity are mostly interchangeable in everyday use, but in scientific usage a distinction can be made. "Gravitation" is a general term describing the attractive influence that all objects with mass exert on each other, while "gravity" specifically refers to a force that is supposed in some theories, for example Newton's theory, to be the *cause* of this attraction. By contrast, general relativity gravitation is due to spacetime curvatures that cause inertial moving objects to accelerate towards each other.

Isaac Newton's theory of universal gravitation is a physical law describing the gravitational attraction between bodies with mass. It is a part of classical mechanics and was first formulated in Newton's work *Philosophiae Naturalis Principia Mathematica*, published in 1687. In modern language, it postulates that every point mass attracts every other point mass by a force pointing along the line intersecting both points. The force is proportional to the product of the two masses and inversely proportional to the square of the distance between the point masses:

> *F is the magnitude of the gravitational force between the two point masses,*
> *G is the gravitational constant,*
> *m1 is the mass of the first point mass,*
> *m2 is the mass of the second point mass,*
> *r is the distance between the two point masses. Einstein made famous his*
>   *equation E = mc2*
> *E is energy*
> *m is mass*
> *c is the speed of light*

Einstein declared that physical matter was nothing more than a concentrated field of force. What we term a physical substance is, in reality, an intangible concentration of waveforms. Different concentrations of structural patterns of waves unite to form the myriad of chemicals and elements which, in turn, react with one another to form physical substances. Different waveforms of matter appear to us to be solid because we are constituted of similar waveforms which resonate within a clearly defined range of frequencies that control the physical processes of our limited world.

Einstein maintained that "m," the value for mass in the equation, could eventually be removed and a value substituted would express the physical in the form of pure energy. In other words, by substituting a value standing for pure energy for "m," a unified equation should result which would express, in mathematical terms, the whole existence (including everything) of the universe. Matter and antimatter are formed by the same wave-motions in space. The waves travel through space in a spiraling motion, and alternately pass through positive and negative stages. Matter is formed through the positive stage, or pulse, and antimatter through the negative pulse. Each spiral of 360° forms a single pulse. The circular motion of an electron around the nucleus of an atom is therefore an illusion. The relative motion of the nucleus and electrons through space gives the illusion of circular motion. The period during the formation of anti-matter is completely undetectable, since obviously all physical matter is manifesting at the same pulse rate, including any instruments or detectors used to probe atomic structures. The period or frequency rate between each pulse of physical matter creates the measurement that we call time, as well as the speed of light, at the particular position in space that we are aware of at any given moment.

If the frequency rate of positive and negative pulses is either increased or decreased, then time and the speed of light vary in direct proportion. This concept explains time as a geometric construct, as Einstein theorized it would be. Light has correctly been described as being both a wave motion and a pulse. The theories of Max Planck would also correspond. Planck reasoned that a pulse of light is manifested when the energy level of an atomic structure is altered by outside influences. In this construct, there would be a twin stream of consciousness on the anti-matter side of the cycle, and this would create a mirror image of our own individual personality. The frequency of manifestation of both streams of consciousness would position our awareness of the illusion of reality at a particular point in space and time. Now we are in a position to travel from one point of space to another without being aware that we have traversed distance in the physical sense. This is the ultimate method used for intergalactic space travel.

Einstein knew that infinite non-constructive compression was the key to solving the Unified Field Theory. Einstein didn't know about fractal geometry. And he didn't realize that the golden mean ratio solves constructive electrical interference. It is the reason modern physics does not claim to know the cause of gravity or light. If you want to make a wheel, you need a circle. If you want to create life with DNA, you need the golden ratio.

NATURE ABHORS A VACUUM

Occultists over a hundred years ago spoke of the aether (also spelled ether), which is the material that fills the region of the universe above the terrestrial sphere. This notion challenged scientific beliefs for many decades. Occult chemists were speaking of proto-aether called *Mulaprakriti*, or an "initial false vacuum" undergoing an expansionary phase-change to become *Koilon*, or what we call today the "normal quantum vacuum" driven by a "superforce." The occultists belabor the point that instead of matter being solid within an empty insubstantial aether, the aether itself is very dense, and matter is really just bubbles, or the absence of aether. What appears as empty space is actually a seething ferment of quantum activity, teeming with "ghost" or virtual particles in a frenzy of complex interactions.

The existence of aether was widely accepted in scientific circles until the early 20th century when the Michelson-Morley experiment of 1887 was co-opted to "prove" that no such hidden energy source exists. Similar to the way cold fusion was denounced and has re-emerged with the new name "Lattice Assisted Nuclear Reaction," just use the benign term "quantum medium" instead of the forbidden word aether, and the mainstream press might just cover the issue. Call it what you like, an unseen energy medium pulsates throughout the universe. The 19th century concepts underlying this occult cosmology are easily visualized in terms of liquid in a cylinder. Fizzing can be induced if a piston is moved. Thus the superforce can induce a quantum-vacuum transition, *Mulaprakriti*, to *Koilon,* releasing energy which can tear the ether into numerous subatomic particles or "bubbles." These can be observed and appears as being substantial even though they are, in fact, the absence of substance. Thus, one could say that matter was sucked into existence by gaps in the cosmic expansion.

It is important to understand that at the quantum level of description, the vacuum is the dominant structure. Particles are only minor disturbances bubbling up over this background sea of activity. The simplest kind of "massive" particle is known as a meson, which is actually a bubble in the ether with its internal "matter" field lines trapped within the bubble. Non-spinning "matter bubbles" would tend to be spherical. They are called scalar mesons and there are 36 different kinds of them in nature. The occult chemists, Besant and Leadbeater, identified both kinds—vector and scalar mesons—as their E3 state of matter in 1895. Thus, the "dense aether," or the quantum vacuum, is scientific dogma today, even though it seemed the height of absurdity when the occultist Theosophists first proposed the notion; proof that in time esoteric theories can, and usually do, become accepted science.

The new quantum sciences also tend to reject the "Big Bang" theory as a universal creation, whereas like the torus, for every expansion there must also be a contraction. There is also a tendency to move away from the theory that the universe is in decay. To prove that the universe is in decay, scientists would have to prove that protons decay, which they have not yet been able to do. The new quantum sciences also throw the free energy debate wide open.

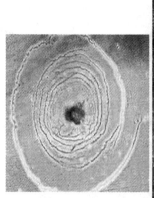

The energy field of a carbon particle looks similar to the spiral arm of a hurricane, which appears similar to the spiral formation of a galaxy. As above, so below. All contain their own toridial field, as does every planet. The power of spin and motion is the key to understanding the Grand Unified Field Theory. All information is available in the event horizon of a "black hole."

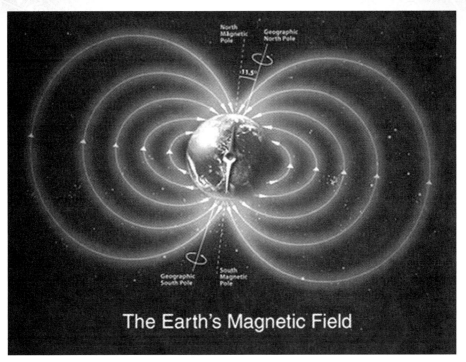

The Earth's Magnetic Field

Earth's magnetic field is a magnetic dipole, with the magnetic field South Pole near the Earth's geographic north pole and the magnetic field North Pole near the Earth's geographic south pole.

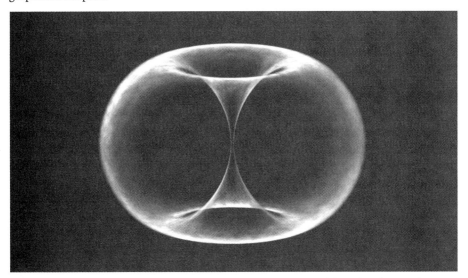

The torus, or primary pattern, is an energy dynamic that looks like a doughnut; it's a continuous surface with a hole in it. The energy flows in through one end, circulates around the center and exits out the other side. We see the torus everywhere in nature and in the universe: from the cross-section of an apple to a tornado pattern; from the magnetic energy flow of a planet to the pattern of an atom; from cells, seeds, flowers, trees, animals and humans to hurricanes, planets, suns, galaxies and even the cosmos as a whole.

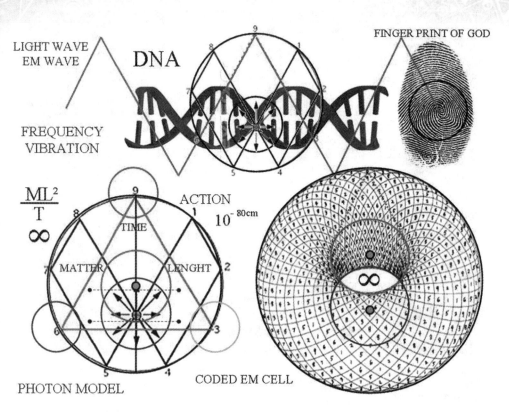

LIGHT WAVE
EM WAVE

DNA

FINGER PRINT OF GOD

FREQUENCY
VIBRATION

$$\frac{ML^2}{T}$$
$$\infty$$

ACTION

$$10^{-80cm}$$

TIME

MATTER   LENGHT

PHOTON MODEL   CODED EM CELL

This diagram depicts the vortex based mathematics involved in the fractal nature of consciousness and the process of Ascension that it goes through. The expression (ML2/T) + X2 + Y2 - DT2 is the formula used to represent the Ascension of consciousness and the soul itself. The symbol (ML2/T) and the photons X2 and the Y2 represent two forms of subtle energies that are present during the time of the Ascension. These help to take distance and time out of the equation for an existence that stretches into infinity all at once. Each consciousness experiences what we call a past a present and a future which are all part of a standing wave that is present in a photon containing a particle and wave aspect. The wave aspect of the photon causes it to spiral in waves much like the pattern seen within DNA. The Rodin coil (2,3,4,5,6,7,8,9,10,11,12,13), which is the atomic model for a photon, shows that it is a captured standing wave of probabilities inside an electromagnetic torus. These electromagnetic toruses are capable of transmitting and receiving information onto themselves as living cells of pure energy.

FREE ENERGY

"If these new energy technologies were to be set free worldwide, the change would be profound. It would affect everybody. It would be applicable everywhere. These technologies are absolutely the most important thing that has happened in the history of the world." –Dr. Brian O'Leary, Ph.D. in Astronomy, UC-Berkeley, NASA Astronaut, adjunct lecturer at Princeton, Cal Tech, Cornell, expert on breakthrough energy technologies

EVERYONE seems to be caught up in a battle or struggle for energy. We eat energy bars to keep apace. People can feel low or high energy, or sense bad or good energy in others. Our energy costs, especially for transportation, continue to weigh heavily on most American budgets. Our conflicts with the people of the Middle East are mostly over energy—our desire to acquire theirs. And as we shall see now, our quest to introduce free energy is one of the major challenges for the future of this world.

The elite controllers referred to throughout this book have a history of obstructing anything that threatens their own power structure, including revolutionary new energy technologies. Today the hydrocarbon and nuclear lobbies represent a multi-trillion dollar per year industry. Those with financial interests in the current global petrochemical industry are literally suppressing the very information and solutions we need to restore our planet to health. Our need for radical energy solutions could not be more urgent.

The current model of burning oil, coal and gas for our energy needs is woefully outdated. Even nuclear energy is not a sustainable or a dependable clean energy source for our future. In choosing an energy path, and it is a choice, we must consider all the living people, animals, plants and general health of the planet, all of which are affected. Burning oil and coal for energy are smokestack relics of the 19th century—the antiquated top hat mentality with no regard for the environment.

POLLUTION PARASITES

Human beings, in the way we pollute without regard to other living organisms, have become a planetary parasite—tainting nearly every ecosystem on Earth with our destructive and wasteful ways. There must be a better choice! We've put a man on the Moon, developed the microchip, and we can communicate and travel globally. Consider the concept of an "over-unity device" where you put a little energy in to get the engine started and then it produces a greater output. Few people are aware that since the 19th century, over-unity devices have been introduced with much fanfare, then have quickly disappeared. But why? Is the 19th century invention of an internal combustion engine which runs on gasoline really the best we can do for personal transportation? Or can the manufacture and marketing of an over-unity device be the downfall of the largest corporations on the planet? It must be remembered that burning hydrocarbons equals making lots of money. And making big money means influence and control.

Scientists as far back as Nikola Tesla in the early 1900s have been developing alternative ways to access electricity without combustion. Tesla's breakthrough inventions and patents (those not destroyed or suppressed) have changed the face of energy technologies in the 20th century. Yet his name and work have been absent in science textbooks—and the reason will become clear, as the reader absorbs the facts and checks reliable Internet sources. Tesla discovered the AC current that is used all over the world today. He also developed the ability to transmit electrical energy through the air like radio waves, where the power could be received by the end user with an antenna. He built the Wardenclyffe Tower to demonstrate this capability to the world, and famously stated: "All peoples everywhere should have free energy sources. … Electric power is everywhere present in unlimited quantities and can drive the world's machinery without the need for coal, oil or gas."

Nikola Tesla was not motivated by the desire for status or wealth. He wanted to give the world free energy. But right before his wireless energy broadcast demonstration, banker J. P. Morgan ceased further funding and the project was terminated. Morgan owned the copper mines and was making a fortune from the copper wire used to conduct electricity. Tesla's invention would have made those copper wires obsolete. It would also have upset the business model of Morgan's rich friends in the petroleum industry. If we are to implement free energy in the tradition of Nikola Tesla, then we need to replicate not only his science, but his humanity.

MOTIVES FOR SUPPRESSION

There is clearly a technology block that continues to choke the planet in order to control all its inhabitants. Big Oil and special interests permeate all branches of government, and many private and public agencies are certainly to blame. Since 1951, the U.S. Government has restricted the release of over 5,000 known energy technology patents that have the potential to end many of today's greatest challenges. For example, in 1955, a car that runs only on nonpolluting hydrogen was shown to the world by completing 110 laps at the Indianapolis 500 Race Track. The plans were bought by Gulf-Western Oil and never seen nor heard about again.

While the nonpolluting aspects of hydrogen are encouraging, the question remains how to create the energy to generate the energy. A number of inventions (some actually patented) have made great strides toward solving this problem. However, it would appear there are powerful individuals in a compartmentalized area of the U.S. Government, together with Big Oil itself, which retain and control all of the patents and breakthrough free energy technologies; but they continue to suppress this vital information intentionally (and intimidate those who wish to share it) because it is seen as a threat to their hegemonic empire. Remember the saying: "What is good for General Motors is good for America, and what is good for America is good for General Motors?" (It is quite possible that various powerful individuals believe this maxim.) Various governmental agencies, or rather, key individuals within these organizations, view free energy technologies as a threat. Conscious or not, the underlying threat and motivation for suppression appears to be the fear of loss of professional identity, status, livelihood (for those dependent on academic support) and, yes, greed and control for those at the top of the pyramid. After all, free energy is exactly what it is, free, which does not turn a profit, make a meter tick, or generate any tax revenue.

The U.S. Patent Office has quietly seized thousands of alternative energy inventions over the decades, and have defended this action in the name of "national security." Inventors such as John Hutchison, Adam Trombly, Thomas Bearden, and John Bedini each have invented similar new energy technologies which have the potential to free us of oil dependency and open up access for everyone to a universally abundant energy source. But the startling fact is that their labs have been raided and their devices destroyed. Claiming national security issues, the U.S. Patent Office has confiscated thousands of alternative energy devices during the application process for patents. If the free energy inventors persist, one of the warnings commonly given is "Cease and desist your operations … We're terminating your project due to the threats it poses to the international monetary system."

If "free energy" were just a hoax, why would the government take such harsh measures to confiscate plans and equipment? If an inventor cannot be bought, the U.S. Government's response to any hint of success from free energy inventors has been to raid their labs with an armed FBI or SWAT team, confiscate their equipment, intimidate the inventor and issue a gag order. They do this because the stakes are very high and the government enjoys huge revenues from taxing the generation of power. As Steven Greer of the Disclosure Project points out, "This information coming out would completely change geo-political power more than anything in human history."

Free energy inventor Adam Trombly maintains that one of the top reasons why the UFO phenomenon is suppressed is because people would clamor to know what drives these crafts, and it would force disclosure of "free energy." If we could eliminate the very powerful special interest blocks on free energy, Trombly states, "we would have universal abundance."

OIL IS NOT WHAT YOU THINK

When the Nazis took power, Germany had resolved to develop enough synthetic oil to wage war successfully, even without abundant national oil reserves. At the end of World War II, U.S. intelligence agents confiscated thousands of German documents on what was known as the "Fischer-Tropsch Process," a series of equations developed by German chemists that unlocked the secret of how oil was formed. For decades, these confiscated Nazi documents remained largely ignored in the United States where petro-geologists and petro-chemists were convinced that oil was a "fossil fuel" created by long-ago decayed biological debris.

The theory that oil is a fossil fuel derived from decaying ancient forests and dead dinosaurs is now challenged on two fronts. Following the war, Stalin demanded his petro-geologists simply "dig deeper." In 1970, the Russians started drilling an exploration well called Kola SG-3. It finally reached a staggering world record depth of 12,260 meters (40,230 feet). Since then, the Russian oil company Yukos has drilled over 310 successful super-deep oil wells and put them into production. The Russian reserves discovered at greater depths, and other Siberian wells which at first appeared to be depleted but then somehow became refilled, has propelled Russia to be the world's top oil producer. A single oil field in Siberia today challenges Saudi Arabia for the lead in oil production and global exportation.

A 2008 study published in *Science Magazine* presented new evidence supporting the abiotic theory for the origin of oil, which postulates that oil is a natural product generated constantly from deep within the Earth. The abiotic theory of the origin of oil directly challenges the conventional scientific theory that hydrocarbons are organic in nature, created by the deterioration of biological material deposited millions of years ago in sedimentary rock and converted to hydrocarbons under intense heat and pressure.

Clearly, big U.S. oil companies have no financial interest in disclosing to the American people that oil is simply a natural product made on a continual basis deep within the Earth. Rather, if there were only so many fossils in geological time as is currently accepted, there could only be so much oil. Big Oil could then charge much more for a perceived finite, rapidly disappearing resource than for a natural, renewable, and probably inexhaustible one. However, not only can oil be produced synthetically, once oil is understood as an abundantly available resource, there is no reason for hydrocarbon fuels to indefinitely remain for sale by Big Oil and according to their prices. And therein is the threat to their dominant position in the global economy. The concept of "Peak Oil" is a scam, meant only to raise the price and profitability of hydrocarbon products.

ENERGY CONTROL IS WORLD CONTROL

For over 100 years, since the time of Nikola Tesla, hundreds of new energy researchers have been suppressed by powerful vested interests in government, industry, science, and the media. Abner Doble was an American mechanical engineer who built and sold steam-powered automobiles. Doble worked in his native America, and also in New Zealand, Great Britain and Germany in the 1920s and 1930s. Abner Doble's work, if not actually suppressed, was certainly thwarted by vested interests, namely the major international oil companies and cartels and giant car companies who manufactured internal combustion-powered vehicles. The electric car has also been subject to suppression, and it has been around even longer than the gasoline car! Electric cars were being manufactured and sold before the advent of the internal combustion engine. Thomas Edison used to drive about town in his 1914 electric car. It should be little mystery who killed these alternatives to "fossil fuel" driven vehicles.

Alternative energy scientist Colonel Thomas Bearden had this to say about free energy suppression: "The people of the world need to know that the oil companies have become the enemies of mankind. They are withholding and suppressing technologies which could save the planet and eliminate poverty and suffering." Bearden does not mince words when he clearly calls out the perpetrators and their world control agenda. He continues: "As long as we allow there to be a 'secret government,' this will continue to be so. Those who toil in basements and garages to bring forth energy from the vacuum in spite of death threats and assassinations are the true heroes of this age." Another free energy device inventor Adam Trombly said: "There is limitless and practically useful energy anywhere you stand or sit. We can feel it and we can be it. We can tap into it with real technologies. We can light our homes and drive our quiet, clean vehicles as the wounds of our tortured Earth are healed forever. Let's take our planet back. Let's start now." According to the free energy inventors, we can develop and make available new energy devices with only modest investments.

Once again, the entire phenomenon of extraterrestrial beings is a critical factor in this global energy problem and its solutions. If even a portion of the millions of UFO sightings worldwide are credible, it is clear that they can travel and communicate (remember the crop circles, for example) with advanced technologies. There must be another method of extracting energy from the universe which neither pollutes nor costs anything. Many scientists who have been forced underground say yes, there is another method. It is called "Zero Point Energy," or "free energy," and it uses the process of cold fusion which does not produce any harmful or polluting byproducts. Such a scientific "discovery" would certainly shake up the status quo and thus render Big Oil soon obsolete. In the eyes of these conglomerates, this cannot be allowed to happen. Since oil companies are among the largest corporations on the planet, it has been far easier (in their view) for them to buy out such companies, suppress the technology, and hire really good lobbyists and PR firms to keep their energy myth alive. The strategy has been to make campaign contributions to the president and members of Congress who steer energy policies behind closed doors. For decades, big business, especially Big Oil and its thousands of derivative companies, have cultivated interdependent ties to top government officials. Each believes it needs the other and this allows Big Oil to operate unimpeded. And even gives them massive tax breaks. Such is the motivation behind energy secrecy.

FREE ENERGY DISINFORMATION

The spin about free energy, largely perpetuated by handlers of the mass media, is that it simply cannot exist. It is a myth. It would seem to violate existing scientific "laws." It is so advanced that its use is far in the future. Thus we must only look backwards to what already exists to keep civilization chugging along. Yet the biggest myth of all is that we can trust governments, Big Oil, or the marketplace to support the necessary research and development to get us out of our current dilemma.

Consider a clever and "scientific" disinformation story. We have all heard the claims of perpetual motion engine falsehoods. It is the most common way to bash free energy devices. A repeating claim (and an invented target) is a car that runs on nothing but water. The car, it is claimed, has an energy generator that extracts hydrogen from water that is poured into the car's tank. No gasoline, no battery recharging, and no emissions. Hard to believe?

It is notable that the critics will refute the idea of producing a water car because the energy to create hydrogen from water is very inefficient. A water-fueled car is a hypothetical automobile that derives its energy directly from water. In the end, where does that energy generator get its energy? Water-fueled cars have been the subject of numerous international patents, newspaper and popular science magazine articles, local television news coverage, and claims on the Internet. Some proposals for these devices have been found to be incorrect and some were found to be tied to investment frauds. These vehicles may be claimed by their inventor to produce fuel from water on board with no other energy input, or may be a hybrid of sorts, deriving energy from both water and a conventional source, such as gasoline.

Therefore, any claim of vehicles which extract chemical potential energy directly from water is media-planted disinformation to muddy the waters. After all, water is fully oxidized hydrogen. Hydrogen itself is a high-energy, flammable substance, but its useful energy is released when water is formed. We all know water cannot burn. The process of electrolysis can split water into hydrogen and oxygen, but it takes as much energy to take apart a water molecule as is released when hydrogen is oxidized to form water. With this process, some energy would be lost in converting water to hydrogen, thus disqualifying the motor from being a free energy device. In addition, by then burning the hydrogen, some heat would also be produced in the conversions. Releasing chemical energy from water would therefore violate the first and second laws of thermodynamics.

The second law of thermodynamics acknowledges that a torus is not a closed or isolated system. It is open to the rest of the universe, as are galaxies, solar systems and the atoms that provide the electricity in our very own bodies. None of these are plugged into a wall socket. They all run off the infinite torque of the universe that is turning every system in existence. What if there were devices that could tap into this system? Like "free air," it is available everywhere, for anyone. Energy is also endlessly available without burning or exploding anything.

The Powers That Were will not allow a new energy revolution. They are masters at deception, able to create confusion within any scientific debate, not only about free energy, but in their full-out assault on climate science. Solutions to the energy crisis already exist, but they are systematically suppressed. These information blocks must be removed. In their place, we need new energy systems which are Earth-oriented, visionary and possible.

COLD FUSION CONTROVERSY

Cold fusion hit the world's stage in 1989 with the announcement of the experiments of respected electrochemists Martin Fleischmann and Stanley Pons. The pair reported anomalous heat production, or "excess heat," of a magnitude they asserted would defy explanation except in terms of a nuclear process. Although decried as non-reproducible in the scientific community, it was revealed that the palladium was defective in subsequent experiments, and that is because all samples came from the same tainted supplier. Beginning to seem suspicious? The pair was forced to release their findings prematurely because another researcher raised a clamor. In order to protect their patent, they announced their findings earlier than they wished, but their earlier findings turned world perception against them for misguided reasons. Fleischmann and Pons were labeled frauds and dismissed from the scientific community.

The ability of palladium to absorb hydrogen was recognized as early as the 19th century, so it was not any kind of big unknown. Over the years the experiments of Fleischmann and Pons have indeed been replicated, but with all the bad press surrounding the term "cold fusion," it is now renamed "Low Energy Nuclear Reaction," "Lattice Assisted Nuclear Reaction," or "Chemically Assisted Nuclear Reaction" to avoid the negative connotations associated with the original name. A small community of researchers continues to investigate cold fusion, claiming to replicate Fleischmann and Pons' results, including nuclear reaction byproducts.

Cold fusion, or a "nuclear effect," can create 25 times the heat of the energy put in, with no radioactivity. The process uses palladium and a form of hydrogen called duterium found in seawater. At the atomic level palladium looks like a lattice; its electrical charge drawing in duterium and creating heat. This provides an electric current (wrapped in insulation) to a storage device. A cold fusion story on *60 Minutes* has debunked the idea that free energy research is usually pegged as a pseudo-science. It is no longer regarded as a misguided attempt at a "perpetual motion" device, long derided by the conservative scientific community. This is encouraging progress toward accurate reporting.

Another encouraging event was the Cold Fusion Colloquium held at MIT in Cambridge, Massachusetts, June 11-12, 2011, which allowed scientists to independently demonstrate their "Lattice Assisted Nuclear Reaction" devices. Two dozen scientists discussed their experimental evidence proving that test tube nuclear fusion is a real effect. Hundreds of other scientists have replicated cold fusion experiments. It seems that changing the mass perception of cold fusion is much harder than replicating the experiments of Fleischmann and Pons, but progress is being made.

THE RISE AND FALL OF TESLA TECHNOLOGY

While scientists in the early 19th century produced rapid developments in electrical science, the late 19th century witnessed the greatest progress in electrical engineering. Through such people as Nikola Tesla, Thomas Edison, George Westinghouse, Ernst Werner von Siemens, Alexander Graham Bell and Lord Kelvin, electricity was turned from a scientific curiosity into an essential tool for modern life, becoming a driving force behind a second Industrial Revolution.

Nikola Tesla (1856-1943) was a physicist and electrical engineer who changed the world with the invention of the alternating electric current, making the universal transmission and distribution of electricity possible. He invented the electric motor, the induction motor, the Tesla turbine, fluorescent and neon lights, radio transmission, wireless communications, wireless electricity transfer, a remote controlled boat, robotics, and Tesla's oscillator. He also discovered rotating magnetic fields, invented the electric car, vertical take-off aircraft which appears to resemble an ion-propelled aircraft or modern Stealth bombers, bifilar coil, HAARP military weather modification, particle beam weapons, and "death ray" guns. All this "advanced" science came from one individual.

Tesla's other discoveries also led to the invention of radio, television, radar, X-rays, the spark plug, and the wireless transmission of free energy. Tesla registered over 700 patents worldwide. His vision included exploration of teleforce, telegeodynamics, electrogravitics, terrestrial stationary waves, solar energy and harnessing the power of the sea. At the very least, his undeveloped inventions, especially those regarding the wireless transmission of free energy, need to be re-examined. Given this array of groundbreaking inventions, Tesla is regarded by many as the greatest inventor of all time, yet few have ever heard of him. This is a stark example of widespread and effective suppression. If the moneyed interests cannot buy out a patent holder, they will systematically harass him and destroy his credibility. Murder is not out of the question.

J. P. Morgan was a shill for the 19th century energy cabal, and he stole a number of Tesla's inventions and technologies. Tesla had submitted 1,800 patents to the U.S. Patent Office, yet for all his work there is only one public statue of Nikola Tesla in the USA, and it is located at the hydroelectric dam he developed in Niagara Falls, New York. J. P. Morgan originally funded Tesla because he needed his work for a telegraph design, among other things. When Tesla's understudy Marconi took the ideas and claimed to invent the telegraph independently, that was enough for J. P. Morgan to demolish Tesla's business and reputation.

Tesla wanted to give us an antenna system that would use the Earth's energy grid to heat homes and run cars from an inexhaustible source. Despite his lab being mysteriously burned down in 1895, he persisted. Prior to the completion of his work on the free energy generator and prior to any patenting, all of his equipment, models, and inventions were destroyed. Nevertheless, he created a wireless electricity transfer system in 1902 at Colorado Springs, Colorado. He was going to offer it to the world wirelessly, so that all people needed was an antenna in their yard for access. Wireless energy could be transferred as easily as cell phones, a radio signal, or television is today.

Finally, having obtained dozens and dozens of patents for his work, he experienced several periods of success, though he struggled to finance the Wardenclyffe project on Long Island, New York. Shrouded in secrecy, the intentions of this project were unclear to the public. However, desperate for money to continue the project, Tesla felt he must reveal the potential for the vast expansion of electricity to J. P. Morgan in order to secure further financing. Margaret Cheney, author of *Tesla: Man Out of Time*, estimates that Tesla had misjudged Morgan. "The prospect of beaming electricity to penniless Zulus or Pygmies," she wrote, "left the financier apathetic about the project." When asked where the meter was, Tesla said there was none; it was free energy for the people. Consequently, this project (among others) was discontinued by his financier J. P. Morgan and never came to fruition.

Besides discrediting or downplaying Tesla technology, the black operations of the U.S. Government have been studying free energy devices since at least the late 1940s when the first extraterrestrial spacecrafts were recovered and back-engineered. As a result they have successfully developed free energy technology, but will not release the information to the public. This blackout of vital energy technology has many casualties in its wake, including Eugene Mallove, who was mysteriously beaten to death in 2004, the day before he was to make a free energy announcement on a nationally syndicated radio program. Despite being America's greatest inventor, Tesla was ostracized and died penniless, simply for trying to implement his vision of unlimited energy for everyone. Shortly before his death in 1943, he affirmed his humanitarian vision:

> *"Out of this war, the greatest since the beginning of history, a new world must be born, a world that would justify the sacrifices offered by humanity. This new world must be a world in which there shall be no exploitation of the weak by the strong, of the good by the evil; where there will be no humiliation of the poor by the violence of the rich; where the products of intellect, science and art will serve society for the betterment and beautification of life, and not the individuals for achieving wealth. This new world shall not be a world of the downtrodden and humiliated, but of free men and free nations, equal in dignity and respect for man."*

Is it any wonder the energy cabal considered Nikola Tesla an enemy?

THE WIRELESS TRANSMISSIONS OF ENERGY

Originally revered in top scientific circles and once considered one of the most famous people on the planet, today Dr. Nikola Tesla is practically written out of our scientific and educational textbooks. What did he discover that caused his fall from grace, in fact, his virtual disappearance from the official history of science? Maybe Tesla's own words give a clue:

> "The transmission of power without wires is not a theory or a mere possibility, as it appears to most people, but a fact demonstrated by me in experiments which have extended for years. Nor did the idea present itself to me all of a sudden, but was the result of a very slow and gradual development and a logical consequence of my investigations which were earnestly undertaken in 1893 when I gave the world my first outline of my system of broadcasting wireless energy for all purposes. ... The transmission of energy through a single conductor without return having been found practicable, it occurred to me that possibly even that one wire might be dispensed with the Earth and used to convey the energy from the transmitter to the receiver."

Tesla's wireless system, in all its essential features, is already used throughout the world in wireless cell phone transmissions, or for conveying data intelligence such as Wi-Fi. But his pioneer efforts in the field of wirelessly transmitting electricity are still largely misunderstood.

> "My efforts to transmit large amounts of power through the atmosphere resulted in the development of an invention of great promise, which has since been called the 'Death Ray,' and attributed to Dr. Grindell Matthews, an ingenious and skillful English electrician. The underlying idea was to render the air conducting by suitable ionizing radiations and to convey high tension currents along the path of the rays. Experiments, conducted on a large scale, showed that with pressures of many millions of volts, virtually unlimited quantities of energy can be projected to a small distance of a few hundred feet, which might be satisfactory if the process were more economical and the apparatus less expensive. Since that time, I have made important improvements and discovered a new principle which can be successfully applied without difficulty for various purposes in peace and war."

Tesla discovered that energy travels chiefly along an orthodromic line, which is the shortest distance between two points at the surface of the globe. It reaches the receiver without the slightest dispersion so that they greatest amount of energy is collected. He has thus provided a perfect means for transmitting power in any desired direction far more economically and without any such qualitative and quantitative limitations as the use of reflectors would necessarily involve. Tesla's system is based entirely on resonance. The foundation for its use was laid down by Sir William Crookes, who in 1876, discovered that a highly heated conductor emits electrified particles. In 1882, a young French electrician named Vissiere observed that a current issues from the filament of an incandescent lamp and he made careful measurements with specially prepared bulbs.

"Nature has stored up in the universe infinite energy. The eternal recipient and transmitter of this energy is the ether," observed Tesla in 1891. He continued, "Of all forms of nature's energy, which is ever and ever changing and moving, like a soul animates the inert universe, electricity and magnetism are perhaps the most fascinating." He asked the question and then gives the answer: "What is electricity, and what is magnetism? All matter comes from a primary substance, the Akasha, or luminiferous ether." He sensed that the universe was composed of a symphony of alternating currents with the harmonies played on a vast range of octaves. To explore the whole range of electrical vibrations would bring him closer to an understanding of the cosmic symphony. Tesla understood that the cosmic symphony is resonance. Nothing exists in the universe that does not have harmonic vibration. As we know today, there is energy and vibrations all around us. Even matter is a potential form of energy. Tesla was right when he observed that free energy could be extracted by exciting the electrons in a steady state which can absorb and drive the electrons to shed even more energy.

THEY WILL KILL YOU

The same banker, J. P. Morgan, who prohibited Nikola Tesla from making abundant energy available wirelessly, was also influential in suppressing key scientific truths about how energy works. In the early 20th century, he used his financial influence on educational policy to delete from textbooks the knowledge which can lead to creating such devices. According to free energy inventor Tom Bearden, author of *Energy from the Vacuum*:

> "J.P. Morgan got Lorentz to cripple the Heaviside equations so that the new electrical engineering concepts being taught in the universities would not ever contain free energy and over-unity systems. This deliberate mutilation and crippling of electrical engineering is the real and single cause of our dependence on oil and of much of the pollution of our biosphere. ... The 'High Cabal'—Churchill's name for the secret consortium of elite families and organizations we loosely refer to as the 'control groups'—has been ruthlessly suppressing free energy inventors for a century, including by direct assassination. Having personally survived several such assassination attempts, I have experienced what I'm speaking of."

The notion of clean, inexpensive energy for all, however, is a threat to those who want to squeeze every last dollar out of hydrocarbon fuels, and especially those who would use the control of energy to dictate people's lives. Shortly before his death in 1943, Tesla had submitted a proposal to the Roosevelt Administration to counter the damaging potential of fission-based nuclear energy development. He claimed in his proposal to the president that he knew of a method by which we could get all of the energy we could ever use from the space that surrounds us. A meeting was scheduled with FDR as a result of this proposal, but the meeting never occurred. Tesla was found dead in his New York apartment. The official report attributed his death to natural causes, but others were not satisfied with this version and suspected foul play.

Along with the questionable death of Nikola Tesla, others who have spoken publicly about free energy have died under suspicious circumstances. Dr. Eugene F. Mallove, the Harvard and MIT trained scientist and engineer who edited *Infinite Energy* magazine, was about to appear with author David Wilcock on the *Coast to Coast* radio show in May, 2004, to announce a breakthrough in free energy. The day before his announcement, he was mysteriously bludgeoned to death.

TESLA'S "WORLD SYSTEM"

Tesla knew his plan to provide wireless transmission to all people of the world was going to flourish. In his mind, it was really just a matter of funding. The fundamental difference between the broadcasting system he expected to inaugurate and what had been in place, is that the current transmitter emits energy in all directions, while in the system he devised, only force is conveyed to all points of the Earth. The energy itself is traveling in definite predetermined paths.

Tesla's "World System" was designed with novel transmitters of great effectiveness and receivers of elementary simplicity. In his apparatus, the isochronism is so perfect and the attunement sharp to such a degree that in the transmission of speech, pictures or similar operations, the frequency or wavelength is varied only through a minute range which need not be more than one hundredth of one percent, if desired. Static and all other interferences are completely eliminated and the service is unaffected by weather and seasonal or diurnal changes of any kind. Tesla also noted in the late 19th century that "the system lends itself particularly to World Wireless Telephony and Telegraphy."

The wireless transmission of free energy around the world had many other practical uses. Tesla noted:

> *"One of the most important uses of wireless energy will be undoubtedly for the propulsion of flying machines to which power can be readily supplied without ground connection, for although the flow of the currents is confined to the Earth, an electromagnetic field is created in the atmosphere surrounding it. If conductors of circuits accurately attuned and properly positioned are carried by the plane, energy is drawn into these circuits much the same as a fluid will pass through a hole created in the container. With an industrial plant of great capacity, sufficient power can be derived in this manner to propel any kind of aerial machine. This I always considered as the best and permanent solution of the problems of flight. No fuel of any kind will be required as the propulsion will be accomplished by light electric motors operated at a great speed."*

Inventor John Bedini began working with Tesla's theories of "radiant energy" decades ago and has produced an assortment of battery-charging devices that generate more energy than it takes for them to run. Devices by John Bedini in the field of radiant energy were reported to operate at over 800% efficiency, according to the *American National News Service*. This document from 1984 reports Bedini's initial intentions to market such devices. He announced that he was going to start offering them at low cost. Soon after that, he was attacked in his lab and warned not to produce the machines. For his own safety he had to discontinue marketing his free energy devices. Similarly, Canadian inventor John Hutchison not only created free energy batteries, but also used Tesla's theories to counter gravity, to make objects float weightlessly. This could revolutionize the field of propulsion. His lab was raided and equipment was taken by police and government officials in 1978, 1989, and again in 2000.

Fast forward to the dilemma of the early 21st century. Oil, coal, gasoline, and nuclear energy remain the dominant paradigm for our energy solutions. Tesla knew that special interests would continue to suppress his technology, but one day it would get another look. "Sooner or later my power system will have to be adopted in its entirety, and so far as I am concerned it is now as good as done. If I were ever assailed by doubt of ultimate success, I would dismiss it by remembering the words of that great philosopher Lord Kelvin who, after witnessing some of my experiments, said to me with tears in his eyes: 'I am sure you will do it.' "

FREE ENERGY FROM THE SUN

The solar-to-electric conversion of energy, used and known throughout the world today as the photovoltaic effect, is no more than the capture of light, a stream of particles called photons. Some photons dislodge some electrons off the silicon atom at an energy conversion point, freeing electrons which are captured by the conducting grid and fed into a battery for later use, or immediately used as controlled energy. That infinite source of free electrons is the major source of natural Earth energy, from its obvious manifestation in lightning bolts, to its unseen but measurable vastness in the ionosphere. Modern solar collectors have to overcome current inefficiencies, but future improvements can make photovoltaics much more efficient and practical.

The ionosphere and the sun shining on the Earth provide literally infinite charging. The sun is made of plasma and no other matter can get so hot. Plasma responds to magnetism. It thus can be molded and shaped and tied to a magnetic field. The natural photovoltaic effect produces limitless, immeasurable amounts of free electrons. This free and natural electricity is more than we can ever use without upsetting the balance of nature. The Earth's magnetic field can also be used to harvest electricity. Magnetic propulsion, anti-gravity and unlimited power generation are the applications.

If free energy discoveries prove valid, it will be necessary to re-examine the implications of the Second Law of Thermodynamics which says energy can be neither created nor destroyed. If the magnet machines pump energy from a heretofore unrecognized background field of energy, then they do not create energy, they just convert it.

BAD ENERGY AND GOOD ENERGY

Let's be very clear. Supplying the world with energy is the biggest and most profitable of all business models. The proven oil, natural gas and global coal reserves are worth over 200 trillion dollars. Let's break it down: as of October 2011, crude oil cost $95/barrel and there were approximately 1.2 trillion barrels of oil reserves on Earth. This equals roughly $114 trillion still untapped. Coal costs $80 per ton and there were approximately 500 billion tons of coal reserves on Earth. This equals roughly $40 trillion. Natural gas cost $400 per ton, and there were approximately 155 billion tons of natural gas reserves on Earth. This equals roughly $62 trillion. The total value of these energy reserves is $216 trillion.

The bulk of energy we use now is obviously unsustainable and is compromising the planet's health through wars of conquest, pollution and irreversible civilization-destroying climate change. Energy non-solutions are all hydrocarbons, nuclear, wind, biofuels and the current models of hydrogen and solar energy. Burning oil, coal and natural gas are highly flawed energy solutions. Nuclear power is expensive and extremely unsafe. Just look at the huge exclusion zones surrounding Chernobyl in the former Soviet Union countries of Ukraine and Belarus, and more recently the disaster in Fukushima, Japan. The dangers of using nuclear power are tragically graphic. Furthermore, there is no safe storage for nuclear waste. While hydrogen burns clean, as a fuel it requires more energy to produce than can be obtained for usage. Only if we can manipulate the chemical nature of the hydrogen molecule can we have a form of over-unity, or free energy. Solar and wind solutions suffer from high costs and expensive materials and require precious land use, making them inefficient. Wind energy turbines and fans also kill huge numbers of birds in flight. Biofuel is just another way of burning carbon. An enormous infrastructure is required for biofuels which compete with agricultural land needed to grow food for a hungry world population.

The new energy technologies include Vacuum, or Zero Point Energy (ZPE); low temperature non-radioactive nuclear reactions like cold fusion; advanced hydrogen and water technologies; and we should always keep the door open to other potential surprises. The ZPE are electromagnetic devices that through the use of vibrating electrons, either through the rotary motion of spinning electromagnets, or the vibrations of electrons within a solid-state device, can tap the enormous energy potential of the etheric field, or vacuum. Advanced hydrogen and water technologies still in development are special forms that can produce more energy than is needed to start the machine running.

ZERO POINT ENERGY

There is energy everywhere in the quantum state yet to be harvested. The astronomy and cosmology sciences have observed that at least two-thirds of the total universe is comprised of an invisible type of energy, about which little is known or only slightly more than the fact that it exists. One cannot see this type of energy, thus it has been given the name "dark energy." The name does not compare with or connote "dark" or some miraculous paranormal forces, it simply points out that this energy is out of view, just like one cannot see anything in the darkness. The name also indicates that we have little knowledge of its nature or origin. This energy is sometimes referred to as "space energy" or "vacuum energy" because it is a property of mere space and is thus a vacuum. If classical physics is right, this energy is everywhere. The engineering goal is to make Zero Point Energy visible and manifest it in the laboratory, leading to an energy harvest for all of humankind's use. That would convert the classical physics dark energy into mechanical energy, thus proving this aspect of the classical theory.

Another portion of this energy is "quantum mechanical zero-point energy," because it is supposed that it originates from quantum mechanical zero-point oscillations. Though these oscillations are rather abstract, they are well-known within quantum mechanics and have been for several decades.

Both motor-run and motionless devices share commonalities: the device can establish or entrain a flow to the ZPE field using high frequency electromagnetic fields. With the ZPE entrained by the electric current, the current is suddenly stopped with a precise timing device. When the electron flow suddenly stops a "radiant energy event" then occurs, which releases a pulse of energy far in excess of the original current flow. The pulse is captured to some degree by a transducer that converts the "radiant energy" back to a usable form, and presumably into the grid for wider distribution. Tom Bearden made public the announcement of a "Motionless Electro-Magnetic Generator" (MEG) in 2002. His patent was an oscillating magnetic field to entrain the ZPE with no moving parts. Another low energy device called a Mighty Engine MYT (Massive Yet Tiny) has been demonstrated to use only 5% of the fuel of a normal engine.

Free energy inventor Adam Trombly had been invited to demonstrate one of his generators at the United Nations and to the U.S. Senate, but these events were constrained by the first Bush Administration. Then the device itself was taken in a government raid. Former Canadian Ambassador, James George, details these series of events in his book, *The Little Green Book on Awakening*. In 1982, Adam Trombly received an international patent (WO/1982/002126) for his and Joseph Kahn's co-invention of the "Closed Path Homopolar Machine," a ZPE device. In 1983, Trombly was issued a gag order by the U.S. Government to stop development of the Closed Path Homopolar Machine. Then sometime before 1989, Trombly's gag order was dropped and he developed another Zero Point Energy device with David Farnsworth, called the "Piezo Ringing Resonance Generator." In June of 1989, Trombly was scheduled to demonstrate a small version of his Piezo Ringing Resonance Generator at the UN in New York, but at the last minute he was forced to move to a church down the street. Afterwards, Trombly gave a speech in Dag Hammarskjöld Auditorium at the United Nations in front of an international audience. A few days later, Trombly was scheduled to demonstrate the same device at the U.S. Senate Banking and Finance Committee in Washington. Only Senator Carl Levin and a "handful" of staff were in attendance because the Senior Bush Administration called hundreds of Senators, Congressional Representatives and their staff members for an "off-the-cuff" discussion of the Clean Air Act at the exact same time as Trombly's demonstration. Thus, the first Bush Administration successfully diverted attention away from the technology in an effort to censor Trombly.

MAGNETIC ENERGY DEVICES

Free energy systems generated by magnets have been independently invented by dozens of people around the world for decades. In the United States, the few people who invent free energy devices most often proceed to take out a patent. Once making their inventions known they will sometimes be offered large sums of money for the plans, or the patent seeker may retreat from advancing the patent, or simply disappear. Inventors are also handicapped by a lack of funding, greedy capital venture groups, naive investors, personal eccentricities, the vagaries and whims of the U.S. Patent Office, and active suppression by shadowy forces. The quest to simply arouse public attention seems more difficult than actually creating the free energy device itself! Dealing with the forces of suppression is one goal, and those who are aware of the dilemma are developing effective tools to counter disinformation as awareness of the problem increases.

The most commonly invented free energy device involves the natural resistance of magnets. Once the magnets are given a start, an engine can produce a steady energy flow, which charges a battery or produces direct electric discharge completely independent of where it was started. Magnetic free energy is produced by an entrainment of ZPE through the use of high frequency electromagnetic fields. When the energy is abruptly cut, the field collapses and a brief burst of energy is captured, apparently from the ZPE field. Inertia and gravity appear not to be fundamental forces, but artifacts of the interaction between matter and the ZPE field. The scientific goal is to improve the design of magnetic generators in ways that would overcome or avoid the counter-force that usually opposes movements of magnets in a generator.

Over-unity, in which a little energy is needed to start the device and then it produces a greater output, is the Holy Grail of energy research. Perhaps reading the writing on the wall, in 2005 GMC Holdings announced the "Rare Earth Magnetic Amplification Tech" (REMAT) which delivers brief pulses to the rotor magnets and then cuts the pulse abruptly. The pulse from the collapsing magnetic field delivers added kick to the rotor magnets and the cycle repeats. Precise and fast timing are part of the operation, capturing the entrained ZPE. A small amount of shared energy is necessary to start and run the motor, which then produces substantial output power during operation, even considerably more than is needed to start and operate the device.

Methernita Commune (near Bern, Switzerland) has a free energy machine, which works on the same principles as the REMAT. It has been producing a constant power output of 230 volts at 13 amperes for a 3kw rating pulsed DC daily rate for over 25 years. A PAPP Engine created by Joseph Papp has also been demonstrated to run without fuel. It utilizes noble gases driven only by anti-gravity, generating 500hp for an engine. Joseph Papp invented and demonstrated a pulsed plasma discharge automotive style piston engine that ran on sealed charges of noble gas mixtures in the cylinders. His electric arc ignition triggered far greater output than input. The superconducting Searl Effect Generator (SEG) by John Searl is another novel magnet-based electrical generator. The SEG is given an initial application of a small amount of electricity to get it going, thereafter accelerating to operating speed on its own, with no further external power being required. It is a demand-driven device system which automatically and seamlessly responds to an increased electrical load, with no spikes or transients in the power being delivered.

... AND BEYOND!

There is a saying that no free thinker is ahead of his or her time, but they are their time. Right now excessive carbon emissions are melting the polar ice caps, polluting the atmosphere and threatening the delicate balance of life on the planet. This carbon-burning energy madness, like war, needs to end on Earth if we hope to survive as a species. Certainly we are clever enough to move past 19th century internal combustion engine technology and to see through the attitudes that treat possible free energy solutions as idle speculation to be ignored, ridiculed or feared. The coming "Energy Revolution" will then change the world immediately. The oil-based economy will have to readjust to clean, unlimited energy for free or little cost to the people of the world. Synthetic or drilled oil can be used for plastics and chemicals, but no longer for fuel. It will become obvious that most remaining oil, natural gas, coal and uranium reserves should stay buried. Embracing the mere *possibility* of a breakthrough energy solution revolution should be and will become a fundamental and over-riding United Nations global mandate. But those individuals who rule the oil-based economy are also the largest banking interests and basically the current masters of the world. Before we can reach our utopia we'll have to overcome these forces, which is no easy task.

In 1989, researcher Stanley Pons and chemist Martin Fleischmann rose to prominence, then quickly fell from grace, after they prematurely announced the discovery of generating power from the elusive "cold fusion." The scientific community rebelled and the U.S. Department of Energy convened a panel led by cold fusion critic, John Huizenga, to investigate the validity of their claim. Needless to say, Pons and Fleischmann were condemned, discredited and forced to do further research in other countries, but are now largely vindicated. With almost three decades having passed since their original claims, independent scientists all over the world are routinely duplicating and continually improving the results of this new energy source.

In 1899, Nikola Tesla moved to Colorado Springs and began doing experiments on transmitting signals from Pikes Peak to Paris. Tesla proved that the Earth was a conductor and he produced artificial lightning, some (as seen here) with discharges emitting millions of volts and extending up to 35 meters in length. Tesla discovered that the resonant frequency of the Earth was approximately 8 hertz (Hz). In the 1950s, researchers confirmed that the resonant frequency of the Earth's ionospheric cavity was in this range, later named the Schumann resonance.

In 1900, Tesla left Colorado Springs. His lab was torn down and its contents sold to pay debts. In June, 1902, Tesla's lab operations were moved to Wardenclyffe from Houston Street in New York City. With $150,000, 51% coming from J. P. Morgan, Tesla began planning the Wardenclyffe Tower facility on Long Island, New York. In one of the most notorious turnabouts in history, J.P. Morgan (with his controlling interest) pulled the plug after Tesla told him he would provide "free" energy to the world. The tower was dismantled for scrap during World War I. Tesla lamented, "My project was retarded (merely delayed). ... The world was not prepared for it. It was too ahead of its time. But the same laws will prevail in the end and make it a triumphal success."

ENDGAME-ENSLAVEMENT

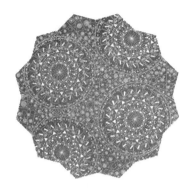

"None are more hopelessly enslaved than those who falsely believe they are free." –Johann Wolfgang von Goethe

THIS chapter is a dystopian scenario, a recap for the reader of what shadow forces have wrought, and of what could happen if nothing changes. *It is included in the Utopia section with the disclaimer that it does not have to be this way.*

We currently find ourselves in a trap which involves money enslavement and the intentional encouragement of stupidity through the "lamestream" media. Apart from a few educational shows on PBS, the rest of television is a vast wasteland of sports, celebrity worship, and make-believe dramas usually of a violent nature. Most Americans are unaware that they are deliberately held in a cycle of bondage by a network of elite families, who are the bankers, developers, CEOs, and corporate business owners. Their aim is to possess a cheap, unquestioning, and compliant labor force who pay high rents, crippling interest, and huge medical bills. They invest in developing such a labor force not by investing in the education and quality of life for anyone, but for their own gain. "Working class Americans were clubbed into submission long ago," wrote Joe Bageant in his book *Rainbow Pie: A Redneck Memoir*. "We now require only enough medication for our high levels of cholesterol, enough alcohol to keep the sludge moving through our arteries, and a 24/7 mind-numbing spectacle of titties, tabloid TV, and terrorist dramas. Throw in a couple of new flavors of XXL edible thongs, and you've got a nation of drowsing hippos who will never notice that our country has been looted."

With the rapid development of telecommunications technology, we are coming into a dualistic era of profound advances in present-day knowledge, plus new methods of surveillance and behavioral engineering. This is both good and bad for us. It allows malicious individuals to conduct disinformation manipulations that in other epochs of history were only evil intentions. Today we live in a disturbing new reality where any psychopath can build a website. On the plus side, the Internet and communications technology allows for an unprecedented connectedness, allowing us to communicate more effectively than ever before. Individuals are empowered in ways that have never before been available to the average citizen. There is now instant collaboration, connecting without meeting, an array of opinions, and uncensored imagery at a time when anyone with a computer and Internet connection can become a publisher of media content.

The Internet enables horizontal communication instead of through the rigid hierarchy system. It is the empowerment of people who have never before had a voice. It's everyone to everyone connected for the first time. Consider how social networks enabled the Arab Spring uprisings starting in December, 2010, and then allowed other social justice demonstrations worldwide to flourish. Social media is a revolutionary tool for spreading information and connecting people worldwide. Over 90% of those under 30 in the Millennial generation in the Western Hemisphere has joined a social network. Google, Facebook, and Twitter connect around two billion people worldwide, close to a third of the planet's population. More video content was uploaded to YouTube in six months than was produced by the three major TV networks in 60 years. Wikipedia has over 13 million articles, all written by volunteers. And through social media a new order has emerged based on open access, decentralized creativity, and freedom of speech. But all this information freedom has its blowback, because now the Internet itself is threatened with censorship.

DUDE, WHERE'S MY COUNTRY?

It would be disingenuous to blame our problems entirely on a dysfunctional elected government. There are puppet masters above our elected officials who really pull the strings. You may not see the strings, but they are there. These seemingly invisible power brokers direct the politicians to enact the laws that will benefit them, and also keep the population in a state of servitude. For starters, under the Constitution, the federal government has never had the legal authority to pass a national tax on income. The law that enacted income tax, the 16th amendment, was never ratified as required by law. The U.S. federal government originally had no authority over states in the republic, and never had the legal jurisdiction to pass laws making any crimes "federal" or subjecting people to a national federal criminal law system. Yet, a combination of illegally passed laws has allowed the federal government to create national federal law enforcement agencies who spy on the American public, seize property, and even kill Americans abroad in drone attacks, all to consolidate their illegal power. The puppet masters of the politicians know that the federal government is top heavy, making it fairly easy to control a few powerful people who make a majority of the big decisions. Establishing a police state is in the best interest of the power elite.

House-to-house searches and seizures are now being conducted without warrants across the land. Mobilization of the National Guard and UN troops are already in place to enforce martial law, and they are prepared to engage in "peace keeping" operations against their own citizens. Surveillance cameras are in place atop tall light posts along highways. To pinpoint them, look for antennas sticking out from black boxes on extremely tall light posts. Police cars are equipped with barcodes and tracking devices. A national I.D. card or RFID implanted chip and a cashless society seems imminent, so we may all be tracked in our every moment with no penny left unaccounted. FEMA detention camps are already built nationwide, possibly to deport dissidents who oppose these plans. The country has already been divided into ten regions for ten regional governments under martial law. Our national media has become nothing but the official "Ministry of Propaganda" mouthpiece of the government and elite, putting forth false "polls" and outright propaganda to sway public opinion, and failing to report countless outrageous abuses of the public by federal agents. George Orwell would roll over in his grave knowing his *1984* prophecy just came true.

Congress has been wholly unresponsive to demands by the American people to revoke these illegal laws, restore the republic, and reserve for the states their own enumerated governmental powers. Instead, Congress has passed, and the president has signed, unconstitutional laws that they have no authority to pass. This has been done because money interests have eroded our constitutional rights, while the rights of the states to self-govern are all but lost.

Future visionary author H. G. Wells wrote of utopian and dystopian societies. In his 1939 book entitled *The New World Order,* Wells makes an interesting prediction of things to come. "When the struggle seems to be drifting definitely towards a world social democracy, there may still be very great delays and disappointments before it becomes an efficient and beneficent world system. Countless people ... will hate the new world order ... and will die protesting against it. When we attempt to evaluate its promise, we have to bear in mind the distress of a generation or so of malcontents, many of them quite gallant and graceful-looking people." This sounds very reminiscent of the Occupy Movement protesting the power of the 1% over the rest of us, which eventually became brutally suppressed.

The military of the United States is currently deployed in more than 150 countries around the world, with more than 369,000 of its 1,580,255 active-duty personnel serving outside the United States and its territories. The U.S. Government has over 700 foreign military bases around the world. However, the United States Constitution only authorizes a Navy and a standing Army for an occupation up to two years. The War Powers Act authorizes 60 days of an undeclared "emergency" war. Therefore in order to restore peace and harmony among all people, a drawdown and eventual departure from all the countries where U.S. military bases exist must occur. The Founding Fathers knew an occupying foreign military presence would be the problem, not the solution. George Washington's farewell address to the people of the United States reflects his idea of foreign policy: "It is our true policy to steer clear of permanent alliance with any portion of the foreign world."

There is still time left to reclaim these United States of America. We need to band together consciously and reassert our sovereignty, restore the republic, and arrest the guilty parties. This is a nation of laws, and we should keep it that way. Rioting will not help, but only inflame the turbulence. Either we come together or else they'll keep us divided and the truth embargo will continue. While we are at it, we will need to rethink our collective consciousness by learning to respect the planet and find peaceful ways to coexist with all in harmony. Our human experience is a world of duality, of yin and yang. With every act of great compassion there is also the potential for extreme evil.

UNCONSTITUTIONAL FEDERAL LAWS AND AGENCIES

A direct result of the events on 9-11-2001 led to the creation of the Department of Homeland Security, and the Patriot Act to become the law of the land. Notice the *1984* doublespeak in those names, when in fact they more closely resemble the Homeland Insecurity Department and the Anti-Patriot Act. The year 2012 started ominously with the reprehensible National Defense Authorization Act (NDAA) signed into law on New Year's Eve when only a minimal number of people were paying attention to the news. After the United States Congress passed NDAA and President Obama endorsed the bill (after he said he would veto it), top experts and even some sponsors of the bill recognized its dangers— one being authorizing indefinite detention of Americans living within the United States. This is in direct conflict with the U.S. Constitution which guarantees every citizen the right to a fair trial. Top legal experts also point out that, according to this bill, the government claims the right to assassinate American citizens on U.S. soil without any charges, trial or other constitutional protections. *Mother Jones* magazine claims that Congress has explicitly authorized, through NDAA, the allowing of Americans residing in the U.S. to be sent to other countries that perform torture, or in doublespeak terms "extraordinary rendition." The Patriot Act eviscerated our 4th amendment privacy protections, is completely unconstitutional, and needs to be repealed. The NDAA also needs to be repealed, and the Homeland Security agency disbanded.

Public condemnation of President Obama was intense on the days following his signing into law the indefinite detention bill embedded in the 2012 National Defense Authorization Act. These denunciations come not only from the nation's leading civil liberties and human rights groups, but also from the pro-Obama *New York Times* editorial page, which ran scathing critiques describing Obama's stance as "a complete political cave-in, one that reinforces the impression of a fumbling presidency," and lamenting that "the bill has so many other objectionable aspects that we can't go into them all." The above-ground television media issued a near complete blackout of coverage exposing the NDAA passage into law.

If American citizens should fail to heed the many warnings such as the enactment of the Patriot Act and NDAA, our future will become a "Homeland Gestapo" police state where all of our constitutional rights are stripped away right before our eyes. If nothing changes, we can expect the reality as described by George Orwell in his seminal work *1984*, wherein he warned: "People simply disappeared, always during the night. Your name was removed from the registers, every record of everything you had ever done was wiped out, and your one-time existence was denied and then forgotten. You were abolished, annihilated: vaporized was the usual word." As William Cooper repeatedly predicted, we are either entering the most illuminated Golden Age in history, or the worst enslavement imaginable.

FINAL GLOBAL GOVERNANCE

And while we can project in our minds a better world, we also need to know what we're up against. This brings us to the 21st century hegemony, not the American nation-state shell, nor the British nation-state shell, but the globalist super-sovereignty which devised this whole scheme. The New World Rulers are the original cabal, described loosely as the elite finance network of the Rothschild's origin, based in England and Europe originally, then on to America with its large military and industrial base in the 20th century. The USA in the 21st century is truly a global super structure of power based on finance and asset control, along with nation-state government ownership through debt.

We have a globalist ruling elite, and they have names. The following are the most dangerous of the elite cabal who call the real shots: Lord Jacob de Rothschild; His son Nathaniel; Baron John de Rothschild; Sir Evelyn de Rothschild; David Rockefeller; Nathan Warburg; Henry Kissinger; George Soros; Paul Volcker; Larry Summers; Lloyd Blankfein; and Ben Shalom Bernanke. These are the most powerful individuals leading the New World Order, with a huge investment portfolio under global sociopathic human management. Their aim is to consolidate, in the 21st century, their power into a one world governmental system—a future One World Company, Limited. For this New World Order, a world government is just the beginning. Once in place, they can engage in their dastardly plan to exterminate up to 90% of the world's population. This would enable the "elite" to rule with far less opposition. Included in their plan is for the select few to live decades longer using the aid of advanced technology.

The Bilderberg Group also functions as a means toward a future One World Company, Limited. This is a private, by invitation only group of world leaders, who have met annually since 1954 to discuss global issues. Some say their ostensibly public website and listing of a global agenda (although meetings are closed) is simply a cover for deeper motives, that of assisting the cabal to gain even tighter control. In fact, they may engineer financial crises toward that end. The nightmarish future these groups represent is to transform Earth into a prison planet by bringing about a single globalized marketplace, controlled by a One World Company, financially regulated by a World Bank, and populated by a dumbed-down class of people whose necessities of life will be stripped to materialism and survival, all connected to a global computer that monitors our every move. "Work, produce, obey, consume, sleep" will be our destiny as they dictate.

Other groups the cabal is attempting to use in their typical disinformation style are the Pentagon "White Hats" and the NASA "good-guys," "riding in to save the day" and telling you not to listen to all those quacks on the Internet. In fact, the White Hats and NASA good guys are former military intelligence operatives and NASA scientists who first became disillusioned and then appalled by their assignments. They believe an elite cabal is implementing an agenda that is unconstitutional and destructive to the foundation of our democracy, seemingly for their own personal gain. They have researched and prepared dozens of reports for members of Congress and the media, but have received only muted response and, in many cases, threats. So NASA science, as well as the barrage of "Internet impostors," are all manipulated by the controllers to indoctrinate and confuse the population, from public school education to the information gleaned from mass media. The confusion stems from not knowing who is working for whom. The numbers of whistleblowers, however, is rapidly increasing. Perhaps we are moving toward a tipping point when it is no longer possible, or even productive, to silence them all. Some insiders estimate that the White Hats are at 90% consensus to move against the cabal, but they are paralyzed to act until a new system is in place. Until then, many Internet impostors receive support from NWO sources to distort the real efforts of those few sane voices that exist in the world today. We watch the news and we watch entertainment and we see the conflicts of people, and it appears this world is a negative and horrendous place. But the media hype is not representative of what the world really is, or what the world wants. Internet information is a particular challenge. When perusing the Internet, it pays to be intelligently skeptical. It takes some patience and a discerning eye to distinguish truth from lies amidst the vast sea of data, distortion and blatant disinformation. Weighing all research and allegations against one's personal experience and higher intuitive instincts is also useful.

A Brookings Institute study determined that the general population could not handle UFO truth. But that "truth" they refer to is that "the handlers" cannot handle us, an angry world population, once the truth breaks free. This "general population" is us, that is, you and me, the useless eaters, the masses, the sheeple, the taxpayers, the patriots, the good people, the brown people, the children, that is, the 99.999% of us. The cabal pretends that we will have a hard time coming to terms with the reality of an alien presence, when in fact, they will lose control if they tell the entire story as it is, unabridged, no spin, no lies, no omissions, nothing but the truth. That would be the end for them; their grip on power will come to an abrupt halt. The elite controllers that are the 0.001%, of those tiny minority of population reductionists (or whatever they prefer to call themselves), those who are privy to the big picture, will see their influence diminish and wither away. Meanwhile, they prefer to do the thinking for the rest of us for as long as they possibly can, that is, until there is a complete global police state to protect them, or they are arrested, brought to justice and prosecuted for their crimes.

CORPORATE AND BANKING TAKEOVER

The Illuminati is another name for the group of individuals functioning as the shadow government. It has simply been reformed as different family empires and private corporations under different names. When it comes to the control of money, some things never change. The individuals behind the organization of the Federal Reserve in 1913 already then appointed their descendents to rule today.

The Bilderberg Group was created to bolster America's extension and zone of influence upon Europe and now Russia. The Illuminati and all its subsidiary influences within religious hierarchies and financial institutions must be investigated and the information made public. There are many examples of their covert dealings that affect the lives of us all.

Back in 1994, *New Scientist* magazine reported that the World Bank wanted to control the International Agricultural Research Centers (IARC) and their valuable collection of genetic varieties of crops. Developing nations protested since most seed varieties come from their countries, thus control should go to them not the World Bank, which uses its backing for economic reform in developing countries. "If the World Bank controls agricultural development and research, then it controls the shape of the world agriculture for the immediate future" according to Pat Mooney of Rural Advancement Foundation International, a development pressure group. If successful, the World Bank would then control the funding research and intellectual property rights of the Earth's agricultural bounty.

The Federal Reserve represents the central planning force behind a global banking cartel that has deliberately impoverished people throughout the world. U.S. politicians have not recognized the problem or taken action to end this system of political bribery. The campaign finance and lobbying racket allows the global bankers to control our political process. In its century long rule, the Federal Reserve has never been audited, not even once, since its inception over a century ago.

Another subsidiary influence of the ruling elite is the black operation groups within the Federal Government's "three 'letter' agencies," the NSA, CIA and NATO. The NSA became operational in 1947 with the passing of the National Security Act, but only announced its existence fairly recently, hence the nickname, No Such Agency. No one really has any idea what the CIA is up to on any given day. Of course the three letter agencies can hide behind the curtain of nation security. The United States contributes about 75% of the monies to operate NATO, up from 50% historically. As the saying goes, the USA is "first among equals" within NATO. Bonding very closely within NATO, the UK and the USA have a military and technology-sharing pact. This sharing pact also includes Australia, New Zealand and Canada. The USA and the UK are leaders in the New World Order because their agenda is set by secretive groups, including the Trilateral Commission (another arm of the "elite") and the Council of Foreign Relations.

EUGENICS

Eugenics is the antisocial practice where some people get to decide who is worthy to live and reproduce, and who is not. Eugenics and de-population programs were initiated at the beginning of the 20th century by powerful family dynasties, including the Rockefellers, Carnegies and Harrimans. Their work inspired later dictators like Adolph Hitler to justify the culling of undesirable portions of the populace. We have been schooled to focus on Hitler as a unique madman who somehow got control of a whole nation by his own cult of personality; but as is usually the case, that is not the whole picture. It is well-documented that Hitler was himself a puppet figure for the international banking cabal that was intent to overthrow Stalin.

Unfortunately, the Third Reich is only one of many governments that have turned against their own citizens. Human experimentation in the U.S. has been documented as early as 1890. The government has been caught, over 30 times, covertly experimenting with toxic chemicals on its own citizens—from soldiers, prisoners, and Native Americans on reservations, to entire towns and counties. Such cases, from syphilis experiments conducted by the Tuskegee Institute in the 1930s, to biological waste dumping in the 1990s and mysterious army vaccine-related deaths in the 21st century, all were considered controlled experiments. Let's not forget how the British gave away blankets deliberately infected with the smallpox virus to Native Americans in the 1700s. The resulting spread of deadly germs, whether purposefully delivered or by accident, eventually killed-off half the Native American population.

Sterilization is another one of the many insidious ways eugenics is being implemented. In 1904, the Carnegies covertly funded the first eugenics laboratory in Cold Spring Harbor, Long Island. The Rockefellers funded involuntary sterilization of people of color through their eugenics programs and funded the Kaiser Wilhelm Institute in Germany to further the racial supremacy agenda later adopted by the Third Reich. The genocidal agenda of the Nazis was forced underground after the defeat of the Germans and the convictions of the Nuremberg Trials, but a similar agenda of aggressive elimination of large numbers of people (in less obvious forms) is re-surfacing all around the world. More recently, in the past decade, mass covert sterilization of women and girls, using secret additives to vaccines, has been exposed in Brazil, Puerto Rico, Nicaragua, Mexico and the Philippines.

Investigative journalist Edwin Black documents the origin of the eugenics movement in the United States in his 2003 book, *War Against the Weak: Eugenics and America's Campaign to Create a Master Race.* In its early years the eugenics movement was financed by large corporate philanthropies, including the Carnegie Institution and the Rockefeller Foundation. Not only did the Carnegies and Rockefellers lend financial support, but the political and social significance of their philanthropic endeavors endowed the movement with greater credibility, which attracted some of the nation's brightest minds—from Harvard, Princeton, and Yale, among others. Black describes a concerted effort to create a master race long before the Third Reich popularized the infamous term. The Rockefellers also founded the World Health Foundation, which on the surface appears to be strictly for humanitarian purposes, but also has a dark history of introducing subversive vaccines. A 1991 publication by the Club of Rome, an international elitist organization, confirms that their dastardly agenda continues in earnest. In this publication, "The First Global Revolution," the authors note that "In searching for a new enemy to unite us, we came up with the idea that pollution, the threat of global warming, water shortages, famine, and the like would fit the bill. All these dangers are caused by human intervention ... The real enemy, then, is humanity itself." The tone of this agenda makes clear that their definition of "humanity" is *lesser others*, themselves excluded.

In 1984, the World Development Report commissioned by the World Bank issued the following statement: "Inaction today could mean that more drastic steps, less compatible with individual choice and freedom, will seem necessary tomorrow to slow population growth." Henry Kissinger cryptically declared in 1978: "U.S. policy toward the third world should be one of depopulation." Crop spraying, aerial chemical trailing, water additives such as fluoride, contaminated vaccines, GMOs, human-created weather catastrophes through HAARP, and endless wars look a whole lot different when viewed through the lens of depopulation. Is it any wonder that human fertility rates are plunging globally?

As more and more people are becoming aware of the dangers posed by the global elite, they are speaking out. For example, research indicates that sodium fluoride, even in weak concentrations, is damaging and destructive to cellular tissue. People are demanding that the fluoridation of our drinking water be terminated. It has nothing to do with preventing cavities and everything to do with eugenics. Our government has known for a long time that sodium fluoride is poison to mammals and collects around the pineal gland. Animal studies of pineal function indicate that fluoride exposure results in altered melatonin production and altered timing of sexual maturity. Recent information on the role of the pineal organ in humans suggest that any agent that affects pineal function could affect human health in a variety of ways, including effects on sexual maturation, calcium metabolism, parathyroid function, postmenopausal osteoporosis, cancer, and a host of psychiatric diseases. However, we are told that fluoride is put into our drinking water because it's "good for the teeth."

Aldous Huxley, author of the dystopian novel *Brave New World*, observed in 1959: "Whereas death control is extremely easy under modern circumstances, birth control is extremely difficult. The reason is very simple: death control—the control, for example, of infectious diseases—can be accomplished by a handful of experts and quite a small labor force of unskilled persons and requires a very small capital expenditure." Does life imitate fiction? The newly manufactured diseases meant to cull human populations include HIV, Ebola and SARS, among others. SARS, or the bird flu, was developed as a specific bio-weapon targeting non-Caucasian people, specifically Asians. When members of the Japanese organized crime syndicate called the *yakusa* learned of the New World Order plotting against their people, they decided to fight back. Instead of enabling the New World Order, they changed their tune and now hire others to expose the cabal's hidden agenda. Their lead spokesperson is Benjamin Fulford, the former Asia-Pacific bureau chief for *Forbes Magazine*, whom they call a "blue-eyed samurai."

THE ALTERNATIVE IS TOO MIND-BOGGLING FOR MOST TO HANDLE

Fulford explains how the financial elite has repeatedly created fake military incidents in order to get the general population motivated to enter into a new war. The bankers stand to gain the most from warfare. Quite simply, they finance both sides of each conflict and make a tidy profit off the interest rates. Fulford urges readers to examine the circumstances around which each military operation began, and ample evidence emerges pointing to false flag operations. From the Spanish-American War to the 9-11 tragedy, almost every American military engagement in the last century involved a pre-emptive strike, a false flag operation, or both. Only in the last decade has it been established that FDR had prior knowledge of the imminent Japanese threat to Pearl Harbor, but let the sneak attack occur without alerting the U.S. Pacific Fleet.

The dilemma that most people encounter is that if the rationale for war was not a real provocation, not the real history we've been told, then the implications are too steep to absorb rationally. It is simply too mind-boggling to consider the "what if" opposite perspective. It involves such a large number of people and so much planning, and so many insiders, that most people just enter into a state of denial. Such a conspiracy is far too complex to be plausible, such as that 9-11 was an inside job. It is simply too huge a conspiracy, too much complicity with elected officials, too many things that could go wrong and, basically, too difficult to fathom, and so the theory is dismissed outright. When people reach this denial point, their minds shut down and reasoning on the subject ends.

Crisis counselors note that people have a natural response to a crisis, especially their post-traumatic stress disorder (PTSD) clients. When someone has been severely traumatized they create a dissociative partition in their mind, a place of denial. It's like a separate personality that handles the trauma, which may or may not be connected to the other parts of the mind. The person will become very defensive around even peripheral issues associated with the trauma. Typically if they get information that brings up the experience that triggered the trauma, their first tendency is to attack the messenger. This defensive behavior, one version of "cognitive dissonance," stems from an overwhelming sense of "no, no, this does not compute; it can't be," while at the same time, a fearful, subconscious part of the person's mind realizes it's true. Similarly, the average American confronted with information in this book likely will first have the reaction of cognitive dissonance, that is, this information doesn't compute; it doesn't fit with anything we've been told or could ever believed. The "messengers" must be crazy.

BREAKING FROM THE PRISON PLANET

David Icke, in his book *Children of the Matrix,* writes: "Most of the human race is so utterly indoctrinated by the externally implanted 'norms' that bombard their minds from the cradle to the grave that they have no comprehension that their 'normal' thinking is their own individual and collective prison." He further points out that the only way the elite can run the planet is if they succeed in their ongoing effort to keep us ignorant. Icke points out what the controllers have done is employ a system that tightly regulates the flow of information that the human race receives. What they have done is de-link us from the information of who we are, our true power, the accurate facts of where we come from, our true history and, until now, the knowledge of their scam. What they have done is taken an inter-dimensional species and created a population of blinded sheep.

Fulford, Icke, Collier, Wilcock and many others who speak out on this sensitive issue assert that it is time for the people of Earth to become sovereign once again.

The ultimate tyranny in a society is not control by martial law. It is control by the psychological manipulation of consciousness through which reality is defined, so that those who exist within it do not even realize that they are imprisoned. The manipulators do not want us to remember that each of us is responsible for our own experience, and each of us can inspire others. But more and more of us can and do understand the "alternative narrative" and can share this awareness with others around us. Anyone has the opportunity to wake up. When enough people awaken to the choice against victimhood, when we all begin to consciously embrace the alternative, then we'll see macro-changes in the world for the better. When we co-create this new reality there can never again be authoritarian control. We all have the potential to become masters. The elites know there is no turning back once human consciousness begins to shift. Creating our own new shift in perspective and the resulting change in experience goes back to the concept that the world is not really a solid. It is a holographic image. At its atomic core all material is constructed of energy, and that holographic energy takes form through the thoughts of those individuals that participate within the world.

HOW CAN WE PROTECT OURSELVES?

The specific aim of the Illuminati and its secret government network is to implement covert mind control methods for a wholesale takeover of the people on Earth. The Draconian reptilians and their servants the Greys also back this agenda. Currently these deceitful ETs and power-hungry humans are working in conjunction with each other to achieve the same goal. These two groups are intimately connected. Most people think of world takeover only in terms of military means such as bombs and guns. But the subversive methods of these groups to control world leaders and the mass public is through mind control, hypnosis, and brain implants. The key question is, "What can we do to stop this?" Our government has sold us out because of greed, technology acquisition and world domination. Now they can't stop what they have started. The first step is for the people of Earth to reclaim the world's government systems and expose the myriad of hidden agendas in which they collude with these groups. A key element in this first step is to force governments to make a complete disclosure about extraterrestrials to the world at large, no matter how disturbing this news may seem at first.

Until they are defeated, the only current way to protect ourselves is through the strength of our consciousness. If a person is attuned to a higher power, controls their own personal strength, and has self-mastery over their personal energies or urges, they have little to worry about. If you ever sense a malevolent presence around, just affirm your nonviolence principles, and visualize protection for yourself. Your connection with service to others will bring you immediate protection. Part of our strength is also to think as individuals. The Greys are a group memory complex that has very little ability to think on its own. It is now time to make people aware of what is really going on. Share this information with your friends and family in a non-threatening discussion. Do more individual research on the subject. If enough people become aware, the one hundredth monkey effect will begin to occur. It is already happening, but time is running short.

The world needs to wake up spiritually and psychologically and stop consenting to victimhood. It is this victim consciousness that contributes to continued alien abduction and manipulation of unsuspecting humans. It bears repetition that change begins in consciousness, which leads to individual and group action. The Illuminati power cabal and their negative ET allies are more vulnerable now than ever before. Their greatest advantage, for both the malevolent ETs and the secret government, is how outrageous these claims will seem to the mass populous. That is why they keep us guessing with just enough information, combined with clever disinformation tactics, to divert us from the truth of what's really going on.

The only real hope for the people of this planet is a mass spiritual awakening which is just beginning to occur. This spiritual awakening must also lead us into political action to remove the secret government and Illuminati from power. They too are capable of becoming aware of their own victimization by the negative extraterrestrials. They too can even begin to realize the dead end and ultimate insecurity of ruling by fear. And for the rest of us, we will have to find a way to forgive them. Change in human perspective is always possible and no one is beyond redemption. The global spiritual awakening already in progress will bring forward a profound new respect for all beings in all dimensions, not the least of which is the terribly mistreated animal kingdom here on Earth.

NONCOMPLIANCE

A specific way we can we stop the New World Order in their tracks is through noncompliance with the system. It is not about quitting your job or burning your money or dropping out of society, but about right actions towards others and ourselves. When in doubt, do what is right in your heart. Disconnect from the system by making a conscious decision such as becoming a vegetarian or not owning a car. Do what feels right. It is not something you have to justify with an inner dialogue. Just think and act like a humanitarian rather than from your social status or how many trinkets you can collect. Be aware of the energy you are projecting on others, and more importantly that you are drawing to yourself.

We must all realize our potential as consciously aware human beings. Look carefully at the whole spectrum beyond the illusions that are created. The institutions of the world will not help us in our advancement. Ignore the imaginary limitations taught and practiced by the world's institutions. Those false institutions include corporations, governments, and religions. Each of them compartmentalizes knowledge by limiting the scope of our understanding. Only when we make the connection between religion and logic, and how an imposed belief system is being forced upon us, can we comprehend the need for spirituality to be infused in science without dogma. What is the true nature of the entity humans call God? It must be a duality of both male and female, an internal expression of us all. There is only one law in the universe and that is love. Evil is the presence of disharmony, those who deny the one law. Look deep within and realize your own unique role in this lifetime, and aspire to your true potential. Stop complying with the system and become aware of the incredible time we are living in when the human race wakes up and moves towards a mass enlightenment.

WHAT NEEDS TO BE DONE

The largest social movement in the history of humankind is happening right now. There are over one million organizations in the world currently working toward ecological sustainability and social justice. There is power in our numbers. We outnumber the architects of the global domination agenda by more than a million to one. All we need to do is awaken against their oppression and demand justice.

The Federal Reserve needs to be audited and dismantled. Next is to disband the International Monetary Fund and World Bank entirely and start over with a new money system with full transparency—or do away with money altogether. Establish a Truth and Reconciliation Commission for the members of these organizations. For example, who are the governors of the Federal Reserve? Nobody knows. Let's investigate every one of them, and even collect testimony and evidence from the central banking system throughout history.

We also need to investigate and report on the maximum security Bilderberg Group. Named for the Bilderberg hotel in Arnhem, Netherlands, where the group first met in late May 1954, it clearly has close ties to the Illuminati or is controlled by them. It was started by a few American delegates tasked to build the USA branch of NATO's new secret service, and it should end with the banishing of all secrets. David Rockefeller and ex-Prime Ministers were among the first speakers. Today there are over 120 participants, mostly bankers, CEOs, ex Prime Ministers and international diplomats, including David Rockefeller and Henry Kissinger, both with considerable influence over the Trilateral Commission. The affairs of the Bilderberg Group have never been disclosed or made public although they publish what they claim is their agenda for meetings. But of course their meetings are by invitation only.

The spy agencies out of purview of Congress or the public, the CIA and NSA specifically, need to be investigated and dismantled. Again, a Truth and Reconciliation panel is the best way to bring to light wrong doing, name names, place responsibility, and if necessary prosecute and jail any living guilty parties. All underground bases must be made public knowledge. The CIA, NSA, MI-5, Mossad and other intelligence agencies must first be constrained, then dismantled and stripped of their resources to watch and control people in a covert manner. This may all seem like a pipe dream, but remember this is a utopian scenario.

We must hold the oil companies legally responsible for knowingly facilitating harmful climate change and suppressing free energy technology. A People of the World vs. Big Oil class action lawsuit would be a good start. If the "People" succeed, a guilty verdict will allow the complete liquidation of all carbon-creating energy companies with all of their assets going into free energy development, or in the event of bankruptcy, all assets applied to correcting climate change and damage done to the atmosphere. According to Lester Brown's Earth Policy Institute, it would take under 200 billion dollars a year to restore the Earth's environment and meet global social goals. Taxpayer funds amounting to billions of dollars, without legally required Congressional oversight, have been applied to "Unacknowledged Special Access Projects" related to black operations. A full and open accounting of all monies spent must be reviewed and reported.

Congress needs to hold open hearings on UFOs. When Gerald Ford was a Michigan Congressman he tried to have UFO hearings in the 1960s, but was denied. He never publicly tried as president. Two U.S. presidents and at least five Congresspersons have tried and failed to investigate the UFO phenomenon.

Governments have been responsible for most of the war, death, and destruction on the planet, with more than 200 million individuals killed in the 20th century alone. If we cut the U.S. military budget in half, it would still roughly equal the defense spending of the entire world's military spending combined. Isn't it time we instituted the Department of Peace? In a utopian society, there will be no need for armed forces, no need to hide anything under the cloak of national security, as heightened awareness will provide only nonviolent solutions to problems.

END OF SUPPRESSED KNOWLEDGE

Releasing information on UFOs and free energy technology only begins the list of suppressed subjects. The Powers That Were still have their tentacles in every sector where their agenda seeks centralized control. Here is a short list, just a few examples, of what else is being suppressed or marginalized, according to the film and website *Thrive*:

Organic Growing
Natural and Raw Foods
Natural Supplements
Natural Cures
Medical Marijuana Dispensaries
Independent Radio Stations
Alternative Currencies
Independent Banks
Generic and Imported Medicines
Independent Investigations into 9-11
Alternate Political Candidates
Voting Machines with Paper Trails
Voting by People of Color and Soldiers
Home Schooling
Freedom from Vaccination
Resistance to and Labeling of GMO Foods
Privacy in the Moving of Personal Money
Internet Privacy and Equality of Speed and Access
Clean Drinking Water and No GMO Foods
Transparency of the Federal Reserve and Black Budget Appropriations

THE ENDGAME TO OUR ENSLAVEMENT

Those who could face prosecution will include active or retired military brass, former and current elected officials and political appointees, top intelligence personnel, defense contractors, top media moguls, corporate executives, the Federal Reserve Board of Governors, and the top Wall Street financiers behind the "too big to fail" financial institutions. Of course, those who are suspected of being guilty will oppose anyone who would suggest they be investigated. But these power mongers must be exposed and given a fair trial, hopefully in the spirit of truth and reconciliation, and in a fully transparent world court.

When this is done, only then can we start building new institutions that are fair, transparent and truly democratic. Service-oriented success, honestly achieved, will be the only success rewarded. The money trough will be removed from the Powers That Were forever, and with its removal goes their power. Those who manipulate and exploit will no longer be rewarded. Instead, a new system will be implemented where anyone can ascend to their highest ability if they are good enough and determined enough. The vice of inbred family groups controlling everything significant to humankind will be broken.

Top Ten Actions we can do now to end our enslavement, also inspired by *Thrive*:

1. *Get Informed, Speak Up and Connect with Others*
2. *Bank Locally*
3. *Buy and Invest Responsibly*
4. *Join the Movement to Audit and End the Federal Reserve*
5. *Keep the Internet Fair and Open*
6. *Support Independent Media*
7. *Support Organic, Non-GMO Farming*
8. *Require Election and Campaign Finance Reform*
9. *Advocate for Renewable and Free Energy*
10. *Take part in Critical Mass Action*

Plus, a particularly important milestone to work toward—let's eliminate the money system altogether.

All you need to tell yourself right now is that things are worse than you could possibly comprehend or imagine. It's worse than the worst nightmare you have ever had. It is something right out of a horror film. At the same time, you cannot let this overwhelm you. It is the fear-based emotions that trigger and drag us down to their level, where we cannot possibly win. Stay informed and always remain aware of what is important in life. Tell yourself every day just how beautiful this world is, reaffirm how important you are, and how every good person you know makes an important contribution in his or her own small way. Just a smile can change another person's day. Stay positive and truthful at all times and you'll be able to detect lies and deceit much easier.

It is very easy to lose hope and lose sight of what really matters in life when you are being bombarded with disinformation and negativity like we are right now. You need to keep your mind and spirit intact in a time of such deception and wickedness. Listen to Bob Marley's *Three Little Birds* song whenever you're feeling defeated, with the encouraging lines: "Don't worry, about a thing, cuz every little thing, is gonna be all right." Give yourself a positive lift when you need to get through a tough day. Make a daily affirmation to continue your personal quest for happiness, truth, justice, and equality for all. Continue the momentum of the 1960s peace movement by advancing their slogan "If you're not part of the solution, you're part of the problem." If appropriate, encourage family and friends to discuss the subjects that are really important to you.

It may sound counterproductive, but the best way to end the prospects of enslavement is to become an advocate for nonviolence and inner peace. Change comes at an individual level. Inspired people can make a big difference just by having a positive attitude toward others. Be active in the electoral process while we still have the power to vote. Part of the end to our enslavement involves the United States becoming a truly peaceful nation by closing all its military bases around the world. A Department of Peace will replace the Department of Defense. A true utopia must resonate true in everybody's mind. No one gets left behind.

Recently passed legislation such as the National Defense Authorization Act (NDAA) enforced by Homeland Security could result in a total corporate global governance with an accompanying police state. In this new system, the role of elected government officials would be to serve as subservient agents for the transnational corporations, while the armies, police, and courts, instead of protecting citizens, would also serve the interests of these transnational corporations.

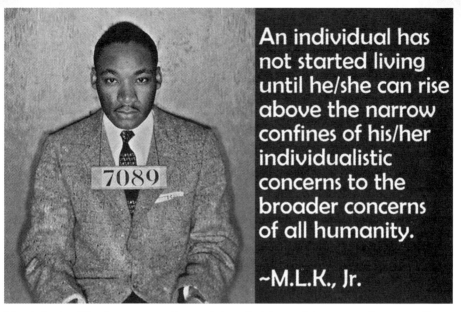

An individual has not started living until he/she can rise above the narrow confines of his/her individualistic concerns to the broader concerns of all humanity.

~M.L.K., Jr.

Martin Luther King Jr. was arrested several times for his nonviolent acts and noncompliance to an unjust system. Now the USA has a national holiday named in his honor.

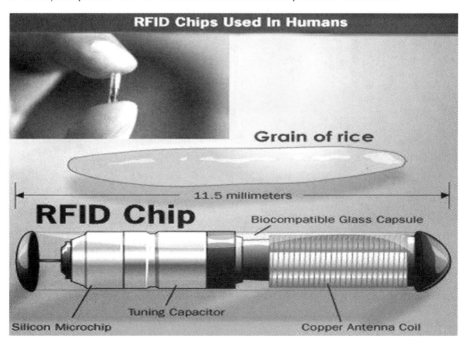

RFID Chips Used In Humans

Grain of rice

11.5 millimeters

RFID Chip

Biocompatible Glass Capsule

Tuning Capacitor

Silicon Microchip

Copper Antenna Coil

"It is no measure of health to be well adjusted to a profoundly sick society," said the mystic Krishnamurti. But your peace of mind will not help if you are implanted with a Radio-Frequency Identification (RFID) chip that can punish or even kill its host.

"And Jesus went into the temple of God, and cast out all them that sold and bought in the temple, and overthrew the tables of the moneychangers ... and said unto them, it is written, 'my house shall be called the house of prayer; but ye have made it a den of thieves.' " (Matthew 21:12) While dishonest "moneychangers" clearly inhabit many of our religious, political, and social institutions, many Biblical scholars agree that this story is untrue and was made up later for political reasons. It is still being used as justification for the use of *attack* to solve problems—a problem-solving approach that not only doesn't work, but invites counter-attack—and so the cycle continues.

THE END OF MONEY

"Permit me to issue and control the money of a nation, and I care not who makes its laws." –Mayer Amschel Rothschild (1744 - 1812)

MONEY is at the intersection of nearly every aspect of modern life. Most of us take the monetary system for granted, but it has a profound and largely misunderstood influence over our lives. Money simply does not "work" any longer. Originally it was an abstract concept that was created to allow a more efficient barter exchange between people. The concept today, that we can make money from money, has been derived essentially from the concept of gambling—creating something from nothing. And what has been deceiving about our accounting standards and financial markets is the concept that money not only does not work, it does not really exist. There is a sheer fantasy behind it all. It can cease to exist in an instant. Thus, we should get rid of it. The sooner the better. The end of money would mark the beginning of a utopian world for the vast majority of people. But what would we do for work in order to acquire the necessary goods to live and put a roof over our heads? What if we were to create a new world without money? How would things get done and how could society persist? Of course, nothing can be so black and white. There are those with supreme control over the money supply and all the inherent power that goes with it, and of course they do not want to see it end. Not now or ever. The elite will fight tooth and nail against such a transformation. And they are a formidable enemy when confronted with the elimination of their power.

As Lao Tzu observed long ago, the more laws we have the more crimes we will have. With an equal life and an equal resource system we will have only one law, that which is best for all life always. *Laissez-faire* will be the foundation for peace and happiness and is actually practical for real enlightenment. Simplicity, not a collection of trinkets, brings contentment. Take it from the Greek philosopher Socrates, "He is richest who is content with the least, for content is the wealth of nature." We can direct each relationship in a way that is best for all, which in turn will produce in every way a society that is best for all. Once we reject money by understanding the inequality it creates, we will fail to see the world as nations of people. Instead we will see one people, on one planet, all connected and interdependent with each other and all life. Instead of the pursuit of money, let's pledge an allegiance to the Earth and all the life that it supports. One planet, in our care, irreplaceable, with sustenance and respect for all. We can make this a planet of abundance for everyone, and the first step is to eliminate the class barriers that money creates.

WHAT IS MONEY, ANYWAY?

Ask yourself, where does money come from? Where does it go? Who makes it? What is it based upon? If we could reveal the money magician's secrets, what would we find? If we could look past their smoke and mirror machines, the pulleys, cogs, and wheels that create the grand illusion called money, we would find the most blatant scam in history. It's the worldwide cause of wars, boom-bust cycles, inflation, depression, prosperity for the very few, and too much disparity for all the rest.

These days, money is not backed by gold, silver or anything of real value anymore, simply because there is not enough of these precious commodities to go around. The leaders of the world were convinced two centuries ago that eliminating all gold-backed currencies was the only solution to this problem, then money could be issued via "fiat" currency. It was impossible, however, for a fiat currency system to co-exist with a gold standard system in any country. Though the term fiat is akin to saying "the Devil's Pitchfork" to any economist, the original idea behind fiat currency was that it would be backed by the wealth created by the people. The British economist Adam Smith made this point in 1776 right from the beginning in *The Wealth of Nations*: "It was not by gold or by silver, but by labor, that all the wealth of the world was originally purchased; and its value, to those who possess it, and who want to exchange it for some new productions, is precisely equal to the quantity of labor which it can enable them to purchase or command." When President Nixon took the U.S. off the gold standard in 1971, the dollar became a fully "fiat currency." The dollar was backed by nothing except the promise of the federal government that it was worth something. This action, referred to as the Nixon shock, created the situation in which the United States dollar became the sole backing of currencies and a reserve currency for the member central bank states around the world.

If any country does have a gold-backed currency they would have an unfair advantage over other nations which can just create money "out of thin air." After all, the people of the world would naturally want to invest in a gold-backed currency over any "worthless paper" counterpart. Therefore, by maintaining fiat currencies the powerful only get more powerful, while the weak become systematically weaker. Power eventually corrupts, and absolute power eventually corrupts absolutely.

ABUSES OF MONEY

"I care not what puppet is placed upon the throne of England to rule the Empire on which the sun never sets," boasted Nathan Mayer Rothschild, who by 1820 had established a firm grip on the Bank of England. He continued: "The man who controls Britain's money supply controls the British Empire, and I control the British money supply." The Second Bank of the United States was also chartered by the Rothschild-owned Bank of England to carry the American war debt. When its charter expired in 1836, President Andrew Jackson refused to renew it, saying a central bank concentrated too much power in the hands of un-elected bankers.

Thomas Jefferson warned us that there are dangers in allowing a private central bank to create America's currency. He said: "If the American people ever allow private banks to control the issue of their currency, first by inflation, then by deflation, the banks and the corporations which grow up around them will deprive the people of all property until their children wake up homeless on the continent their fathers conquered." How prophetic are Jefferson's words today, with the overreaching power of the banks, the record number of home foreclosures and citizens who cannot escape perpetual debt.

Between 1923 and 1929, the concentration of wealth at the top of the country's economic ladder was at the highest point in U.S. history. Then the stock market crashed in 1929, followed by the Great Depression, which sent millions of Americans into abject poverty. For decades afterward, the middle class grew within society at a quickened pace. As recently as 1976, America's wealthiest 1% took in only 9% of the country's income. That figure has skyrocketed in the last few decades. Today, America's wealthiest 1% accumulate 24% of all income generated each year. *Time* magazine, hardly an organization full of liberal extremists, warns that the concentration of wealth has again reached 1929 levels. To illustrate, America's wealthiest 1% own over 40% of the country's total wealth, with the bottom 80% owning a mere 7%. America's wealthiest 1% own 51% of all of the country's stocks, bonds, and mutual funds, where the bottom 50% own just one-half of one percent. It is no wonder the Occupy Movement in the fall of 2011 took off like wildfire, exposing the greedy 1% for who they are. The chokehold on wealth distribution has not been this grim since the last depression.

Clearly the current system of wealth distribution in America and around the world is terribly flawed. Powerful investors and financial institutions have abused the use of currency and the whole concept of investment. The system is completely rigged in favor of the elite. Because it is a system based on money, the result is an inadequate social arrangement which produces hunger, poverty, and scarcity. As long as there is the use of money in society, which inevitably spawns the creation of debt and economic insecurity, these conditions will continue to perpetuate crime, lawlessness, and resentment.

CONTROL OF THE WESTERN WORLD

There's nothing new about the concept of a New World Order with its aim to control all people through the use of money. The term has been in use since at least 1915, but the idea that a shadowy cabal beyond the reach of rulers and presidents is controlling world events and manipulating the masses is far older. However, the cabal is now much closer to establishing its long-desired one-world government than ever before. In fact, plans are already underway.

The original Illuminati, who took great pains to keep their personal identities unknown, were around at least since the 1780s when they stopped using the name "Illuminati." By whatever name their offspring go by today, you can be sure their influence still persists and has only gotten stronger. Their descendants are still on track to create a one world centrally controlled government, and have even been instrumental in fomenting the communist revolution which set the stage for World War II. They now operate through such organizations as the United Nations, The European Union, the Bilderbergs, the Trilateral Commission and the various banking cartels. The original Illuminati were infiltrated and taken over by Jewish bankers in 1782, when the headquarters of Illuminated Freemasonry moved to Frankfurt, Germany, a financial center controlled by the Rothschild family. Jews were admitted into the order of Freemasons for the first time in Masonic history. If indeed members of the Rothschild family or their close associates were polluted by the occultism of Adam Weishaupt's Illuminated Freemasonry, then there is a direct link between the occult and the world of finance.

Napoleon Bonaparte recognized the danger and power of the bankers when he observed, "The hand that gives is above the hand that takes. Money has no motherland; financiers are without patriotism and without decency. Their sole object is gain." With early information gained on the outcome of the Battle of Waterloo in 1815, Nathan Mayer Rothschild went on to famously bluff traders of the English Stock Exchange that Napoleon had won, and very publicly began to sell his stocks, creating a selling panic in the market. Only hours later he began to buy huge amounts of shares back (when they were pennies on the dollar) from the same investors he fooled. It is also suspected that at this time Nathan Mayer Rothschild took control of the Bank of England, the first privately owned central bank, and used this as a model for new central banks to be established worldwide.

The Rothschild dynasty remains the most dominant banking entity in the world. They have been the wealthiest family in the world for the last three centuries. The early Rothschilds soon learned that making loans to governments and kings was more profitable than giving credit to private individuals. Not only were the loans bigger with more interest, but they were secured by the nation's taxes. By the 1850s, James Rothschild in France was several times richer than all the other French bankers combined. The Rothschilds were the masterminds behind fractional reserve banking. By the end of the 19th century, one estimate put the Rothschild wealth at half of the entire world. In the early 20th century, with the Rothschild investments,

J. P. Morgan created an artificial crash so their central bank could be implemented. They succeeded in creating the U.S. Federal Reserve in 1913. Paul Warburg, architect of the Federal Reserve System, was a Rothschild agent.

Representing the interests of British aristocracy and Rothschild-front bankers such as the Warburgs, Schroders and Lazards, the Round Table promoted and continues to advance the notion of a New World Order based on Freemasonic and Illuminist concepts. The Rothschilds were known to have financed the founder of the Round Table, diamond-mining magnate Cecil Rhodes, while he lived in Africa. The Round Table advocated, both then and today, a clear reflection of Illuminist ideas including the destruction of all national sovereignties and the surrender to an elitist ruling body. The prototype is the high-sounding New World Order, an esoteric theme that inspired the philosophy of occult groups since at least the pre-Masonic Rosicrucians of the 1600s. The Round Table group was patterned (according to Cecil Rhodes) along "Masonic lines" with an inner "Circle of Initiates," including Rhodes, Lord Milner, future prime minister Arthur Balfour, and Lord Rothschild, whose banking cabal financed and influenced the English Round Table meetings. The modern incarnation is the Committee of 300, which is an international council that dictates the direction of politics, commerce, banking, media, and the military for centralized global efforts.

Today, Lord Evelyn Rothschild is the most trusted advisor to Elizabeth, Queen of England. The Houses of Rothschild, Schiff, Oppenheimer, and Warburg are among the 13 powerful banking families who form the "Ring of Power" and run the "City of London," which are all Crown holdings. Lord Rothschild is the second richest man in the world, with a controlling interest in the three leading TV networks as well as the AP and Reuter's news agencies.

FOLLOW THE MONEY

The flow of money is the flow of power. Dollars are the amoral units of power around the world, used to exploit, impoverish and enslave others. Dollars are overwhelmingly held by the super rich who are seemingly unaware of the suffering their indifference to others causes. Some of the super rich have developed altruistic programs and charitable foundations with their wealth. Unfortunately many of these agencies have been corrupted by greed and the lust for power on the part of individuals within who call the shots and hoard the assets for their own self-interests. The closer a person is to the flow of money, the more that person can divert money into their own pockets, hence the incredible wealth of bankers. The further a person is from the flow, the poorer they are. Ideas such as the public good, merit, morality, fairness, justice and rationality eventually play no part at all in the money flow. Money is entirely a "proximity phenomenon," which means the closer you are to its source, to its flow, the better. So, the rich ensure they are in closest proximity, while ordinary people find themselves estranged. Those who are furthest of all from the money flow require State handouts, charity, or must beg. In poor countries they go to sleep every night malnourished or starving. There must be a better way.

The elite 1% who control most of the world's assets appear to live in an insulated, rarified, removed and amoral domain. They control the law so they are rarely prosecuted and are so audacious that they have arranged for their unlimited theft from the public coffers to be declared legal. The bailouts that took place all over the world to save insolvent banks and thus prevent the global economy from collapsing in 2008 were actually criminal acts of theft from the elite to prevent their own from going bankrupt. They caused the financial crisis in the first place, yet the poor picked up the tab. The elite are wealthier now than they have ever been, even though most of them are not even taxpayers. The trend for the super rich is to keep their assets in hidden overseas accounts and renounce their citizenship of any country so they can avoid paying taxes entirely. The elite are largely responsible for the devastating economic situation that is currently gripping the world. While their ill-gotten gains have only increased, the taxpayers are the fools who have been saddled with the debts of the elite. The debt of the nations is now so large that it is impossible to see how it can ever be paid off without catastrophic, value-destroying hyperinflation on the same basis that swept the Third Reich to power in Germany in 1933.

The elite have ruined the world for everyone else. By any civilized rule of law, they are criminals. If the money system in which they rely upon were obliterated, it would bring about a radical improvement around the world. Because the elite show no sign of reversing their abusive pattern of hoarding wealth, money should be regarded by the rest of us as a deadly disease that must be eradicated, just as if it were smallpox. Eliminating money altogether is the only way to completely undermine the cabal's authority and power.

END THE FEDERAL RESERVE

The descendants of the Bavarian Illuminati went on to create and control the World Bank and other large financial institutions. It is the World Bank that covertly dictates global oil prices and other commodities. Individual shareholders of the World Bank also control the Federal Reserve banking system. Each Western government has the right to control its own money supply, but few exercise that right mainly because they've all been compromised by the central bankers. Countries of the world have little choice but to borrow money from the various privately run central-banking systems. Through the magic of fractional reserve banking, these central banks can create money out of thin air via the creation of money as debt, then profit on it by charging interest on the loan.

The private individuals who control much of the money and resources in the world also wield tremendous control over all Western governments, and own the largest mainstream media outlets, which means they can control the message. This private covert empire continues to use the one square mile "City of London" as its center of financial control, with the Vatican City tasked with spiritual control and Washington D.C. designated the center for military control. All are under the control of a corporate state, that is, a gigantic business enterprise. The private individuals who control this covert empire are the most powerful individuals in the world because they rule over the world monetary system. The Bank of

England was the first model for other central banks now operating in nearly every country worldwide. Within these privately owned central banks, the plutocracy is able to control each country where it operates; yet the names of these directors and investors are never revealed. Although this information is a closely guarded secret, there have been enough leaks to confirm the identities of the key banking families who own the Federal Reserve.

According to the National Association of Retired Federal Employees (NARFE) the Federal Reserve System "is not a Federal entity but a private corporation owned in part by the following: Rothschild banks of London and Berlin, Lazard Brothers bank of Paris, Israel Moses Seif banks of Italy, Warburg bank of Hamburg and Amsterdam, Chase Manhattan bank of New York, Kuhn & Loeb bank of New York, and the Goldman Sachs bank of New York." Researcher and CPA Thomas D. Schauf came to almost exactly the same conclusions, adding that ten banks control all 12 Federal Reserve bank branches. He names N.M. Rothschild of London, Rothschild Bank of Berlin, Warburg bank of Hamburg, Warburg bank of Amsterdam, Lehman Brothers of New York, Lazard Brothers of Paris, Kuhn & Loeb Bank of New York, Israel Moses Seif Bank of Italy, Goldman Sachs of New York and JP Morgan Chase Bank of New York. Schauf lists William Rockefeller, Paul Warburg, Jacob Schiff and James Stillman as the four individuals who own the largest shares of the Federal Reserve. The Schiffs are insiders at Kuhn & Loeb. The Stillmans are Citigroup insiders who married into the Rockefeller clan at the turn of the century.

The United States Federal Reserve is not federally operated at all; it is a private corporation of bankers. These bankers "volunteered" to finance the United States government when it became bankrupt during World War I. Special legislation was then passed to allow these bankers to print paper money, regardless of the fact that only the Treasury is legally allowed to coin its own money. Creating the money would be called a "loan" by the U.S. government. In turn, the U.S. government agreed to repay this loan by taxing American citizens. At this point, only a fraction of the interest is being paid on the national debt, and none of the principal. These same bankers set the national interest rate and control the economy. Our national debt is the amount owed to these bankers and our tax dollars line their pockets. The country is literally bankrupt and beholden to the banking oligarchs.

But the problem only grows exponentially. It turns out the Federal Reserve is at the epicenter of a vast "interlocking directorate" of companies that earn upwards of 80% of the entire world's wealth. In author David Wilcock's groundbreaking 2012 series of essays aptly titled *Financial Tyranny: Defeating the Greatest Cover-Up of All Time*, he reveals a "core" of 1,318 companies that directly control 20% of the world's wealth. In addition, these corporations also can be linked to owning the stock in a majority of the world's largest companies, which are the majority of the world's largest blue chip and manufacturing firms whose profits add up to an additional 60% of global revenues. A full 75% of the corporations within this "super-entity" of 147 interlocked companies are financial institutions. They include Barclays Bank, JP Morgan Chase, Merrill Lynch, UBS, Bank of New York, Deutsche Bank and Goldman Sachs. The directors and board members of the 12 Federal Reserve banks are also heading the top financial institutions.

Just five banks—JP Morgan, Bank of America, Citigroup, Wells Fargo, and Goldman Sachs Group—together held $8.5 trillion in assets at the end of 2011, equal to 56% of the U.S. economy, compared with 43% in 2006, according to central bankers at the Federal Reserve. Five years after the financial crisis, not a single one of the "too-big-to-fail" banks is smaller. In fact, they all continue to grow in size and risk.

FRACTIONAL RESERVE PYRAMID SCHEME

Our current "fractional reserve" currency system is completely dependent upon more debt in order to grow. It is a statement that may sound illogical, but it's factual. If there is less debt in the system, the system itself becomes deflationary and begins to collapse. It is important to reiterate that every single dollar is borrowed into existence, and it is then owed back with interest. Clearly it's a scam, based on a devious pyramid scheme. We pay tax for the privilege to have currency printed by a private cabal of bankers. Our entire currency system is purely phantasmal. It doesn't really exist. It's just that we are all dreaming the same dream and as soon as we wake up to these abuses, it will be all over for the global bankster cabal.

It could start like this: Let's say there was a movement to ensure that all eighth graders, or high school seniors, or even college freshmen, were required to truly understand what fractional reserve banking is, how it operates in the real world, and the toxic consequences of its very practice. Many would begin to question almost everything they had been told their entire lives on the assumption that now they were being told the truth. Clearly, this is not taught to students for a reason. Fractional reserve banking using inherently worthless fiat currency is the most cunning and destructive ruse that has ever been perpetrated upon humankind.

Fractional reserve banking as state doctrine is akin to having a system in place whereby all children are born pre-addicted to a potent drug, and then kept on that drug for the rest of their lives. The Powers That Were withdraw it or provide it in excess, depending upon what behavior they want to induce from the populace. Fractional reserve banking allows a handful of people to create a broken-willed herd of debt serfs, and it is extraordinarily efficient. If they can make individuals believe that they alone are to blame for their own misfortune because of their lack of intelligence, their inability to create wealth, or their poor work ethic, people will not rise up to overturn the system. Instead of rebelling against the economic system, individuals are manipulated into believing they are helpless and conditioned to blame themselves. This leads to a depressive emotional and mental state which undermines motivation and inhibits action. And without action, there is no revolution.

While the present currency system "is what it is" and we have to operate within it for now, it is in our best interest to learn more about how this system of creating currency really works. We can still individually choose to not participate by never taking on debt, that is, excessive or risky debt. If we choose to "opt-out," it will not feed the system and may possibly lead towards more individual liberty, freedom, and independence. An individual can begin by taking a stand against being a debt serf-slave who is beholden to their financial masters.

You can be sure this same bankster cabal has plans for our monetary future. The global elite are intentionally collapsing the U.S. dollar and attempting to replace it with a global IMF currency. Several nations, including China and Russia, have proposed replacing the dollar as the world's reserve currency. The 2009 United Nations Trade and Development Report endorsed this solution as well, blaming the current system of currencies and capital rules for the financial and economic crises. The UK newspaper *The Telegraph* claimed that the report's proposed changes represent the "biggest overhaul of the world's monetary system since the Second World War." Not only does the UN suggest a new global currency should replace the dollar, but the Vatican has endorsed this deal as well. Here again are the same perpetrators proposing a lofty-sounding *faux* solution. Sound familiar?

THE ESOTERIC NATURE OF MONEY

The provocative financial journalist Benjamin Fulford claims the people who run the financial system use an instrument known as a "Black Screen." Fulford describes this as the ultimate high-tech computer network where an enormous sum of money is supposedly hidden. These Black Screens are part of the same financial system that was created at Bretton Woods, the location where the creation of a fiat currency system occurred. The Bretton Woods Agreement set the methods of management and control over the world of banking. The post W. W. II conference also created the International Monetary Fund and the Bank for Reconstruction, now known as the World Bank. There are now quintillions of dollars that they've tried to put into the system. And, according to Fulford, that's about 33 orders of magnitude more than there is of money in the real world economy. Fulford notes that this is financially "esoteric stuff," involving thousands of trillions of dollars. He reminds us of the illusionary aspect of money with this factoid: "You've got to remember that 95 percent of the money in the world exists only as numbers in a computer. Only five percent of it exists as cash money."

As a result of Bretton Woods, central banks were forbidden from directly trading with one another. They had to have civilian intermediaries who were actually the bondholders, those investors who kept the equity in their own private accounts. Part of the Bretton Woods Agreement was that these people were supposed to deposit 80% of the yield (although this money was created out of thin air) into humanitarian relief programs, including those at the United Nations.

Fulford also says the cabal has obtained something known as the "Book of Maklumat." This is a book that details the historical ownership of much of the world's gold by a group of Asian royal families called the Dragon Family. They also have copies of the original cash certificates and evidence of how this money was transferred to the custodianship of the UN and the United States Federal Reserve for use on behalf of the international community. This evidence is hyperbole for a lawsuit with the potential to prove the private owners of the Federal Reserve Board stole this money and have been using it illegally for over 60 years. In the end, if successful, revealing this technology and all potential lawsuits will clearly illustrate how rotten to the core our current financial system has become.

VISUALIZE A WORLD WITHOUT MONEY

Imagine no banks, no cash, no wages, no bills, and no money of any kind whatsoever. What do you see? Do you imagine everyone going back to a primitive barter-lifestyle like peasants? Would there be a complete breakdown in society with no laws or social order, where people desperate or too lazy to grow their own food would steal from others to survive? Not if we are prepared first before money is completely phased out.

Think of the benefits. A deliberate decision to stop using money would make our lives many times better. Just look at your life as it is today. How free are you? Do you owe any money to anyone, or to a bank, credit card debt, college loan or a mortgage? Certainly you can't ignore these things, because if you did, you might end up losing your home, or be cut off from credit.

What about your job? Most people only work because they have to, because we all have to pay our bills. If we don't work the lights will go out, water gets turn off, phones disconnect, and we can't buy food. So you're not really that free at all. Like most people you probably think this is sadly just a fact of life—you have to work to make money to live, just like our parents did. But this is not a fact of life anymore.

Bear in mind we don't really *need* money itself. We just need the things that money buys for us, such as food, clothing, shelter, electricity, a computer and so on. Money itself is just a middleman; on its own it is completely useless. Indeed, it just causes misery to anyone who doesn't have enough of it, which is just about everyone.

CHASING THE ILLUSION

Let's start with throwing the concepts of society, religion, politics, money, and statutes into the trash can. They're all an illusion. But sometimes people don't want to hear the truth because they don't want their illusions destroyed. Like the proverbial fish who doesn't know what water is, we swim in an economy built on money that few of us can comprehend. A look toward the next stage in money's evolution can liberate us from the current grip of centralized and politicized money power. However, what is needed is not another "improved" money-based system, but specific new design proposals and exchange system structures for local, regional, national and global financial systems. The new "legal tender" takes on innovative forms that will be developed to promote local economies in communities around the nation and the world. In the transition, if we are to keep some kind of money or barter system (such as non-monetary exchange of services), the first thing we need to do is democratize the economy and restore the "credit commons," that is, access to necessities available to all based on "service" credits.

Having new road maps for healthy money in a healthy world is as vital to our souls as food, air and water are to our bodies. A new financial system should be based on merit, such as sweat-equity or a person's knowledge. When someone creates a good or service, they will have created value or wealth. It is creating something of value or backed by equity with worth such as real estate or precious metals. Currently, to make money we lose our health, and then to restore our health we lose our money. We live as if we are never going to die, and we die as if we never lived. Let us affirm instead that money and commerce could work for our deeper values of justice, caring, community, and preserving the Earth. However, since it is routinely abused, it is better in the long run to abolish money as soon as possible.

The current system is so monolithic that it's hard to remember money being anything more than just a mirage, like all power. It's hard to remember that the money system is another set of illusions, like advertising and pornography, whose functions are to generate fear and desire and keep us mesmerized, inert, and debilitated by self-doubt. These sets of illusions tell us that our souls feel empty or in pain because we don't yet have this or that, him or her, and that the people who do are somehow superior to us, and that there's something out there you can buy or achieve that will finally stop the fear and aching inside that says you're nothing until you have it. The illusion creates shame if you don't have it, or desire to gain more even if you do have it. Capitalism and greed carry no limitations.

The current system has made us feel secondary for being unemployed, or underemployed, indebted, disabled, disrespected, and otherwise judged to be inferior in our society if we are anything but rich. These are not just the downtrodden on skid row anymore; it's nearly everyone. And if we can stop hating ourselves because the system devalues us, if we can start loving ourselves and each other for exactly who we are, the world will become radically changed and beautifully different. The illusion of inescapable power we suffer under, which makes us enslaved and oppressed and willing to abuse each other over acquiring money, will simply cease to be. The end of money will be a glorious moment for humanity.

CAPITALISM FAILURES

Capitalism is about growth, progress, and change. Under capitalism the virtues of ambition, initiative, and competitiveness are praised, because those virtues serve the dynamics of capitalism. People are encouraged to always accumulate more, and never be satisfied with what they have achieved. Under capitalism, people need to have a bit of liberty, and a bit of prosperity, so that the dynamics of capitalism can operate. Without some liberty, ambition cannot be actualized, and without some prosperity, how could accumulation be pursued? Capitalism also needs the best and the brightest, but at what cost?

Pulitzer-winning journalist and best-selling author Chris Hedges has some interesting insights on the failure of education and capitalism: "We've bought into the idea that education is about training and 'success,' defined monetarily, rather than learning to think critically and to challenge. We should not forget that the true purpose of education is to make minds, not careers. A culture that does not grasp the vital interplay between morality and power, which mistakes management techniques for wisdom, fails to understand that the measure of a civilization is its compassion, not its speed or ability to consume, condemns itself to death."

It is clear the pursuit of money drives some people to be unethical. It is clear that our capitalist system, which began so optimistically as a tool for growth, progress and positive change, has become corrupt and wasteful. Perhaps capitalism is inherently corrupt because it encourages greed and mindless consumption. People struggle to compete with one another, to "get ahead" in the rat race. How much more sensible is the idea of production brigades, producing only what is needed, and using only what is sustainable. How much wiser may it be to live within our ration quotas and to accept our assigned duties, whatever they might be, in service to humanity?

In this current gradual awakening and regime change, ushering in the post-capitalist era, we are seeing a conscious orchestration of economics, politics, geopolitics, and mythology—as one coordinated consequence of a more aware populace. A whole new reality is being created; a whole new global culture. When it comes down to it, the ability to transform culture is the ultimate form of power. In only a single generation, a new culture becomes the way things are and people look back at the old ways and find it hard to believe people once lived that way.

Let's consider how the bankster royal families might respond to this threat of ongoing regime change. One likely scenario is that in the post-capitalist NWO plan, entrepreneurial virtues will be demonized. This will be important, because it could manipulate people into accepting poverty and regimentation.

NEW MODELS TO END MONEY

To summarize the current dilemma, in today's modern culture of profit, we do not produce goods based on human needs. We do not build houses based on population needs. We do not grow food to feed people. Industry's major motivation is only profit. The monetary system is currently functioning as an impediment to survival rather than a means of facilitating individual existence and growth. This imaginary tool has outlived its usefulness. What if there were a better way, a path without any money system at all, and the inherent power it provides to only a few individuals? There is no reason for a single person to suffer from malnutrition, let alone our current one in six worldwide who will go to sleep tonight hungry. Money only has power because we believe it should. If we change our perception of what money represents then we can change the way we take care of ourselves. After all, money is simply a way of distributing obligations among people.

The current faulty monetary construct which places tragic limitations on Earth's population should be phased out immediately. It is not money that people need, but the access to goods and services. Since humanity requires resources to exist, the replacement system should provide those resources directly to people without the impediment of selfish financial and political interests. The replacement system is therefore a resource-based economy as proposed by the think-tank called the Venus Project, a comprehensive plan for a sustainable society. This global resource-based economy would be gradually phased in while the monetary system is phased out. It is our birthright to have healthy food, unpolluted water, and fresh air. When the people of the world unite, the current system of control will come crashing down like a house of cards. The veil of secrecy that has controlled the masses of people for millennia is only now being lifted. Until then, as long as a social system uses money or barter, people and nations will seek to maintain positions of differential advantage. If they cannot do so by means of commerce they will resort to military intervention. This too must be unraveled by the same process of awakened and direct action.

A moneyless society would also frown upon a bartering society because bartering is similar to money and can be abused in the same way. In the beginning, money was designed to overcome the need for barter but did not solve the problem. The true reflection of a moneyless society would encourage an individual's highest passion and excitement in service to others. Specifically this would be a society based upon an individual seeking a career that seems best suited for them in an organic system where all basic necessities are provided and where routine and mundane tasks are carried out automatically using technology developed by those with passion and excitement for a particular invention. This would allow others to spend more time following their highest passion and excitement, which in turn would increase and speed up the evolutional and spiritual advancement of humanity. Plus, if everything were free and accessible, there would be little incentive to steal or cheat.

Moving up in society entirely based on a person's ability is called a "meritocracy," where anybody can advance if they really apply themselves and develop their talents. This used to be the American dream until the forces of wealth and power took over. A moneyless meritocracy will effectively destroy much of the corruption now plaguing the existing system and significantly improve the quality of life for everyone on Earth. This is only a transitional stage to a system in which money will be completely superfluous. Another idea in the transition is reissuing a commodity-based currency, in which a country's currencies are issued against commodities. These assets such as wheat, corn, steel, copper and all other commodities can be stored in a warehouse and considered as collateral.

THE GIFT ECONOMY

The gift economy, or the free economy, is a model where people can share their excess goods and acquire items they need. In a gift economy, there is no need to give if it is not possible, because giving or receiving is completely optional. In the spirit of generosity and reuse, a "free box" has been operating in Telluride, Colorado, since 1976. Visitors to the Telluride free box are encouraged to take only what they can use, or bring something of value for the next "shopper." A flagship shop based on the Telluride model has opened in Long Beach, California, and new free stores are opening in other cities.

The gift economy is alive and global among an improbable network of "couch surfers." Since its launch in 2003, the website couchsurfing.org has become an international phenomenon. It has attracted over two million registered couch surfers from around the world and facilitated millions of successful guest and host experiences. Free night stays on couches are offered in 230 countries and 74,000 towns and cities.

The Burning Man Festival in Nevada operates strictly on the gift economy. Outside vendors are not permitted at Burning Man, except for the organization selling of ice and one central café. The success of Burning Man to foster a gift economy amongst participants has the net result of raising the kookiness level of the event, simply by encouraging all to give instead of charge.

There is a peculiar response which happens when people become charitable— they become happier! Neuroscientists have located the brain's "charity spot," an area at the top and back of the brain that is busier in altruistic individuals. This region of the brain determines whether we put others before ourselves. Science has grappled with why people will put the welfare of others ahead of their own, even at a personal cost. From a standard evolutionary viewpoint it makes little sense because it does not increase the chances of someone passing on their genes. However, research shows that serving others will boost the immune system. Furthermore, the act of being charitable involves the uppermost portion of the brain, allowing a warm glow that many donors report receiving from the act of giving. Being generous stimulates the same brain mechanisms that evoke pleasurable sensations after sex, eating good food, and using heroin or other euphoric drugs.

A leading expert on gratitude, University of California-Davis professor, Dr. Robert Emmons, finds that people who faithfully cultivate generosity report a host of physical, psychological, and social benefits. Gratitude celebrates the present, blocks negative emotions, and affirms goodness by recognizing external, greater-than-self factors. People who are grateful have a higher sense of self worth because they are continually aware that others are looking out for their best interests. It is also gaining the satisfaction of giving simply for the love of sharing. For example, hedge fund billionaire Warren Hellman bequeathed the resources for the Hardly Strictly Bluegrass free concert in San Francisco's Golden Gate Park to continue a decade past his unfortunate passing in December, 2011. Who will be remembered more favorably, Warren Hellman or an anonymous billionaire who died with a pile of "fuck you" money? As we wake up, a more enlightened objective might be not how much you can earn, but if you do make it, how much you can give away. There's no reason to be the richest dead guy in the graveyard.

The gift economy will change the current culture of greed and competition, to a society focusing on cooperation and sharing, eliminating the need to compete for limited resources. With enough to go around it would be reasonable to ask every adult to set aside several hours of each working day to contribute something for the common good. All of people's needs would be met and society could then function. Call it a new currency of love. Call it people working together to share and help elevate other people. Selfishness is no longer an operative word when all strive to serve, such as the ultimate lesson taken from the Hermann Hesse novel *Journey to the East*: "the servant is the master."

THE RESOURCE-BASED ECONOMY

A resource-based economy is a social system concerned with the sustainability of human health and our planet. Believe it or not, our planet has plenty of resources to provide for everyone. The only thing we're short of is money. So why not just make everything free? Forget about money all together? Why not? It's our world, so we can make our own rules! Human conduct should be aligned to how our reality works by recognizing sound scientific principles. All humans really need for a healthy life is clean air, fresh unpolluted water, arable land, fresh food, and adequate shelter. Include technology and mechanization and we can all enjoy a high standard of living. The real wealth of any nation is measured in its potential and actual resources, plus the development of a more humane way of life. A resource-based economy would use technology to overcome apparent scarce resources by utilizing renewable and free sources of energy, while people can work towards the elimination of previously perceived scarcity. Technology will also allow computerized and automated manufacturing, inventory and distribution. We can use technology to design safe and energy-efficient cities. Technology will provide universal health care and relevant education for all. And most of all, technology will generate a new incentive system based on both human and environmental concerns.

International economist David Korten, who has set up business schools in low-income countries, proposes that we create real wealth through increased political participation. This can be achieved by basing value on living systems rather than on the money system, by shifting power from global financial markets to local, community-controlled economies, and by expanding the areas of our lives that are based on gift economies, selfless barter, mutual aid, and caring for the greater good. All social systems, regardless of political philosophy, religious beliefs, or social customs, ultimately depend upon natural resources, that is, living systems rather than a money system.

The human aspect must be of prime concern to any future society, with technology subordinate to this goal. This would result in a considerable increase in leisure time for all. We can harken back to emulate the ancient Greeks who considered daily discussions of philosophy and exercise on the beach as among the highest callings. In a modern economy where production is accomplished primarily by computers or machines, and products and services are available to all, the concepts of "work" and "earning a living" will become irrelevant. A community that extols the splendor of sharing also cooperates more, which leads to less crime, conflict and inequalities. It also makes individuals feel better about themselves and other people. Cybernation, or the application of computers and automation to the social system, could be regarded as an emancipation proclamation for humankind if used humanely and intelligently. No longer will people have to toil away at jobs they hate. Its thorough application could eventually enable people to have the highest conceivable standard of living with practically no labor. A resource-based economy could free people for the first time in human history from a highly structured and outwardly imposed routine of repetitive and mundane activity. It could enable us to return to the Greek concept of leisure, where slaves did most of the work and men had time to cultivate their minds. However, in the future, each of us will command more than a million slaves, but they will be mechanical and electrical slaves, never again our fellow human beings.

A resource-based economy by definition includes the necessary participation of all people to share in its benefits. Plus, there are some things that money just cannot buy, such as manners, morals, intelligence, or as the Beatles suggested, "love." In a monetary system there is an inherent reason for corruption, and that is to gain a competitive advantage over someone else. Without vested interests or the use of money, there is no benefit in falsifying information or taking advantage of anyone. There would be no need for any underlying rigid social barriers that would limit the participation of anyone or restrain the introduction of new ideas. Truth would never be withheld, not even from children. The main objective would be the access of information and the availability of goods and services to all people. Without greed or competition, people would be far better prepared to participate in the exciting challenges of this new society. Learning would become a lifelong pursuit. If overpopulation became a burden, trained personnel could volunteer to colonize other Earth-like planets, or even a terra-formed Mars.

The method for the distribution of goods and services without the use of money or tokens could be accomplished through the establishment of distribution centers, which would be similar to a public library or an exposition, where the advantages of new products would be explained and demonstrated. With the infusion of a resource-based economy, we will soon have new, clean and free sources of energy in unlimited quantity that will serve civilization for many thousands of years.

It cannot be stressed enough that it is not money that people need, but rather it is freedom of access to most of their necessities without having to appeal to a government bureaucracy or any other agency. Just walk right up and get anything you need at any time. In a resource-based economy, money is completely irrelevant. All that would be required are the resources, manufacturing, and distribution of needed products.

INTO THE SPACE AGE

With today's technology just about everything we produce for ourselves is done by machines or computers. This is one reason we have high unemployment everywhere, because machines have taken over so many jobs. But maybe this is a good thing. After all, technology can completely free us from hard labor, so we should be grateful. If we don't need people to produce the stuff we consume, then surely the producing is easy, and if producing stuff is easy, then there's absolutely no reason we shouldn't be doing it for everybody, not just the ones who can pay. Think how much less waste there would be. At the moment our economy is all about moving money around and making a profit. It has nothing to do with actually providing for the people of the world what they need. The only constraint to producing the goods we need should be what's physically possible, not what's affordable.

The only thing money creates is terrible inequality, a scoring system for humanity that decides who gets what and most people end up with the short end of the stick. For the first time in history our technology allows us to do away with this notion of haves and have-nots. But that's only the beginning. Making our world money-free would unleash our full technological potential and allow us to tap into revolutionary clean and free energy sources. It would bring meaningful prosperity and knowledge all across the world, and it would even put an end to war and injustice forever.

Our world will be much better without money. Just imagine food produced to the highest standards in plentiful supply. Starvation would be completely wiped out forever. We could have bigger and better hospitals and schools without any budgetary problems. There would be abundant energy, easy communication, space exploration, and underwater cities available to everyone. All of this would facilitate a peaceful transition toward meaningful contact with benevolent entities of other worlds. Sound too utopian? What about UFOs or time travel? Legendary scriptwriter Gene Roddenberry was supposedly inspired by séance sessions foretelling future worlds, including on Earth. There is no episode in the *Star Trek* series where the use of money is seen. Just speak out loud what it is that you desire, and out it comes. No tokens, credit cards or money in any form is ever used in the entire *Star Trek* franchise of TV shows or movies.

Take away costs, and the only limit is our imagination and the raw materials needed to make whatever we want. In today's society, if you don't have money, basically you die. This is not just wrong, but completely immoral, simply because it's unnecessary. There is another way, a new way, a better world without money, where everything is free, where you are free, where we can provide for everyone and finally see an end to malnutrition, poverty, and all social injustices. This will be the Golden Age on Earth. We can live in a world where society is as fair as it possibly can be, and where technology is unhindered by costs so advanced that we would hardly recognize ourselves in a generation or two. It's all possible right now if we choose a money-free future for our children and for the sake of our planet. Exploitation of everything would end.

FOUR PRINCIPLES

Every animal species takes care of its own, except oddly the human species. This has to change if we are meant to reach our fabled utopia. Every enlightened society is able to provide basic care for all its citizens. No one falls through the cracks ever again. This is not only do-able but absolutely necessary for our collective advancement. However, in creating a egalitarian new world without money, we have to define our terms. The first principle is that no human will have to go hungry ever again. The weakest link is always a barometer for the best and worst potential of the entire population. The second principle is that everyone should be given free access to the basic necessities such as shelter, electricity, clean water, nutritious food and adequate health care. The third, which we already have, is the right to a basic education, but the learning process can continue for a lifetime, and higher education is also free. In this utopian unified theory model all people would participate in the Laws of Consistency, which allows for each upcoming generation to receive all the new information gathered when it becomes known, and then they can improve upon it as matured adults and continue to make new breakthroughs. Nothing is ever withheld from anybody in the Age of Transparency, and every asset that is available to one is available to all. Lastly, the fourth principle is that our educational system becomes completely uncorrupted, and geared towards universal truths. As such, we'll see the introduction of personal holographic technology and lessons geared to teaching people meaningful spirituality on a macro and individual basis. All will voluntarily seek inner peace, their peace with others, and peace with the natural world.

In this enlightened society, children from an early age will be taught tasks that are useful to a free energy, resource-based society. After receiving a high school education each individual is given an aptitude test. If a person does not wish to continue on to college they are given the choice of any labor-related job, or no job at all. If they want to sit in their dorm room and play video games all day that's fine. Everybody chooses for themselves what they aspire to do with their life. Those who wish to extend their free education into specific professions may do so, but they must prove their aptitude at different levels to continue. When adults leave school they know they are required to donate part of their day to the career they have chosen in service to others. The man who loves animals will go to work at a ranch, just as the woman with an aptitude for science will enjoy going to the laboratory on her workdays. Work is no longer a chore, but a personally rewarding experience, as everyone knows that the fruit of their labor contributes in a small way towards everyone's benefit. When people perform their tasks at an optimum level, they are given rewards and, as their education and experience has taught them, these will not necessarily be material. Those who do not strive for personal perfection or who are handicapped will always have their essential needs provided. Those who decide to help in service to others and advance civilization will be rewarded in ways they prefer as the most fulfilling. In a new world without money, we must develop new ethics that will not allow anyone to be abandoned no matter what their circumstances, have all their basic necessities met, and even provide spiritual training. In the end, such a system will elevate every person and preserve the planet for future generations growing up in an ever-dynamic utopian society.

This is a "Continental dollar," actually based on something of worth, redeemable for actual silver dollars during the colonial era. The stunning conclusion is that the financial system in the West is an illusion used by a secret cabal to keep us enslaved. This growing awareness suggests we are now about to become truly free in ways that will exceed many people's most optimistic expectations.

The Federal Reserve System constantly decreases the value of our dollar by printing money out of thin air. The fiat money we now use is based on nothing, unlike the dollar when it was backed by silver or gold. The Federal Reserve Act of 1913 must be revoked, and Executive Order 11110, still valid, must be reinstated, authorizing the Treasury Department to print, issue, and distribute United States Notes that are interest and debt free. The United States government and the American citizens must no longer be dependent on and in perpetual debt to the elite banking cartel for their privately issued money.

ANNUIT COEPTIS 'announcing conception'

Illumined eye Great architect 'Lucifer'

NOVUS ORDO SECLORUM 'Secular New Order'

13 letters in motto E PLURIBUS UNUM 'One of Many'

13 illuminated Stars - 13 enlightened Colonnies

13 Layers of Brick - 13 Original collonies 72 Bricks - 72 Powers of the name of God in Qabbalah

MDCCLXXVI - 1776 Date 'illuminati' formed mDCcLXxVI = 666

13 Arrows, 13 leaves 13 Berries - Different powers possessed by the 13 colonies

Pheonix not an eagle rising from the ashes, or ignorant world

9 Tail feathers - 9 spheres risen through to return to heavenly state

Why is there occult symbolism on the U.S. dollar bill? Some say it symbolizes the true controlling forces of the United States, those who own and control the puppet government. *E pluribus unum* means "Out of many, one" which some translate to mean "Out of many governments, a one world government."

What do we need money for anyway? To get the goods and services we need. This is the free box at Burning Man, an event that runs strictly on the "gift economy."

ENDGAME-LOVE

"Act boldly and mighty forces will come to your aid."
-Johann Wolfgang von Goethe

SEEING is not always believing, much less understanding. What matters is seeing with a conscientious and open perspective. History provides many examples of people witnessing phenomena that were refuted outright by higher authorities. A good example is Renaissance astronomer Galileo Galilei who failed to get the pope, priests, and even scientists of the period to look at Jupiter's moons through a telescope. They knew they would see new things and their world quite literally would be turned upside down—so they refused to look through the telescope. The lesson is that nobody can see new horizons until they are willing to look beyond their own shoreline. Perspective is everything.

Consider your life and those around you. We are living on a stunningly beautiful planet with so much wonder, magnificence and abundance. We do not seem to comprehend how lucky we are to be alive right now on this planet we call Earth. Nature is such a beautiful gift that it is hard to appreciate the forest for the trees. Many feel lost because we've become cogs in the wheel of the mass madness called society. Look at the species of animals that live in your neighborhood and think of how astonishing these animals are to have evolved to the point they are now. If you don't care about yourself and your own future, then at least do something for the sake of the animals that depend on the planet just as much as we do. Don't go around accusing the average person for being who they have become. We are the outcome of multiple, mostly negative determinants. There are the societal forces that intentionally molded us this way. There are the toxins people consume on a daily basis which harm our natural survival instincts and even affect our ability to think. Yet, our alleged victimhood is only superficial. There is a beautiful endgame for us, but only if we can change our focus to loving all that is around us, even, as Jesus preached, our "enemies" who caused this mess.

A good way to start embracing love is to find easy ways to practice compassion. This is amazingly simple. Remember, there can be no such thing as a small act of kindness. Every act creates a ripple effect with no logical end. A kind and compassionate act is often its own reward. The Greek philosopher Socrates observed "The highest realms of thought are impossible to reach without first attaining an understanding of compassion." All living beings seek happiness, so let your compassion extend itself to all. Do it for your own self-betterment. A compassionate world begins with each one of us as an embodiment, and if we all practice it, the world will be transformed. How could it not be? "Compassion, in which all ethics must take root, can only attain its full breadth and depth if it embraces all living creatures and does not limit itself to mankind," said Albert Schweitzer, "It is a man's sympathy with all creatures that first makes him truly a man."

NOOSPHERE AND THE PSI BANK

The "noosphere," according to the understanding of Vladimir Vernadsky and Teilhard de Chardin, denotes the "sphere of human thought." The word is derived from the Greek word *nous*, meaning "mind," and *sphaira*, meaning "sphere." In lexical analogy it is related to "atmosphere" and "biosphere." The noosphere is in the upper atmosphere, located between the radiation belts. By the constructs of Vernadsky and de Chardin, our brains are electromagnetic and can thus affect the electromagnetic fields. Author José Arguelles calls the noosphere a circumpolar Rainbow Bridge surrounding the planet. A new phase change occurred at the end of the year 2012, and this has taken us into the beginning of the Psychozooic Era.

The noosphere is best described as a sort of "collective consciousness" among all human beings. It emerges gradually from the highest interaction of human minds. The noosphere has grown in step with the organization of the human mass in relation to itself as it populates the Earth. As humankind organizes itself in more complex social networks, the higher the noosphere will grow in awareness. This is an extension of Teilhard's Law of Complexity and Consciousness, the law describing the nature of evolution in the universe. Teilhard de Chardin added that the noosphere is growing towards an even greater integration and unification, culminating in the Omega point, which he saw as the goal of history. The goal of history, then, is an apex of thought and consciousness. Teilhard de Chardin commented that, "The more complex a being is, so our Scale of Complexity tells us, the more it is centered upon itself and therefore the more aware does it become. In other words, the higher the degree of complexity in a living creature, the higher its consciousness; and vice versa. The two properties vary in parallel and simultaneously. If we depict them in diagrammatic form, they are equivalent and interchangeable."

If it is possible to spiritually unify and coordinate ourselves telepathically all over the planet, we will need a common goal. How can this be done? First, by understanding the how. The global memory matrix is known as the "psi bank," which regulates all of the thinking layers that exist. The psi bank is a magnetic memory field around the Earth which is influencing biological evolution. These thinking layers act much like a membrane, similar to the membrane of a eukaryotic cell. There are also layers on the physical, the spiritual, the astral and the etheric planes. These outer layers exist in the Earth's spheres, including the radiation and magnetic belts. They are fourth- and fifth-dimensional zones of consciousness wherein structural codes of harmonious growth and development are stored. These codes can be accessed through the use of sacred rituals, metaphysical arts, and esoteric sciences. They can also be accessed by looking within.

KNOW THYSELF

Many neuroscientists and psychologists agree that we consciously use only a small fraction of our brains. What if we were able to tap into the major portion of our unused mental capacities? Could it make us extremely smart? That depends how you define smart. Having book smarts or street smarts will not help us heal our own selves. Your mind is powerful enough to make you sick. It is also powerful enough to allow you to heal yourself. This will be the real therapy process in the future. Eventually there will be a step-by-step process where every individual can get in touch with his or her subconscious mind and in turn gain access to the "universal mind." Technology therapy using ET headbands that can access our past lives will recover vast amounts of lost, forgotten or hidden knowledge relevant to who we really are as spiritual individuals.

Our lesson in this age is to know ourselves. If you want to live in a beautiful, peaceful world, it is your choice. Conversely, it is also your choice to live in fear and anger. It does not matter if you have had a horrible domestic life or a bad childhood. That focus is what holds us to "old" Earth. What's important is letting go of the negative emotions. Let go of fear. Embrace forgiveness. Focus on peace and harmony and you really can have that in your life. We all have the power to heal our lives and everyone needs to know that. We think so often that we are helpless, but we're not. We always have the power of our minds. Claim and consciously use your power. We can change the future with our thoughts. Until we have access to the headbands, this form of self-therapy still works best.

In the end, developing a personal philosophy that feels right to you is the best solution. A personal philosophy should be concerned with questions of ultimate meaning, such as the purpose of life, the relation between mind and body, and an understanding of a higher power in the universe. The primary religious values of love and compassion appear to be almost completely divorced from shaping the economic and political life of our culture. Most politicians and corporate decision makers focus on fame and fortune for themselves, which is in service to self. An ego-based philosophy that does not value kindness, that does not seek to share its bounty, and that measures its self worth according to wealth, status, and reputation will ultimately fail. The same is true for organized religions when they become biased against selected groups and driven by political ambitions instead of loving and kindness. Poet Ella Wheeler Wilcox observed, "so many gods, so many creeds, so many paths that wind and wind, while just the art of being kind is all the sad world needs." So simple.

Love is the primary philosophical value common to the origin of all the world's religions; a simple four letter word that means so much. The religions of the world are aligned when they agree that "divine love" is the force which creates and sustains our world. Our primary purpose, when embodied, is to grow in our ability to understand and express this divine love. The majority of the world's religions advocate that we practice compassion and forgiveness towards others, that we treat people as we ourselves would like to be treated, and that we not obsess over material possessions. The good life according to religion consists not in the pursuit of money, reputation, status or power, but rather in the pursuit of the right relationship with the divine. Access to the divine is through learning to know the deepest part of ourselves. This will lead to the belief that "success" by afterlife standards is measured not in terms of publications, grants, wealth or reputation, but rather by acts of kindness and compassion towards others. Thus, materialism is false, and consciousness can and does exist independently of the body. Those who are aware of this truth have been dubbed "quantum activists."

NO FEAR

When each of us can banish fear from our lives we will have the ability to expand in amazing ways. By losing fear, the challenges we face in life will then become great opportunities. For if it were not for the challenges, the opportunities we are provided would not be so profound. Losing fear is a power we all have, and it has the capacity to unite the human family. It will help us embrace unity consciousness. It will allow us to develop peaceful noncompliance to an unfair system and yet remain focused on happiness and staying positive.

Sound too difficult to lose fear? Then try a little experiment. Begin each day with a random act of kindness. By doing this we instantly change the energy field. Polarized energy—the cultivation of conflict and differences, with its accompanying distrust, anger, violence and fear—is promoted by the Powers That Were to keep us divided. Once we see through their program, we can truly break the bonds of subservience and unify the human race. Just remember—there is a lot of trickery in the world. Sometimes it is difficult to deal with angry people, a broken system, or the very real threat of physical violence, but with motivation and discipline you can remember that fear will keep you down while love will bring you up.

Human evolution is the evolution of consciousness. Even the Earth we live on is a living and conscious life form with complete awareness of itself. In turn, humans are evolving alongside it. Consciousness itself is evolving, creating a new reality, and humans are the vector, as above so below. The choice between love and fear lies within all of us. When we forget, we can always choose once again. The entire human race is in reality one singular consciousness. What keeps us united is our collective focus on love; what divides us is going into fear. Remain centered in your heart, with a connection to the heart of the Earth, and spread goodness wherever you go. This will be the best way to prepare for the coming changes. But the most important factor is letting go of fear. Release negative emotions, no matter how bad, no matter how much a condition or circumstance is "someone else's fault." Don't give away yourself. Forgive yourself. Forgive others.

We've all heard of karma. When you create fear you create a great deal of karma. This is an assurance you'll be reborn on Earth time and again until you embrace love and forgiveness. Follow the one universal law of unconditional love and it will return back to you many fold. Besides, after we die what is there to fear, or to hate, or to judge any longer? Understand that the life we are living in this reality is a game of free will being played out of single consciousness in which we are all frequencies and shafts of light in the holographic universe. Embrace it, become it, and willfully bring it into your life, because pure love energy is the essence of what we are and from whence we've come. If you want a second opinion, then take it from Albert Einstein. He said, "Everything is energy and that's all there is to it. Match the frequency of the reality you want and you cannot help but get that reality. It can be no other way. This is not philosophy. This is physics."

Next time you feel fearful, try to remember the Mayan wisdom term *In Lak'ech*, which means "I am Another Yourself," or I am you, and you are me. We are all one, we are all in this together, and fear will only hold us back. If still in doubt that fear-based emotions should no longer have a place in your life, remember these words from the Dalai Lama, "Anger is the ultimate destroyer of your own peace of mind."

THE LOVE VIBRATION

Japanese author Dr. Masaru Emoto has conducted worldwide research on the effect of thoughts, words, music and intentions upon water molecules. His extensive research concluded that words can actually convert the vibrations of nature into sound. According to Dr. Emoto, an emotional discharge by a person can alter the structure of localized water crystals. Positive emotional changes can be achieved through prayer, music, or by attaching written words to a container of water. Dr. Emoto claims that there are many differences in the crystalline structure of the water depending on the type of water source. He collected samples from all over the world and documented that a water sample from a pristine mountain stream, for example, will show a geometric design that is beautifully shaped when frozen. On the other hand, polluted water sources will show a definite distortion and their structure is more randomly formed. Displaying a more neutral pattern, an ice crystal of distilled water exhibits a basic hexagonal structure with no intricate branching.

His research further indicates that when human speech or thoughts are directed at water droplets before being frozen, images of the resulting water crystals will be "beautiful" or "ugly" depending upon whether the words or thoughts were positive or negative. Our intention with the words we choose has a real effect on the material world. Considering that the human body is made up of over 80% water, it really *does* matter how we speak and think about ourselves and others. Thoughts as well as words are things. Choose them wisely. Love needs to be based in gratitude, and gratitude needs to be based in love. According to Dr. Emoto, these two words together create the most important positive vibration in water crystals.

Cymatics is the study of visible sound and vibration. In the living as well as non-living parts of nature, the trained eye encounters widespread evidence of systems in a periodic state of vibration. The systems of sound and vibration show a continuous transformation from one set of conditions to the opposite set. We see everywhere examples of vibrations, oscillations, pulses, wave motions, wind patterns, pendulum swings, rhythmic courses of events, serial sequences, and their effects and actions. Everything owes its existence solely and completely to sound. Indeed, according to cymatics, vibration creates matter. Sound is the factor which holds it together.

Similarly, our reality is holographic, with each portion or segment containing the whole. If you amplify its frequency, the structure of matter will change. It becomes evident that there is a predictability about the study of harmonics and their standing wave patterns. Not surprisingly, this predictability expresses itself in a series of mathematical relationships which correlate the wavelength of the wave pattern to the length of the medium. Additionally, the frequency of each harmonic overtone is mathematically related to the frequency of the first harmonic. All matter originates and exists only by virtue of a force which brings the particle of an atom to vibration and holds this most minute "solar system" of the atom together. Everything from the atomic level to the far reaches of the galaxy has this same correlated frequency, vibration and sound, suggesting we are all existing in a holographic universe. Knowing that any one thing influences everything else, how could we strive for anything less than being the best possible person we can be? Again, whatever the question, love is the answer.

THE EARTH VIBRATION

The incredible truth is that we humans vibrate at the same pulse rates as the living planet Earth. This aligns the human race with all other living organism and sentient beings, including light, in the ladder or chain of existence. This alignment is the vertical axis of consciousness, linking us outward towards the noosphere and the psi bank. We can think of our levels of consciousness in vibrational terms. The iron-core crystal in the center of Earth vibrates at 40 hertz (Hz), which is equal to 40 pulses per second. When the mind is most active and creative, it pulsates with the core at 40 Hz. This is the beta wave state associated with normal waking consciousness. When we are in this beta state, we are resonating with the Earth's inner iron-core crystal. When the mind is relaxed and meditative it vibrates with the Earth's inner spheres, those from the core to the crust. We pulse progressively slower from 40 Hz down to 7 Hz as our relaxation increases.

Alpha waves are reduced with open eyes, drowsiness and eventually sleep. In the beta through alpha states we are resonating with the inner Earth. Our brains vibrate in alpha at 13 to 8 Hz, so we resonance with the inner Earth when in both beta and alpha waves. The Earth's crust vibrates at around 7.5 Hz. This is the transition between alpha and theta waves. When we are drowsy or in light sleep, alpha waves are reduced and our minds pulse with theta waves at 7 to 4 Hz as our consciousness begins to move out into the atmosphere. The Earth's Van Allen belt, the inner belt of radiation that contains charged particles held in place by the Earth's surface, is 7 to 4 Hz. This means that when our minds pulse in theta, we are resonating with the atmosphere and the inner Van Allen belt.

When we are in a deep sleep, our minds are in the delta range at 4 to 1 Hz, which means we are resonating far outside the planet. In the deepest stages of delta sleep, we are vibrating with the outer Van Allen belt and out to the magnetopause, the interface between Earth's electromagnetic fields and the solar system. The magnetopause is where the pressure from the solar wind and the planet's magnetic field are equal. In other words, when we are thinking the most intensely and having creative flashes of genius, we are vibrating with the iron-core crystal. When we are in the deepest states of concentration, we are connected directly to the core of Earth's central intelligence, and when we let go, relax, and fall asleep, our minds move out of the fields of the planet. When we move out into space, we leave our bodies, the Earth and move into the celestial realms. Similarly, the first dimension is the iron-core crystal in the center of the Earth. The second dimension is the outer and inner core. The third dimension is the crust. The forth dimension is Earth's atmosphere extending all the way through the inner and outer Van Allen belts and out to the magnetopause. The fifth dimension and higher are beyond the magnetopause. Of course, we are living our waking hours in the third dimension.

BE THE CHANGE YOU WISH TO SEE IN THE WORLD

We wait for the day when all people of all races and colors can live together in total respect and trust on a planet that is clean, healthy and abundant. In fact, we can bring this into the world fairly easily and efficiently, but it must begin within each of us. In our daily lives, we can start each day by seeking wisdom, being truthful, practicing generosity and hold the conviction that compassion for all life is important.

In our hearts and minds, we must first develop a love for ourselves, then for those around us, and eventually for every living person and every living thing. This is gained by a sense of reason and compassion. We must move toward bringing an end to all aggression, conflicts and acts of violence, as well as criminality and discord, and we must do so without hate, revenge, jealousy, privation, misery, murder, terror or wars. We must recognize creation and life through evolution as the highest goal and meaning of life, manifesting true peace and love for all despite skin color, race or faith. Eventually we must forgive everyone, even if certain individuals brought us harm. Let go of all grievances. Our personal grudges will be our baggage to carry until we can finally lay them aside. Forgive those "who spitefully use you" is what Jesus meant by expressing unconditional love.

For those fed up with the financial world and all its inequalities, simply do not participate until we can abolish money. Stop paying for credit, stop paying the bankers' tax, use interest-free credit schemes. Buy your consumer durables second hand. Buy all market goods from family businesses, farmer's markets and charities. Stop watching TV news. Avoid violent movies or video games. Stop reading mainstream newspapers. If possible, leave your publicly limited company job. Demand that bankers give back the wealth they've robbed from humanity.

"In the end, we return to the question, just how much do you love truth?" inquires author Scott Mandelker. "Do you really love truth or are you just curious? Do you love it enough to rebuild your understanding to conform to a reality that doesn't fit your current beliefs, and doesn't feel 120% happy? Do you love truth enough to continue seeking even when it hurts, when it reveals aspects of yourself (or human society, or the universe) that are shocking, complex and disturbing, or humbling, glorious and amazing—or even, when truth is far beyond human mind itself? Just how much do we love truth? It's a good question to ask ourselves, I think." We need to strive to be completely truthful as individuals if we are to fully embrace love. Never forget that truth is a constant in the universe, no matter how much any truism may appear to hurt. Just as George Orwell noted, "In a time of universal deceit, telling the truth is a revolutionary act."

MANIFEST YOUR DESTINY

The goal is to reach universal consciousness, when one will become the many. To achieve this, focus on positive good thoughts. Laugh out loud and be happy to quicken it into existence. Love, happiness, joy, and laughter at the exact moment you focus your creation, manifests what you want instantaneously. Thoughts without emotion dissolve. Here are five simple rules for happiness: free your heart from hatred; free your mind from worries; live simply; give more; expect less. You must be happy with what you wish to manifest. Pay no attention to that which makes you sad, angry, frustrated or depressed. Pay full attention to love, peace, abundance, truth, honesty, justice, and caring. These positive emotions add energy to the positive vibration of unconditional love. Adding energy to this vibration of love brings it into being effortlessly. Collective consciousness of love manifests into our reality almost instantly. When happiness and love are combined it brings manifestation into existence rapidly to all those around you.

Get ready for your own graduation process.

Humanity is lifting the veil of illusion. All participants are advised to distinguish between literary dogma and universal truth. This universal truth is to be found inside each and every one of us. We've learned it all, and we have all the wisdom and knowledge of the universe within us. It is time for the human race on planet Earth to turn inside out, and collectively reach for our highest potential, a true one world order benefitting all. Great truths are deceptively simple, just as profound truths are always right before our eyes, yet often masked by clever deceptions.

In our modern world, the most insidious deception is the illusion of separation. Religions, nations, races, and politics keep us divided, but in truth each and every individual alive in this world is a unique expression of planet Earth itself. Our very flesh, the air we breathe, the food we consume, the water we drink, the blood in our veins, every component of the instrumentalities of our technological society, down to the smallest microchip, all come from the living planet Earth. We are inextricably one with the world we inhabit. We are each of us, individualized expressions of the consciousness of the Earth itself, just as it is an individualized expression of the consciousness of our galaxy, just as our galaxy is an individualized expression of all creation. The great masters fully understood this ultimate truth of spiritual unity. Jesus said, "Verily I say unto you, inasmuch as ye have done it to one of the least of these my brethren, ye have done it to me."

DESIDERATA

Max Ehrmann was a lawyer and poet from Terre Haute, Indiana, who lived from 1872 to 1945. He wrote *Desiderata* in 1927 at the age of 55, which made him famous, but only after his death. The title means a list of desirable items. It has been reported that *Desiderata* was inspired by an urge that Ehrmann noted in his diary: "I should like, if I could, to leave a humble gift—a bit of chaste prose that had caught up some noble moods." Like Lao Tzu in his book *The Way*, Max Ehrmann captures the essence of being and correct living in such concise prose. Here is *Desiderata* in it entirety:

"Go placidly amid the noise and the haste, and remember what peace there may be in silence. As far as possible without surrender be on good terms with all persons. Speak your truth quietly and clearly; and listen to others, even to the dull and the ignorant; they too have their story.

Avoid loud and aggressive persons, they are vexations to the spirit. If you compare yourself with others, you may become vain or bitter; for always there will be greater and lesser persons than yourself.

Enjoy your achievements as well as your plans. Keep interested in your own career, however humble; it is a real possession in the changing fortunes of time.

Exercise caution in your business affairs, for the world is full of trickery. But let not this blind you to what virtue there is; many persons strive for high ideals, and everywhere life is full of heroism.

Be yourself. Especially do not feign affection. Neither be cynical about love; for in the face of all aridity and disenchantment it is as perennial as the grass.

Take kindly the counsel of the years, gracefully surrendering the things of youth. Nurture strength of spirit to shield you in sudden misfortune. But do not distress yourself with dark imaginings. Many fears are born of fatigue and loneliness.

Beyond a wholesome discipline, be gentle with yourself. You are a child of the universe, no less than the trees and the stars; you have a right to be here.

And whether or not it is clear to you, no doubt the universe is unfolding as it should. Therefore, be at peace with God, whatever you conceive Him to be. And whatever your labors and aspirations in the noisy confusion of life, keep peace in your soul. With all its sham, drudgery and broken dreams; it is still a beautiful world.

Be cheerful. Strive to be happy."

AND BACK TO OUR UTOPIA

Let us assume the endgame will be love and there will be world peace. Let's say a younger generation will come together in unity consciousness, and by doing so put an end to all wars, poverty and a reversal to environmental destruction. Money will lose its power to enslave. Problems are solved nonviolently and no one is left behind. Utilizing new technologies will produce opportunities on the horizon never before imagined. Humanity will be set free.

Breakthroughs will include the introduction of free energy available to all people with no pollution. With unlimited free power, energy companies will have to re-invent themselves. As their markets wind down, oil companies will realize they are in the liquid transportation business and can start moving fresh water supplies to needy locations around the planet. Oil refineries can be rebuilt as desalinization plants. Major engineering companies can respond to rising sea levels by creating canals that divert the excess seawater into barren lowlands inside the continents to form wetlands where it is needed. Neighborhoods will take on a wide variety of energy producing solutions to become fully independent, but not totally separate from the power grid.

Small acts, when multiplied by millions of people, can transform the planet. In a peaceful world, the military and police forces will have to find a new relevance or be disbanded. The national military forces of the planet can merge to form natural security teams to restore the eco-systems of their respective regions, for example, or help others in their time of need. The newly disarmed forces will find plenty of work in restoring the Earth's forests, plant life, watersheds, wildlife, and while we're at it, let's focus on the entire biosphere.

Governments will decentralize into bio-regions and organize their former military and other departments to generate crop growing regions in all available locations to ensure total global food abundance. Railheads, airports, and warehouses will converge to facilitate and launch global air rescue missions that deliver major emergency supplies to any needy group globally within hours of a disaster. All will recognize the karmic benefits of helping others in need. Post-disaster aid will make the stricken cities and villages habitable again by quickly restoring people's lives. The rescued will in turn gratefully volunteer to help in the next disaster effort. All will know the importance of karma and the great benefit in helping others and working together.

Colleges will adapt to the vast quantities of content that is already available on-line, and change their courses to teach personal learning-based pursuits, practical life skills, and a new partnership with nature. The teaching services will include mental, physical and spiritual therapy available to all, where all traumas can be resolved on a personal basis. Medical practices and the health industry will be radically restructured. Helping each other learn and heal will be a very rewarding pursuit for many as we recognize the positive karmic importance of "service to others." Universities will expand upon the science of conscious evolution, enabling a visionary mindset with emphasis on the life force of living intelligence. We will reintroduce creativity as a replacement for the elusive satisfaction of physical belongings and mindless entertainment. An experience-based curriculum will become the new standard of learning. This will include a global embrace of profound simplicity, a freedom from want, and an elevated level of compassion for all living things.

Citizens will form web-based democracies to attend to their regional, national and world needs. Open voting in a completely fair and level platform will enable everyone to voice their concerns in their community, weigh in on global issues, and reflect on everyone else's vote in a completely transparent forum. Facial recognition and retina identification is already an inexpensive technology that can ensure open and fair elections. Everyone will want to vote because each vote will count for the decisions that will affect their lives. No longer will the inherently corrupt representative government be needed, and corporations will not be allowed the same rights as individuals. Locally based constituents will use the global web intelligence system to optimize local living. Micro farming at an individual level will be encouraged as we strive to get back to nature. The global public will achieve a clear unifying identity with connections to all people on Earth. Pre-emptive political power will defang any future conflict. There will no longer be fear-based factions that offer military industrial complex product lines for the creation of war. Engaging in warfare or any kind of violence will become reprehensible.

Finally, we will come to terms with the notion that intelligent life exists in the galaxy and has already made contact with Earth. It will become common knowledge that the UFO phenomenon was real all along, and we will discover the motives of the four races of ETs that have been in contact with certain members of humanity for thousands of years. Those races are the small Greys, tall Greys, Nordics, and Reptilians. We will come to terms with the malevolent ETs who have selfishly done us harm in their "service to self." With Looking Glass technology, all events from all time will be openly viewed by everyone. Talk about the next killer smart phone app! There can be no more secrets and no more lies as we enter the Age of Transparency. History will become completely clear with no more conspiracies or mysteries. With the assistance of those ETs oriented towards "service to others," we will experience real planetary benefits from these new connections. No more starvation or homelessness. No more monetary injustice. All life is held in the highest regard. The endgame is love. The planet becomes a paradise. Utopia on Earth is achieved.

"The yogi who knows that the entire splendor of the universe is his, who rises to the consciousness of unity with the universe, retains his divinity even in the midst of various thoughts and fancies. This entire universe is a sport of consciousness. One who is constantly aware of this is certainly a liberated being." –Jivanmukta, *Tantric Scriptures*

Cymatics is the study of visible sound. The literal meaning concerns matters pertaining to waves. The higher the frequency, the more complex the wave shapes produced. Waves appear to interact with molecules. Molecules are atoms that are bonded together. Dr. Masaru Emoto has conducted worldwide research on the effect of ideas, words and music upon water molecules, with some astonishing results.

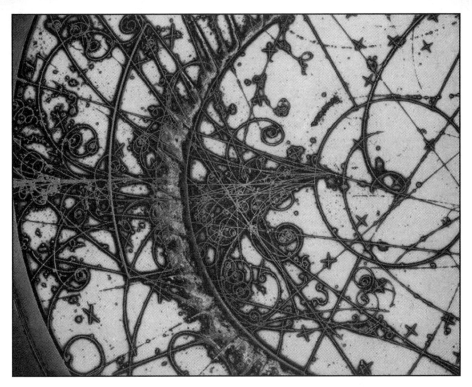

Our minds output a powerful broadcast of energy. This determines how we experience the world and what we create. Our thoughts are magnetic. They go out from us and draw to us those things we think about. Our inner dialogue is also important, for the way we speak to ourselves determines the events, people, and objects we will attract. The mind works sub-atomically, spiraling out superluminal frequencies of divine energy.

"The thought manifests as the word; the word manifests as the deed; the deed develops into habit; and habit hardens into character. So watch the thought and its way with care, and let it spring from love, born out of concern for all beings. As the shadow follows the body, as we think so we become." These are sayings of the Buddha, from the *Dhammapada*. Although our experience is of a very dualistic reality, we can "watch the thought" and "let it spring from love."

CONCLUSION

"Your time is limited, so don't waste it living someone else's life. Don't be trapped by dogma—which is living with the results of other people's thinking. Don't let the noise of others' opinions drown out your own inner voice. And most important, have the courage to follow your heart and intuition. They somehow already know what you truly want to become. Everything else is secondary." -Steve Jobs, 2005 Stanford University Commencement Speech

WHEN I started composing the chapters of this book in 2008, what simply began as jotting down information and observations in a journal, I had no concept of where this project would lead. All I knew is there were many subjects out there that I had a passion to understand and articulate. These subjects received little if any attention, and wove such a fascinating and comprehensive "alternative narrative," that I feverishly pursued my writing. Eventually the book title came to me (in the shower) and all the sections and additional chapters started to fall into place. I didn't know how any of this would materialize, and on occasion I wondered if it was all worthwhile. As I progressed, I was reminded that many artistic and literary masters also grappled with self-doubt. Even the great Ernest Hemingway reflected similar feelings on the subject when he observed: "I was completely ashamed of myself as a writer. I felt that I was simply a carpenter with words, picking up whatever was furnished on the job and nailing them together and sometimes making an okay pig pen." As a travel journalist, writing this book was a total departure for me. Yet, I followed the course wherever it would take me, and my strokes had some of the qualities of my travel writing. Similar to Hemingway, I hope to have constructed an okay pig pen. As my own worst critic, I wrote this book as much for me as for you. I have always looked at writing books with the idea that if I were buying my own book, what would I want to learn and discover inside? Would I reference the content of these pages and use it for years to come? Would I recommend it to others?

If this book ever receives the wide attention which I think it greatly deserves, I have a feeling there will be critics who will say I have no authority to write this book. They could be correct, because I have not written on most of these subjects before. I will be the first to admit that apart from one sighting, I do not consider myself a UFO expert, nor am I even a substantiated eyewitness. I am not an insider who became a whistleblower and I have never taken a security oath. I am not a scientific expert, nor do I hold an advanced degree in some of the topics I cover. What I am is a good storyteller who has an unlimited curiosity about the workings of everything around us and the seemingly suppressed human condition. As such, I have been researching these subjects for decades, mostly in my own personal quest for self-betterment and intellectual inquiry. Many new subjects also came to my attention during the writing of this book. Ralph Waldo Emerson once said, "Talent alone cannot make a writer. There must be a man behind the book." Behind this book is a person who has always searched for truth, even if some of those avenues of discovery, such as UFO research, were unpopular. I strongly believe world peace is possible, and with others I have established an educational nonprofit organization devoted to the philosophical pursuit of defining "benevolent" technology that could positively advance the human race. I have no agenda in presenting this book other than to offer the "alternative narrative" as comprehensively and accurately as possible. The information in this book is the result of a decades-long collection of data, recognizing patterns, and having the courage to follow my intuition. I feel this *Future Esoteric* manifesto has the potential to greatly impact future generations. It is either the most important information held back from the human race, or it will go down in history as the defining mythology of our age. I am content with either outcome.

DEBUNKERS OF A MODERN ENIGMA

As I was compiling the text for the first two books in the *Esoteric Series*, it was abundantly clear that the information contained would seem to many readers as phantasmal, if not outright impossible. As someone who believes in logic and the scientific method, I welcome debunkers or skeptics to join the debate. I was brought up by two atheist parents who encouraged my two siblings and me to explore life and anything beyond for ourselves. As a teen I subscribed to the *Skeptical Inquirer* magazine and attended American Atheist meetings. Yet as we grow older we have the advantage of accumulating experiences and knowledge, with the result that our convictions have a tendency to change over time. Even though pride is a basic human flaw, wisdom allows us to grow intellectually. I am grateful that I have continued to be curious and to grow and change, and that is never something to be ashamed of. Knowledge is power and questioning is patriotic.

Why will many people resist or find the information contained in this book difficult to digest? Each of us has a worldview which is largely conditioned and formed by the culture in which we grew up, particularly what our parents taught us. When we hear information that contradicts our core worldview, social psychologists call the resulting insecurity "cognitive dissonance." One cognitive belief is the official story that UFOs do not exist, repeated over and over. On the other hand, there is a growing body of evidence that tells us the official story cannot be true. Now we have lost our sense of security. Now we are vulnerable and confused. When a person's core beliefs are questioned, or when two compelling beliefs are inconsistent, there is cognitive dissonance. Most people know if they peek into Pandora's Box, that it will challenge their fundamental beliefs. When our worldview is challenged, fear and anxiety are created. In response, our psychological defenses activate, and we are protected from these emotions. Denial is most likely to kick in when our core beliefs are challenged, and denial is one of our most primitive psychological defenses. Because it is so important to protect core beliefs, people confronted with contrary new evidence will often rationalize, ignore, and even deny anything that does not fit with that core belief. Eventually our minds get overloaded and we shut down. It's easier to deny new information and move on, or just stick with the original story. Beliefs are not scientific facts, and beliefs can keep us from looking critically, even at empirical evidence. Denial protects people from anxiety. The emotion of fear makes people afraid of being ostracized, alienated, shunned, their lives being inconvenienced, or feeling helpless, confused or vulnerable. We want to protect and defend ourselves and often how we do this is to become angry. We become offended, indignant, or we want to ridicule and censor the messenger.

Regarding the extraterrestrial phenomenon, here is a typical example of handling upsetting new information.

> "If the huge number of 'contacts' and abductees are telling even a particle of the truth, then it follows that their alien friends are not attempting to keep their own existence a secret. Well, in that case, why do they never stay still for more than a single-shot photo? There has never been an uncut roll of film offered, let alone a small piece of metal unavailable on Earth, or a tiny sample of tissue. And sketches of the beings have a consistent anthropomorphic resemblance to those offered in science-fiction comics. Since travel from Alpha Centauri (the preferred origin) would involve some bending of the laws of physics, even the smallest particle of matter would be of enormous use, and would have a literally Earth-shattering effect. Instead of which—nothing. Nothing, that is, except the growth of a huge new superstition, based upon a belief in occult texts and shards that are available only to a favored few."

The professional debunkers, such as the view of Christopher Hitchens above, whose ideological denials boil down to the claim that such things never happened, or, if they did, that they are just "anecdotes" unworthy of our careful thought and serious attention. Such mock rationalisms, such defense mechanisms, such cowardly refusals to think outside of the box will only resign these authors to obscurity and irrelevance. Because, by doing so is to deny each of us the irreducibly, unrepeatable, unquantifiable and subjective ability to be an anecdote. By framing the argument and reducing the discussion to a casual dismissal, Hitchens bundles the entire ET phenomenon into a comic book-like farce. By being ruthlessly pragmatic he closes the door to all alternative study and, by doing so, essentially ends the discussion and deprives himself of future discovery on the subject.

Hitchens and other UFO debunkers also flatly deny, let alone fail to weigh, the overwhelming physical evidence, much of it presented in this book; nor do the naysayers consider the millions of mass sightings and the majority perception on the subject. It bears repeating that a report by the United Nations says since 1947 more than 150 million people have been witnesses to UFO sightings throughout the world, and of those more than 20,000 have been documented landings. A recent Roper poll conducted in the United States reported that 70% of the U.S. population believes that the government is not telling the public everything it knows about UFOs and extraterrestrials. Taken together with the abduction, cattle mutilation, and crop circle phenomenon, there is clearly something very large at hand being controlled under the strictest of secrecy.

ALWAYS FOLLOW YOUR PASSION

I have never been involved in any organized religions per say, not even Buddhism for which I have great respect but would not consider myself an adherent. Yet I have considered myself spiritual since my late 20s. I do examine the many religious texts out there because I believe they all include intriguing aspects of the same story. One can find profound knowledge from various New Age books and from the annals of ancient religious texts. Many of these sources are quoted in the *Esoteric Series* of books. I believe that we as humans are inherently creators, like the one creator, and we are all one with that creator, by whatever name that creator is called. I also believe we will be moving into a higher level of consciousness where we can consciously and physically co-create in our world, since we are only *unconsciously* co-creating at the moment.

Our lives are lined with signposts to help guide us along our life's path and remind us of our goals and intentions. It's just that most of us forget to watch out for the signs or are unmindful that we are following a course unique to each one of us. Sometimes we cannot remember the lessons, but they still influence our life's path. If you can follow your intuitive lessons from day to day you will be on course to a happy and healthy life. Your higher self never forgets your life mission. We are all learning our life lessons every day while we strive to graduate from "Earth School," whether we are aware of it or not. Before being born, we were all given a glimpse of our life path, for a labyrinth of choices always comes our way as we navigate towards our chosen goal. All lives are chosen, as are the lessons we encounter. We may sometimes feel the need to improve a certain aspect of our being, such as making a commitment to honesty. A life path is chosen to help us with this learning. A lifetime of stealing will frequently get the person in trouble, or a prison sentence, and their life's lesson can be lost. Often we are distracted, the chosen path forgotten, and therefore the lesson does not take place, so we must then attempt it over again. For some, this can happen many times before any progress is made. Karma is a very real law throughout the universe. The glimpse of your life before it manifests is to help you remember which choices to make if you are to reach your goal, but still it is easy to forget. Just as you forget your dreams when you awaken from sleep, it is easy to forget your chosen path once you are born. Practice makes perfect, as they say, and as one lives through more and more experiences, it is easier to focus on goals that you've set for yourself. Thus, the older, more experienced soul has fewer distractions and does not get hooked into power plays, does not sell out to the highest bidder, and usually stands out for totally different reasons than those who are glorified by the promoters of fame and fortune.

All of your emotional energy, including your intent, your joys, your pain and your sorrows, all become your emotional imprint. By following your passions, your soul (the spirit of your higher self) is given the opportunity to bathe in the wondrous excitement of these physical endeavors. By the very act of following what excites you, there is little negative energy attaching itself to your physical framework. Negative energy is what causes most illnesses among people. Stay positive and your world will change around you in so many positive ways. Just as violence begets violence, and negativity in turn draws in more negativity, conversely, positive behavior attracts positivistic returns.

A WEIRD UNIVERSE

There is a process we all had to go through upon our arrival back on Earth that normally edits our memory of everything that has happened off planet, and in our past lives. It is the physical process of fitting us back into the normal state, what you might call a denser being, a more compressed self. In other words, in each new lifetime we are really spiritual beings simply having another physical experience. The new material we have absorbed as non-physical entities, the new information gathered, hardly ever holds. It is like our dreams. In fact, it is exactly like a dream memory. We might remember some very small fractions, but quickly the details will fade and, try as we might, we will lose most of our recall. However, in the near future we may be in contact with technology that will allow us to traverse time, space, and dimensions just as easily as we would cut a cake. Imagine a cell phone-sized device that could interact with your mind and pull up a holographic video of any historical event, or could completely reveal all of your past lives in the greatest of detail. Talk about the next "killer app!"

When I began writing this book I believed in aliens visiting Earth from afar, but in a touch-and-go, non-malicious kind-of way. Now I suspect we're under a collective spell from entities that have been on this planet for a very long time. Before, I believed in the Greys visiting Earth, and still do, but now enter their masters the Draconian reptilians. "Our planet is run by telepathic Alpha Dracos who possess the minds of human leaders by blackmail, by corruption and by force," says Andromedan contactee Alex Collier. He continues, "Alpha Dracos are attempting to conquer this whole Galaxy utilizing trickery and deceit." I may lose credibility with some readers for promoting this viewpoint, but I believe it to be true, and in time I feel it will become common knowledge. I could be wrong and the Greys and Dracos are only part of the mosaic of our modern folklore, but if I am right we are talking of no less than the worst assault on humanity in all time. For this reason alone I implore the reader to seriously consider this scenario, do your own research, and come to your own educated conclusion. We fear being attacked by an outright alien invasion, but they've been here all along with an agenda to enslave the human race. Being strong, intelligent, telepathic and much ahead of us technologically, they live in underground bases here on Earth and have a huge advantage over humans. It would appear many top decision makers in the world today are compromised under their control via implants, telepathy or blackmail. We may be superior in numbers, but they are much farther advanced technologically, with the added protection of the extreme secrecy granted to them by the cabal and secret government who seem to be in a lock-step alliance. The mere fact that revealing their presence would be so beyond belief to most people remains their greatest protection. The Greys and their Alpha Draco masters are the baddies, while the "theomorphic" inter-dimensional beings in contact with the "higher mind" and who travel in plasma ships are the goodies. This is again a dramatic example of the duality of the universe.

There seems to be a kernel of truth in all folklore, both ancient and modern. As someone who was not raised a Christian, I've tended to reject the stories of the Bible and the principles of the Judeo-Christian faith. Since starting this book, I've re-evaluated my position on Christianity. Jesus preached peace and love which is always a good thing. Maybe heaven is an allegory for the post-death experience. It could be that "extraterrestrial humans," widely regarded in ancient folklore as angels, elves, leprechauns, faeries, jinn and others, have been guiding and helping us all along. Virtually every ancient culture reports human-looking "gods" who came and brought them written language, mathematics, agriculture, irrigation, animal husbandry, building techniques, astronomy and extensive spiritual teachings. But most revealing is the notion of hell which is presided over by Satan and his legion of demons. What was once easily dismissed as a fantasy now appears to me to hold that kernel of truth. Could the concept of Satan be a description of the Alpha Dracos with their Grey minions? Draconians are described as tall, muscular and scaly like the devil, both sporting horns and goat-like slits for eye pupils. Both the devil and reptilians are at odds with the good people, and part of their sinister nature is that they can mentally take over and coerce unsuspecting humans. Could this be the allegory of evil humans making a pact with the devil? Both reptilians and the devil are said to live below the surface of the Earth. These masters of the underworld maliciously manipulate and control humans with a penchant for what we would call evil. Could the age-old image of the devil be the same as the Draconians? Is this the hideous creature that appears in a sorcerer's spell, or a black magic ritual? After all, the greatest trick the devil ever played on humans was to make us believe he didn't exist.

As people turn away from spirituality, some turn to cult worship. These misguided individuals might attract, from whatever reality or dimension, unknown alien creatures sometimes referred to as "archons" which could potentially migrate this way from planet to planet, seeking those who call in their dark energy. It would seem that the agenda of Dark Forces is part of an unseen war, which is in fact, a war for the human mind. UFO researcher Jacques Vallée noted in his book *Confrontations*, "The medical examinations to which abductees are said to be subjected, often accompanied by sadistic sexual manipulation, is reminiscent of the medieval tales of encounters with demons."

AND IN THE END ...

Age-old questions relating to the fear of death, where we go when we die, and whether we need to be reincarnated have been the subjects examined by mystics and masters since time immemorial. There are reports of ghost hauntings, the light at the end of the tunnel, the astral healing center, and soul families. There are activities in the afterlife, communications beyond the grave, and preparations for the next life to consider. We each have two bodies back on Earth, the physical and the non-physical, so we never walk alone. Most people on Earth intrinsically know this, but our science is working hard to distance itself from merging with spirituality. The greatest human advancements, the ultimate modern esoteric study, is to fuse these two aspects of humanity into one whole. In other words, for us to be fully aware of our other self. The human potential, our real human experience on this planet, and many other fascinating subjects are included in the two companions to this book. The first book in the *Esoteric Series* is titled *Modern Esoteric: Beyond Our Senses*, and the final book is *Beyond Esoteric: The Ultimate Journey*, due out in 2018.

For the human race to reach its full potential we need access to the absolute truth. So many lies, spins and half-truths have been cast that no one really knows what to believe anymore. No wonder there is so much mistrust in government these days. We have long since passed the point where we can trust government on any level. We must insist on complete transparency in any government that claims to work for the people and be representative of the people, including everything that is happening with the military, spy agencies and the black operations. The agenda of the New World Order must be revealed and defeated. The exploitative money system, especially the American system of capitalism, absolutely must change or be eliminated altogether. We need to know our real Earth history, both past and present, even beyond our galaxy. We need to come to terms with and understand other ET civilizations, some who come from way out there in the far reaches of the universe, and others that are already here. But most importantly, we need to know who we are as spiritual individuals on a personal level, and rediscover the tools we need to reach our highest potential.

The hero's journey can become the journey of each individual. A journey that reunites us with the natural order along a path. I can only hope your life journey has been as rewarding as mine. Remember that every breath you take is a blessing, and you always have the freedom to choose and align yourself with the light. Until the Age of Transparency is a foregone conclusion, strive to know everything and believe nothing until it's proven. Most importantly, just love yourself.

Happy travels!

Christian and Apollyon.

CHRISTIAN'S COMBAT WITH APOLLYON

The Book of Revelation, clearly metaphorical and open to widely-divergent interpretations, twice refers to "the Dragon, that ancient serpent, who is called the devil and Satan." The Book of Revelation also refers to the deceiver, from which is derived the common epithet "the great deceiver." An example is Revelation 9:11, in the King James Version of the Christian Bible: "And they had a king over them, which is the angel of the bottomless pit, whose name in the Hebrew tongue is Abaddon, but in the Greek tongue hath his name Apollyon." This is the great dragon of Chapter 12, Satan or Azazel. He has a number of names, but in each case he is the king of all the demons, Lucifer, who became Satan.

Cognitive dissonance is a discomfort caused by simultaneously holding differing cognitions, such as beliefs, values, or emotional reactions which conflict with incoming information. After a person has performed the (reactionary) dissonant behavior, they may, in defense, find external consonant elements. A snake oil salesman may find a justification for promoting falsehoods, such as his own personal gain, but may consequently need to change his views about the falsehoods themselves.

REFERENCES

"Somehow tied into the fate of our species are transcendental objects made manifest." –Terence McKenna

SIMILAR to the content of *FUTURE ESOTERIC*, the metric system was designed to be universal, that is, available to all. The metric system was designed for ordinary people, for engineers who worked in human-related measurements and for astronomers and physicists who worked with numbers both large and small. The metric system was, in the words of the French philosopher Condorcet to be "for all people for all time." Such is the reason why the metric system is used in this book. May they both stand the test of time—always subject to the rigors of truth and the advancement of knowledge.

The following are some references that inspired the contents of *FUTURE ESOTERIC*:

AUTHOR'S KARMA STATEMENT
"American's Seeing Things?" Chronicle of the 20th Century, Mt Kisco, NY, 1988.

FUTURE ESOTERIC INTRODUCTION
www.thrivemovement.com, Movie/DVD: *Thrive* (Foster Gamble, producer).

SECRETS

SECRETS NO MORE
"Bloomberg Briefing: Numbers of the Day, More Millionaires" *San Francisco Chronicle*, Business Report, June 23, 2011

www.truthdig.com/chris_hedges

A Disturbing Tale: Why we may never see government UFO disclosure:
www.starpod.org/news/100910.htm

THE FOURTH REICH IN AMERICA

Good, Timothy, *Above Top Secret*. William Morrow and Company, 1988

Marrs, Jim, *The Rise of the Fourth Reich: The Secret Societies That Threaten to Take Over America*. William Morrow and Company, 2008

Nazi connection to the U.S. Government:
www.brasschecktv.com/videos/government-corruption/almost-true-story-about-the-nazius-connection.html

SECRET GOVERNMENTS

www.hereinreality.com/carlyle.html

Majestic 12 Group, "Special Operations Manual, SOM1-01 - Extraterrestrial Entities and Technology, Recovery and Disposal," April 1954 Pt 2, http://209.132.68.98/pdf/som101_part2.pdf or www.majesticdocuments.com/

Bill Wood, former Navy Seal, Unit 9 (a unit whose existence was denied): www.YouTube.com/watch?v=C1BEHxB0xJM&feature=related

Milton William Cooper, "Origin, Identity, and Purpose of MJ-12," www.geocities.com/Area51/Shadowlands/6583/maji007.html also in Cooper, *Behold a Pale Horse*

For discussion of U.S. strategy in dealing with extraterrestrials, *see* Michael Salla, *The Failure of Power Politics as a Strategic Response to the Extraterrestrial Presence – Developing Human Capacity as a Viable Global Defense Strategy*, (January 1, 2004). www.exopolitics.org/Study-Paper-7.htm

For a comparison of US official positions with European positions on extraterrestrial phenomena, see Leslie Kean. *UFOs. General, Pilots, and Government Officials Go on the Record*. Three Rivers Press, an imprint of Crown Publishing, A division of Random House, New York, 2010

MEDIA MANIPULATION

Bagdikian, Ben H. *The New Media Monopoly*. Boston: Beacon Press, 2004

Robert Kennedy, Jr. interviewed on Tavis Smiley: www.pbs.org/wnet/tavissmiley/interviews/environmental-advocate-robert-f-kennedy-jr/

SHADOW GOVERNMENTS

http://educate-yourself.org/nwo/ (New World Order site)

Alexander, John, B. *UFOs: Myths, Conspiracies, and Realities*. New York, NY. St. Martin's Press, 2011

21st Century Radio's Hieronimus & Co. "Illuminati a myth?" updated March 1, 2011 www.youtube.com/watch?v=0PLhBECS7oA&feature=share

SECRET SCIENCES

Gatto, John, *Underground History of American Education*. New York: Oxford Village Press, 2006

Horowitz, Leonard, *Emerging Viruses: AIDS and Ebola*. Tetrahedron, 1998

A disturbing video documenting the manufacture of the AIDS virus on U.S. laboratories:
www.YouTube.com/watch?v=OOzuFsdmSfI&feature=related

BACKWARD ENGINEERING

Corso, Phillip, *The Day After Roswell*. Pocket Books, 1997

General Ramey's wife speaks out about Roswell: www.huffingtonpost.com/2011/07/22/roswell-ufo-cover-up_n_904039.html

Farrell, Joseph, P., *Roswell and the Reich: The Nazi Connection*. Kempton, IL: Adventures Unlimited Press, 2010

WEAPONS IN SPACE

Lasker, John, *Technoir*. The eBookSale Publishing, 2010

Patton, Ron, *Kinetic Retaliation:* http://www.groundzeromedia.org/kinetic-retaliation/

Testimony of Dr. Carol Rosin , Dr. Steven Greer, et. al. at the National Press Club, Washington, D.C. for *The Disclosure Project*, 9 May, 2001

"Report of the Commission to Assess United States National Security Space Management and Organization," Washington, D.C. (Public Law 106-65), 11 January, 2001

UNDERGROUND BASES

www.anomalies-unlimited.com/Bases.html

www.YouTube.com/watch?v=XzWGsO0F3b8

http://369news.net/2015/12/16/the-dulce-underground-base-how-deep-does-this-rabbit-hole-go/

Stevens, Henry, *Hitler's Suppressed and Still-Secret Weapons, Science and Technology*. Kempton, IL, Adventures Unlimited, 2007

Wolf, Michael, *The Catchers of Heaven: A Trilogy*. Torrance Pub Co. 1996

Barry King on the Peasemore UK base: www.youtube.com/watch?v=nLVfCWz8XvE&feature=share

Phil Schneider, "MUFON Conference Presentation, 1995," available online at: www.anomalous-images.com/text/schneid.html

COSMOS

TO FLY A UFO

21st Century Radio's Hieronimus & Co. "Transcript of Interview with Bob Dean, March 24, 1996
www.bibliotecapleyades.net/vida_alien/cosmic_topsecret03.htm

"Bob Lazar on the Billy Goodman Happening" December 20, 1989 www.swa-home.de/lazar3.htm

ANTI-GRAVITY

An excellent YouTube collection of instructional videos:
www.peswiki.com/index.php/Review:_Anti-Gravity_/_Cold_Fusion_Explained_In_Detail:_A_New_Era_in_Physics#Part_2

Spacetime and Spin: http://einstein.stanford.edu/SPACETIME/spacetime4.html

Element 115 references:
www.unsolvedrealm.com/2011/06/26/element-115-does-this-prove-bob-lazars-claims/

www.webelements.com/ununpentium/

UFOs COSMIC TOP SECRET

William Moore, "UFO's: Exploring the ET Phenomenon," *Gazette* (Hollywood, CA., March 29, 1989). Available online at:
www.presidentialufo.com/ike&the.htm

John Spencer, "Light, Gerald," The UFO Encyclopedia: Inexplicable Sightings, Alien Abductions, Close Encounters, Brilliant Hoaxes (Avon Books, 1991) 188

"A Covenant With Death by Bill Cooper," www.alienshift.com/id40.html Also in William Cooper, *Behold a Pale Horse* (Light Technology Publishing 1991), 203

Personal notes from William Hamilton from a 1991 interview with Sgt Suggs. See also William Hamilton, *Cosmic Top Secret* (Inner Light, 1992)

John Lear Disclosure Briefing," Coast to Coast Radio (November, 2003) www.coasttocoastam.com/shows/2003/11/02.html

www.thetruthbehindthescenes.org/2011/02/15/dod-confirms-reality-of-secret-solar-warden-space-project-to-ufo-researcher/

21st Century Radio's Hieronimus & Co. "Transcript of Interview with Bob Dean, March 24, 1996,"
www.planetarymysteries.com/hieronimus/bobdean.html

See also Larry Lowe, "Perspective on Robert O. Dean: Let's Listen to the Man," (CNI News, 1995)

Chris Stoner, 'The Revelations of Dr. Michael Wolf on the UFO Cover Up and ET Reality," (October 2000)
www3.mistral.co.uk/futurepositive/mdrwolf.htm

Richard Boylan, "Official Within MJ-12 UFO-Secrecy Management Group Reveals Insider Secrets," www.drboylan.com/wolfdoc2.html

"Testimony of Don Phillips," Disclosure, ed., Stephen Greer (Crossing Point, 2001)

'Chris Stoner, 'The Revelations of Dr. Michael Wolf on the UFO Cover Up and ET Reality," (October 2000)
www3.mistral.co.uk/futurepositive/mdrwolf.htm

See Michael Salla, "Disinformation, Extraterrestrial Subversion & Psychological Reductionism – A Reply to Dr. Richard Boylan,"
www.exopolitics.org January 7, 2004. http://exopolitics.org/Exo-Comment-11.htm

A. Craig Copetas, "Extraterrestrial edge helps the balance sheet," Bloomberg News (01/21/04). Available online at:
www.chron.com/cs/CDA/ssistory.mpl/business/2365195

www.bibliotecapleyades.net/esp_autor_lyssaroyal.htm. See "Contact and the Power Struggle," a channeled perspective on overall purpose, what to expect, how to hold one's center.

SPACE AND TIME

Doctrine of the Convergent Time Lines: www.bibliotecapleyades.net/dan_burisch/esp_dan_burisch_29.htm

Looking Glass: www.youtube.com/watch?v=C1BEHxB0xJM&feature=related,
Bill Brockbrader, aka, Bill Wood, former Navy Seal

Time travel devices based on multiple YouTube video interviews with Dan Burisch. The Project Camelot series is good:
www.youtube.com/watch?v=KhK3Os_eE4g&feature=relmfu

Lecture delivered by Dan Burish at Caltech: https://eaglesdisobey.net/Caltech2008.htm

The human mission to Serpo: www.serpo.org

"Are We Living in a Holographic Universe? This May Be the Greatest Revolution of the 21st Century" www.dailygalaxy.com/my_weblog/2011/07/are-we-living-in-a-holographic-universe-this-may-be-the-greatest-revolution-of-the-21st-century.html

EBEs

Perhaps the first ever comprehensive and face-to-face interview with a living Grey alien:
www.theparacast.com/alieninterview/AlienInterview.pdf

For description of Wolf's association with the Greys, see Chris Stoner, *The Revelations of Dr. Michael Wolf on the UFO Cover Up and ET Reality*, (October 2000) www3.mistral.co.uk/futurepositive/mdrwolf.htm

Scientists create human/animal hybrid embryos:
www.dailymail.co.uk/news/article-2017818/Embryos-involving-genes-animals-mixed-humans-produced-secretively-past-years.html#ixzz1T3SJajHc

Good' versus 'Bad Alien,' www.presidentialufo.com/good_bad_alien.htm

ABDUCTIONS AND CATTLE MUTILATIONS

An examination of all the known EBEs and their motivations for interacting with Earth:
www.bibliotecapleyades.net/vida_alien/esp_vida_alien_19a.html Ashtar Command

www.reptilianagenda.com/research/r110199j.html

Contributors: Michael E. Sala, Ph.D. various research studies, www.exopolitics.org

MEN IN BLACK

Andrews, George, C. *Extraterrestrial Friends and Foes.* Illuminet Press, Lilburn, GA, 1993

The Men in Black Unmasked: http://theparanormaleffect.wordpress.com/2011/05/28/men-in-black-unmasked/

CRYPTOZOOLOGY

Chinese Sea Monster: www.thesun.co.uk/sol/homepage/news/3652122/Chinese-find-55ft-sea-monster.html#ixzz1QDKB9i00

Guiley, Rosemary Ellen, *Atlas of the Mysterious in North America.* New York, NY: Facts On File, 1995

Kelleher, Colm & Knapp, George, *Hunt for the Skinwalker: Science Confronts the Unexplained at a Remote Ranch in Utah.* Paraview Pocket Books, 2005

Clark, Jerome *Unexplained!* Visible Ink Press, 1993

Mysteries of the Unknown: Mysterious Creatures, Time-Life Books, 1988

Bord, Janet and Colin, *Alien Animals.* Stackpole Books, 1981

Keel, John A., *The Mothman Prophecies.* Saturday Review Press, 1975

CROP CIRCLES

Pringle, Lucy, *Crop Circles: The Greatest Mystery of Modern Times.* London, UK: Thorsons, 1999

Silva, Freddy, "Does Sound Create Crop Circles?" Nexus, (Mapleton, Australia), Sept.-Oct., 2005

Spignesi, Stephen J. and Andrews, Colin. *Crop Circles: Signs of Contact.* Franklin Lakes: Career Press, 2003

OTHER PLANET STRUCTURES

The standard atmosphere (symbol: atm) is a unit of pressure and is defined as being equal to 101.325 kPa. Bar and kPa are metric measurements of atmospheric pressure. The pascal (Pa) or kilopascal (kPa) as a unit of pressure measurement is widely used throughout the world and largely replaces the pounds per square inch (psi) unit. Atmospheric air pressure is often given in millibars where "standard" sea level pressure (1 atm) is defined as 1013.25 mbar (hPa), equal to 1.01325 bar. Despite millibars not being an SI unit, meteorologists and weather reporters worldwide have long measured air pressure in millibars.

Amateur Astronomer discovers Mars Structure: www.dailymail.co.uk/sciencetech/article-1394322/Armchair-astronomer-discovers-structure-Mars-Google-earth.html#ixzz1PgJzb8jd

An information site on the UFO phenomenon by and for professional scientists: www.ufoskeptic.org/

Here is the NSA-released document of scientists discussing the meaning of the Sputnik messages: www.nsa.gov/public_info/_files/ufo/key_to_et_messages.pdf

Alien Presence on the Moon? - Moon Anomalies: www.ufocasebook.com/moon.html

"UFO Quotes by Astronauts and Cosmonauts," ufos.my100megs.com/ufoquotes.htm

Reports of secret space projects: www.thetruthbehindthescenes.org/2011/02/15/dod-confirms-reality-of-secret-solar-warden-space-project-to-ufo-researcher/

Artificial Mars moons: www.ufodigest.com/article/scientist-claims-mars-moon-phobos-hollow

UTOPIA

UTOPIA

Kripal, Jeffrey J. *Authors of the Impossible: The Paranormal and the Sacred.* Chicago, IL: The University of Chicago Press, 2010

One in 10 Wall Street workers is a psychopath: www.huffingtonpost.com/2012/02/28/wall-street-psychopaths_n_1307168.html

AGE OF TRANSPARENCY

Sifry, Micah L. *Wikileaks and the Age of Transparency,* Counterpoint, 2011

More explanation on 4th and 5th dimensional beings here: http://accnl.tripod.com/chakras2.html

SUPER HUMAN ABILITIES

Armstrong, Karen, *A History of God.* New York, NY: Ballantine Books, 1993

Horowitz, Len, *DNA is a Torsion field antenna:* www.YouTube/Z6adHSKxF2A

Sagan, Carl, *The Demon Haunted World.* Ballantine Books, 1997

Sargant, William, *Battle for the Mind.* Malor Books, 1997

Placebo Effect, *The Guardian,* 22 December, 2010

Wormholes in Our DNA: wakeup-world.com/2011/07/12/scientist-prove-dna-can-be-reprogrammed-by-words-frequencies/

David Wilcock on the Source Field Investigations: www.YouTube.com/watch?v=nR-klTa1y54&feature=player_embedded

The man who does not need food to survive: www.riseearth.com/2011/07/indian-who-doesnt-need-food-to-survive.html

GRAND UNIFIED FIELD THEORY

Vortex Based Math lecture on TED/Charlotte by Randy Powell: www.YouTube.com/watch?v=Yzfgq1zv8jg&feature=player_embedded

Childress, David Hatcher, *Anti-Gravity & The World Grid.* Kempton, IL: Adventures Unlimited Press, 1987, 1997, 2001

FREE ENERGY

Tesla, Nikola, "World System of Wireless Transmission of Energy." Originally published in *Telegraph and Telephone Age*, 16 October, 1927

Bearden, Colonel Thomas, "Motionless Electro-Magnetic Generator" patent # 6,362,718 03/26/2002.

Corsi, Jerome, *The Great Oil Conspiracy: How the U.S. Government Hid the Nazi Discovery of Abiotic Oil from the American People*, Skyhorse Publishing, 2012

George, James, *The Little Green Book on Awakening*. 2009. Barrytown, NY: Barrytown/Station Hill Press, 2009

Suppression of free energy, and much more: www.thrivemovement.com

ENDGAME-ENSLAVEMENT

Black, Edwin. *War Against the Weak: Eugenics and America's Campaign to Create a Master Race.* Dialog Press, 2008

New Scientist, 2, July, 1994 "Battle for Control of World's Seeds"

THE END OF MONEY

Bretton Woods gatherings:
www2.econ.iastate.edu/classes/econ355/choi/bre.htm

A great essay by the Venus Project on the resource-based economy: www.thevenusproject.com/a-new-social-design/essay#the

David Wilcock's essay on "Financial Tyranny": http://divinecosmos.com/start-here/davids-blog/1023-financial-tyranny

Altruism's positive effects: www.bhutanobserver.bt/good/

http://psychology.ucdavis.edu/faculty/Emmons/

ENDGAME-LOVE

Jampolsky, Dr. Gerald, *Love is Letting Go of Fear*, Celestial Arts, 1979, 3rd ed. 2010

Renard, Gary R. *The Disappearance of the Universe. Straight Talk about Illusions, Past Lives, Religion, Sex, Politics, and the Miracles of Forgiveness.* Fearless Books, 2003, Hay House, 2004

A few views of Masaro Emoto's work: www.life-enthusiast.com/twilight/research_emoto.htm

http://is-masaru-emoto-for-real.com/

www.cymatics.co.uk/

CONCLUSION

Hitchens, Christopher. *God is Not Great: How Religion Poisons Everything.* Hachette Book Group, New York, NY, 2007

ACKNOWLEDGEMENTS

Foremost, this book was hugely inspired by the Australian magazine *Nexus* and the provoking stories and issues they fearlessly exposed. Another invaluable tool was the online encyclopedia Wikipedia. Both were invaluable assets in the research, fact checking, and inspiration for the vast wealth of knowledge contained in this volume. I consider both to be game-changing media resources. Thank you Duncan Roads for *Nexus*, and thank you Jimmy Wales and the fantastic contributors @ Wikipedia. The Wikimedia Commons, a media file repository making available public domain and freely licensed educational media content, was instrumental in the collection for most of the images used in this book. Keeping it real under all odds, & the open source sharing of information is the inevitable direction of the future.

The following individuals were instrumental in making this book possible: lead editor Doris Lora, co-editor Jennifer Fahey, Edward Taylor, Jerry Nardini, Michael O'Rourke, Justin Weiner, book design and co-editing by Mark J. Maxam, cover design by Robert Kidwell, and my family members, mother Elaine Olsen, father Marshall Olsen, brother Chris Olsen, and sister Marsi Sweetland. I am also indebted to Mary Rowles, Jen Wisnowski, Sporty, and Annie Johnston of Independent Publishers Group, plus David Hatcher Childress and Chris O'Brien of AUP. Thank you all for the editing, guidance, support and invaluable suggestions.

This book is in memory to those who have been persecuted or killed for their commitment to truth and justice. I gratefully invoke their courage in making the ultimate sacrifice to defend equality and transparency, with an aspiration for unity consciousness, so the human race may collectively ascend in peace during this enormously transformational period.

INDEX

Symbols

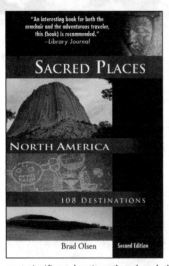

SACRED PLACES

NORTH AMERICA

108 DESTINATIONS

Brad Olsen   Second Edition

Sacred Places North America: 108 Destinations
– 2nd EDITION

by Brad Olsen

This comprehensive travel guide examines North America's most sacred sites for spiritually attuned explorers. Spirituality & Health reviewed: "The book is filled with fascinating archeological, geological, and historical material. These 108 sacred places in the United States, Canada, and Hawaii offer ample opportunity for questing by spiritual seekers."

$19.95 :: 408 pages   **paperback: 978-1888729139**

all Ebooks priced at $9.99

Kindle: 978-1888729252
PDF: 978-1888729191
ePub: 978-1888729337

SACRED PLACES

EUROPE

108 DESTINATIONS

Brad Olsen

Sacred Places Europe: 108 Destinations

by Brad Olsen

This guide to European holy sites examines the most significant locations that shaped the religious consciousness of Western civilization. Travel to Europe for 108 uplifting destinations that helped define religion and spirituality in the Western Hemisphere. From Paleolithic cave art and Neolithic megaliths, to New Age temples, this is an impartial guide book many millennium in the making.

$19.95 :: 344 pages   **paperback: 978-1888729122**

all Ebooks priced at $9.99

Kindle: 978-1888729245
PDF: 978-1888729184
ePub: 978-1888729320

SACRED PLACES

OF GODDESS

108 DESTINATIONS

Karen Tate

Sacred Places of Goddess: 108 Destinations

by Karen Tate

Readers will be escorted on a pilgrimage that reawakens, rethinks, and reveals the Divine Feminine in a multitude of sacred locations on every continent. Meticulously researched, clearly written and comprehensively documented, this book explores the rich tapestry of Goddess worship from prehistoric cultures to modern academic theories.

$19.95 :: 424 pages   **paperback: 978-1888729115**

all Ebooks priced at $9.99

Kindle: 978-1888729269
PDF: 978-1888729177
ePub: 978-1888729344

Sacred Places Around the World: 108 Destinations
– 2nd EDITION

by Brad Olsen

The mystical comes alive in this exciting compilation of 108 beloved holy destinations. World travelers and armchair tourists who want to explore the mythology and archaeology of the ruins, sanctuaries, mountains, lost cities, and temples of ancient civilizations will find this guide ideal.

$17.95 :: 288 pages   **paperback: 978-1888729108**

all Ebooks priced at $8.99

Kindle: 978-1888729238
PDF: 978-1888729160
ePub: 978-1888729313

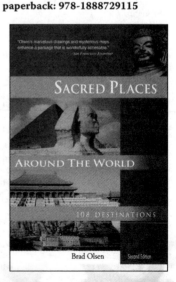

SACRED PLACES

AROUND THE WORLD

108 DESTINATIONS

Brad Olsen   Second Edition

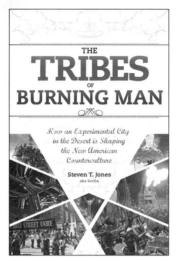

The Tribes of Burning Man: How an Experimental City in the Desert is Shaping the New American Counterculture

by Steven T. Jones

The Burning Man Festival has taken on a new character in recent years, with the frontier finally becoming a real city and the many tribes of the event—the fire artists, circus freaks, music lovers, do-gooders, sexual adventurers, grungy builders, and a myriad of other burner collectives—developing an impactful perennial presence in sister cities all over the world.

$17.95 :: 312 pages   **paperback: 978-1888729290**

all Ebooks priced at $9.99

Kindle: 978-1888729443
PDF: 978-1888729450
ePub: 978-1888729436

The Key to Solomon's Key: Is This the Lost Symbol of Masonry?

– 2nd EDITION

by Lon Milo DuQuette

Is King Solomon's story true? Is his account in the Bible to be considered historical fact? Or do myth and tradition hold the key that unlocks mysteries of human consciousness infinitely more astounding than history?

$16.95 :: 256 pages   **paperback: 978-1888729283**

all Ebooks priced at $9.99

Kindle: 978-1888729412
PDF: 978-1888729368
ePub: 978-1888729375

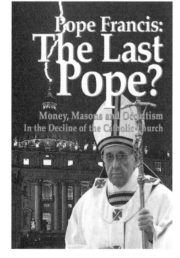

Pope Francis: The Last Pope? Money, Masons and Occultism in the Decline of the Catholic Church

by Leo Lyon Zagami

This book examines the possible reasons for the abdication of Benedict XVI and the election of Cardinal Bergoglio: the Pope who many have prophesized will be the last and will bring the Catholic Church to its end. The book details the history of this prophecy, which was hidden away in the Vatican for hundreds of years and predicts that the reign of the last Pope will herald the beginning of "great apostasy" followed by "great tribulation."

$16.95 :: 288 pages   **hardcover: 978-1888729542**

all Ebooks priced at $9.99

Kindle: 978-1888729566
PDF: 978-1888729559
ePub: 978-1888729573

World Stompers: A Global Travel Manifesto

– 5th EDITION

by Brad Olsen

Here is a travel guide written specifically to assist and motivate young readers to travel the world. When you are ready to leave your day job, load up your backpack and head out to distant lands for extended periods of time, Brad Olsen's "Travel Classic" will lend a helping hand.

$17.95 :: 288 pages   **paperback: 978-1888729054**

all Ebooks priced at $8.99

Kindle: 978-1888729276
PDF: 978-1888729061
ePub: 978-1888729351

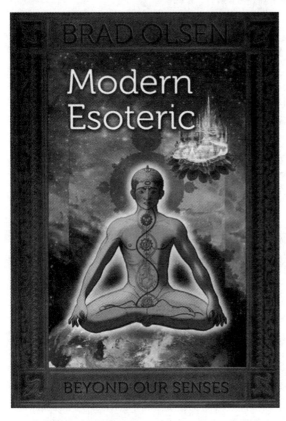